Women in the Ancient World

SUNY Series in Classical Studies
John Peradotto, Editor

Women in the Ancient World
The *Arethusa* Papers

John Peradotto and J. P. Sullivan
Editors

State University of New York Press

Albany

Published by State University of New York Press, Albany

©1984 State University of New York

Printed in the United States of America

For information, address State University of New York
Press, State University Plaza, Albany, N.Y., 12246

Library of Congress Cataloging in Publication Data
Women in the Ancient World.

    (SUNY series in classical studies)
    Bibliography: p.
    1. Women — Greece — Addresses, essays, lectures.
    2. Women — Rome — Addresses, essays, lectures.
    3. Civilization, Greek — Addresses, essays, lectures.
    4. Rome — Civilization — Addresses, essays, lectures.
    I. Peradotto, John, 1933-   .   II. Sullivan, J. P., 1930- .   III. Series.
HQ1134.W63 1984   305.4'0938   83-4975
ISBN 0-87395-772-5
ISBN 0-87395-773-3 (pbk.)

10 9 8

CONTENTS

ABBREVIATIONS

ABV	Sir John Beasley, *Attic Black-Figure Vase-Painters* (Oxford, 1956).
AC	*L'Antiquité Classique.*
AJA	*American Journal of Archaeology.*
AJAH	*American Journal of Ancient History.*
AJP	*American Journal of Philology.*
AncSoc	*Ancient Society.*
Arch	*Archéologia.*
ArchAnz	*Archäologischer Anzeiger.*
ARV²	Sir John Beasley, *Attic Red-Figure Vase-Painters*, 2nd edition (Oxford, 1963).
ASNP	*Annali della Scuola Normale Superiore di Pisa.*
BSA	*Annual of the British School at Athens.*
CAH	*Cambridge Ancient History* (Cambridge, 1923-).
CE	*Chronique d'Égypte.*
CH	*Cahiers d'Histoire.*
CIL	*Corpus Inscriptionum Latinum* (Berlin, 1863-).
CJ	*Classical Journal.*
CP or *CPh*	*Classical Philology.*
CPCP	*University of California Publications in Classical Philology.*
CQ	*Classical Quarterly.*
CR	*Classical Review.*
CULR	*Catholic University Law Review.*
CVA	*Corpus Vasorum Antiquorum.* Volumes identified by city and by numbers in the series for that city.
CW	*Classical World.*
G & R	*Greece and Rome.*
HJ	*Historisches Jahrbuch.*
HSPh	*Harvard Studies in Classical Philology.*
JDAI	*Jahrbuch des Deutschen Archäologischen Instituts.*
JHS	*Journal of Hellenic Studies.*
JRS	*Journal of Roman Studies.*
JTS	*Journal of Theological Studies.*
MEFR	*Mélanges d'Archéologie et d'Histoire de l'École Française de Rome.*

Para	Sir John Beasley, *Paralipomena: Additions to Attic Black-Figure Vase-Painters and to Attic Red-Figure Vase-Painters*, 2nd edition (Oxford, 1971).
PBSR	*Papers of the British School at Rome.*
PCPhS	*Proceedings of the Cambridge Philological Society.*
PP	*La Parola del Passato.*
RE	A. Pauly and G. Wissowa (eds.), *Realencyclopädie der classischen Altertumswissenschaft* (Stuttgart, 1894-).
REA	*Revue des Études Anciennes.*
REG	*Revue des Études Grecques.*
RhM	*Rheinisches Museum.*
RSA	*Rivista storica dell'Antichità.*
RSR	*Revue des Sciences Religieuses.*
StEtr	*Studi Etruschi.*
StudMisc	*Studi Miscellanei, Seminario di Archeologia et Storia dell'Arte Greca e Romana dell'Università di Roma.*
TAPA or *TAPhA*	*Transactions and proceedings of the American Philological Association.*
YCS	*Yale Classical Studies.*
ZPE	*Zeitschrift für Papyrologie und Epigraphik.*

Names of ancient authors and their works are generally abbreviated according to the practice of H.G. Liddell, R. Scott, and H.S. Jones (eds.), *Greek-English Lexicon*, 9th edition (Oxford, 1940) for Greek, and the *Oxford Latin Dictionary* (Oxford, 1968-82) or C.T. Lewis and C. Short, *A Latin Dictionary* (Oxford, 1879) for Latin.

INTRODUCTION

PREJUDICE AGAINST WOMEN, avowed or covert, institutionalized or personal, goes back to the very beginning of western culture, to its foundations in Greece, Rome, and Israel. Greece gave us the idea of democracy; Rome gave us most of our legal systems; and Israel ultimately provided the basis for all Judaeo-Christian forms of religion. This book concentrates on Greece and Rome. The influence of Judaeism and its offshoot Christianity on the status of women must be left to other concerned scholars.

We owe much to Greek and Roman civilization, and perhaps because of their contributions to Western culture, we are prone to idealize these cultures. We speak of the Glory that was Greece and the Grandeur that was Rome. Without belittling their achievements and their contributions, however, we ought not to blind ourselves to the seamier legacies they left us: often brutal competition in games and public life, their ideals of warfare and martial virtues, which are not irrelevant in what some may see as the closing days of our conventional and nuclear arms races. To all of these one would have to add the practice and philosophical defense of slavery, which helped perpetuate the "peculiar institution" long after its demise was due. As nations they were not unique in all this, but it was Graeco-Roman literature, jurisprudence, and philosophy, along with the Bible, which moulded the literature, philosophy and legislation of the states that emerged after the breakup of the Roman Empire. Not the least significant of the traditions we inherited from them were based on their legal, social, and religious views regarding the position of women in an advanced society. Greek myth, for instance, embodies an implicit antagonism between the male and female principles as opposed to the sympathetic polarity of the oriental principles of YIN and YANG, and it has been argued that in Greece a patriarchal theology was grafted onto, thereby obscuring, a more maternal religion. In no set of myths then is the antagonism between the male and female principles so acute and so variously ramified as in the elaborate mythology of Greece, subsequently inherited by Rome, and therefore dominant until the advent of Christianity. Almost every problem involving the sexes, whether of cooperation or hostility, was explored by the Greeks in powerful and vivid narratives and symbols, whether centering on Olympus, Thebes, or Troy, on Heracles or

1

Oedipus, not to mention the more peripheral legends of Teiresias, Narcissus, Hermaphroditus, and the Amazons. We may perhaps even descry in Danae and Andromeda Ms. Collette Downing's notorious Cinderella-complex.

Indeed, the vision of woman as the root of all evil is best expressed by Hesiod in the story of Pandora's jar. The corollaries of this antifeminist mode of thinking are to be found in the many myths of women as sexually uncontrollable and powerful beings, both human and divine, whether Aphrodite, Stheneboea, Phaedra, Pasiphae, Circe or Calypso: the female figures that trap and destroy men are multifarious in Greek mythology. Against this background may be set the supremacy of sky-gods, supremely male like Zeus and Apollo, over the earth-goddesses like Demeter and Pytho, exemplified for instance, in the usurpation of primary female powers by phallic gods. Zeus, for example, gives birth, by himself, to both Dionysus and Athena. Some might argue that this is coupled with denying to the more powerful goddesses such as Artemis and Athena female attributes of sexuality and childbearing by elevating them to the deceptively honorific pedestal of virginity.

What sort of society then is fostered by such influential symbols and the social and economic factors that underlie them? The Athenians may have invented democracy, but they gave the vote neither to women nor to slaves. An obvious consequence of this sort of social system was, from a feminist standpoint, the abiding predisposition of mythmakers, poets and philosophers to justify the *status quo* in which women are subjugated and regarded as both dangerous and inferior, whose sexual subjectivity must be rigidly controlled in order to sustain a social system based in part on the exchange of women.

It is therefore not surprising that, in Aeschylus' *Eumenides*, Apollo justifies Orestes' slaying of his mother, Clytemnestra, by what could only be called sexist biology: the male-oriented *polis* is more important than blood ties, but even if blood is important, then the son is really the blood-relative only of the father, the mother being merely the receptacle for the bearing of the child.

It is more startling that Aristotle translated into "scientific terms" the myth dramatically presented by Aeschylus more than a century before. He defined a female as a "mutilated male", and the female body as a departure from the norm of the male body. Women and slaves, then, are the natural and biological inferiors of the

2

patriarchal male citizen. Marriage therefore is *ipso facto* an unequal relationship, since justice is giving each one his due. Unequals receive unequal treatment.

It is impossible to exaggerate the influence of Aristotle's claims that women are physically, mentally, and socially, although not sexually, inferior by nature to men. These ideas were to pervade the theological, philosophical, medical, and political writings of later ages.

Rome's myths, social organization and legal system, set up by a warrior society, where the emphasis was on martial strength and courage, were equally unlikely to foster high aspirations in women or male admiration of their particular virtues. The Romans gave all power to the head of the family, as they gave all power initially to the Kings of Rome, and as they would give later all power to the Caesars under the Empire. Yet, for reasons we cannot go into here, Rome's legal system actually contributed to the *de facto* liberation of Roman women. Indeed, it is not too much to say that the ladies of Rome, on the levels of society most visible in our evidence, enjoyed a personal, sexual, and economic freedom unparalleled before the latter half of the twentieth century in America, England, and some parts of Europe. Only the advent of institutionalized Christianity changed this state of affairs.

There is a complex of assumptions not uncommon among classicists, who are perhaps unfamiliar with the work of H. G. Gadamer and others, that there are such things as translucent or "neutral" translations of the works we study, "objective" descriptions of historical processes, evaluations of classical poets and philosophers unaffected by contemporary literary values or philosophical methods. Insofar as this set of beliefs promotes a high regard for facts and accuracy, evidence and historical circumstances, this is to the good; insofar as it promotes a contempt for theory, for the discernment of patterns, inter-relationships, and chains of causality other than the most obvious, it works to our detriment. The debatability of a thesis does not make it somehow inferior to the establishment of a fact. Truth may be sometimes trivial.

A great many *facts* about the condition, social, legal, and personal, of woman in classical antiquity have long been known. But books and articles dealing with the subject have been essentially a detailing of *Realien*, except for the occasional Marxist or Freudian critic. Attempts to explore systematically the underlying roots of the lowly status of women have been few and much work remains to be done.

One of the alleged reasons for the study of the Classics is their perpetual relevance. In no area can this position be more clearly defended than in the investigation of the feminine condition in Greece and Rome. For it was here that basic derogatory attitudes about the sex were moulded by legal and social systems, by philosophers and poets, and by the thinking of men long since gone.

Many of those attitudes (much as with the institution of slavery) were transmitted, indeed reinforced, by the Christian church, along with analogous Judaic beliefs, so that views formulated by fallible Greek thinkers remained, until quite recently, unquestioned assumptions about the nature of things. The history of slavery and the origins of racial prejudice has been to a large extent written. It is now the turn of another oppressed segment of humankind. But we must not anticipate the findings of our authors.

It was of course impossible to do justice to such a vast subject as Women in Antiquity, particularly as so much innovative work still continues. The editors and the contributors had to content themselves with surveying the territory (no longer, luckily, *terra incognita*) by a series of forays, as it were, into such areas as we could reach. Sexual matters have not been burked by the contributors, whether male or female. The editors hope that frank discussion of this sort of material will help rather than hinder modern thinking on these delicate or repressed subjects.

The history of this collection of papers may be of interest. A conference on Women in Antiquity, held at the State University of New York at Buffalo led to the publication of the papers there presented in the Spring issue of *Arethusa* in 1973. The popularity and usefulness of that issue, for scholarly citation and as a textbook for the classroom, stimulated a further and more ambitious gathering of articles and reviews on the subject (*Arethusa*, 11.1 & 2, 1978). Some differences may be discerned between the contributions to each of the issues. Two things at least emerge from such a comparison. One is a reduced sense of urgency, of the need for overstatement or for something approaching the polemical in the face of letheragy or hostility, now that the study of women in antiquity has demonstrated what it should never have been required to demonstrate: its legitimacy as an area of serious scholarly endeavor. The other is a sharpening of methodological reflectiveness — not as much or as evenly evidenced, perhaps, as might have been hoped for, given the intensity and prominence of such concerns in some other disciplines, but certainly more than what found its way, with a few notable exceptions, into the earliest examples of Classical Women's Studies. Several of the essays in this collection, with varying degrees of explicitness, show an awareness that the attitude toward women and even the very definition of sex itself are organic parts of an anonymous, complex, highly structured cognitive system for understanding and expressing world, society, and self — a system which places both societal demands for clarity and logical demands for consistency above considerations such as justice, mercy, cruelty, indecency, the limits of which are themselves defined by the system and variable from culture to culture — a system of standardized analogies nearly impervious to change in the part without change of the whole. It is regrettable that we have here but one study of Plato and none of Aristotle, in whom the Greek cognitive system is most open to awareness of alternatives and most fully available to analysis. (One should not overlook M. C. Horowitz' "Aristotle and Woman" in the *Journal of the History of Biology* 9 [1979] 183-213.) It would, we think, be interesting, for example, to explore the extent to which, in Aristotle's view, the defining characteristic of human nature, its capacity for reasoned choice, enables it, if at all, to break free of or at least to alter what are represented as universal characteristics of the sexes in this symptomatic passage from the *Historia Animalium* (608b):

> With all other animals [except the bear and leopard] the female is softer in disposition than the male, is more mischievous, less simple, more impulsive, and more attentive to the nurture of the young; the male, on the other hand, is more spirited than the female, more savage, more simple and less cunning. The traces of these differentiated characteristics are more or less visible everywhere, but they are especially visible where character is more developed, and most of all in man. The fact is, the nature of man is the most rounded off and complete, and consequently in man the qualities or capacities above referred to are found in their perfection. Hence woman is more compassionate than man, more easily moved to tears, at the same time is more jealous, more querulous, more apt to scold and to strike. She is furthermore, more prone to despondency and less hopeful than

the man, more void of shame or self-respect, more false of speech, more deceptive, and of more retentive memory. She is also more wakeful, more shrinking, more difficult to rouse to action, and requires a smaller quantity of nutriment.

[D'Arcy W. Thompson, trans.]

It is hoped that such studies as this are in the making and that this collection may act as a spur to their early appearance.

Our gratitude for assistance is owed to many people. Ms. Agnes Mitrision, typesetter, lay-out artist, and factotum for many years in the service of the journal, provided a stable, calm center of patient competence to offset the tardiness, negligence and vacillation of authors, referees, subscribers, and editors. Our contributors obligingly shortened, revised, or updated their sections in the light of our editorial exigencies and constraints. Professors Averil Cameron and Froma Zeitlin were particularly helpful with their editorial counsel in the production of *Arethusa* volume 11. Last but by no means least, we would like to convey our thanks to Eric A. Havelock, who, during his tenure as Andrew V.V. Raymond Professor of Classics at SUNY/Buffalo, helped sponsor the initial conference on Women in Antiquity, through which the first volume of *Arethusa* on this subject was generated.

J.P. & J.P.S.

EARLY GREECE:
THE ORIGINS OF THE WESTERN ATTITUDE TOWARD WOMEN*

THE STUDY OF CLASSICAL ANTIQUITY is unique in that it is quite clearly and self-consciously the study of the crucible in which the forms and the spirit of Western civilization were first mingled, and as such it has been throughout Western history notoriously susceptible to depiction alternatively as a barbarous crudity from which the further development of science and morality has fortunately delivered us, or as a primitive simplicity whose unique harmonization of the natural and physical with the rational and spiritual life, we can only seek in vain to recover. The matter of woman's position in antiquity, together with the question of slavery, have been focal points in this dispute, and have often been the bases on which the liberal-democratic ideal has fallen or risen. The question remains: can we seek to discover in classical antiquity an understanding of our present historical moment and a perspective on our own values, and yet remain both free from ideological compulsion and unburdened by the tyranny of raw data?

The impulse given to the study of woman's position throughout history by the recent women's liberation movement, invites us to do just that. In the following pages, we shall attempt to correlate various aspects of the political, socio-economic and cultural position of women in ancient Greece, in order to present an intelligible whole, and a picture which will not force us to choose whether women in ancient Greece were despised or revered, but will enable us to understand how they could seem to be both simultaneously. In order to do this, we must of course consider the position of women in relation to the particular historical moment in which they found themselves, and we must consequently be aware that any change in the status of women is always an *aspect* of a whole social movement. This article will therefore take the form of an abbreviated history of the emergence of the Greek city-state, with special emphasis on the position of women and

* This article developed out of a lecture on the same subject delivered at Wesleyan University (Middletown, Conn.) for a course on Women in History in the Spring of 1971. To Sheila Tobias, who directed this course (the first of its kind at Wesleyan) I owe special thanks for both her inspiration and her sometimes much-needed encouragement to pursue my investigations in this area.

with special attention to those cultural documents that are relevant to an assessment of the status of women. We shall focus primarily on the period between the ninth and sixth centuries (inclusive), as the era in which the basic framework of the polis was set down. It will be assumed that the period before the Dark-Age migrations was essentially irrelevant to the particular form that the polis took, and that political and social developments in the post-sixth-century polis were, for the most part, extensions or intensifications of already well-established patterns.

Our source for the Dark-Age period will naturally have to be the Homeric poems, which were composed in the eighth century and whose outlook reflects, at least in part, Dark-Age life. They are thus our only cultural documents for a period that was crucially important in the development of Greece. For it was the time when the political, social and cultural forms of Greece were first taking shape, and along with them everything that was later to become known as specifically and peculiarly "Greek." Hesiod will provide us with information about the seventh century which, when taken together with the Homeric evidence, will enable us to construct a fairly complete picture of social life just before the decisive transformations of the sixth century which brought the polis into being as a legal and political entity. For the period of sixth century, our primary historical focus will be on Athens, as our best-documented example of developments that were taking place all over Greece. For while Athens' development toward a democratic form of government took place fairly late (in comparison with the same movements elsewhere on the mainland and in the islands), it soon became evident during the sixth century that a peculiar combination of geographical, cultural and other factors was thrusting her forward into a position of economic and, later, political leadership of the entire Greek world. As such, her achievements, as well as her failures, can be fairly understood to represent the outer limits of development of the democratic Greek city-state. Only the states of Sparta and Crete developed in radically different ways from the rest of Greece, and as such offer an interesting commentary on certain aspects of Athenian life. These will not, however, be the subject of discussion in this paper.

For cultural documents in which we may find reflected the social developments of the sixth century, and in particular the attitude toward women, we shall be obliged to abandon Athens (except for the poems of Solon) and turn for evidence to the literary remains of the lyric poets of the Greek islands. Taken all together, our varied sources will enable us to construct a complex picture of the emergence of the

Greek city-state in which various and sometimes contradictory forces were at work and in which the position of women and the social attitude towards her were correspondingly diverse. Our procedure will be to first define the historical characteristics of each period or era, and then to deduce from cultural documents the social attitudes of that period, especially the attitude towards women.

The Homeric poems were composed in the eighth century B.C., but the world which they portray both reflects backward on the age of great kingdoms, and looks forward to that form of social organization which Homer in the eighth century only just saw emerging about him — the polis.[1] The setting of the poems, in the heroic era of great wars and great kingdoms, ostensibly looks back to Mycenean times. But recent investigation has demonstrated that the social institutions in particular, as well as many other features of the poems, reflect Dark-Age culture. Although there is still considerable dispute as to which "background" predominates, it is still evident that the juxtaposition of old and new afforded Homer an opportunity for making a complex and comprehensive statement about the meaning as well as the evolution of social forms. We shall examine these in some detail, paying particular attention to differences in social practice that have ramifications for the status of women.

In the view of those who defend the thesis that the background of the poems roughly reflects conditions as they would have been in Mycenean Greece, the political background is that of "a simple tribal monarchy,"[2] with a warrior aristocracy, and a highly cultured, highly commercialized bureaucracy centered around the palace of the king, to whom every member of society owed allegiance, and who presided over the dispensation of justice, religion, and material goods. The family of such a society was a loose conglomeration of husband, wife, children, close relatives, concubine's children (see V.70f., VIII.283f., and 14.202ff.), and incorporated strangers of various kinds (like Phoenix in IX.485ff.). M. I. Finley, who is the main spokesman for the thesis that the action of the poems takes place against a background of primarily Dark-Age institutions, describes this world as follows:

> It was a world of petty kings and nobles, who possessed
> the best land and considerable flocks, and lived a seignio-
> rial existence, in which raids and local wars were frequent.
> The noble household (*oikos*) was the centre of activity and

9

power...The king with power was judge, lawgiver and
commander, and there were accepted ceremonies, rituals,
conventions and a code of honour by which nobles lived,
including table fellowship, gift exchange, sacrifice to the
gods and appropriate burial rites. But there was no bureaucratic apparatus, no formalized legal system or constitutional machinery. The power equilibrium was delicately
balanced; tension between king and nobles was chronic,
struggles for power frequent.[3]

On the whole, this is the view which will be followed in this paper,
with the one exception that we shall treat the evidence for certain
Mycenean practices not as mere "survivals," not as lifeless shells
of long-dead customs, but as one half of a polarity which is presented
in the poems as a dynamic tension out of which new social forms
eventually break forth. So, for example, Homer's portrayal of Priam's
palace, which houses his fifty sons and their wives as well as his
twelve daughters with their husbands, suggests the large, loosely-knit
type of family associated with the Mycenean age. In such a context,
Homer's focus of interest on the relationship between Hector and
Andromache emerges as something of an anachronism, more appropriate
to an era of small families. Conversely, the heroic code by which the
warriors fight in this poem is inconsistent with an emphasis upon the
nuclear family, and more appropriate to the age when the warriors
formed a class apart. As we shall see, the manner in which Homer has
developed the character of Hector, as both a warrior and a family man,
has enabled him to deal directly with this clash in social forms and
cultural values between the old, heroic society, and the new world
of pre-polis society. And an important aspect of this conflict is a
striking difference in both the position and the attitude toward the
women of the society in question.

As Sarpedon explains the heroic code to Glaucus in the famous
passage in Book XII of the *Iliad*, he and Glaucus are honored above all
others in Lycia with a position of preeminence and choice tracts of
land, because they fight in the front ranks of the Lycians; they fight
in the front ranks in turn, so that the Lycians will honor them (310-
321). It is a circular argument in which the rewards of the heroic life
are identified as its rationale. It contrasts quite strikingly with Achilles' refusal in Book IX to find in the traditional rewards of excellence
a sufficient reason to rejoin his comrades on the battlefield; his
rejection of the heroic code is never repudiated — when he does return

to the fray he does so only to avenge the death of Patroclus, in the
service, that is, of a close and personal friendship. The heroic code
as Sarpedon defines it is implicitly rejected by Hector as well, who
justifies his life as a warrior by a very different rationale; as he
explains it to Andromache in the famous homilia of Book VI:

> But my concern is not so much for the suffering of the Trojans
> nor [of my mother and father and brother]
> but for your suffering, [on the day when some Achaean
> leads you away as his slave].
>
> VI. 450-455 (abridged)

That is to say, Hector affirms himself as a warrior by recognizing the
bond that he has with his family and with the city as a whole, and he
claims that his activity as a warrior is on behalf of them all. In this,
Hector is the prototype of a new type of Greek hero whom Werner
Jaeger identified as "radically different from those truly aristocratic
Greek heroes who fought not for their native land but only for their
own personal glory. His personality is already an example of the in-
filtration of the new ethics of the polis .... "[4] To put it differently, in
the character of Hector Homer had attempted to present a more integrated and whole person, whose activity as a warrior was the expression of the totality of his human relations. This he achieved by
developing an elaborate portrayal of Hector as a "family man" in
Book VI. There Hector is shown in the company of friends and family,
whom he approaches in the course of the book, in an "ascending scale
of affections"[5] at the apex of which stands Andromache, his wife.
Andromache, for her part, reciprocates with an assertion of Hector's
primary importance to her, again presented in the form of an ascending
scale of affections:

> But Hector, you are father and noble mother to me
> and brother as well, and you are my tender husband.
>
> VI.429-430.

Such a code as Hector articulates is clearly more appropriate in
a social milieu like the polis, in which social relationships begin with
the central importance of the nuclear family and encompass, in successively larger concentric circles, the whole of society. The heroic
code which Sarpedon espouses is better suited to a bureaucratic state
of the Mycenean type, in which the warriors were a military aristocracy.
And yet, as we have stated, such a world is not predominant in the

11

poems; most of the warriors have, like Hector, a wife and child, and a household to which they will return. However, with the exception of Hector, the private lives of the Homeric heroes, and the great affection which they may have felt for their wives and children, have no place in their code as warriors. The explanation that the Greeks were fighting offensively and the Trojans were defending their homeland, is not sufficient: in the picture which Nestor presents in Book IX (705 ff.) of the attack on his homeland by the Epeians, it is still booty and the honor to be gained from fighting gloriously that is uppermost in the minds of the Pylians. And in Book V, Dione comforts her daughter Aphrodite, whom Diomedes has just wounded, by reminding her of the anguish which would await Diomedes' wife and children, should he meet death at Troy. Yet at no point is any of the heroes other than Hector said either to fight for the sake of the glory which would accrue to his family (in the manner of the career which Hector foresees for Astyanax in Book VI.479–481), or to fear death for their sakes. Booty and fame and honor *(geras* and *kleos* and *timē*) are the only considerations which have a place in the heroic code.

The distinction which we have been delineating between the two types of warrior codes is obviously one of great consequence for the position of women. The traditional heroic code reflects a society whose ideal was exclusively and uniquely male, in which all of the socially relevant transactions took place between the males of the community. The "family" of such a community was, as we have noticed (see above, page 9), a loose conglomeration of persons related to one another in various ways. In the "new" code which Hector articulates, and which reflects the organization of society around small, nuclear families, the position of the wife is upgraded and the concubine fades or disappears.[6] Socially relevant transactions were still the province of the males of the community, but these men were increasingly defined as heads of families, and not as members of a class apart from the rest of society. The new heroic code therefore embodies a new type of humanism, in which man is defined as a total being, and not on the basis of one special function, and in which his rights as a member of society proceed from an acknowledgment of that which he has in common with the rest of society, rather than from his particular and special abilities.

The incorporation of the wife into the warrior's code involves as well a new attention to her social function, and a new concern to delineate its limits. This is evident from Hector's use of what was to later become the traditional male/female polarity, in his final words to

12

Andromache in Book VI:

> But go into the house and attend to your own work,
> the loom and the distaff, and tell the servants
> to set to work; as for fighting, that will be the
> concern of all the men, especially myself, who are sons of Troy.
>
> VI.490-493

We should emphasize here that the distinction we are discussing does not involves any new social functions for the wife — but a revaluation of her traditional duties and an incorporation of her functions into a new social ideal. So the warrior went on fighting wars as before, but in the service of a different set of values. The women we see in the Homeric epics are performing all of the traditional duties: Helen is on call for Alexander's sexual needs, no less than any concubine; women's normal sphere is the home, which they leave freely, but only on unusual occasions (and ordinarily in the company of attendants — see VI.388f., cf. 1.331); women are solicitous of their children as well as their husbands, and perform such domestic services as seeing that a hot bath is drawn when the man of the house comes home from "work," or urging on him food or drink. As was true in Athens of the fifth century, the performance of certain religious rites was reserved to the women of the city, and the goddess celebrated in both cases is Athena. The goddess is propitiated with a robe of the women's own handiwork; for from Mycenean times forward to the Hellenistic period spinning and weaving was the province of women, be they domestic slaves or royalty.[7]

Does this mean that we have to accept as substantially correct the statement of M. I. Finley to the effect that "there is no mistaking the fact that Homer fully reveals what remained true for the whole of antiquity, that women were held to be naturally inferior and therefore limited in their function to the production of offspring and the performance of household duties..."?[8] I do not think so. The first objection to Finley's statement is that it assumes a connection between women's social function and an active desire on the part of society as a whole to establish their inferiority. Yet nowhere in the *Iliad* or *Odyssey* do we find any disparaging remarks about women's role, nowhere do we encounter the expressions of misogyny which appear so frequently in later Greek literature. Although it may be true that the position of women in Homeric times was little different from that of later times in Greece, there *is* a difference in the Homeric attitude toward this social role. The Homeric poet focusses almost exclusively on the positive side of the position of women; it emphasizes women's *inclusion* in society as a whole, rather than her *exclusion* from certain roles; it celebrates the importance of the functions that women do perform, instead of drawing attention to their handicaps or inabilities. Of course, this is not to say that Homer was unaware of the negative side of this picture: certainly the use of the formulaic lines which distinguish the male and female spheres (quoted above, page 13) demonstrates this. For these lines appear at those points where the women involved (Andromache and Penelope) threaten to overstep the limits of their prerogatives as females, and in a context which makes it clear that they are being deliberately excluded from participating in decisions which affect them directly. In Book VI.431 ff., Andromache's advice on military matters may be unfeminine,[9] but, as she had made clear in the preceding lines of her speech, her life is as much involved as Hector's in the war which rages outside the walls. In the *Odyssey*, Penelope's tearful appeal to the bard not to remind her in his songs of the husband for whom she longs, is cut short by Telemachus' reminder (in 1.356-359) that *mythos* is the province of the men; and in 21.350-353 Telemachus prevents her from further participating in or even witnessing the contest of the bow which will decide her husband. Nevertheless, Homer does not seek to explore the implications of this negative side of the picture of women's status, or to condemn his society on account of it; in fact, the only extended treatment of the "war of the sexes," the marital squabbles of Zeus and Hera, is done with humorous wit. In the figure of the goddess Hera we have a clever and intelligent woman who is impatient with the restraints to which her position as Zeus' wife subject her. She is jealous of his love-affairs, and determined to use feminine and other wiles to get around him. Fourth-century New Comedy has hardly anything to add to Homer's picture of the nagging wife.

If we can generalize, then, from the examples which have been before us, we can say that the social position of women in Homeric times was roughly the same as in later times in Greece, but it is notable that Homer treats as part of the challenge of the new social system, and as part of the forward-moving element in society, the new importance of man's personal life, especially the life of the family. As a result, woman's position was upgraded *ideologically*; the everyday relations between man and wife especially were the subject of a romanticization which contrasted strongly with the epic emphasis on heroic exploits. Hector and Andromache were the great example in the *Iliad*, but the relation between Penelope and Odysseus is even more fully developed, mostly because Penelope is characterized in the *Odyssey* much more fully than Andromache had been. Now certainly the plot line is responsible for some of this: since Odysseus is absent from home, Penelope is thrown into a situation where her own resourcefulness and character not only count for a great deal, but are allowed their full scope of expression. In addition, since the focus in the *Odyssey* is on domesticity, our attention is drawn very naturally to the wife of Odysseus. However, the famous romanticization of Penelope's relationship with Odysseus stands out as a striking example of that mutual respect and affection which characterized the Homeric ideal of marriage. This is particularly demonstrated by the episode in Book 23 in which the secret of the marriage-bed is disclosed. Not only is Penelope's cleverness revealed by the trick she plays on Odysseus, but in making knowledge that is shared between them alone the basis of their reunion, Homer has celebrated not the institution of marriage, nor the social role of either husband and wife, but the peculiarly personal and intimate aspects of the relation between these two individual persons. It must be emphasized here again that there is no indication that Penelope suffered any less from the disability that came from being a woman in ancient Greece, than any other woman in these poems. We have mentioned Telemachus' rebuke to her, but we should note as well that her marriage was to be arranged between the men involved; the questions about her eligibility derived mainly from the confusion as to who her *kyrios* was.[10] And the consulting of her wishes was no more than the respect owed and characteristically paid to a mature and noble woman, and the presentation of a choice which, as it seems, it was later given to her to make in Attic law.[11] Homer does not seek to conceal Penelope's status, or to diminish its consequences for her freedom of action. However, in the case of Penelope, her desirability as a rich widow and her eligibility for remarriage is converted into the arena where her qualities of endurance and perseverance can be tested. The feminine craft of weaving and her family obligations as the chief woman in the house are not presented as limitations for her, but become in her hands the devices for cheating the suitors and for demonstrating, at the same time, her considerable inventiveness and intelligence. The simile with which the poet describes Penelope's joy and relief at being reunited with Odysseus recalls in form both the simile and the description in 5.394 ff., where Odysseus finally reaches the land of the Phaeacians; it thus formally suggests a complementarity which Homer has developed throughout the poem between the trials of Penelope and those of Odysseus, and between the qualities of endurability and wiliness in Odysseus and the similar qualities of character in Penelope.

If we saw in the *Iliad* a new interest in the social role of women which portended a new upgrading of their position from the ideological point of view, then we are confronted in the *Odyssey* with a particular example of this new social ideal, with its separate but complementary spheres, in each of which the same human qualities are valued and in each of which they can find expression, albeit in different ways. The marriage of Penelope and Odysseus is an example of that partnership of husband and wife in the household which Odysseus had celebrated in Book 6 as the "best of all things":

> For nothing is stronger and better than this:
> when a man and a wife live together in their home,
> their thoughts of one accord – a great pain to their enemies
> but a joy to their friends, as they themselves especially know.
>
> 6.182-185

It was Homer, then, who was the first to formulate that promise of a position of worth and honor which even today is glorified by the defenders of the traditional separation between the sexes. Such hopes have been revealed as a sham for our own times, but for the Greeks of Homer's time the negative side of this ideal had not yet fully revealed itself.

For the sake of completeness in our discussion of women in the Homeric poems, we should include mention of the two Homeric women who are most often instanced as examples of Homeric women's "higher status," as compared with her fifth-century Athenian counterpart: Helen and Arete. It must of course first be remarked that both of these women are anomalous; that does not mean that they have nothing to tell us about the women of their society, but it does mean that not every aspect of their positions can be regarded as typical.

Helen, in both the *Iliad* and *Odyssey*, is a demi-goddess, and the special position that she occupies, and her special and magical powers, derive from this. Even Menelaus is given special treatment by the old man of the sea,

> since you have Helen as wife, and you are the son-in-law of Zeus

and is guaranteed immortality on the same account (4.569). In both poems Helen is notoriously free from the disgrace which later attaches to adulterous women. Although she certainly regards herself as blame-

16

worthy (see III.173, VI.344 and 4.145), the Greek expedition is concerned only to exact retribution from Alexandros, and to recover Helen "and all her possessions," and not to punish Helen. Menelaos' hostility and his feelings of outrage are directed only at Alexandros:

> Lord Zeus, grant that I may avenge the evil which he did to me first,
> godlike Alexandros, and vanquish him at my hands,
> so that some man even of those who are yet to come may shudder
> to do wrong to a host who has extended kindness to him.
>
> 3.351-354

Such an attitude does not betray any recognition of sexual freedom for women, but rather proceeds from a social climate in which the moral code encompassed men alone. Chastity or faithfulness for women in such a period was not a moral obligation but a simple regulation which was ordinarily adhered to; when the rule was broken it was a matter between the men in whose power the women were understood to be and whose responsibility they were. Furthermore, in the context of the looser family structure which certainly characterized such a period these transgressions on the part of women had less consequence for society as a whole. Since heirs were freely bred from concubines, or freely adopted, the child-bearing services of the wife were less critically essential than in an era when only the legitimate wife could produce a legitimate heir. Such a system doubtless prevailed in Mycenean times, but survived as well into later society when the small family was not as yet a legal entity, but only a cultural tendency. It is, however, the case that the Homeric poems contain also evidence of the disposition to call into account the wife in cases of adultery, a practice which is normally associated with the later, bourgeois state. This evidence is the condemnation of Clytemnestra by Agamemnon's shade:

> So nothing is more dreadful or disgraceful than a woman —
> at least the kind that devises such deeds in her mind,
> planning death for her wedded husband . . .
> But she, the deviser of such great sorrow,
> heaped disgrace upon herself and upon all the tribe of females
> that is yet to come, even upon those who do good deeds.
>
> 11.427-434 (abbreviated)

It is notable that only in Agamemnon's eyes, for whom Clytemnestra's betrayal had a personal rather than a social aspect, does Clytemnestra

17

stand so condemned. Otherwise, the focus of wrath in the poems is on Aegisthus alone, in the matter both of Agamemnon's betrayal and his murder, and the demand for vengeance is from Aegisthus alone (1.30 ff., 1.193 ff., 3.255 ff.). In the case of Agamemnon and Clytemnestra, then, Homer has anticipated a negative feature of the new emphasis on the husband-wife relationship, and has anticipated as well the misogynistic form in which this negative attitude is most often expressed. In the cases of Hector and Andromache, and of Penelope and Odysseus, as we have said, the positive features of this relationship predominate.

In the case of Arete, the honored position which she holds in Phaeacia is isolated by Athena as anomalous:

[Alcinous] honored her as no other woman on earth is honored,
of such women as now live and keep house for their husbands.

7.67-68

and in addition it is fairly clear that her participation in the life of Phaeacia is based upon her husband's willingness to share authority: although Odysseus supplicates Arete, it is Alcinous alone who has the power to accept him as a suppliant (7.167 ff.); and regardless of her respect for her mother's judgment and intelligence, Nausicaa is clear that Alcinous is the ruler of Phaeacia (6.195 ff.). Modest though Arete's participation is, it is still surprising to see the distortion to which it is so easily subject by modern commentators: Finley describes Arete as a figure with "strange, unwomanly claims to power and authority"![12] Furthermore, even if Arete's position were not anomalous, we would not be justified in deducing from it a position of greater worth for the women of Phaeacia. However, since Phaeacia is the Homeric Utopia, the domestic harmony and high respect for Arete which are part of it may represent Homer's commentary on the traditional divisions, and on the usual exclusion of women from public life.

In the cases of both Helen and Arete, their presence in the *megaron* after the meal when the men are drinking has often been cited as evidence of a greater degree of incorporation of Homeric women into social life. However, aside from the fact that much of the evidence having to do with the "seclusion" of women in fifth-century Athens affords proof of a highly questionable kind,[13] and so offers a less striking contrast with the Homeric practice than might have been previously thought, the Homeric practice is to be attributed, at least in part, to the fact that the palaces in question were centres of the social and political activity of the ruling classes. In neither case is anything like a symposium suggested, but rather the scenes represent

18

the reception of a *xenos*. Furthermore, a comparison with a similar scene in Nestor's palace at Pylos reveals that his wife does not join the men, although she was presumably available, since she later "sleeps at his side" (3.404). This leads us to suspect that the presence of Helen and Arete in the *megaron* does not reflect the usual practice, but is allowed by the poet on the grounds that a special interest attaches to each of these women.

The examples of Helen and Arete, then, do not provide us with any information which might cause us to modify our assertions about woman's place and role in Dark-Age Greece. And so we must conclude that where claims are made as to the "high" position of Homeric women vis-à-vis their later counterparts, scholars either illegitimately infer higher social status for women on the basis of Homer's favorable attitude toward the marriage relationship, or depend upon an unfairly and incorrectly negative evaluation of women's position in later times. On the other hand, where it is maintained, as by Finley, that Homer's picture of women confirms the negative judgment of antiquity as a whole, then the difference between the positive emphasis in Homer's presentation of women and their role, and the misogynistic tendency in later literature, has not been given sufficient weight.

The poems of Hesiod, although from about a century later than those of Homer, provide us with enough evidence to allow us to infer some of the economic and political characteristics of the period which gave birth to the tendencies which Homer described. In Homer, as we noted, the ideological upgrading of women's position, and the romanticization of the marital relationship, was the outgrowth of an impulse to find fault with the values of the heroic age, and a search for a more humane basis on which to define social relationships. Homer, therefore, focusses on the importance of ideas and of changes in value in bringing about social change. Hesiod, in the *Works and Days*, at any rate, is explicitly concerned with the economics and politics of his day, and consequently provides a valuable complement to the Homeric evidence. In using these two poets in complementarity I am not ignoring the century or so which separates them from one another – but since the dating of Homer's outlook which I use makes his poems a reflection of Dark-Age life, and since the elements which especially concern us look forward to women's status in the polis, and since Hesiod's outlook is clearly that of early Archaic society, the evidence of the two sets of poems taken together probably provides us with the best possible coherent account of this crucially important transition phase in Greek history.

From Hesiod we learn that social conditions in the seventh century in Greece were close to those of the later polis. The picture that Hesiod presents is one in which the polis as a form is already well-established, with an urban nucleus but an agricultural base. The religious, military and political offices — and therefore the state itself — were controlled by an hereditary aristocracy, called Eupatridae in Athens. Clan ties were still strong, although the division of society into clan groups no longer reflected the real social divisions which were increasingly between the emerging "classes": the interests of of the upper, richer, aristocratic classes were reinforced and defended by traditional clan associations, but for the impoverished and exploited small peasant, and the enterprising and increasingly important group of prosperous farmers, craftsmen, merchants and traders, clan associations had ceased to be a meaningful source of support and influence. From the *Works and Days* of Hesiod we can derive a picture of the situation of this latter type. In this poem Hesiod emerges as an aggressive individualist, extolling the virtue of hard work and its ability to keep the farmer a free and self-sufficient person. The tutelary deity of the poem is what Hesiod calls the good strife:

> This Eris incites even a witless kind of man to work.
> For the lazy man studies the example of his neighbor
> who is richer, and who busily plows and plants
> and puts his house in order. And so the neighbor
> competes with his neighbor
> who is busy pursuing wealth. This is the Eris that
> is good for mortal men.
>
> WD 20-24

Although there are elements in such an attitude which we might call petit-bourgeois, in Hesiod's time such a philosophy was a statement of faith that men were viable without the supportive protection of the clan or tribe and without the protective paternalism of the upper classes. The spirit of the poem seems conservative, not revolutionary, to us, precisely because it is not the voice of the people who have become declassed, who live in serfdom or wander about as beggars (whose situation is an object lesson for Hesiod — WD 394-395). But it is the voice of those people who, in the unsettling and chaotic social situation which developed out of the breakdown of the great empires of the Mycenean ages and the Dark-Age resettlement in small towns and cities, could turn such a situation to their own use. The new widespread availability of metal (iron) for tools[14] and slaves for labor[15] meant, on the one hand, that the large landowning and ruling classes could consolidate their position and increase their wealth, but it meant, on the other hand, that those members of the lower classes who were not reduced to serfdom, extreme poverty, or forced to become beggars, could, by maximizing the efficiency of the land which they held or their small workshops in the cities, produce a surplus which would enable them to engage in trade both in the marketplace in the city and overseas. Their position, however, was highly precarious, since all judicial and other authority was vested in the *basileis* of the upper classes (see the famous passage at *WD* 37 ff.), and at any moment an arbitrary decision by a covetous aristocrat could wrest their means of livelihood from them.

In the *Odyssey*, we encounter a similar social situation, but from the perspective of the aristocratic nobleman, rather than the well-to-do peasant. There we find, in the persons of Odysseus and Penelope, as we noted earlier, the same emphasis on individual resourcefulness and self-reliance. But here the arena of struggle is the ruling class, the wealthy landowners. Although Odysseus seems to have held the kingship among them, there are several indications that it was as *primus inter pares*, not as king in the Mycenean sense,[16] and that his prominent position nevertheless made him subject to envy and so to constant attempts to undermine his authority or to seize his property.[17] In this struggle, the people (the *demos*) had little interest or stake, but were nevertheless available as a force which one or the other side could try to manipulate: in 16.375 ff. Amphinous fears that the *demos* might be incited by Telemachus to rise up against him and his cohorts, if report of their attempt on Telemachus' life gets abroad; in 1.239 ff., Mentor rebukes the *demos* for not coming to the aid of Telemachus against the suitors. But perhaps the most eloquent commentary on the constant strife and petty quarreling of this class is the picture that Homer presents of an analogous situation in Phaeacia. There the aristocratic class is filled with spirited and competitive young men: Nausicaa speaks of the reproaches to which she might be subject from one of the "haughty" men of her community, were she to accompany Odysseus to the palace herself (6.274 ff.); and Euryalus clearly speaks for his whole circle in 8.158, when he attempts to goad Odysseus into competition. In Phaeacia, however, the unquestioned authority of Alcinous is able to keep this group in check (in 8.396 he forces Euryalus to apologize to Odysseus), and so to guarantee for Phaeacia that political stability and freedom from constant shifts in the balance of power that was so notably absent from the early polis.

The conclusions that we can draw about early polis- and pre-polis-society from juxtaposing Homer and Hesiod, then, are as follows. This was a world of fairly small and independent communities, whose social and political structure was fluid, and in which power and authority were decentralized. The ruling aristocratic class was subject, not only to internal strife and power struggles, but to the increasing hostility and opposition of the lower classes, who still retained some vestige of political authority through their participation in the assembly. In addition, a "middle" class of enterprising and prosperous farmers, composed of men like Hesiod himself, were increasingly dissatisfied with their exclusion from all social and political privilege. They were shortly to develop enough economic leverage in the society to challenge this exclusion, but in Hesiod's time the focus is still on their weakness and subjection to the authority of the aristocratic class. In both the upper and lower classes, however, individual family units were increasingly emerging as the principal social nucleus, although clan ties still existed and were still strong. In particular, there were some significant restrictions on the right to dispose of land. Early Greek land tenure is, of course, a very complex question, and the rules which governed it have been for a long time the subject of considerable scholarly debate. However, it seems clear from references in both Homer and Hesiod[18] that there was some family property which was obliged to be returned to the clan in default of male heirs. And of course the legislation of Solon and other early lawgivers which instituted the practice of making wills (see below, page 28) would have been superfluous, had complete freedom of disposition existed prior to these reforms.

But even though it was not until Solon's time that the primacy of the individual family unit was established in the state, Solon's reforms themselves were only the consolidation of a trend that had its beginnings centuries before. We saw in Homer the idealization of the family, and especially of the relations of husband and wife. We see in Hesiod a picture of the everyday functioning of a family farm very much like the *oikos* of classical times. In addition, however, we come up against the earliest and most extensive formulation of the misogynistic attitude that was to become a veritable *topos* in Greek life and literature of later periods. What accounts for this, and what accounts for the absence of this type of misogyny in the Homeric poems, which also foreshadow, as we saw, household life?

We have discussed how, in Homer, the emphasis on the warrior as a family man entailed a new importance for his wife as well. The

22

domestic functions which she performs are celebrated as an integral and valuable part of a society increasingly inclined to incorporate the private side of man's existence into its cultural ideals. The other side of this picture is, of course, that the failure of the wife to fulfill her functions takes on a correspondingly greater importance, and represents a more significant threat. From the aristocratic point of view which the Homeric poems represent, however, and which is especially reflected in the treatment of Helen, such a threat is not altogether serious. In the context of large and loosely structured families, and of a secure class position, women's philandering is an aspect of the internal strife among the families and clans that characterized this period. As we saw, it represents an insult to the woman's husband rather than a threat to social stability, and since social status involved only the men of the community, women's faithlessness initiates a quarrel only between the men involved (whether mortals, as Alexander and Menelaus, or divine, as Hephaestus and Ares). We saw as well that in the one case which did involve reproach for the wife in question, Clytemnestra was rebuked by Agamemnon alone, for whom her adultery was a personal betrayal. Yet the fact that Agamemnon indicted the whole female sex on the basis of his own wife's crime, is an indication of the negative side of the incorporation of the social role of women into the cultural ideal: for there is a new insistence on strict adherence to a "type," and a corresponding disposition to construe moral failings as deviations from that type. But the Homeric picture does not focus on this aspect of women's position, as we have said, but where it treats the marital relationship it concentrates upon domestic harmony and the romantic aspects of the husband/wife relation, and where it reflects the mores of society at large (as in the matter of adultery) it takes advantage of the insignificance of women in the heroic or aristocratic codes of honor, in order to exonerate them of blame or reproach.

In the rising "middle" class which Hesiod represents, on the other hand, there was far greater fragmentation and far deeper divisions between class members. For these people a policy of aggressive individualism and fierce competition was dictated; the nuclear family was a necessity of life for this group, and the wife was part of a corporate effort which made possible her husband's ascent up to the economic and social scale. In particular, the most important function of women, that of providing an heir, was crucial to the survival and countinuance of the family in an era when availability of land was increasingly restricted, and continuance of rights over family land dependent upon the existence of an heir (see above, note 18). From the point of view of this class, women's sexuality emerges as a threat and as a potentiality which required regulation and supervision. In the classic expression of misogyny in the Hesiodic poems, for example, Pandora's attractiveness, her sexiness, makes her

> an evil thing, in which all men
> may rejoice in their hearts as they welcome their own destruction.
>
> *WD* 57-58

Apart from their sexuality, hostility to women was a product of the perception that women had no concrete stake in any particular social or political order, or even any particular family. The liability of women to be transferred from one family to another, and their freedom from any of the major social and political responsibilities, caused fears about the fickleness of their allegiances. This is a point which is made even in the *Odyssey*, and even about Penelope herself (Athena is urging Telemachus on his way, reminding him that his mother is beset with pressure from all sides to marry one of the suitors):

> For you know the kind of sentiments that woman has in her heart —
> she wants to increase the house of whomever she marries,
> but of her former children and of her dead husband
> she takes not a thought after he is dead, nor does she long for him.
>
> 15.20-23

Just such an attitude toward women informs the whole of Hesiod's *Theogony*, and determines its structure as well as the content of the ideology which it, as one of the principal cultural documents of the Greeks, presented to the Greek peoples of its own and succeeding eras. Hesiod makes a polar tension between male and female a primary fact of his cosmogony. The succession-myth provides the structure on which the whole poem is built, with the stories and other genealogies sandwiched between the three stages of the master-myth. In that succession-myth the female and her progeny are allied against the male, and are locked into a cycle of victory and defeat. It is only Zeus who finally succeeds in escaping from the cycle, and he does so by learning to assimilate, rather than simply repress, the forces which threaten him. Zeus' other children (Dike, Eunomia, Eirene, etc.) are not only tokens of his sponsorship of a moral order which brings peace and progress, but since they are nearly all female, they signify the beneficence of the female principle when it is subjected to regulation by

24

the patriarchal authority of the male. In the light of the Hesiodic model for the cosmos, then, the female appears not only as hostile to civilization, in that she is allied with the monsters and beasts who wreak chaos, but she appears as well as a being without moral dimension, as a force which needs direction and control to become truly human. Such a sentiment lies behind the truism about women which is frequently encountered in Greek literature – that she is both a great good and a great evil:

> For a man carries off as his prize no better thing
> than a good wife, and nothing to chill him to the bone like a bad one.
>
> WD 702-703

In the story of Pandora in the *Works and Days*, Hesiod makes the same point, both in the comment quoted above (page 24), and in his description of her creation. For in describing the positive aspects of this creature, Hesiod focusses upon those qualities which make her a useful partner for men in the household (beauty, skill in handiwork – 63 ff.), and regards as negative those qualities which involve open or secret assertiveness of her own will (a shameless mind and a deceitful character – 67).

The Hesiodic attitude toward women and their social role, then, is part and parcel of the developing trend toward a society made up of individual, small families, but an attitude formulated from the perspective of that class for whom the small family was an economic and political necessity and for whom, consequently, woman's enforced participation in a society in which she had no concrete stake posed a problem. From the Homeric or aristocratic point of view, this evolution was part of a promising movement toward a new humanism, and no immediate threat to a class for whom the small family was only part of a larger network of clan affiliations which assured the security of their political positions.

Perhaps we should pause briefly here and emphasize the point that the relation of the attitudes which we have been discussing to the particular realities of the historical era in which they appear is far from simple or direct. We have noticed how the economic and political situations of the day affected class outlook, but we should be wary of assuming that the fears or the ambitions of any one class or social group represented anything more than the recognition of the *limits of possible progress or decline*. That is to say, it is not necessary for 51% or more of women in eighth and seventh century Greece to have betrayed their husbands or families, for there to have existed the perception that, since women were regularly transferred from family to family, their allegiances were not necessarily steadfast. The well-known *topos* in Greek literature, whereby a woman betrays her family or state for love of a visiting stranger (Medea or Ariadne) did not represent a simple truth about Greek society; it was rather a rendering of the typical Greek ambivalence about woman's position: the awareness of her potentiality coupled with fears about her allegiances. And the realization that women were an element in the society whose participation had to be regulated or controlled by the patriarchal authority of the male, need not presuppose a majority of recalcitrant females. One needs only presume an increasing awareness of the paradox of a social order in which women's role was crucial and integral, but in which women's rights, in either the family or the state, were minimal. And as we shall see especially in the poetry of Solon, the Greeks were highly conscious of their polis as an artificial, or man-made creation, consciously embodying certain rational and universally valid principles. They were from earliest times sensitive both to women's new position in the city-state, and the need to justify her exclusion from public life. We need not therefore infer any kind of "agitation" on behalf of women in this period, in order to realize that the concern with women in Greek literature, both to idealize and to depreciate her, to celebrate and to deplore her position in society, was part and parcel of a whole sphere of philosophical speculation which sought to understand and to justify the particular features of the Greek city-state.

In the century after Hesiod a series of developments which took place nearly simultaneously all over the Mediterranean produced the cluster of small, independent city-states which was to be "Greece." Beginning in the late seventh century or even earlier, a wave of colonizations which swept east and west across the Mediterranean established a network of Greek cities around the entire basin. There was a tremendous resurgence of commercial activity, and by the sixth century several cities like Miletus were established as mercantile centers. The class tensions which we saw reflected in Hesiod's poems were intensified as the growing importance of the urban centers fostered an increasingly strong middle class. Control of the state by an aristocratic nobility defined by birth no longer served the interests of the state as a whole, and the polis underwent a long period of class strife followed by political reorganization. The outcome was the middle-class city state which Aristotle in the fourth century described as the ideal form of association:

It is therefore clear both that the best kind of political association is that which is administered by the middle class, and that those states are capable of being well governed in which the middle class is more numerous and stronger than the other two . . . .

Pol. 1295b35

This middle class had developed out of a broad spectrum of interests representing all social and economic groups: wealthy landowners interested in trade, younger or illegitimate sons of the nobility who had become involved in maritime ventures and other kinds of commercial enterprise, the growing number of craftsmen and other specialists, and peasants like Hesiod of Boeotia. In some cities, like Athens, a catalyst was provided by the agitation of the increasingly desperate poor peasants, whose exploitation had gone so far as to resemble slavery. In the final stages of progress toward the middle-class city state, one or both of two figures usually appeared: the tyrant and/or the lawgiver. They appeared at a time when civil strife had reached a critical point, and they were conciliators of social factions. The tyrants especially are associated with the sponsorship of arts and crafts, the promotion of industry and commerce, the minting or revaluation of coinage, and the first programs of public works. The effect of their rule was therefore to strengthen the economic position of the middle class and to promote the development of their cities into centers of commerce and industry. By their interest in the arts and through their public works the tyrants both opened new avenues of employment and helped to foster a sense of pride among the people as well as a new basis on which to identify with each other – as citizens (*politeis*).

The earliest lawgivers, such as Draco of Athens, were associated with the first setting down of that elaborate complex of rules and customs by which men lived. The fixing of these regulations in the form of a code accessible to everyone was the first step in freeing the population from the arbitrariness of the aristocratic nobility in whose hands the administration of justice still rested at this early period; codification of the laws was thus also the first step toward the abstraction of the laws and toward the conversion of them into that *nomos* which later was famous as "the master" of the Greeks. Later lawgivers, like Solon of Athens or Andromedas of Rhegium, were responsible for instituting a constitution, and for setting up the legal machinery which allowed the city to transform itself from a mere agricultural center into a hub of commerce and mercantilism. Although

27

Athens had its tyrants as well as its lawgivers, Solon performed the functions of both, though holding the office of only one (but the story that he was offered the tyranny indicates that some of the changes he was expected to accomplish were associated with the rule of a *tyrannos*). We can therefore achieve a more exact notion of how the classical polis arose if we examine his program in some detail. Although some of its features were peculiarly Athenian, like the Seisachtheia, even this was only the Athenian program for coping with a problem that had arisen all over the Greek world: inequality of land distribution. Pheidon of Corinth, for example, suggested keeping the number of family plots and the number of citizens equal to one another.[19]

The Seisachtheia (as Aristotle called it)[20] or the freeing of the debtors and their land, and the laws forbidding debt-enslavement, were a brake on the power of the wealthy classes, as well as a revolutionary proclamation of the right of every citizen to be free. For debt-enslavement was the primary method by which the estates of the rich had been enlarged.[21] Solon liberalized the laws of succession to allow for the making of wills, and this was a first step towards private property in that it freed the individual *oikos*, or family holding, from the obligation to be returned to the clan in default of male heirs.[22] Such is the importance attributed to these laws by Plutarch:

> But [Solon], by allowing a man who had no children to give
> his property to whomsoever he wished, ranked friendship
> above kinship and freedom of choice (*charin*) above neces-
> sity, and made property the possession of those who held it.
>
> *Sol.* 21.2

Solon was thus the first to institute "ownership" of property in the Aristotelian sense: Aristotle defines ownership as the right of alienation (*apallotriōsis*) which consisted in gift (*dosis*) and sale (*prasis*).[23] However, at the same time Solon limited this right of alienation of property to fathers without sons and to one generation[24] to prevent this new freedom from being used as a new method of accumulating estates. These limitations were probably unpopular with the large landowners, who had in all likelihood agitated for loosening of the restrictions on buying and selling family property, but who certainly did not have in mind the plurality of smallholders which Solon's restrictions produced. The rulers in an oligarchy, says Plato, when he is discussing the transition to democracy,

> do not want those of the youth who would become wild

> (*akolastoi*) to be held back by law so that it is not allowed
> for them to waste and ruin their property; for the rulers
> want, by buying the property of such men and lending
> money on the security of it, to become even richer and
> more honored.
>
> *Pol.* 555c

Solon's laws about property were instead primarily of benefit to peasant
and middle class landowners, and a first step in providing for these
classes a measure of the individual freedom which the wealth of the
upper classes had always guaranteed that group.

The reforms which concerned themselves with trade and manu-
facture were equally important in determining the course of the future
development of Athens and in ensuring the increasing dominance of
middle class interests. According to Plutarch, "[Solon] allowed for the
export of oil alone of natural produce, and he prohibited the export of
other products" (*Sol.* 24. 1). This restriction is generally understood to
have been aimed against the export of grain, one of the chief means by
which the large farmers had enriched themselves and created misery
for the poor (by driving up the price of grain at home).[25] Others of
Solon's new laws encouraged the development of craft-industry:

> [Solon] did not allow citizenship to be granted except to
> those who left their own countries by a decree of permanent
> exile (*aeiphygia*) or to those who fled with their whole
> families and settled in Athens to practice a trade. He is
> said to have done this not so much with the intention of
> driving away others as of inducing the above-mentioned to
> come to Athens by offering the assurance of participation
> in the state.
>
> Plut., *Sol.* 24.2

Another law mentions a penalty which a father who does not teach his
son a trade is liable to incur.[26] By such laws Solon forged a new alliance between the producers of oil and wine and the rising class of
craftsmen, mostly potters. Shortly thereafter Athenian pottery achieved
a dominance of the market which soon developed into a monopoly which
drove all competitors from the field.[27]

Bullion and coinage were in use in Attica prior to Solon's mone-
tary reforms, and had in fact been a factor in accelerating the process
of enslavement of the poor by the rich.[28] But under Solon the first
general issue of Athenian coinage took place, and his adoption of the

Corinthian or Euboic standard[29] and his abandonment of the Aeginetan or Pheidonian standard[30] meant that there would be "increased contact with the rich Corinthian trade with the Greek settlements in Italy and Sicily."[31]

The constitution was reformed under Solon so as to have an economic basis: "in using the four property groups for his work on the constitution, Solon clearly intended to base his constitutional reform on the facts of Athenian agrarian economy. Landed property and its income, not birth, was to be the basic principle."[32] The assembly was now open to *thetes*, the lowest property-class, and there was some loosening of the rules of eligibility for public office which had been altered as well by the new definition of the classes. But the features of his constitution which were most influential in initiating a move toward the democratic principle of judicial equality among all citizens (Solon's reforms were far from ensuring any other kind of equality) were those which Aristotle himself termed "most democratic":[33] (1) the law forbidding loans on personal security, which effectively guaranteed that no citizen was in danger of enslavement; (2) the right of every citizen to go to law on behalf on anyone who had been wronged, which established the principle that the state as a whole was involved in an assault on any one of its members: "for force belongs to the few, but the laws to all,"[34] as Demosthenes commented in referring to this law. And (3) the right of appeal from the decision of the magistrates to the popular courts, which Aristotle identifies as the most important reform in terms of increasing the power of the people, for, as he says, "when the people have a right to vote in the courts, they become masters of the state" (*Ath. Pol.* 9.1.)[35] Although the establishment of the courts of law was probably the work of Cleisthenes, the increased importance of the assembly after Solon (a result, not so much of alterations in its power and composition but of the substantiation of its powers by the new rule of law) caused him to be regarded as their originator.

In all areas, then, it was the work of Solon which was decisive in establishing the foundations for the development of a full democracy. Although the constitution as he had set it up was immediately challenged, neither the tyranny of Peisistratus nor the reforms of Cleisthenes did more than perfect and elaborate the system which Solon had conceived. It was his economic and legislative reforms which had ensured the viability of a state composed of a plurality of independent smallholders. It was Solon's *eunomia* which had designated the victory of a constitutional state after the arbitrary rule of the aristocratic

period, and which had first established the principle that every citizen
in the state had certain inalienable, if minimal, rights and freedoms.
Solon had thus paved the way for the Cleisthenian principle of equality
under the law — *isonomia* — under which all citizens, rich and poor,
shared equally in political office. And it was this principle which was
understood to express par excellence the democratic spirit. As Theseus
explains it to the Theban messenger in Euripides' *Suppliants*:

> For there is no rule
> by one man here, but the city is free.
> The people rules, taking turns
> in yearly succession, not giving to the rich
> the most power, but with the poor man having an equal share.
> . . . .
> At the very beginning, when there are no common
> laws, one man rules, having himself set down the
> law according to himself — this is no kind of equality.
> But when the laws are written down and the weak and
> the rich have the same equality of justice . . .
> [then the one with right on his side wins out].
>
> 404-407; 430-437

It was Solon who had written down the laws, Cleisthenes who had
established equal justice for all.

The other area in which Solon legislated extensively was the
family. Here too, the names of several others of the early lawgivers
(such as Philolaus of Thebes, Andromedas of Rhegium, Charondas of
Catana) are associated with family law, and so indicate to us the
importance of family relations in the formation of the Greek polis. And
it was these laws especially which were instrumental in establishing
for women that position in Greek society which appeared to later
generations especially as degraded or demeaning. The recent book by
W. K. Lacey, *The Family in Classical Greece* (Oxford, 1968) has set
forth in some detail the complex of laws and customs governing the
operation of the family and family relations in Greece. Lacey follows
Aristotle in defining the *oikos*, the household, as the smallest unit of
the state and in affirming its primary importance in the organization of
the Greek city-state, but he does not sufficiently emphasize the fact
that all aspects of women's position in antiquity followed directly
from this essential truth: that the state was conceived as a union of
oikoi, each of which was an association of husband, wife, children
and slaves, together with the property which supported them and whose

growth their association was designed to promote.[36] A. R. W. Harrison, in *The Law of Athens: the Family and Property* (Oxford, 1968), more consistently attributes the "rights" as well as the restrictions on women to her primary function, that of perpetuating her father's or husband's *oikos*.[37] Most of his observations in this regard, however, are derived from the work of Hans Julius Wolff[38] who, in several articles on Greek marriage law, has demonstrated that the fundamental principle which governed the legal relations between individual, family and state in the Greek polis was that which defined the polis as an aggregation of *oikoi*. Wolff has, in other words, demonstrated that this truth about the polis is not a mere *fact*, but a *principle* of law. Laws governing marriage therefore focus exclusively on the procreative function of the woman, and reserve that function as a duty owed ultimately to the *oikos* into which the woman was born. It was the laws of Solon which, as they regulated every other aspect of Greek life for the benefit of the middle class, assured the continuation and the perpetuity of that system through laws which systematized the succession to the headship of the *oikoi* which were its base. Although our greatest amount of evidence derives from the extensive litigation involving inheritance of the fourth century, and although the laws which governed inheritance changed from time to time, the basic principles on which they were based, as well as the most important of the laws themselves, were always understood to derive from Solon. And since the codification of the laws which began shortly after the first restoration of the democracy following the oligarchic revolution of 411, and continued throughout the fourth century, emphasized the legislation of Solon as the basic code and insisted on continuity with it,[39] it is altogether likely that we do have preserved, in spirit if not in letter, the most significant provisions of Solon's laws.[40]

The most famous of Solon's laws on women had to do with *epikleroi*, heiresses, and were a subdivision of his general program for revolutionizing the laws of succession (see above, page 28f.). As a result of Solon's reforms, brotherless daughters now had an enforceable right to inherit their father's property: "Whenever a man dies without making a will, if he leaves female children [his estate will go] with them" (Dem. 43.51).[41] They, in turn, are to be married or dowered by the next-of-kin on the father's side:

> let it be necessary for the next-of-kin to give [the heiress] in marriage or marry her himself. If he fails to do this, let the archon compel him to do it.

> Dem. 43.54

The rights over property which a woman thus acquired were, therefore, strictly limited: according to the Aristotelian definition (see above, page 28) they did not entail ownership at all. Strictly speaking, *epikleroi* only transmitted ownership of the property which they "inherited," and only to a male child related through his father to the same family from which his mother came. For all women, including *epikleroi*, were limited by Athenian law in their right to dispose of property to that valued at no more than one *medimnos*.[42] Therefore, even the limited rights over property of an *epikleros* were not so much an affirmation of her, as of her father's, rights. Lévi-Strauss has explained an analogous situation in kinship terminology: "Matrilineal filiation is but the authority of the woman's father or brother rather than husband which extends back to the brother's village."[43] The right, indeed duty, of an *epikleros* to inherit her father's property was the assertion of the primacy of the father's family over that of the husband, and expressed itself as a principle according to which a woman never passed out of the family into which she had been born. Through marriage, she was only "loaned out" to another family. Wolff, in his work on Athenian marriage laws,[44] has demonstrated that *ekdidonai*, the legal term for "to give in marriage,"

> always implies that someone gives up power over a person or thing for a specific purpose, and its effect is the transfer of rights insofar as this is required by the purpose. But it is at the same time understood that no definite severance of the relationship between the transferor and the object will take place.[45]

The duty of *epikleroi* to inherit, dictated as it was by the necessity to keep the father's *oikos* in his family, coupled with their inability to actually own the property, required in addition legislation that would assure the speedy production of an heir to the *oikos*. Hence the law which Plutarch called strange (*atopos*) and ridiculous (*geloios*): the law which "allows an *epikleros*, if the man who has power over her and who is her legal kyrios is unable to have intercourse with her, to be married by one of her husband's kinsmen" (*Sol*. 20.2). This man in turn is required "to have intercourse with her at least three times a month" (*Sol*. 20.3).

Adopted sons were subject to similar limitations: they could not make wills,[46] they could not return to their own families without leaving behind a legitimate son,[47] and they could not be registered as *kyrios* of the *oikos* until they had produced a legitimate son.[48]

The restrictions on *epikleroi* and on adopted sons had a common object: to ensure a descendant for any one *oikos*, and to prevent that *oikos* from being absorbed by inheritance into that of another family (that of the *epikleros'* husband, if she had one, or of the adopted son).

The only other form of property which needed similar protection was the dowry. Here, too, the laws benefitted women, but only incidentally, since the intention was to protect the interest of the father against that of the husband. The dowry was not required by law (except in the case of *epikleroi*, for whom the father's next-of-kin were required to provide a dowry, the amount of which was specified by law and was determined in accordance with the father's property qualification (see the law quoted above on p. 32, Dem. 43.54), but it was a customary contribution to the estate of the husband. It was not an outright gift, however, since the husband's rights over it were limited by a law which reflects the principle that the dowry continued to belong to the woman's family, and which incidentally protected the woman against divorce. For a husband was required by law "if he divorces his wife to give back the dowry, and, failing that, to pay interest on it at the rate of [eighteen percent]" (Dem. 59.52).

Solon is credited with some other legislation affecting women which does not have to do directly with the *oikos*, but reflects the need to regularize the marriage procedure, in view of the new importance of the household headed by a legally married husband and wife. Solon is recorded by Plutarch as the author of a regulation which called for "a bride to be shut up together with her husband after having eaten a quince" (*Sol.* 20.3); there was also a regulation that "a bride carry a vessel for roasting barley as a symbol of her household duties (*alphitourgias*)" (Pollux, I.246). Furthermore, it was Solon who regularized, even if he did not introduce, a different status for men and women in the matter of sexual freedom. He did, it is true, introduce strict laws against homosexuality,[49] but otherwise the double standard was not only tolerated by Solon, but encouraged, since it was he, according to tradition, who first set up brothels and even founded a temple of Aphrodite Pandemos using the profits collected by the madams.[50] Adultery in a free Athenian woman made her liable to exclusion from participation in religious ceremonies and festivals, and her husband was compelled to divorce her.[51] The adulterer, according to Solonian law, could be killed with impunity.[52] Both rape and seduction of free women Solon punished with a fine, and an unmarried daughter was allowed to be sold if she was caught having intercourse with a man.[53] It was only, however, under the latter circumstances that a woman could be sold by her *kyrios*, and so the law actually represented a step in the direction of freedom from the complete discretionary power which, prior to this legislation, a man had exercised over the women under his *kyrieia*.

The rest of Solon's legislation on women comes under the heading of sumptuary laws: he supposedly introduced a restriction on bridal gifts (*phernai*) and a limitation to "three pieces of clothing and household items of small value"[54] (i.e. the traditional *himatia kai chrusia*) on the property that a woman could bring with her when she married. He further

> regulated by law the public appearances of women and their mourning and their festivals, prohibiting disorderly (*atakton*) and intemperate (*akolaston*) conduct. He ordered that a woman going outdoors not have on more than three garments, nor carry more than an obol's worth of food or drink, nor a basket larger than a cubit, and that a woman not go abroad at night unless she travelled in a wagon with a lamp shining before it.
>
> Plut., Sol. 21.4

Such legislation, characteristic of the early lawgivers, was primarily intended to put a check on display and extravagance among the wealthy families, which was occasioned primarily by marriage celebrations, funeral solemnities or parties of various kinds. Solon consequently regulated the conduct of men as well as of women at funerals;[55] he specified the time and manner in which boys were to go to school or to the gymnasium;[56] and he prohibited unemployment (*argia*) among citizens.[57] It was in all likelihood the conservative spirit of such laws that encouraged the growth of that bourgeois morality which later thought it unfitting for Athenian matrons to appear in public at all.

It is necessary to emphasize that all of the laws which we have been considering applied only to middle class women, to that group in other words who, together with their husbands and children, were intended to be the bastion of the new state. As the state increased in size, there arose a very large number of metics, freedmen and slaves who were excluded in varying degrees from citizen rights. None of this group could, except by special dispensation, own land, and so the regulation of their marriages would have been superfluous, except when they married Athenian citizens. Yet the fact that there were laws governing marriage, succession and related matters among metics and freedmen (administered by the polemarch rather than the archon), and that these laws seem to have duplicated those governing full-fledged Athenian citizens, is an indication that the laws and customs of the middle class citizens, while applying directly to only a fraction of the population of the city-state, provided nevertheless the dominant cultural pattern.[58] This is further demonstrated from the fact that informal unions between men and women in Athens, whether citizens or not, seemed to have mimicked, in several important respects, the arrangements of legitimate marriage.[59]

Let us now attempt to draw out some of the implications for women of the Solonian program of legislative and constitutional reform. It is clear that the program as a whole was a progressive one, and women derived some particular benefits from it. The social role which women had always played, that of wives and mothers, was now legally established as their right as well as duty, and was recognized, through various festivals,[59a] as a vital and honored contribution to the state. However, Solon's re-introduction into society of the distinction between public and private, albeit in a new form, had some important ramifications for women. In Dark-Age society, as we remarked, the heroic code reflected a culture which conceived of the female and male spheres of activity as two separate entities, existing of necessity side by side, but fundamentally unrelated to each other. In the city-state, the private side of man's existence, his headship of an *oikos*, is the condition for his incorporation into the state as a citizen. The distinction between public and private is therefore maintained, only now the private life of man is a sub-category of the public sphere. Insofar as women continued to be associated with the private side of life alone, they now appear as a sub-species of humanity. That is to say, women had before been conceived as an aspect of life in general; now they are seen as an aspect of men's existence. The difference is an important one, for it means that the inferiority of women, their subservience to men, has to be explicitly recognized. Formerly, women's inferiority was merely implied by the fact that the cultural ideal (the hero) was male. Now, the social and legal structure of the state specifically endorses and prescribes the subservience of women to men. The difference, as we see, is not one of quality of life – for women's social role and function did not undergo any fundamental transformation. Rather, the difference in status has to do with the *manner* in which women's function is incorporated into the state. The Greek city-state gave women status as an aspect of men's existence, rather than as existants in their own right. That this was necessary is a commentary on the limited and partial nature of Athenian democracy.

For the social and political history of Athens, as of every pre-capitalist state, is a history of constant trade-offs of prerequisites and rights. Where the early aristocracy had ensured a free and leisured life for itself by the concentration in its hands of all economic and social privilege, the democracies of ancient Greece secured liberty for all of its citizens by inventing a system of private property[59b] which required women to legitimate it and slaves to work it. However, such considerations must not blind us to the fact that, insofar as the polis was founded on the ideal of guaranteed rights and freedoms for all its citizens, it was a progressive step forward from the arbitrary rule by a nobility of birth which had characterized the aristocratic state. The principle of freedom and equality, once adopted for some, strives by the necessity of logic to incorporate all under its aegis, and the history of the Greek state from the time of Solon is one of an ever-expanding citizen body.

When we turn to the poetry which arose in the democratic city-state, we find that the challenge which women's exclusion from public life posed, is immediately taken up. There emerges as well a clear division between the aristocratic and the "bourgeois" outlooks. On the whole, the trends which we discovered in Homer and Hesiod continue in evidence throughout the archaic and classical periods – but the differences which we noted between their outlooks harden into a real division between the aristocratic and the bourgeois poets. Now although we noted that in Homer's poems, and in the *Odyssey* especially, the particular features of aristocratic culture and life-style were represented, Homer's point of view did not represent that class alone. Rather, he concerned himself with changes in social forms and in cultural values that affected society as a whole, and that represented a whole social transformation, not the interests of a particular class. Similarly, in Hesiod, although his point of view in the *Works and Days* may have been more demonstrably class-determined, his *Theogony* voiced the beliefs and the values of society as a whole. However, in the next great era of literary production after the age of the epic, that is to say the lyric age, the intense class conflict of this period finds expression in a marked difference of outlook between the poets whose sentiments express the views of the rapidly-declining rich nobility, and those poets whom we have called "bourgeois," who seem to voice, in one way or another, the aspirations as well as the doubts, the hopes as well as the fears, of that emerging middle class whose economic and political interests were soon to dominate the state, and whose ideals were shortly to become identified with the spirit of the polis itself. In aristocratic poetry the romantic attitude toward women continued to prevail; it is a wholly different kind of romanticization, however, from what we found in Homer. For it focusses neither upon women's position in society (as in the *Iliad*) nor on individual women (as in the *Odyssey*). Here the love-relationship (rather than the marriage-relation) is prominent, and the attitude toward them has to be deduced from their portrayal as love-partners. In the bourgeois poetry of this same period, as we shall see, the love-relationship is prominent also, but it has a completely different character; and in bourgeois poetry we have as well direct comments (or attacks) on both individual women and on women seen as a class apart.

Among the aristocratic poets of the lyric age are Alcaeus, Sappho, Ibycus and Anacreon.[60] Although we have direct evidence about the political views of Alcaeus alone of this group, we can infer from indirect evidence the typically conservative outlook of the aristocrat in the cases of the other poets. Alcaeus was an outspoken opponent of Pittacus and other political leaders of Lesbos. Since Pittacus' tyranny was, like the archonship of Solon, distinguished by its fair-mindedness and sympathy toward the widespread demand for a fairer distribution of power and privilege, Alcaeus' opposition to it marks him as a die-hard aristocrat, utterly opposed to any concessions to the agitators, and bitterly resentful of Pittacus' popular appeal.[61] There is very little indeed in Sappho's poems to indicate her perspective on the burning political questions of the day, but what little there is certainly suggests that her sympathies were similar to those of Alcaeus.[62] Ibycus and Anacreon were court poets to the tyrant Polycrates of Samos in the second half of the sixth century. Now we have already identified, in the cases of Athens, Mytilene and other cities, the period of the rule by tyrants as an era of great progress for the middle class, and in the case of Alcaeus his opposition to the Mytilenean tyrants marked him as an aristocrat. Polycrates was no exception to this rule, for he sponsored many public works, encouraged industry, and promoted trade, in the usual manner. But he also maintained his court as a bastion of the old aristocratic way of life, conspicuous for its elegance and luxury, and famous for its cultivation of the fine arts. A short-lived but immensely powerful piratical thassalocracy, for which Polycrates was single-handedly responsible, was the background against which there flourished side by side in Samos this unique combination of aristocratic elegance and solid bourgeois accomplishment.

The works of these aristocratic poets are especially distinguished by their portrayal of a world of youthfulness, beauty and grace, peopled

by gods, heroes, or luxuriating aristocrats, and characterized especially by the absence of conflict. There are hymns to deities, stories of the
old heroes, celebrations of the pleasures of love and wine. It is a
world, and a way of life, which contrasts quite strikingly with the
struggle – social, political and economic – that was going on all
around these poets, and as such it represents something of an anachronism. For it looks back to an era when aristocratic manners dominated
the culture, and when the aristocratic class ruled society. This is
nowhere more clearly demonstrated than by Alcaeus' poem on Lesbian
armor (Z34), in which the epic type of armature, is described in ad-
miring detail, rather than the hoplite type of arms which were current
in Alcaeus' own day, and whose advent had betokened an important
advance for those non-aristocratic members of society who were increasingly demanding the right to fulfill major social functions.

Otherwise, the fact that sumptuary laws were a significant
feature of the legislation of the early lawgivers (see above, page 35)
leads us to suspect that the style of life celebrated by the aristocratic
poets was just that which promoted resentment and bitterness among
the rest of society, and so the aristocratic poets' insistence upon
glorifying the habits and manners of their class emerges as something
of a polemic against the increasing "vulgarization" of political and
social life. Pittacus, for example, the tyrant of Mytilene, was especially remembered as the sponsor of laws against drunkenness;[63] Alcaeus
was equally famous as a lover of wine. Now we must believe that it
was not the drinking of wine, as such, which was objectionable in the
early polis, but the extravagant and sometimes raucous gatherings of
young aristocrats at which wine flowed especially freely. It is just
such elegant parties which Alcaeus' poems on wine suggest, which
emphasize the luxuriousness of the occasions: Alcaeus drinks from
large ornamented cups (Z22), and with his head resting on a soft
pillow (Z14).

The pursuit of love by these poets is equally refined and voluptu-
ous. In the first place, there is quite an emphasis on homosexual
love, of which both the practice and the subject were especially associated with the aristocratic way of life in this period. The tradition
of Solon's legislation prohibiting pederasty among citizens (see above,
page 34) may have been part of his effort to restrict aristocratic display. Some at least of the extant fragments of each of the poets under
discussion refer to a homosexual love. The love-affairs of these poets,
whether heterosexual or homosexual, are invariably pursued in cultivated gardens or rural sanctuaries, in an atmosphere of refined beauty

and elegance:

> The Cyprian goddess [has found you] in good season,
> Damoanactidas; . . . beside the lovely olive-trees, . . .
> delights; when the gates of spring are opened . . . with
> ambrosia scented . . . .
>
> Alcaeus, P 26 (trans. D. L. Page)

A similar delicacy and elegance characterize Sappho's Fr. 94 (addressed to an absent girl) and Fr. 2, in which Aphrodite is summoned to appear in "a pleasant grove of apple-trees." The aristocratic outlook of Ibycus and Anacreon is reflected mostly in an exaggeration and amplification of the Lesbian emphasis on refinement and delicacy, which expresses itself in these two poets as highly-wrought artifice. Ibycus, for example, consistently employs the opening of blossoms in a carefully cultivated garden as a metaphor for the love-experience, and Anacreon's characterization of a young girl as a Thracian filly whom he wishes to "mount" is particularly famous as an example of risqué metaphor.

The attitude toward passion in the aristocratic poets especially distinguishes them from their bourgeois counterparts. For the idea of love as suffering, and, especially, of passion as dangerous, is entirely absent from these poets. This is not to say that the aristocratic poets, and especially Sappho, do not flirt with such ideas – but in the end they are revealed as only one move in what is essentially a game of love. The famous *phainetai moi*, (Fr. 31), for example, which is the archetype for all subsequent expressions of the physical manifestations of *eros* in love-poetry, is structured around a tension between passion and control which has often been obscured by the omission of the last line of the poem: "But all must be endured, since . . ." (ἀλλὰ πᾶν τόλματον, ἐπεὶ . . .).[64] There is a playful tension in this poem between the passions aroused by love and the decorous restraint of aristocratic *eros*. The poem opens with a scene of lovers' dalliance, in which the tenderness of the girl and the fascination of the boy are the central elements of the picture: the boy sits and listens closely to the sweet voice and pleasant laughter of the girl; then the force of Sappho's passion, with its extreme physical manifestations, suddenly intrudes, but only to be checked by her a few lines later. Clearly, Sapphic love, famous though it was, was not the stormy violence of that destructive *eros* which we encounter in other Greek poetry. Its passion, though hyperbolically exaggerated, was always controlled. Similarly, in Sappho's first fragment the anguish of the poetess is

40

regarded by Aphrodite (and hence by the poetess herself) with tender and amused indulgence (13-16). Her ability to smile at her own extremes of emotion reveal an attitude toward the pursuit of love which regards it as something of an amusement or diversion, and which is wholly consistent with other aspects of the aristocratic outlook which we have discussed. A short fragment of Anacreon reveals a similarly light-hearted attitude:

> Once more I am in love and not in love
> and both maddened and not mad.
>
> Fr. 428

For the aristocrats, then, love is a game, but it is a sport which is to be played only among the aristocrats themselves. Anacreon, as well as Sappho and Alcaeus, condemn love with whores (*pornai*). In Anacreon's satire on the ostentatious Artemon (Fr. 388), it is a mark of the latter's vulgarity and lower-class origins that he associated "with bread-sellers and volunteer prostitutes." Sappho disapproved of her brother's emancipation of an Egyptian courtesan; according to Herodotus, she "railed at him in a poem."[65] And we have a fragment of Alcaeus which claims that "anything given to a whore might just as well be tossed into the waves of the grey sea" (F3[b] 26 f.)

Women in these poems are beautiful goddesses and heroines, the wives, mothers and daughters of the gods and heroes, or else they are the idealizations of the aristocratic female "type": tall and stately, proud, slightly haughty, and cultured. In aristocratic as well as bourgeois poetry this type is symbolized by the mare. We have already referred to Anacreon's address to the Thracian filly; we should mention as well the comparison of the choral leaders in Alcman's *Partheneion* to thoroughbred and prizewinning mares. And Alcman too is very much an aristocratic poet, for he was associated with Sparta in that brief period in the seventh century when it was a flourishing and highly cultured aristocracy, and when there was a great influx of foreign poets and musicians. The women, like the men in these poems, appear exclusively at aristocratic feasts, in religious celebrations and in the dance; they inhabit a dreamlike world much like some of the fantasy lands in the *Odyssey*, where, as on the island of Aiolos,

> [The sons and daughters of Aiolos and their consorts]
> evermore beside their dear father and noble mother
> sit feasting; and beside them are lain assorted delicacies,
> and the house is fragrant with sacrifice and resounds with

41

the echo of their celebrations in the courtyard all day long.
But at night they lie down once more beside their wedded wives
in beds strewn with coverlets and with bored bedsteads.

                                                    10.8-12

    This idealization of aristocratic manners and the creation of a
fantasy-world of peace and harmony, was the aristocratic counter to
the progressive spirit of the times; their world of sensuality and beauty
was an answer to the stark political realities of the day. In such a
context the emphasis on women's beauty and sexual appeal, and the
lack of any expression of misogyny, cannot legitimately be construed
as either an indication of women's favorable position or of the aristocratic poets' favorable attitude toward them. For it is evident that
women's social role was of no concern to these poets. Although we
may perhaps infer from the interest in romantic love a certain greater
degree of sexual freedom for women, there is no indication anywhere
in lyric poetry that aristocratic women participated any more (or less)
in public life than their later counterparts. And certainly any liberties
which they were allowed were a bonus deriving from the prominence
and wealth of their fathers, brothers or husbands. Only to the extent,
then, that we say that women were limited in their social function to
the sexual partners of men, can we say that they were honored in
aristocratic society. And since even this deference is paid to them as
part of a program of idealizing the aristocratic way of life, it cannot
be interpreted as a true representation of the mores or the values of
the times.
    If we consider briefly the circle of Sappho, whose existence
has suggested to many that women in aristocratic society occupied a
"higher" position than their later counterparts in Athenian society,
I do not think that we shall find anything to contradict the assertions
we have just made. It is difficult to define the exact nature of this
circle, but since it was frequented by girls only during a brief interval
between childhood and marriage, it is perhaps most analogous to a
finishing school. Its existence is nevertheless testimony to the high
degree of culture and independence in the life of aristocratic women,
and suggests a favorable contrast with the largely uncultured and
home-keeping life of the fifth-century Athenian woman. We should be
wary, however, of making inferences like that of Rostovtzeff:[66] "Women
did not play that part in the life of Athens in the fifth century which
they had played when Greece and Ionia were ruled by aristocracies."
For aside from the fact that such contrasts depend upon an overly and

incorrectly negative evaluation of the fifth-century woman's status, the existence of Sappho's circle does not imply a larger role in the public life of Mytilene for its members. Quite the contrary, Sappho's group is quite self-consciously outside of ordinary political and social life. And we should not forget that the disapproval of intelligent women which we find voiced by characters in fifth-century literature[67] is part of a general hostility to intellectual sophistication.[68] What we can infer from the existence of a group like that of Sappho in seventh-century Mytilene is evidence of an atmosphere in which the pursuit of culture and the leisured life which the wealth and prestige of their families allowed women, was not only tolerated but encouraged. This has been a feature of aristocratic life and mores in all cultures in every era, and carries no implication that aristocratic society either consciously or unconsciously accepted the principle of women's basic equality with men. We do not lack a voice enjoining women from competition with men even among antiquity's female practitioners of the "masculine" art of poetry:

> I myself reproach Myrtis, lovely-voiced
> though she is, because she entered into
> rivalry with Pindar, though she was born a woman.
>> Corinna of Boeotia, 664 (a)

On the other hand, it is the case that in just the conditions of aristocratic life, in which all members of the upper class are freed from the burden of daily toil, a radically different style of life for men and women seems least rational and least necessary. In such circles, therefore, life styles of men and women are likely to gravitate toward one another; and it is no accident that the basis for Plato's equality of men and women in the *Republic* was a division of labor in society as a whole much like that which prevailed in the early aristocracy.

Aristocratic poetry, then, romanticizes women and the love-relationship as part of its idealization of an age prior to the one of chaos and struggle in which aristocratic domination of society was swept away. It is a kind of propaganda which associates peace and harmony between the classes and sexes with a period when the aristocratic monopoly of society assured the stability of values and customs. Similarly, the seemingly higher status of the women of this period was, in the first place, an incidental benefit accruing to them from their class position and, in the second place, consisted not in a greater role in public life but in the freedom to lead a more civilized and cultured private life.

The "bourgeois" poets (as we have designated those figures whose life or whose work reflected the problems of the emerging middle-class state) were acutely aware of their society as an order born out of chaos and struggle. Their response to the turbulence of their times was not to oppose to it a fantasy world of peace and harmony, in the manner of the aristocratic lyric poets, but to see in the social and political upheaval which surrounded them the model of the world itself, in which struggle was constant and success never sure. This group includes philosophers as well as poets, in whose works there is represented a great diversity of themes, as well as a variety of genres. In our discussion, we shall concentrate primarily on those poets whose works have direct relevance to an evaluation of the attitude toward women. We shall therefore just briefly characterize some of the other aspects of the bourgeois outlook.

The mutability of fate, the caprice of fortune, life's frustrations and the constant necessity of toil are the themes of these bourgeois poets. A spirit of pessimism, which runs as an undercurrent throughout all of this poetry, especially distinguishes the bourgeois from the aristocratic attitude. This is not to say that the poets whose basic outlook was aristocratic were not deeply disturbed by the turmoil of their times, and that they did not acutely feel the need for struggle and conflict. On the contrary, we saw in Alcaeus a hostility to certain political developments of his time that was certainly heartfelt, and the poem of his often called "the ship of state" clearly expresses a genuine concern and feeling of helplessness. But what especially characterizes the aristocratic attitude is the tendency to turn one's back on the troubled world of reality, and find in the world of aristocratic manners and ideals an "answer" to the problems of the day. The bourgeois poets deliberately focus on the chaos of their times, and derive from it a philosophy which defines the world itself as hostile, its gods as inscrutable, and the only safe course one of moderation and compromise. Solon of Athens was, of course, the great example of the thinker who combined a deep sense of pessimism with an ability to see in a policy of moderation and balance the possibility of ultimate redemption. As his poetry expresses this conviction, so his constitution was the concrete realization of these ideals. Hesiod's *Theogony* celebrated the final emergence of order and peace out of strife and chaos by means of Zeus' policy of compromise. Other philosophers of this period like Anaximander and Anaximenes sought to explain the dynamics of the world order; the world for them was not a static and unchanging harmony, like the magical realm of the gods and heroes, but a system which was constantly being transformed, in which stability was only an ultimate fact, invisible in the constant whirl of the cycles of nature.[69] The warring of opposites is a particularly prominent feature in the poetry as well as the philosophy of this period. Both Anaximander and the later Empedocles made pairs of opposites a feature of their cosmologies; and in the Pythagoreans this tendency evolved into a fundamental dualism which produced, among other ideas, the Table of Opposites.

The biographies of these poets and philosophers are as diverse as their works; some of them, like Solon or Archilochus, were aristocrats by birth, but found themselves, by choice or necessity, casting their lot with the émigrés, colonists, peasants or other social groups who together made up the new middle class. Simonides of Ceos was a "court poet," but rendered his services not to a tyrant whose court was a preserve of aristocratic mores, like that of Polycrates, but to the Peisistratids, one of the most progressive tyrannies in a city-state which was at that time the most progressive in the Greek world. In contrast to the aristocrats like Alcaeus and Theognis who deplored the new power of money and lamented the debasement of the nobility by the influx of *nouveaux riches*, Simonides (in the famous Fr. 4, discussed by Socrates in the *Protagoras*) gave a new definition to the ἀνὴρ ἀγαθός which recognized nobility as a moral virtue rather than the prerogative of a single social class acquired by birth; and so far from lamenting the new power of money, Simonides was quick to turn the situation to his own profit, and became famous as the first poet to write for money.[70] In the case of another poet such as Archilochus, the details of his biography themselves make up an anti-aristocratic polemic. His famous boasting claim to have saved his skin at the expense of his shield (Fr. 6) has a parallel in Alcaeus (Z105b) but, according to what we can determine from the corrupt fragment, Alcaeus forewent Archilochus' defiant inversion of the warrior's code. Archilochus' small and bandy-legged general, whom he prefers (in Fr. 60) to the conventional aristocratic type, expresses similar scorn for traditional values, as does his dismissal (in Fr. 64) of the hero's ideal of the noble and glorious death.

As we might expect, the attitude toward women in the bourgeois poets is quite different from what we found to be the aristocratic view. For one thing, it is far more complex. The portrayal of women in aristocratic lyric can be summarized simply as an idealization of the sexual and procreative aspects of woman, whether on the divine or the human level. Bourgeois poetry both praises and condemns women,

45

and for a variety of reasons. The picture of women which this poetry offers is full of contradictions — but they are contradictions which correspond with ambivalences in the world view and in the social philosophy of the bourgeois poets.

The willingness of the bourgeois poets to relate directly to the realities of the world around them results in a kind of poetry which is altogether realistic, whether on a somewhat mundane or elevated level. Satire and lampoon appear as a genre of bourgeois poetry, and one of its earliest targets is woman — individual women and women seen as a class apart. Archilochus and Hipponax, like the aristocratic poets, portray love-affairs in their poetry; but Archilochus and Hipponax are both involved with real women, who have names (Neobule and Arete), and who involve the poets in conflicts which have to do directly with the everyday realities of social life.[71] The aristocratic poets, we recall, were in love with nameless, godlike beauties, whose favors they courted in a dreamlike world of peace and luxury.

Semonides of Amorgos was also an iambic poet, and according to tradition turned his art to the service of his personal hostilities. But he is most famous to us as the author of a long diatribe against women. This tirade against women divides them into types, each associated with a particular animal. The poem has obvious affinities with Hesiod's elaborate simile in the *Theogony* (592-599), which compares women to the drones in a beehive, and men to the busy bees, and which is our earliest example of misogynistic poetry. In Semonides, however, the bee is associated with the good woman:

> To her alone no blame is attached,
> but life flourishes and prospers under her care.
>
> Fr. 7, 84-85

As in Hesiod, woman's sexuality is maligned; an interest in sex appears as part of the complaint against two of the ten types: the donkey-woman ''who'll sleep with anyone'' (48-49) and the weasel-woman ''who is always crazy to make love'' (53). Furthermore, one of the distinguishing features of the good woman, descended from the bee, is that she

> does not take pleasure in sitting among the women
> when they are discussing sex.
>
> Fr. 7, 90-91

Another prominent complaint against women in Semonides' poem, and one which figures importantly in Hesiod's condemnation of women, is their laziness. This complaint is voiced against several types, the mud-woman, the donkey-woman, and especially the mare-woman. The latter animal, as we mentioned in our discussion of aristocratic poetry, is the bestial representative of the type of the aristocratic woman. Her laziness is not so much a matter of a slothful character, as of a contemptuous disdain for household drudgery:

> She maneuvers her way around the slavish and
> troublesome housework,
> and wouldn't put a finger to the mill, or so much as lift
> the sieve, or sweep the dirt out of the house,
> or go into the kitchen, for fear she'll get dirty.
>
> Fr. 7, 58-61

The prominence of this type of complaint against women is certainly part of the bourgeois polemic against aristocratic luxury (and the legislation against such extravagance is testimony to the importance of the issue), and indicates as well a tendency to associate the participation of women in social life and their freedom from daily household chores with the prodigality of the aristocratic class rather than to view it as a neutral issue. Not only, therefore, is misogyny itself a *topos* peculiar to bourgeois poetry, but certain ways in which it is expressed are specifically class-determined.

The second fragment of Phocylides, in which women are divided into types associated with animals, in the manner of Semonides' diatribe, with the bee-type outstanding for her virtue, makes it clear that by the sixth century not only was misogyny established as a *topos* of Greek poetry, but that it already had associated with it a particular set of conventions. It contrasts with the romanticism of aristocratic Greek lyric in the same way that the Medieval Romances, written by court poets, were opposed to the "writings of bourgeois inspiration, which attacked women with malignancy: fables, comedies and lays charged them with laziness, coquetry and lewdness."[72] Such satire and lampoon in the Middle Ages were, however, the merest superficial manifestation of an altogether serious debate concerning the Christian life, in which the demands of the spirit are opposed to those of the flesh, and woman is associated with the seductive enticements of the latter. This debate took the form especially of a controversy over the value and place of marriage in the Christian life.[73]

A similar contrast can be observed in the Greek literature of our period, in which the misogyny of Hesiod, Semonides or Phocylides reflects a far more serious strain of thought which assimilated the

47

differentiation of the social roles of male and female to the polarities whose opposition defined the world-order. So, in the Pythagorean Table of Opposites, the female is associated with the boundless, dark, and bad, etc., and the male with limit, light, and good, etc. Such a dichotomy is already visible in Hesiod's *Theogony*, which presented the progress of history and civilization in terms of a triumph of the male over the female forces. But this was only the first example of a long tradition which persists throughout the history of Greek literature. In the Homeric Hymn to Delphian Apollo, for example, the successful establishment of Apollo's oracle depends upon his defeat of the Pytho, by which he establishes his preeminence over the spring Telphousa, the older, female, and more established deity of the region, who had sent Apollo to meet the dragon. The story of the foundation of Apollo's oracle has within it another tale of conflict between god and goddess, a tale which displays suggestive affinities with the succession-myth in the *Theogony*. This story of strife between male and female deities reverses the Hesiodic succession, since it presumes the successful establishment of the kingship of Zeus, and is initiated by Hera's anger at the birth of Athena, which occurred in the last part of the *Theogony*. This birth represents, in the Homeric Hymn as in Hesiod, an interruption of the normal procreative relationship between the male and female, and the male god's assumption of the female's potency. Also as in Hesiod, the female goddess is identified with the impulse to destruction and with the chthonic powers. The male deity is victorious over the theriomorphic symbol of chaos and disorder which is called into being by the female. An era of peace and prosperity is immediately consequent upon the final victory of the male god – the reign of Zeus itself which is the background for the sub-story in the Hymn, or the establishment of Apollo's oracle in the main story. The fact that, as we have mentioned already, the female is represented as beneficent when her creative potential is subjected to the regulatory power of the male, is highly important. For it forms the basis of another tradition in Greek literature – one which commends the faithful wife and mother, and finds in her an outstanding example of moral virtue. To understand the meaning of this tradition, we must discuss it in the context of the bourgeois poets' attitude toward love, *eros*.

We have mentioned in connection with our discussion of aristocratic love-poetry the fact that what especially differentiates this poetry from the bourgeois type is a concentration in the latter on the suffering which love involves, and on the violent and destructive character of *eros*. We mentioned that the aristocratic poets, and especially Sappho, flirted, as it were, with the idea of love as suffering. But the idea of love as anguish, and, especially, as violent and dangerous, especially dominates bourgeois love-poetry and mythology. And just as we discovered in the aristocratic poets' romanticization of the love-relationship a tendency to idealize women, so do we find in the stories of violent and destructive love of the bourgeois poets an inclination to associate women with this passion. Part of Stesichorus' famous innovatory treatment of the old myths, for example, consisted in a retelling of the stories of Helen and Clytemnestra which stressed the immorality of these women, and which called them a curse to their father (Tyndareus – the story of Helen's divine birth is suppressed), "married twice and three times, and husband-deserters all" (Fr. 223). In his story of the Trojan War Aphrodite was apparently far more prominent as the originator of the strife than in the *Iliad* (which only alludes to the judgment of Paris at XXIV.25 ff. and otherwise focusses on Alexander's violation of the guest-friend relation as the cause of the war). Stesichorus was probably the originator of the tradition which made Clytemnestra alone responsible for the death of Agamemnon (a treatment of the myth which similarly contrasts with the Homeric exoneration of Clytemnestra).

The converse of this disposition to condemn women for adulterous transgressions was a corresponding tendency to use faithful women as examples of moral probity. We saw the beginning of this trend in Homer, in his romanticization of the relationship between Hector and Andromache, and in his presentation of Penelope's character. One of the few long fragments of the poet Simonides portrays Danae afloat at sea in a chest with her infant son Perseus (Fr. 12). There is evident in Simonides' description a real appreciation of the tender love of mother for child, and in addition, Danae's apology in the final lines of the fragment, for possible presumptuousness in her prayer to Zeus, is intended to commend her to us as a model of endurance and moral probity in the face of possible disaster.

It is evident, then, that the view of love as destructive, and the association of women with the violence of passion, is an aspect of the bourgeois world-view which focussed on chaos and associated women with the destructive forces in the universe. But as in the world at large the presentation of the goddesses who regulate the seasons (Horai) and who betoken social stability (Dike, Eunomia), as the daughters of Zeus, signified the beneficence of the female potency when it was regulated by the male principle of order, so in the everyday world of social reality did the ideal of the virtuous wife and mother represent the potentially destructive and violent power of *eros* (which is associated with the woman) subordinated to the regulatory agency of the family structure.

The attitude of the bourgeois poets toward women, then, was profoundly affected by their tendency to accept the reality of the struggle and chaos of their world, and to generalize it into a condition of existence. For the polarity of the male and female roles in their culture, which assigned to the female the office of procreation and nourishment, and to the male that of achievement and ambition, led these poets to assimilate this opposition, in an exaggerated form, to the metaphysical polarities which governed the world order.

This ideological polarity, which identified women with passion in the love-relationship, with the family in all social relationships, and with the chaotic in the world-order, was a product of the social and political structure of the polis, in which women were recognized as an aspect of men's existence rather than as existants in their own right. However, just as we discovered that the polis did in fact accomplish some movement toward the acceptance of women as full human beings, and as such represented an advance over the aristocratic state, so do we find in bourgeois poetry, even of the misogynistic variety, a recognition of women's claim to full human status. For the perception of women as a threat, and the hostility toward them as sexual beings, implicitly expects them to assert their claims in these regards, and implicitly understands the need to justify the prevailing order against such claims. In the Homeric Hymn to Delphian Apollo, Hera appears as a powerful and formidable foe to Zeus, conscious of her own prerogatives, jealous of their usurpation by Zeus, and altogether capable of retaliation. Only the most thoroughgoing romantic will oppose to this portrait the ideal of aristocratic womanhood, with its dream-like perfection, its glorification of the submissive, yielding aspect of the female, and claim that the latter betokens a greater respect for women. For in fact, the favorable portrait of woman's role which we find in aristocratic poetry is no more than an idealization of her sexual and procreative function in which she remains, as she was in bourgeois poetry, an aspect of life in general — in this case of the luxurious life of the aristocrat. The bourgeois attitude, insofar as it perceives women as a powerful political threat, recognizes their reality as a social and political force. By its very resistance to the idea of women's full incorporation into political and social life, bourgeois ideology undermines its own ideal of human dignity — that of a legally and socially free and independent individual. The very heights of the aspirations toward human freedom and dignity which were first given expression in the middle-class democracy of the city-state there collided most violently with the reality of the partial and incomplete emancipation of the majority of the population. And to the extent that, in any given society, the nature of the relation of man to woman especially reveals the most basic truths about the level of human and social development, then the inferior position of woman in the Greek city-state, for all that it was a vast improvement over what had been, must be understood as the great stumbling-block to the true realization of the democratic ideal. We need look no further than the early fourth century, to the *Ecclesiazusae* of Aristophanes and the *Republic* of Plato, to understand that the Greeks themselves were conscious of the disparity between the ideal of human freedom and the reality of women's inferior status in the city-state. And yet it is unfortunately true that, as Plato and Aristophanes perceived, the only solution possible at that relatively primitive level of economic and historical development, was to purchase freedom for some at the expense of the enslavement of others. Praxagora's revolutionary program includes leaving all labor to "the slaves" (hoi douloi - 651), and ensuring as well that sexual intercourse ceases to cross class lines:

> no-let [the slave girls] sleep only beside slaves.
>
> 723

The new gynokratic state will realize the fantasy world of the Aeolians (described above, page 41 f.), for

> [the citizen's] only concern will be
> to arrive on time for luxuriating at the dinner-table.
>
> 651-652

In Plato's *Republic*, as we have already remarked, the division of labor and the class structure approximated closely the social and political arrangements of the early aristocracy. The basic humanism of Plato's impulses has been distorted into a totalitarian program which most tragically betrays that which is most noble and enduring the heritage of ancient Greece — the longing for a freedom that is grounded in social relationships, a freedom which is no mere libertinism or anarchism, but which finds its expression in the constitution of society as a union of free, yet mutually interdependent, individuals.

We have sought in this article to demonstrate that the study of women's position especially offers a most searching and most profound commentary on the nature of social and political life in ancient Greece. Since, as Aristotle perceived, the relation of man to woman is at once the most natural and the most elementary form of association, it is therefore a paradigm of all social relationships. It follows that, whenever the nature of man as a social being is under consideration, the position of women will be directly relevant. Women's role will be justified or repudiated, idealized or depreciated — in each case something of the thinker's basic attitude about social life in general will be revealed. This is true for our own time no less than it was for the Greeks. And if the understanding of the past is truly, as is claimed, the revelation of the present, then we may hope that such efforts as this have, in some small way, increased our understanding of our own historical moment.

Yale University

NOTES

[1] Victor Ehrenberg, in "When did the *Polis* rise?", JHS 57 (1937), 147-159, discusses especially the inscriptions dealing with the constitution of the Chians, and dates the appearance of the polis in the Greek world to the eighth century.

[2] George Calhoun, "The Homeric Picture," *A Companion to Homer* (ed. Wace and Stubbins), New York (1963), 431-452; appended to this article is a piece by T. B. L. Webster, "Historical Commentary," which attempts to rebut some of the claims of Finley regarding the "outlook" of the poems (see below, note 3).

[3] M. I. Finley, *Early Greece: the Bronze and Archaic Ages* (London, 1970), 84-85. Finley recapitulates in this work (and elsewhere) the view which he first set forth in *The World of Odysseus* (New York, 1954), to wit, that a comparison of the evidence offered by the Linear B tablets with that in the Homeric poems demonstrates that the outlook of the poems is early Dark-Age, not Mycenean.

[4] Werner Jaeger, "Tyrtaeus on True Arete," *Five Essays* (Montreal, 1966), 121.

[5] J. T. Kakridis, *"Meleagria,"* Philologus 90 (1935), 1-25, where he first discusses the "scale of affections," and *"Hectoreia,"* Hermes 72 (1937), 171-189, where it is applied to the scene between Hector and Andromache.

[6] We note that although the poems contain ample evidence of the incorporation of concubines and their children into the same household with the "wedded wife," at several points it is admitted that such a practice is not consistent with marital love and with a husband's respect for his wife: Phoenix reports that his father, by loving a concubine, "dishonored his wife"

52

(IX.450); and we are told that Laertes did not sleep with Eurykleia, "and so avoided the wrath of his wife" (1.433).

7 Arete recognizes Odysseus' clothes in 7.234-235 as the ones which "she herself with her serving-women had fashioned." And the Linear B tablets, which provide us with evidence of the significant number of female slaves, indicate as well that carding, spinning and weaving were the women's occupations.

8 Finley, *The World of Odysseus*, rev. ed. (London, 1956), 149.

9 This passage was athetized by Aristarchus on the grounds that it is unfitting for Andromache "to compete with Hector's generalship" (antistratēgein).

10 See W. K. Lacey, "Homeric *HEDNA* and Penelope's *KYRIOS*," JHS 86 (1966), 55-68, and M. I. Finley, "Marriage Sale and Gift in the Homeric World," *Révue int. des droits de l'antiquité*, ser. 3 vol. II (Brussels, 1955), 167-194.

11 Dem. 42.27 and the note *ad loc.* in Murray's (Loeb) edition: "After the death of her husband a woman might return to the house of her kyrios ... or, if there were children, she might live with them in her husband's house. In this case the marriage portion became the property of the son. In return he was bound to give his mother maintenance."

12 *World*, 150.

13 Donald Richter, in "The Position of Women in Classical Athens," *Classical Journal of the Midwestern States*, (1971), 1-8 has made a thorough review of most of the evidence. He has corrected the erroneous picture of the Athenian wife as a harem prisoner, although in this he has done little more than Gomme and Kitto, who in 1925 and 1951 (respectively) composed polemics against the view that women were held in contempt by Athenians of the fifth century. From a modern vantage point, we would hardly consider decisive the arguments of Gomme and Kitto that the position of Athenian women differed but little from that of women in modern times. For, as women and men have become newly aware in recent years, such a claim hardly argues for a very high position of woman in the classical era in Athens. But these scholars were countering a tendency to sentimentalize terribly the Homeric and aristocratic periods, and to wax indignant over the shortcomings of Athenian democracy. It is somewhat more surprising to find a scholar of our own period making a statement such as the following: "There is, of course, a healthy strain of misogyny and misogamy running through Greek literature, especially that of the Lyric age." Richter seems to feel that hostility toward women, when it is not so extreme as to strain the limits of gentility, is not only normal, but altogether acceptable. Clearly, the whole question still awaits analysis by a scholar who is free, not only of Victorian taste, but of simple prejudice.

14 See Margaret O. Wason, *Class Struggles in Ancient Greece* (London, 1947) for a discussion of the development of iron in antiquity from both a sociological and metallurgical point of view. She concludes that "the importance of iron was not its superiority to other metals. Its fundamental importance was this. It revolutionized productive methods. For the first time metal

was available in considerable quantities and at a low cost, and without long, laborious and expensive transport." (28).

[15] The employment of slaves on a large scale in this period is much debated; the reader is referred to M. I. Finley, *Slavery in Classical Antiquity: Views and Controversies* (London, 1960).

[16] In 1.394 ff. Telemachus admits that there are many other men in Ithaca besides himself who might be entitled to the kingship.

[17] See especially Leocritus' threats in 2.245 ff.

[18] Hesiod depicts the sad fate of the man who has no children:

> He doesn't lack for livelihood
> while he lives, but when he dies remote kinsmen *(cherestai)*
> divide up his property.
> *Th.*605-607

And Homer confirms this picture; for when the only sons of the old man Phainops are slain by Diomedes, the poet remarks:

> To their father was left mourning
> and bitter sorrows, since he did not welcome them home alive
> from the battle; and remote kinsmen *(cherestai)* divided up his property.
> V.156-158

Plutarch reports that "before the time of Solon it was not allowed [to dispose of property by will], but it was necessary for the *chremata* and the *oikos* to remain in the clan *(genos)* of the deceased" (*Sol.* 21.2).

[19] *Politics* 1265b 13.

[20] *Ath. Pol.* 6.2.

[21] See Aristotle *Ath. Pol.* 2 and Plutarch *Sol.* 13. The precise mechanics of this process have been discovered by Woodhouse, *Solon the Liberator* (London, 1938). Woodhouse there proposes the thesis that a form of contract called "sale with option of redemption...came into use in Attika before the time of Solon, and that it was in fact by this means that the noble families of early Attika had by Solon's time succeeded in bringing under their control perhaps the majority of the holdings of the peasantry of their day, and not the holdings alone, but also, by the operation of the law of personal security for loans, the bodies of a large number of the peasants themselves" (97). This practice, Woodhouse says, applied only to family allotments in the seventh century. Woodhouse's interpretation is accepted by, among others, Gregory Vlastos in his article "Solonian Justice," *CP* 41 (1946), 65-83; see note 57, p. 73, where the article by Napthali Lewis ("Solon's Agrarian Legislation," *AJP* 62 [1941], 144-156) is also mentioned.

[22] See above, note 18.

[23] *Rhet.* 1361a 21-22; G. de Ste. Croix's article, "Some Observations on the Property Rights of Athenian Women," *CR* 20 no. 3 n.s. (1970) has corrected the misleading assertion of A. R. W. Harrison (in *The Law of Athens: the Family and Property* [Oxford, 1968]) that "a woman's capacity...to own either chattels or land was on all fours with that of a man who was of age [subject to certain unimportant limitations]" (236).

[24] This law is quoted, explained, and attributed to Solon in Dem. 44.64 and 67-68.

²⁵ Starting with this period, Athens was an importer of grain. See G. Calhoun, *The Business Life of Ancient Athens* (Chicago, 1926), 21 ff. and 43 ff., and A. R. Burn, *The Lyric Age of Greece* (New York, 1960), 294: "Corn for sale must therefore be sold in Attica at a price which Attic consumers could pay, no matter what higher price might have been obtained oversea."

²⁶ Plut., *Sol.* 22.1., cf. Michell, *Economics of Ancient Greece* (Cambridge, 1940): "So marked was the superiority of Attic pottery that craftsmen from Ionia and the islands betook themselves to Athens, and it is more than probable that most of the Attic potters were in reality Metics." (296-297).

²⁷ "The victory of the Athenian potters was overwhelming... Not long after 600 Attic products began to appear in Naucratis, etc.... and by the middle of the sixth century they had penetrated everywhere, and the great Etrurian market was in the hands of a monopoly which they held undisputed for a century," Michell, *op. cit.*, 296.

²⁸ "The burden of indebtedness was of course no new or recent experience of men in the Attika of those years ... But the situation had been aggravated within the two or three generations immediately before Solon's time by the transition from natural economy to money economy based on a metal currency," Woodhouse, *op. cit.*, 136.

²⁹ In which the mina = 100 drachmas.

³⁰ In which the mina = 70 drachmas.

³¹ A. French, *The Growth of the Athenian Economy* (London, 1965), 25. And further: "The sudden appearance of Athenian pottery in western sites which had hitherto shown only Corinthian ware suggests that the pots were taken along the usual trade-routes by Corinthian shippers, and the implied increase in commercial cooperation between Corinth and Athens is consistent with Solon's measure to put out an Athenian coinage on the Corinthian standard."

³² V. Ehrenberg, *From Solon to Socrates* (London, 1968), 64.

³³ *Ath. Pol.* 9.1.

³⁴ Dem. 21.45.

³⁵ It should be remarked that a great deal of controversy surrounds the question of the exact meaning of the word *ephesis*, here translated as "appeal": see esp. H. J. Wolff, "The Origin of Judicial Legislation Among the Greeks," *Traditio* 4 (1946), 31-87.

³⁶ *Oikos* included the land and buildings on which family life took place.

³⁷ As in his discussion of the laws on adultery (p. 38) or on the dowry (p. 46).

³⁸ "Marriage Law and Family Organization in Ancient Athens," *Traditio* 2 (1944), 43-95; "Die Grundlagen des Griechischen Eherechts," *Tijdschrift voor Rechtsgeschiedenis* 20 (1952), 1-29, 157-163.

³⁹ See Lysias 30 (against Nichomachus).

⁴⁰ The recent edition of the fragments of Solon's laws by Eberhard Ruschenbusch, *SOLONOS NOMOI* (Wiesbaden, 1966), argues, especially against the contrary assertions by C. A. Hignett (in *An History of the Athenian Constitution* (Oxford, 1952), that "the ancient tradition regarding the laws of the axones is relatively trustworthy" (58). Ruschenbusch is especially cautious in his use of the orators and the comic poets as evidence for the tradition of Solonian laws, although he does accept in some cases the

testimony of Demosthenes. In the following pages, we shall be somewhat less restrictive in our application of the designation "Solonian" to laws which, as they are transmitted to us, must date from a later period than that of the Solonian codification, but nevertheless represent provisions that clearly accord with the intent of Solon's reforms.

[41] This law is attributed to "the lawgiver" *(nomothetes)* and some parts of its provisions are late (especially that which completely excludes illegitimate children, explicitly dated to the archonship of Eucleides in 403), but it is in the main the law of Solon, who was traditionally understood to be the originator of the "laws about inheritances *(kleroi)* and heiresses *(epikleroi),*" as Aristotle calls them in the *Ath. Pol.* (9.2).

[42] The rule about the limitation on women's and minors' ability to make legally valid contracts above the value of one *medimnos* is actually introduced by way of an explanation for a minor's (and hence a woman's) inability to make a will: "For it is not possible for a minor to make a will. For the law explicitly forbids a minor or a woman to make a contract for more than one *medimnos* of barley" (Isaeus 10.10).

[43] Lévi-Strauss, *Les Structures élémentaires de la parenté*, quoted in de Beauvoir, *The Second Sex* (New York, 1953), 65.

[44] See note 38.

[45] *Ibid.*, 49.

[46] See above, note 24.

[47] Isaeus 6.44.

[48] Dem. 44.33-42.

[49] Aeschines 1.14: "[The lawgiver] has imposed the heaviest penalties if anyone procures a free-born boy or a woman."

[50] Athenaeus in the *Deipnosophistae* 569d-e reports this and quotes a fragment of Philemon, a comic poet of the late fourth century:

> But you discovered a universal law:
> For they say that you, Solon, were the first to perceive this
> democratic principle and safeguard, by Zeus —
> and it "fits in well" for me to say this, Solon —
> when you saw that the city was full of young men
> and that they were under nature's compulsion
> and so were doing wrong in prohibited quarters,
> you brought women and set them up in various areas,
> so that they were all prepared and ready for all comers.
> 2.479 (Kock)

[51] Dem. 59.87: "Whenever a man has caught the adulterer, let it not be allowed for the man who has caught him to continue living with his wife; if he does so, let him be disbarred from citizenship *(atimos)*. And let it not be permitted for the wife with whom the adulterer was caught to enter into the public sacrifices; if she does, let her suffer whatever she might suffer, except death, with impunity." Aeschines 1.183-185 attributes the law to Solon.

[52] Plut., *Sol.* 23.1.

[53] *Ibid.*

[54] There is a question as to whether a restriction on the dowry proper *(proix)*

is meant: while Plutarch mentions *phernai*, which can mean either dowry or bridal gift (see Eur. *Med.* 956) rather than *proix* which always means dowry after Homer, he also uses the term *epipheresthai* which is regularly applied to the dowry (see Dem. 40.19). Erdmann, in *Die Ehe im alten Griechenland* (Munich, 1934), 223-224, thinks that this restriction "stands in such complete contradiction to the just-cited principles [about dowries] that we do not make any mistake if we see in this regulation an order about funeral gifts." Wolff (*op. cit.* 58) insists that bridal gifts, as opposed to the dowry proper, must be meant, especially since Plutarch mentions in 21.4 restrictions on funeral gifts: "a suppression of the *proix* in the true sense would have been contrary to its social function."

55 Plut., *Sol.* 21.4-5 and Dem. 43.62.

56 Aeschines 1.6-12.

57 Plut. *Sol.* 22.3: "[Solon] arranged for the council of the Areopagus to look into the source of each man's livelihood (*epitēdeia*) and to punish the unemployed (*tous argous*)."

58 See Harrison, *op. cit.,* 148-149 and 184 ff. for succession- and marriage-laws governing metics; see 196, 199 for marriage laws applying to freedmen.

59 See Harrison, *op. cit.,* 13 ff. and Wolff, "Marriage Law," 69 ff; the details are too complex to present here, since they involve an elaborate web of inferences based on a good deal of indirect evidence.

59a The Panathenaic Procession, especially, which was instituted in all likelihood during the sixth century, recognized and celebrated the importance to the state of the contributions of those groups — women and metics above all — who did not participate in the state as full citizens.

59b It should be remarked that the terms "private property" and "bourgeois class" are, strictly speaking, only applicable to certain institutions which exist under that economic form known as capitalism. It is only by analogy that such terms can be applied to the ancient world, in which capitalism did not exist. Marx discusses the economic forms of the ancient world (Greek, Roman and Oriental) in a section of the *Grundrisse der Kritik der Politischen Ökonomie* (written in 1857-8, but only first published in Moscow in 1939-41) which is entitled "Formen die der Kapitalistischen Production vorhergehen." This section is published separately in English as *Pre-Capitalist Economic Formations*, trans. J. Cohen, ed. and intro. E. J. Hobsbawn (International Publishers, 1965). In this work, Marx mentions the "error" of "philologists who speak of the existence of *capital* in classical antiquity, and of Greek and Roman capitalists .... Were the term capital to be applicable to classical antiquity — though the word does not actually occur among the ancients — then the nomadic hordes with their flocks on the steppes of Central Asia would be the greatest capitalists, for the original meaning of the word capital is cattle." *op. cit.,* 118-119. A more modern scholar who discusses the inapplicability of the term "capitalism" to the ancient world is H. Bolkestein, *Economic Life in Greece's Golden Age*, rev. and annot. E. J. Jonkers (Leiden, 1958). I shall make use of the terms "private property" and "bourgeois" nonetheless, since as applied to the ancient world they do properly designate certain institutions or developments which, when they occurred at a later historical period (namely, that of the late feudal era), did result in the creation of private property, the bourgeois class, and capitalism.

[60] Sappho and Alcaeus are cited according to the numbering of the fragments in Page, *Sappho and Alcaeus* (Oxford, 1959); the rest of the Greek lyric poets are cited from D. L. Page, *Poeti Melici Graeci* (Oxford, 1962); the elegiac and iambic poets are quoted from Diehl; *Anthologia Lyrica Graeca,* rev. Beutler (Leipzig, 1949, 1952).

[61] Limitations of space prohibit a full discussion of Alcaeus' political views, or the citation of poems illustrating his outlook. Readers are referred to Page, *S & A* (see note above), for this information, and to A. Andrewes, *The Greek Tyrants* (New York, 1963) for a discussion of the political situation in Mytilene at this time.

[62] Page, *S & A*, 130 ff.

[63] Aristotle reports that he instituted a severer penalty for crimes committed while drunk (*Pol.* 1274b 4).

[64] On the translation as well as the transmission of this incomplete line, see Page's commentary in *S & A ad loc*. The line just before this one has been recently completed by the discovery of a new papyrus fragment: see D. A. Campbell, *Greek Lyric Poetry* (New York, 1967) for the text and notes.

[65] 2.135.

[66] In *Greece* (New York, 1963), 176.

[67] E.g. by Hippolytus in Euripides' play (640 ff.).

[68] See Euripides' *Bacchae*, 395 ff. and *passim*.

[69] See G. Vlastos, "Equality and Justice in Early Greek Cosmologies," *CP* 42 (1947), 156-178.

[70] Pindar, in *Isth.* 2.10, speaks of a time when the Muse was not yet "a money-grubbing professional" (οὐ φιλοκερδής ... οὐδ᾽ ἐργάτις) and the scholiast refers this to Simonides who, he says, "began the practice of composing epinicians for wages."

[71] Note that it matters not at all whether Neobule or Arete *actually* existed and were amorously involved with the respective poets; the important fact is that the beloved, whether real or imagined, is portrayed realistically by both poets.

[72] De Beauvoir, *op. cit.,* 96.

[73] E.g. the *dissuasio Valerii ad Rufinum philosophum ne uxorem ducat* (ca. 1190), in Walter Map's collection of anecdotes *De nugis curialium.*

"REVERSE SIMILES" AND SEX ROLES IN THE ODYSSEY

Helene P. Foley

TWO SURPRISINGLY SIMILAR similes mark the first meeting of Penelope and Odysseus and their hard-won reunion. In the first (19.108-14) Odysseus compares the reputation (*kleos*) of Penelope to that of a good and just king whose land and people prosper under him. Penelope replies that the gods destroyed her beauty on the day of Odysseus' departure for Troy; if he were to return her life and *kleos* would be fairer and greater. In the second (23.233-40) Odysseus is as welcome to Penelope as land to a shipwrecked sailor worn down by his battle with the surf. This simile at once recalls the situation of Odysseus before he struggles to land on Phaeacia (5.394-8). Thus both similes equate Penelope with a figure like Odysseus himself, as he has been and will be.

These two similes comparing a woman to a man form part of a group of similes of family or social relationship clustering almost exclusively around the incident in Phaeacia and the family of Odysseus as it struggles to recover peace and unity on Ithaca.[1] Many of these similes, like the two mentioned above, also evoke in the comparison an inversion of social role or a social theme with an equivalent difference of focus or point of view. Men are compared to women. In Book 8 (523-31) the weeping Odysseus is compared to a woman weeping over the body of her husband lost in war. As she mourns him enemy soldiers strike her shoulders and lead her off to slavery. The conqueror of Troy is identified with the most helpless of his former victims. Fathers are equated with children; Odysseus finds the land of Phaeacia as welcome as the life of a father recovered from sickness is to his children (5.394-8). Telemachus in his reunion with the swineherd Eumaeus is greeted as a loving father greets a son returned from ten years of travel; yet it is Odysseus, the real father who is present to observe this embrace, who has returned from travels of considerable length (16.17-20). Telemachus and Odysseus lament at their reunion more intensely than sea-eagles robbed of their unfledged young (16.216-18). Odysseus has just regained his son; yet Homer marks the moment with an image of bereavement, of parents deprived of their young.

59

These "reverse similes," as I shall call them, seem to suggest both a sense of identity between people in different social and sexual roles and a loss of stability, an inversion of the normal. The comparison of the joy of Penelope to that of a shipwrecked sailor has been interpreted, for example, as Homer's deliberate identification of Odysseus and his like-minded wife, or as one of a series of images of safety from the sea.[2] In this paper, however, I am interested in the larger pattern: why are these so many similes with this consistent change of perspective or reversal of social role in the comparison, and in particular, what is the meaning of the elaborate images of sexual inversion? How do these reverse-sex similes clarify the overall structure and meaning of the relations between man and wife?[3]

The history of festival and comedy provide numerous examples of a world disrupted or inverted, then restored or renewed. Symbolic inversion of the sexes is frequently part of the process. From Aristophanes' Lysistrata to Shakespeare's Rosalind women in literature have assumed men's roles to restore and redefine the institutions of peace — marriage and the family — and to provide an avenue for corrective criticism of the status quo. In festival and comedy the marriage relation, in which the female is subordinate to the male, is used to express, reinforce or criticize a far larger range of hierarchical social and economic relations.[4] In the *Odyssey* direct symbolic inversion of the sexes is delicately reserved for a few prominently-placed similes. Yet these similes can be interpreted as a significant part of a larger pattern of social disruption and restoration in the epic. Throughout his journey Odysseus experiences many cultures whose social order is an incomplete or inverted version of his own Ithaca, including variations on the place of women and the limits on their sexual, social and political roles. In a similar way, voluntarily (through disguise) or involuntarily, Odysseus adopts or experiences a wide range of social roles other than his own. Penelope does not take inappropriate advantage of her opportunity to wield power in Odysseus' absence; yet to maintain his kingship she must come close as a woman can to doing so.[5]

Odysseus regains home in the wake of a disruption of normal economic, social and ethical relations on Ithaca. Yet neither the characteristic form of social reproduction on Ithaca, nor its particular hierarchical social and sexual relations are fully resumed until, through the events of the poem, they have been re-argued, reclarified

60

and voluntarily reaffirmed by all parties concerned. The continual play with social and sexual categories in the poem results not in social change but in a more flexible interpretation of social roles, and in a new understanding of what form of social and economic relations makes possible the continuity of culture on Ithaca. In the elaborate negotiations leading up to the recognition of Penelope and Odysseus, Homer, like Shakespeare in his middle comedies, manipulates the potential threat of social inversion which underlies the travels and the reverse-sex similes.[6] The power which Penelope has legitimately and skillfully wielded is not transferred by her to Odysseus until she has — albeit unconsciously — regained both his complete trust and power in her own domestic sphere. Homer's extensive treatment of Penelope's role in maintaining the kingship for Odysseus' return, and the length and elaboration of the recognition process between men and women throughout the poem reveal the mutual interdependence of husband and wife in the structure of Homeric society.[7]

The poem begins with a family and society barely maintaining order in the absence of its father and king Odysseus. The suitors continually waste Odysseus' economic resources in direct violation of the fundamental principles of "Odyssean" society, the mutual obligations of host and guest. The young men of the island insist on wooing a woman of an older generation instead of reproducing their households with women of the appropriate age. The Ithacan assembly has not met in years, and public opinion no longer effectively protects the household of its king. Telemachus, having no room to grow into into his patrimony, finds his relations with his mother becoming difficult. Odysseus' mother has died longing for her son; his father still pines for him in lonely squalor.

In this situation Penelope plays a critical role. She alone engages in an active struggle to maintain the cultural norm. She, not Odysseus' *dēmos*, dares to reprove the suitors' violation of the social order. Despite her difficult situation she periodically attempts to renew Odysseus' wealth by extracting bridal gifts from the suitors. The Homeric king makes such gift-getting a primary object. She distracts the suitors from quarreling by exciting their hopes of gaining her hand. The dissolution of such quarrels of the young is a kingly function, as is confirmed by both Alcinous' role in Phaeacia and the simile at 12.439-441, where Odysseus clings to a fig tree over Charybdis until the time when a man leaves the assembly for supper, a man who decides the many quarrels of litigious young men. Penelope receives and cross-examines visitors, and tries to maintain standards of hospitality and a network of communication in Odysseus' disrupted family. She keeps Laertes informed with messages; her deceiving web was an act of familial piety, a shroud for her father-in-law. With the exception of the weaving, these are all social functions which Penelope ultimately transfers to the male members of her family, first to Telemachus, then to Odysseus. At 4.791-3 Penelope is compared to a beleaguered lion.[8] Lion images are typically reserved for heroic men. In the disrupted Ithaca of the early books of the *Odyssey* Penelope, far from being the passive figure of most Homeric criticism, has come remarkably close to enacting the role of a besieged warrior.[9]

Penelope achieves this uneasy victory by a woman's weapons: her Athena-like intelligence, her weaving, and her power to order the household. Circe, Calypso, the Sirens, Helen and Penelope all have a special power to stop or transcend change in the sphere under their control. In the pursuit of Helen and immortality in war, Helen's former suitors give up ten years of their lives at Troy. The Sirens offer immortal knowledge to those who surround them, but at the sacrifice of natural life. Circe maintains an unchanging existence on her island by transforming her guests from threatening humans to tame animals. At Sparta, Helen relieves her guests from painful memories with a drug which numbs the effects of time. Like Circe, Penelope has turned her guests into swine, into unmanly banqueters, lovers of dance and song rather than war, who are shown, in their failure to string the bow, to be no match for Odysseus.[10] To keep open a place for Odysseus she has symbolically stopped change on Ithaca. All the young men of the kingdom woo Penelope; they are thus prevented from maturing into husbands and warriors, potential rivals to Telemachus or Odysseus. Whatever the true social status of Penelope — and it has aroused much controversy — the poet suggests that she has the power to bring the kingship with her; the suitors explicitly compete not merely for her beauty but to achieve this political ambition.[11] Similarly, she controls the sexual feelings which might lead her to a new marriage by deliberately maintaining a state of frozen grief. In Book 19 Penelope compares herself to the nightingale, daughter of Pandareus, who eternally bewails the loss of her child (518-23). The image expresses Penelope's suspension of time on Ithaca, as does another image, continually evoked, of the youthful Odysseus before his departure for Troy.[12] In a comparable position Penelope uses on the men surrounding her the weapons of Helen and Circe not to destroy but to maintain the cultural order. Yet in her effort to preserve Ithaca for Odysseus she cannot stop change entirely; thus the maturing of Telemachus creates increasing tensions for Penelope at the opening of the poem. The unnatural situation on Ithaca comes playfully close to an unintended solution; Telemachus emerges as the only man aside from Odysseus who can win his mother in the contest of the bow.

For all her feminine intelligence in maintaining the material conditions for the survival of Odysseus' household, and thus for his kingship, and even in performing such kingly functions as mediating the quarrels of the restless young, Penelope, because she lacks physical force, can only stop change on Ithaca. She cannot restore it to full social growth. From this perspective we can begin to understand Odysseus' compliment in comparing her fame to that of a just and pious king (19.107-14), following a teasing — or hinting — refusal to discuss his own identity:[13]

Lady, no mortal man on the endless earth would have cause
to find fault with you; your fame goes up into the wide heaven,
as of some king who, as a blameless man and god-fearing,
and ruling as lord over many powerful people,
upholds the way of good government, and the black earth yields him
barley and wheat, his trees are heavy with fruit, his sheepflocks
continue to bear young, the sea gives him fish, because of
his good leadership, and his people prosper under him.

These are Odysseus' first words to Penelope. The moment is full of dramatic tension. In the wake of the dangerous and tricky women of Odysseus' journey, of Agamemnon's warnings about faithless wives, of the song of Aphrodite's adultery with Ares, and of Penelope's own possibly ambiguous act in soliciting bridal gifts (Book 18) before she knows of Odysseus' return, the simile poses a question to Penelope. Her reply shows a clear perception of and assent to the model of kingship suggested by Odysseus, if she does not yet recognize her husband. We have seen the suitors awed by her beauty, and heard them paying tribute to her remarkable skill and cleverness.[14] Yet Penelope now repeats her disclaimer that her fame, beauty, and excellence have been lost in the absence of Odysseus and goes on later in their conversation to describe how through chastity and care for Odysseus' goods and family she has circumspectly attempted to preserve his place (19.124-7 and 524-529):

> Stranger, all of my excellence, my beauty and my figure,
> were ruined by the immortals at that time when the Argives took ship
> for Ilion, and with them went my husband, Odysseus.
> If he were to come back and take care of my life, then
> my reputation would be more great and splendid.
> . . . .
> so my mind is divided and starts one way, then another.
> Shall I stay here by my son and keep all in order,
> my property, my serving maids, and my high-roofed house,
> keep faith with my husband's bed and regard the voice of the people,
> or go away at last with the best of all those Achaians
> who court me here in the palace, with endless gifts to woo me?

She accepts Odysseus' compliment to her abilities by taking pride in her own exemplary — almost, she suggests in her elaboration on her theme, masculine — treatment of strangers; yet in the same speech she denies that she is capable of offering full hospitality — gifts, transportation to another place — without Odysseus (19.309-16, 325-334):

> If only this word, stranger and guest, were brought to fulfillment,
> soon you would be aware of my love and many gifts given
> by me so that any man who met you would call you blessed.
> But here is the way I think in my mind, and the way it will happen.
> Odysseus will never come home again, nor will you be given
> conveyance, for there are none to give orders left in the household
> such as Odysseus was among men — if he ever existed —
> for receiving strangers and sending them off on their journeys.
> . . . .
> . . . for how, my friend, will you learn if I in any way
> surpass the rest of women, in mind and good sense,
> if you must attend, badly dressed and unwashed, the feasting
> in the palace? Human beings live only for a short time,
> and when a man is harsh himself, and his mind knows harsh thoughts,
> all man pray that sufferings will befall him hereafter
> while he lives; and when he is dead all men make fun of him.
> But when a man is blameless himself, and his thoughts are blameless,

> the friends he has entertained carry his fame widely
> to all mankind, and many are they who call him excellent.

Her response to the stranger tacitly reaffirms the traditional relation of subordination between husband and wife, reaffirms the limits of her own power and the particular forms necessary for social reproduction on Ithaca.

The vision of kingship in the simile implies a complex symbolic connection between government, agriculture, the worship of the gods and human fertility, as well as a special relation of mutual consent between the sexes.[15] Social reproduction in Ithaca involves dealing creatively with change, exchange and conflict. War, the advent of strangers, the quarrels between families, the need for cooperative organization of agriculture to produce food, the succession of father by son in a kingship all demand a particular control over nature and time. Thus the long process of restoration for Odysseus is appropriate to the challenge of reproducing a continuous culture on Ithaca, not a function of Homer's desire to create suspense. Society in Ithaca is more complex than others we encounter in the poem and its restoration must be correspondingly delicate and complex. As P. Vidal-Naquet has pointed out, the world of the travels is radically simplified in the areas most significant to Ithacan culture: agriculture, marriage and social relationships within the family.[16] There is a correspondingly diminished need for kingship, marriage and social hierarchy. Without war or the necessity to organize labor to reproduce agriculture, the attenuated social structures that we find on some of the islands without hierarchy and with a female on top appear perfectly viable. Life in Ithaca is uniquely characterized by a range of mediating structures organized and unified by a male leader. Through Odysseus' travels we recomprehend the complexity of Ithacan culture and the particular form of male-female relations within it.

On Circe's island or Calypso's, for example, economic production in the household alone is sufficient to sustain her limited social world. It is of parenthetical interest to an evaluation of women's role in Greek literature that their work — weaving, cooking and the guardianship of the household — is present even on Olympus and in utopia. Household economics does not require men or the establishment of a sexual hierarchy and women's control over this sphere is seen as natural, unproblematic. The absence of male agricultural work defines the golden age, just as its presence defines the break into culture, into a world ruled by men. Cooking and weaving on Ithaca are activities dependent on prior agricultural production. The household, as in the analysis in Xenophon's *Oeconomicus*, processes and makes useful and permanent goods produced by men through agriculture and herding.[17] Because both cooking and weaving retard or conquer change they logically have a more primary association with the divine and eternal than male-controlled agriculture. Thus the products of weaving are in Homer sometimes forms of art comparable to poems.[18]

As an example, we may contrast the Homeric *oikos* with the cave of the nymphs (13.102 ff. and 345 ff.) where Odysseus stores his treasures on Ithaca. In this cave the nymphs perform in perpetuity the female functions of an Homeric household. The cave is filled with stone looms, bowls and jars; it protects Odysseus' goods. Here the divine and human intersect; gods and men through separate entrances communicate indirectly through sacrifice. But this cave world of Circe, Calypso and the nymphs with its endless weaving and banqueting admits neither social change nor exchange. This is both its value and its limitation. The female protects what is permanent and unchanging in the Homeric *oikos*, the male its changing place in historical time.[19] Penelope uses powers natural to her sphere when she temporarily transforms Ithaca to a domestic island in which the minimum of change and exchange takes place.

In a similar vein the islands, with the exception of Phaeacia, are too remote to need a foreign policy, to conduct war or to maintain the complex exchanges of favor between host and guest. Yet it is significant that the arrival of the stranger Odysseus, and the experience of the Trojan war he brings with him, radically disrupt the cultural balance of every world which does not reject him with instant hostility. In Ithaca, by contrast, the continual necessity to recognize boundaries, make economic exchange and declare new areas of influence demands the presence of an authoritative male.

Last and most important for our purposes, the islands of Odysseus' travels organize sexual reproduction on a different basis. If Odysseus had accepted Calypso's belated offer of immortality, he would have avoided the necessity of sexual reproduction altogether. Hesiod's Odysseus has offspring by Circe and Calypso. Homer's has none. The gods of the *Odyssey* disapprove of goddesses mating with mortals (5.118 ff.). In a similar vein Hesiod's goddesses mate rarely

66

with men. Their offspring are obscure or short-lived. Yet Zeus and the other male gods sire innumerable culture heroes on mortal women. Where culture, as in Ithaca, cannot be reproduced without the male, there is a corresponding emphasis on sexual reproduction through the male.[20] In Hesiod's *Works and Days* agriculture and mortality come to men simultaneously. In a fallen world men reproduce property (through agriculture) and sons to inherit their property. Similarly, Zeus' achievements are more social than biological, although without females he cannot give birth to Athena, or father other children whose names indicate the development of sophisticated social structures (such as *Dike*). In the island worlds of Circe or Calypso, Homer appears to abstract an incomplete "domestic" world from a larger social reality. Insofar as we accept that these worlds fully represent the domestic sphere, the absence of sexual reproduction suggests that in the larger reality women do not culturally reproduce children. Telemachus cannot attain maturity without the support of other men, nor his full inheritance without Odysseus. Apollo in Aeschylus' *Eumenides* makes a similar point when he argues that the father is the only real parent.

Alternatively, in the stable societies of Aeolus and Phaeacia marriages are between familiars (incestuous or endogamous), not between strangers (exogamous). Without war they need not create a complex network of external alliances to protect and reproduce the social order. In Ithaca relations between strangers are of primary importance; marriages are on the same pattern, between strangers. The success of the marriage depends on the consent of the wife to count her husband's interests as her own, and Penelope's creative fidelity is viewed as remarkable. Thus Homer's selection of the contrasting marriage pattern, marriage between familiars, for his utopian society seems appropriate to its isolation from the external world. Similarly, Odysseus' recovery of his natural relations with Telemachus and even with Laertes are relatively brief, while the redevelopment of his relationship with Eumaeus, and more particularly with Penelope, are long delayed and elaborate.[21] Through Eumaeus, Odysseus symbolically recovers an understanding with those men, often originally strangers, who maintain the external economics of his household. In Ithaca kings play an active role in agriculture. In contrast the other Homeric warriors live off the economic surplus of their society in exchange for offering protection; outside Ithaca we thus find little mention of the peasant classes in Homeric society. In sum, by presenting in isolation these aspects of the more complex Ithacan culture, the islands of the travels clarify the nature and range of female power over the inner sphere of household production, and of the male power over the external world of agriculture, diplomacy and exchange.

The two tokens by which Odysseus is united with wife and father demonstrate clearly the special quality of social relationships on Ithaca. Odysseus identifies himself to Laertes by means of an orchard. There he finds unchanged the trees his father planted for him in youth. Odysseus depends on others to accomplish the laborious and deliberate ordering of nature over time necessary to economic reproduction on Ithaca. Yet only Odysseus can assure economic reproduction; without him the products of agriculture and herding are dissipated, not accumulated as wealth. Laertes lives in poverty and isolation; Eumaeus cannot marry; Penelope cannot give gifts.

The secret of Penelope's life with Odysseus is symbolized in their bed. Odysseus built the bed around a living tree trunk. One post is immovable, rooted in nature. Yet the resulting creation is more lasting than nature. Odysseus depends on Penelope to protect this symbol of the internal continuity of the family. Through this power over their bed we see her out-maneuver the ever-crafty Odysseus. While she accepts her renewed sexual subordination to Odysseus, she is not forced to capitulate to him on his own terms. In contrast, Circe fails to trick Odysseus when she uses her power over bed (10.333-5) and food for treacherous purposes.

The long recourting of Penelope by Odysseus, beginning with the simile of the just king and ending with the simile of the sailor, arises in part, as A. Amory has sensitively suggested, from Penelope's psychological reluctance to recognize Odysseus — a reluctance born of her twenty year vigilance against deception and the protective freezing of her own sexuality.[22] Yet the recourting is primarily a mature renegotiation between two potential strangers, two established powers, which ends in a recreation of trust and a mutual establishment of the limits within which their future relationship will take place. The process begins with Odysseus' tacit recognition of Penelope's role in preserving his kingship, and his testing of her apparent unwillingness — unlike Clytemnestra — to misuse her power. This hint of dangerous potential sexual inversion shapes our reading of the rewooing of Penelope by Odysseus. Shakespeare's Rosalind also ends by consenting to her marital subordination to Orlando at the close of *As You Like*

It. Yet what has passed between them in the period of disguise is surely not irrelevant to our sense of the outcome. Rosalind has won for herself no ordinary wifehood, however it may appear, as the couple joins a throng of other newly-weds at the end of the play. Similarly, by the time Penelope recognizes Odysseus they have, even if subconsciously, recreated the ideal marriage which Odysseus describes to Nausicaa in Book 6.180-185:

and then may the gods give you every thing that your heart longs for;
may they grant you a husband and a house and sweet agreement
in all things, for nothing is better than this, more steadfast
than when two people, a man and his wife, keep a harmonious
household; a thing that brings much distress to the people who hate them
and pleasure to their well-wishers, and for them the best reputation.

Despite his initial caution Odysseus comes to rely completely on Penelope's strategems to set the stage for his revenge. Their final reunion takes place not on his terms but hers: she accepts not the bloody man of force but the verbal and orderly man of peace; she controls the token of the bed. Her feelings about her dream in which the eagle destroys her pet geese (19.536-550), her winning of gifts from the suitors, and her establishment of the contest with the bow before she knows of Odysseus' return are not consciously intended as hostile to her husband.[23] Yet she weeps at the slaughter of the geese and feels frightened and angry at the eagle. Again, while Odysseus dreams of a mature Penelope supporting him with full recognition of his identity, Penelope dreams of the young Odysseus before he went to Troy.[24] They dream together; yet the two images still separate man and wife. The images converge only in their final reunion. In the simile of the shipwrecked sailor Penelope takes on the mature Odysseus' experiences as her own. They meet again in a new present as she finally breaks her almost enchanted attachment to the past, to the stopping of change which was her central weapon. Penelope's dreams and dream-like decisions reflect simultaneously her emerging acceptance of Odysseus' return and her instinctive reluctance to relinquish full control over the household. By eschewing her opportunity for usurping or misusing power Penelope secures from her husband a different kind of power and a marriage clarified by their mutual recognition of like-mindness.

69

Odysseus' experiences with Nausicaa and Arete on Phaeacia prepare us to understand the importance of the form of negotiation between husband and wife and the nature of the outcome. In Phaeacia the figure of Arete is mysteriously central. Alcinous hold the power (*kratos*). Arete, relying on her husband's reverence for her, and accepting her subordination to him, is allowed the limited public role of resolving disputes between the husbands of wives who are in her favor (7.73-74). Yet Odysseus is twice advised to make his pleas to her alone. Bernard Fenik has gone far in exploring this question.[25] He suggests that Arete's importance emerges in one particular scene, the scene where she tests Odysseus with questions about his clothing. Phaeacians are reportedly suspicious of strangers. We are thus prepared dramatically for Odysseus' fate to depend on his answer to this awkward question. Odysseus shows himself, as he did earlier with Nausicaa, to be the ideally tactful man, and Arete is presumably satisfied. Yet Odysseus woos her again in his tale of the underworld by featuring his reunion with his mother and the stories of famous wives. Silence follows the ensuing pause in his story. Then Arete proposes that more gifts be given to Odysseus. The disguised Odysseus makes a comparable indirect compliment to Penelope when he describes the cloak worn by Odysseus in a fictional encounter on Crete. There he emphasizes how impressed the other women were at the workmanship of the cloak (19.234-235).

Alcinous — like Menelaus at Sparta — is more satisfied by appearances than his wife. But even in the most civilized contexts the basis for agreement and understanding between men and women remains problematic. The complexity of these negotiations of the inner domestic world — later perfected in the novel — seem to strain Homer's stylistic repertoire.[26] Interpreters of the scenes between Odysseus and Arete, Odysseus and Penelope, or Helen and Menelaus have turned to an analysis of a variety of stylistic devices such as type-scenes or patterns of repetition for clarification of their unspoken logic. Homer uses and may even have further developed the reverse simile and the dream to express more precisely the ambiguity of Penelope's position and her inner life. Similarly, the obliquely uncomplimentary tales of Helen and Menelaus, and the presence of drugs at their court subtly express uneasy relations in the domestic realm at Sparta.[27] In contrast Odysseus' tact and skill with words neutralizes the potential uneasiness of his relation with Arete and her daughter.

70

At Ithaca the like-mindedness of Odysseus and Penelope is continually recreated through the long recognition process. Through this like-mindedness women like Arete and Penelope win from their husbands influence even in the external world of their society. The woman's consent is in both cases shown to be essential to the male's success in ruling, and it must be won with a special form of gentle, uncoercive negotiation. Odysseus, contrary to Agamemnon's advice in the underworld or Telemachus' rough manners with his mother, is consistently kind (*ēpios*), not forceful to Penelope.[28] In both Phaeacia and Ithaca Homer gives the central place to Odysseus' ability to be indirect and graceful in his dealings with women. If this is not fully borne out in the case of Arete, it is with Penelope. Arete's role probably also pre-figures Penelope's in a restored Ithaca. I see no reason to assume, from Telemachus' adolescent attempts to break out from his mother's influence, that Penelope is to live the rest of her life isolated in the women's quarters.[29] Rather she will take her turn at giving gifts (see 19.309-11) and receiving visitors publicly at Odysseus' side. Like Arete she has won her husband's trust and shown her ability to settle disputes even among men.

This mode of complex and indirect negotiation for male-female relations in the poem becomes in Ithaca symbolic of an important dimension of Odysseus' kingship. Ithacan culture requires a comparable subtly established like-mindedness between the king and his domestic and agricultural subordinates like Eumaeus, Eurycleia, the bard and the herald. The apparent lack of contradiction in the poem between recovering *oikos* and state (the second mysteriously and abruptly accomplished by Athena-ex-machina) suggests that we can interpret Odysseus' elaborate recovery of his marriage and family as symbolic of a wider restoration of his kingdom on the same pattern.[30] Because the marriage is, as here, apparently used to express a larger range of hierarchical relations between "strangers" in the society, women have, not surprisingly, a correspondingly powerful and highly-valued social and ideological position in the poem.[31]

In order to evaluate fully the reverse-sex similes we must briefly return to an examination of the role of inversion in the structure of Odysseus' journey as a whole. Odysseus gains understanding of Ithaca, an ever-increasing desire for home and Penelope, and a renewed social flexibility through his experience of the incompletely human. Odysseus tests all the limits of his culture. He rejects the choice of becoming a god. He enters and returns from the world of the dead. At one moment he is nameless, without identity; at another he is already the hero of undying fame (Phaeacia). With Nausicaa he has the opportunity to relive a youthful marriage. On Ithaca he experiences before his time the indignity of poverty and old age. He explores the full range of nuances in the host-guest relationship. He visits cultures which, because of their isolation from war or their lack of need for agricultural or sexual reproduction offer him no social function he can recognize and accept. Odysseus never experiences the ultimate reversal from male to female. Yet numerous critics have commented on Odysseus' special ability to comprehend and respond to the female consciousness, on his ''non-masculine'' heroism and on his and Penelope's special affinity with the androgenous Athena.[32] The simile comparing Odysseus to a woman weeping over her dead husband in war (8.523-31) perhaps suggests how close Odysseus has come in the course of his travels, and in particular on Calypso's island, to the complete loss of normal social and emotional function which is the due of women enslaved in war. The earlier comparison of Penelope to an entrapped lion suggests her beleagured position in Ithaca, and thus resonates with this simile as well.[33] Once conqueror of Troy, Odysseus now understands the position of its victims; and it is as such a victim, aged, a beggar, and no longer a leader of men, that he reenters Ithaca.

On Circe's island his men flock around Odysseus like calves about their mother (10.410-415), and in recovering Odysseus they feel they have symbolically recovered Ithaca (10.416-17). Yet Odysseus is not Ithaca; and in his journey to the underworld he rediscovers how much of his identity depends not only on his own heroic and warlike powers but on mothers, fathers, sons, and wives. Ithaca, too, cannot fully reproduce itself without Odysseus. The cluster of reverse similes surrounding the return of Odysseus reinforce and clarify the nature of this interdependence of identity in his own culture. Odysseus regains his son and father by sharing action and work. Yet the key to his return is and has been Penelope. With Penelope he recreates mutual trust both verbally and through a gradual and delicate re-awakening of sexual feeling. The characteristics associated with both the male sphere — with its special relation to war as well as agriculture — and with the female sphere — weaving and maintaining the domestic environment — are each shown to be potentially unstable in one dimension. Odysseus' warlike virtues did not provide a safe return for his men, and sometimes, as with the Cyclops, they are directly responsible for their deaths; his armed presence violates the cultural balance of many peaceful islands on his journey. In contrast, he recovers Ithaca not merely through carefully meditated violence, but also through indirection and gentle persuasion. Conversely, uncontrolled female sexuality or irresponsible guardianship of the domestic environment are directly destructive to the cultural order of Ithaca. Yet I would emphasize here that Homer is not criticizing these "male" or "female" powers per se. Purely warlike qualities are appropriate at Troy. Circe's behavior is not inappropriate to a world where agriculture is automatic and foreign policy can be conducted by magic. After all, without the weapon of her sexuality Penelope could not have preserved Ithaca for Odysseus. Instead the poem argues the necessary limitation of each for a stable Ithacan culture.

Thus the *Odyssey* argues for a particular pattern of male-female relations within Ithaca. The reverse similes which frame the return of Odysseus reinforce and explore these interdependent relationships. The two famous similes comparing Penelope to an Odysseus-figure accomplish this purpose with particular subtlety. In contrast to the *Iliad*, where such reverse-sex similes cluster randomly around the relation of Patroclus and Achilles, the Odyssean similes are integral to the structural development of the poem.[34] Penelope's restraint in preserving Odysseus' kingship without usurping his power reveals the nature of her own important guardianship of the domestic sphere. During the period of tacit negotiation which takes place before their final recognition, Odysseus and Penelope recreate a mature marriage with well-defined spheres of power and a dynamic tension between two like-minded members of their sex.

Stanford University

NOTES

A draft of this paper was originally presented at the December, 1976 meeting of the First Greek, Roman, and Byzantine Studies Conference at Briarcliff College, New York.

I wish to thank Carolyn Dewald, Mark Edwards, Rick Griffiths, Duncan Foley, Michael Jameson, and Michelle Rosaldo for their helpful comments and criticisms, and John Peradotto for his editorial suggestions.

[1] Hermann Fraenkel, *Die Homerischen Gleichnisse* (Gottingen 1921), A. J. Podlecki, "Some Odyssean Similes," *Greece and Rome* 18 (1971) 82, and W. C. Scott, *The Oral Nature of the Homeric Simile, Mnemosyne* Suppl. 28 (1974) 123, all notice the structural position of these similes of family relation. Carroll Moulton, "Similes in the Iliad," *Hermes* 102 (1974) 390 and Podlecki note the inversion technique in the *Iliad* and *Odyssey* respectively. "Here we have the merest hint of a unique feature of Odyssean similes . . . by which the poet reminds us of an important theme in the poem, but with a slight difference of focus or point of view" (Podlecki, 82). I was first introduced to the notion of a "reverse simile" by John Finley, Jr. in 1970. None of the above interpretations attempt to explain these similes in the light of the social and sexual logic of the poem as a whole.

[2] The first interpretation is common: for example, Podlecki (above, note 1) 90, and Marilyn B. Arthur, "Early Greece: The Origins of the Western Attitude Towards Women," *Arethusa* 6.1 (1973) 15. The second occurs in C. P. Segal, "The Phaeacians and the Symbolism of Odysseus' Return," *Arion*, 1.4 (1962) 43. Anne Amory, "The Reunion of Odysseus and Penelope," in Charles H. Taylor (ed.), *Essays on the Odyssey* (Bloomington, Indiana 1963, rep. 1969) 100-1 and Podlecki, 87, comment on how the king simile identifies Penelope and Odysseus.

[3] In this paper I shall treat the *Odyssey* as a coherent text (including, for example, the disputed books 11 and 24), whether its coherence arises from its being the product in its final form of a single artistic consciousness or in some other way (for example, from its being the product of a coherent oral or cultural tradition).

Other recent work on Odyssean similes has tended to emphasize that the similes are few and carefully positioned. The content of many is unique, and thus, some argue, more probably composed for the place in which they appear although in conformity with an oral tradition. Among those works not included above are C. M. Bowra, *Tradition and Design in the Iliad* (Oxford 1930, rep. 1950), D. J. N. Lee, *The Similes of the Iliad and Odyssey Compared* (Melbourne 1964), and C. R. Beye, "Male and Female in the Homeric Poems," *Ramus*, 3.2 (1974) 87-101. G. P. Shipp, *Studies in the Language of Homer* (Cambridge 1953, 2nd ed. 1972) argues for the late date of the language of the similes.

[4] The bibliography on this topic is extensive. I found particularly suggestive Natalie Z. Davis, *Society and Culture in Early Modern France* (Stanford 1975) 311, note 12 and her chapter "Women on Top," 124-151.

[5] Jean-Pierre Vernant, *Mythe et Société en Grèce Ancienne* (Paris 1974) 57-81 and especially 77-81 emphasizes how real and important the power of a royal wife was in the absence of her husband. One has only to compare Clytemnestra's role in the *Agamemnon* of Aeschylus.

[6] Many critics have treated the *Odyssey* as high comedy. Interestingly, women in Greek comedy (for example, in Aristophanes) are allowed to overstep domestic boundaries in a limited manner without incurring the

disasters met by their counterparts in tragedy. In part this is because women in comedy act creatively to restore the damaged status quo. Even more important they remain chaste.

Penelope's suspension of time on Ithaca, to be discussed shortly, is also characteristic of the suspension or inversion of natural and social reality in festival and comedy.

7 Bernard Fenik, *Studies in the Odyssey* (*Hermes Einselschr.* 30, Wiesbaden 1974) in his otherwise excellent book does not fully bring out the important implications of this repeated type scene in the *Odyssey* for an interpretation of Penelope. See pp. 18-19 of this paper. Anne Amory (above, note 2) 116 comments that any recognition based only on an external sign would be anticlimactic for Penelope and Odysseus. Thus the recognition is delayed even though we might expect, based what happens in the cases of Helen and Arete (in my interpretation of the type scene), some earlier response.

8 Podlecki (above, note 1) 84 thinks this simile also identifies Penelope with Odysseus. Lion similes are used elsewhere only of Odysseus with one exception (of the Cyclops, 9.292-3).

9 Both Amory and Beye (above, note 2) have recently reinterpreted Penelope's passivity as being a form of activity, of deliberate passivity. I think all critics put too much emphasis on Penelope's constant weeping. Odysseus, Menelaus and Telemachus weep frequently also, but weeping prevents none of them, or Penelope, from acting wherever possible.

10 Helen, like the other archetypal female figures in the poem, also tries to delay Telemachus on his journey of maturation. It is amusing — and psychologically apt — that Telemachus' fears about his mother's fidelity reach their peak in his warning dream at Sparta. In a similar vein Odysseus is compared to a bat above Charybdis. The powerful female figure surrounded by tamed beasts is drawn from the archetypal goddess figure, the mistress of animals.

Beye (above, note 2) 97 notes that both Penelope and Circe are surrounded by suitors dependent on them for food. He sees a common threat of sexual dominance, however benign in most cases, in all the women of the poem.

11 See among others, M. I. Finley, *The World of Odysseus* (New York 1954, rep. 1965) 92 ff., Vernant (above, note 5), and M. P. Nilson, *Homer and Mycenae* (London 1933) 225 ff. Space does not permit a discussion of this complex question.

12 Penelope's discussion of Helen's misjudgment after her recognition of Odysseus (23.215 ff.) shows how much this freezing of her own sexuality to avoid deception by strangers was an act of imagination and an achievement. In contrast, Penelope melts at Odysseus' return like snow on the mountains (19.205-209). For an excellent discussion of Penelope's virtues in this respect see Amory (above, note 2) 120-1.

[13] All the translations in this essay are from Richmond Lattimore's *The Odyssey of Homer*.

[14] See 2.115 ff., 18.212-13, and 245-49. Odysseus thus offers in part a tacit recognition of the exceptional tact and self-restraint with which she has executed a role abnormal to her sex.

[15] Finley (above, note 11) 102 wants to see this simile as anachronistic. Yet its imagery is entirely in keeping with other parts of the poem.

[16] Pierre Vidal-Naquet, "Valeurs Religieuses et Mythique de la Terre et du Sacrifice en Grèce Ancienne," in M. I. Finley (ed.), *Problèmes de la Terre en Grèce Ancienne* (Paris 1973) 269-292. This excellent article differs from my analysis here mainly in emphasis. I agree that sacrifice, marriage and agriculture are the defining features of human culture in the poem and that the world of the islands with their golden-age environment and different social structures should be categorized as supra- or infra-human. I simply wish to apply this analysis to the problem of women's role; thus I am led to analyze the "incompletely human" female-dominated environments in terms of the female sphere of the Ithacan household. Vidal-Naquet's article emphasizes instead that the islands have no need to maintain a pious — or limiting — relation to the gods. Thus they do not sacrifice.

[17] Xenophon, *Oeconomicus* VII, 17 ff. In this model the male produces the goods in the external sphere, the female ("the queen bee") processes and orders goods in the internal sphere. The separation of the two spheres is natural and efficient.

[18] Like the poet, Helen in the *Iliad* (3, 125-128) records on her web the battles fought for her at Troy.

In Lévi-Strauss' structural analysis cooking marks the special quality of human culture by mediating, through the use of fire, between the categories of perishable goods, the raw and the rotten. Goddesses like Circe cook; on Olympus the gods eat uncooked but imperishable ambrosia, although they apparently savor the smoke of cooked sacrifices.

[19] I do not mean to assert that males in the *Odyssey* are primarily associated with change — especially change in the sense of "progress" — but simply that the male is uniquely qualified to handle or neutralize sources of instability external to the domestic world and thus to assure its continuity. Men's work — agriculture, war — is special to the fragile world of human culture. Any complete treatment of the role of the civilized male in the poem would also have to contend with Odysseus' contemporaries Nestor and Menelaus, and is beyond the scope of this paper.

Homer does not make as rigid a differentiation between the female domestic sphere and the male political sphere as the poets of the fifth century. In the fifth century the female sphere continues to be associated with the continuity of the household (the family cult is also located within the *oikos*): the Furies are older gods; Antigone argues for the timeless unwritten laws, etc. In contrast the exclusively male political world of fifth-century Athens was continually in danger of falling prey to extreme innovation, whether internally or in the realm of foreign policy.

[20] Hesiodic and Homeric fathers ideally expect sons in their own image. Again, the emphasis falls on the male parent.

[21] Odysseus' relationships with Telemachus and Laertes are, of course, extremely important. Yet throughout the poem Odysseus' blood relations pose no serious threat to his return. Telemachus does not even require a token to be convinced of his father's identity. The recognition with Laertes is complex, and for many, disturbing. Yet its late appearance in the poem makes clear that the success of Odysseus' homecoming does not depend on his father. Odysseus renegotiates his social not his natural relationships.

[22] See note 2 above, especially page 106.

[23] Both the dream about the geese (19.536 ff.) and her dream about Odysseus as a young man at Troy (20.86-9) are not explicitly sent by gods, so that we can associate them even more directly with Penelope's own inner feelings.

[24] 20.86-89 and 93-94. I do not share Amory's feeling that this dream is simply an image of like-mindedness between husband and wife.

[25] See note 7 above, especially pp. 105-132.

[26] See G. Germain, *Homer*, trans. R. Howard (London 1960) 126 ff. on the novelistic qualities of the *Odyssey*.

[27] See Robert Schmiel, "Telemachus in Sparta," *TAPA* 103 (1972) 463-72 on the uneasy atmosphere at Sparta. Women dream more often than men in the *Odyssey*, and Penelope more than any other character.

[28] Agamemnon at 11.441 counsels Odysseus not to be *ēpios* to Penelope.

[29] Most students of the poem assume that the chaste Penelope will play a different role from that of Arete or Helen in the future. See, for example, M. Arthur (above, note 2) 18-19.

[30] See Natalie Davis (above, note 4) for the widespread use of the marriage relation to symbolize other social relations. Homer's audience would perhaps have found Athena's role startling if this were not the case. Given the very limited role of the Homeric king in ordinary community affairs as opposed to war problems this does not seem as surprising as it would in another context.

[31] Arthur (above, note 2) 13-14 and Finley both comment on the relation between a positive evaluation of women and the development of the nuclear family. Recent anthropological literature finds a similar positive evaluation of women in cultures, like that on Ithaca, where there is a relatively limited separation between the domestic and public spheres. See, for example, Louise Lamphere, "Strategies, Cooperation and Conflict Among Women in Domestic Groups," in Michelle Z. Rosaldo and Louise Lamphere (edd.), *Woman, Culture and Society* (Stanford 1974) 97-112. Finley does not, in my view, go far enough in examining the almost complete isolation of

the ruling family on Ithaca. Odysseus apparently — perhaps simply for dramatic reasons — has no close kin.

[32] See especially W. B. Stanford, *The Ulysses Theme* (Ann Arbor, Michigan 1963) on Odysseus' untypical heroism. The positive attitude towards women in the *Odyssey* has been made famous by Samuel Butler's classic *The Authoress of the Odyssey* and Robert Graves' novel *Homer's Daughter*.

[33] See Podlecki (above, note 1) 86 on the possible reference to Penelope here. Segal (above, note 2) 28 interprets the Book 8 simile in terms of the contrast between Odysseus' real suffering and the Phaeacians' aesthetic distance from it.

[34] Moulton (above, note 1) 391 ff.

WORKERS AND DRONES; LABOR, IDLENESS AND GENDER DEFINITION IN HESIOD'S BEEHIVE

LINDA S. SUSSMAN

ROLAND BARTHES, IN THE PREFACE to his *Mythologies* describes his impatience with the "falsely obvious."[1] Perhaps something of this attitude should govern our approach to Hesiod's account of the creation of women and its consequences for human male kind (*Works and Days* [*WD* hereafter] 47-105, *Theogony* [*Th.* hereafter] 567-613).[2] It is an eye-opening experience to present a group — say a class in classics in translation — with this story and find out just how many people regard it as "natural," not to say inevitable. I'm not sure whether we react this way because we assume that the things Hesiod says about women are true, or because they have been said so many times that they might as well be true.[3] In any case, the cosy familiarity of Hesiod's misogynistic sentiments has tended to obscure the fact that his brand of virulent sexism is neither a natural or inevitable expression of the relationship between men and women.[4] The literary expression of sexism is a phenomenon that requires an explanation.

Hesiod calls the first woman a beautiful evil (*kalon kakon, Th.* 585) and says that she was bestowed upon male kind as a punishment (*Th.* 54-87, *WD* 570-589). Before the creation of Pandora people lived on the earth "without evils or hard labor or grievous sicknesses" (*WD* 90-92). But just how does Pandora bring all this upon the male half of the human race? Disengaging her from the mythical apparatus of Prometheus, Epimetheus, the jar etc., we come down to a very specific charge which is implicit in the context of the *Works and Days* narrative, and is stated most explicitly in *Theogony* 590-602. This is the famous passage where Hesiod compares women to drones. (Hesiod, along with Virgil, had a problem about who does what in the beehive, a problem not shared by Semonides, as we shall see, or by Xenophon.)[5]

And as in thatched hives bees feed the drones whose nature is to do mischief — by day and throughout the day until the sun goes down the bees are busy and lay the white combs, while the drones stay at home in the covered skeps and reap the toil of others into their own bellies —

79

even so Zeus who thunders on high made women to be an
evil to mortal men, with a nature to do evil.[6]

What this amounts to, obviously, is that women do not do their
share, or at least are in a position where they do not *have to* do their
share — an especially devastating situation in the context of the
Works and Days where men, that is, males, are forced to engage in
unremitting, back-breaking labor in order to assure not only their own
survival but that of their families. I should note that in *Works and Days*
304 Hesiod also compares men, i.e. males, to drones:

> For hunger is very much a companion of the man (*andri* =
>   male) who does not work.
> The gods and man are indignant with a person who lives
>   without working,
> Whose disposition is like that of the stingless drones,
> They waste the product of the bees' labor,
> Not working, they consume.
>
> (*WD* 302-306)

Several interesting observations can be made about this passage.
First of all, Hesiod tells us in no uncertain terms that hunger is
invariably a companion of the idle male. Yet, although an idle male
might well starve, we hear nothing about an idle woman going hungry.
(And in Semonides quite the contrary; cf. Semonides *On Women* 106,
quoted below.) Presumably the female drones of *Theogony* 590-602
will be taken care of by the (male?) workers. All of which suggests a
considerable difference in the expectations and valuation of men and
women's work. Also, and just as important, for a male idleness may
result not only in starvation but in the diminution or loss of social
status; such an individual is of no value in the eyes of either gods or
men.[7] The implication is clear. Males who do not work are threatened
with starvation and loss of status. Women who do not work will presumably be taken care of, and perhaps for that very reason, seem to
have very little status to lose. Interestingly enough Semonides' more
colorfully phrased comparisons of women to animals[8] suggest exactly
the same accusation; women have the option of being idle, while men
do not. This is suggested at the very beginning of the poem: (The
following quotations are from Hugh Lloyd Jones' illustrated translation, text and commentary.)[9]

> In the beginning the god made the female mind separately.
> One he made from a long-bristled sow. In her house every-
> thing lies in disorder, smeared with mud, and rolls about
> the floor; and she herself unwashed, in clothes unlaunder-
> ed, sits by the dungheap and grows fat.   (1-6)

The motif is reinforced by the description of the mare woman:

> Another was the offspring of a proud mare with a long
> mane. She pushes servile work and trouble on to others;
> she would never set her hand to a mill, nor pick up a
> sieve nor throw the dung out of the house, nor sit over
> the oven dodging the soot; she makes her husband ac-
> quainted with Necessity. She washes the dirt off herself
> twice, sometimes three times, every day; she rubs herself
> with scents, and always has her thick hair combed and
> garlanded with flowers. A woman like her is a fine sight
> for others, but for the man she belongs to she proves a
> plague, unless he is some tyrant or king (who takes pride
> in such objects).   (57-70)

I am going to return a little later to the observation than an idle but
decorative wife may be an appropriate possession for a tyrant or a
king, though not for anyone else, but first let us consider the only
"good" woman – the bee woman:

> Another is from a bee; the man who gets her is fortunate,
> for on her alone blame does not settle. She causes his
> property to grow and increase, and she grows old with a
> husband whom she loves and who loves her, the mother of
> a handsome and reputable family. She stands out among
> all women, and a godlike beauty plays about her. She
> takes no pleasure in sitting among women in places where
> they tell stories about love. Women like her are the best
> and most sensible whom Zeus bestows on men.   (83-93)

We might observe that while the bee-woman is characterized as a
loving wife and mother, her first and presumably primary attribute is
her ability to increase the value of her husband's property. (It is
interesting to note that for Xenophon, some 300 years later, the maintenance and augmenting of property is the chief if not the sole reason
for getting married,[10] and the training of a wife to do her share seems

to constitute the most important part of the husband's obligations.)[11]
But by the end of the Semonides poem as we have it the poet seems
to regret any concessions he has made to the industry and utility of
the bee-woman:

> Zeus has contrived that all these tribes of women are
> with men and remain with them. Yes, this is the worst
> plague Zeus has made – women; if they seem to be some
> use to him who has them, it is to him especially that they
> prove a plague. The man who lives with a woman never
> goes through all his day in cheerfulness; he will not be
> quick to push out of his house Starvation, a housemate
> who is an enemy, a god who is against us.   (94-102)

All of which implies that women are not or need not be economically
productive. And, by implication, women's work, in dramatic contrast
to men's, is not perceived as essential or important for the functioning
of the society or the family.

This, of course, is not to suggest that in the real world of the
eighth century B.C. women did not work. Except perhaps for a relatively small number of aristocrats (like Semonides' mare-woman, a suitable possession for a tyrant or king) women have always worked – in
the household, outside the household, paid or unpaid. What is at issue
here is not the fact but the *status* of women's work and its *perceived,*
rather than actual, importance for the society. At one point Hesiod
enjoins his ideal farmer to procure a house, a woman and an ox, "a
purchased woman, not a wife, who will follow the ox" (*WD* 405-406).
The work of a slave woman who trudges along in the fields behind
the ox is, like woman herself, presumably low status. But more noteworthy is Hesiod's failure to suggest anywhere in his poem about work
that the work of *any* woman, regardless of her status, can be of real
value. Regardless of whether or not the society described by Homer is
precisely "historical"[12] and if it is, what period of history is reflected,
I think we can safely assume that the poems represent some assumptions
about how things were "before." And in contrast to Pandora and her
descendents we find that the women of the *Odyssey* and even the *Iliad,*
while inevitably prized for their looks and their capacity to produce a
new generation of warriors, are universally valued for the work that
they do.[13] Even the immortals are busy at their looms. And the Linear
B tablets suggest that some women may have had a place in agriculture

as land users[14] but the whole question of land tenure in the Mycenaean period is by no means clear.

So perhaps we can assume that Hesiod's exclusion of women from the economy is not "natural" or "inevitable," but that, on the contrary, it represents a change, and perhaps a drastic one, from an earlier situation. But we are still left with the problem of how and why this change should have taken place, and how it relates to the role of the male as Hesiod depicts it. As I said, Hesiod's complaint is not only that women can survive in idleness, but that they do it by living off a man who, like the bee, must work from morning till night, day after day and, as the *Works and Days* makes clear, year after year as long as he lives. Hesiod's description of the farmer's life is rendered especially poignant by the mythological contrasts. Life doesn't have to be like this[15] and there was a time, a golden age of no work, when things were different.[16] All of which might lead us to suspect that just as the economic role of women in society had altered sometime during or, more likely, prior of Hesiod's lifetime, so, perhaps for the same reasons, men's roles had also changed. This again leads us to some interesting but highly speculative theorizing. In her article "Linear B and Hesiod's Bread Winners"[17] Thalia Phillies Howe postulates on the basis of the Linear B evidence that sometime between the end of the Mycenaean and the beginning of the historical period where we traditionally place Hesiod a major alteration took place in the agricultural basis of the Greek economy — a shift from an essentially pastoral economy featuring meat as a major dietary staple to an economy based largely on grain-raising. It is obvious, as Howe points out, that raising grain is or at least appears to be much more labor intensive than sitting around watching sheep and goats, and it is also obvious that drastically increasing the amount of time and energy needed to produce a given amount of food is bound to have enormous social and psychological repercussions. And whether or not Howe's conclusions are correct,[18] we do find, turning again to Homer, that his ideal warriors eat a good deal of meat. Perhaps more important, these people lead an exciting and highly mobil existence with conspicuously little concern about who is tending to the spring plowing in their absence. Regardless of the extent to which this reality is "historical," I think we can imagine the psychological effect the heroic epic might have on people who are tied to their farms and dependent on the soil for their sustenance.

In any event, there are some ramifications to Howe's hypothesis that go beyond a possible transition from meat eating to bread eating. We tend to assume that "primitive" people, i.e., gatherers and farmers practicing neolithic techniques on virgin soil, have a narrow margin of survival and consequently must work hard all the time to avoid starvation. In fact exactly the opposite seems to be true, which gives us another perspective on Hesiod's golden-age of no agricultural work. Kent V. Flannery, writing on the origins and effects of the domestication of animals in the ancient Near East says, "Even the bushmen of the relatively desolate Kalahari region appeared to get 2100 calories a day with less than three days of foraging per week. Presumably hunter-gatherers in lusher environments in prehistoric times did even better."[19] Similarly, traditional methods of agriculture practiced on virgin land cleared by burning (which requires neither fertilizing, plowing nor weeding) or on land which has lain fallow for several seasons, i.e., long fallow agriculture, are much less labor intensive than the annual or even semi-annual planting of the same land or short fallow agriculture that Hesiod describes.[20] Unfortunately, we seem to know very little about land use patterns in the Mycenaean and even less about the Dark Age which followed.

There is, however, some evidence from the Linear B tablets that the rate of seeding of the land being described was much lower than in later times, leading to Chadwick's suggestion that at any given time in this period as much as one half of the arable land was permitted to lie fallow.[21] The case may be similar in Mesopotamia; prior to 1000 B.C. the rate of seeding seems to be lower than in earlier periods.[22] And while we have no documentary evidence for the rate of planting during the Dark Age, there are some archaeological indications of alternation at a given site between settlement and "nomadism."[23] In other words, people who had at one time practiced relatively intensive agriculture may have shifted to less labor intensive pastoralism or long fallow agriculture during a period of population decline.

Thus on the basis of both archaeological and anthropological studies, we can speculate on why and under what circumstances people made the transition from relatively leisurely long fallow agriculture to the highly labor intensive short fallow agriculture pattern of Hesiod's overworked farmer. This transition, of course, is highly complex and many variables have to be considered, but the one variable which seems to recur most consistently is an increase in population. There is an extensive literature documenting the relationship between population growth, changes in land use, technology, and labor productivity. One of the most important examples is Esther Boserup's *Conditions of Agricultural Growth*[24] which deals for the most part with contemporary traditional societies in transition. This kind of analysis has also proved fruitful in connection with ancient populations; Kent Flannery, whom I quoted before, has worked along these lines with the neolithic populations of Iran.[25] It is important to note that this kind of analysis is anti-Malthusian, that is, while classic Malthusian theory assumes that population change is dependent upon increase or decrease in food supply, anthropologists like Boserup assume that population level determines the method and intensity of food production (and hence supply). Assuming that the population change is an independent variable obviously raises the question of what, if not food supply, regulates population size, a question much easier to ask than to answer. Some anthropologists and population biologists[26] maintain that human populations like those of other mammals are capable of a kind of homeostatic regulation of their numbers in relation to their environment, and that mechanisms, conscious or unconscious for limiting population and/or increasing food supply come into play long before starvation or even the threat of starvation is a factor. And while I am here chiefly concerned with measures to increase productivity, and the effect of these measures on the economic status of women, it is obvious, perhaps even more obvious, that the mechanisms by which populations control fertility or limit the number of births or of childbearing age women in the society are going to have a profound effect on attitudes toward sexuality in general and women in particular. This is a problem to which I think more attention might be paid in the future, but in any case, for the period we are dealing with — ca. 1150-750 B.C., historians and anthropologists assume a decline in population at the beginning[27] and, more important, a dramatic increase at the end.[28] J. Lawrence Angel, in his article "Ecology and Population in the Eastern Mediterranean"[29] has a chart which details not only the relative population density of the area, but also the birth/death ratios, the longevity rates (broken down by sex), types and sources of food supply, and major climatic and other ecological changes from 30,000 B.C. to the present. This chart suggests just such a decline at the beginning of our period and an increase in total population during the late Geometric and early Archaic.[30] It is precisely this kind of increase in the birth rate that provides one impetus towards increasing productivity by intensifying land use which means in practice that people have to work harder to get less.

Thus it is easy to see how such a shift in agricultural techniques could produce despair and resentment among people who retain the memory, historical or mythological, of a time when things were different. It is less easy to see how and why it should result in the virtual exclusion of women from the economic community. In fact, Marylin Arthur, in her article "The Origins of the Western Attitude Toward Women"[31] has suggested that exactly the opposite is true, that is, that Hesiod's characterization of women as nonworkers constitutes a recognition of the vital importance of women's work for the survival of the nuclear family, and simultaneously, a recognition of the fact that, given the existing social structure, women had no real stake in the success of their efforts. Arthur emphasizes the attitudinal changes which result less from a shift in the economic base of the society than from the increasing importance of the nuclear family (as opposed to the 'clan' or extended family) as the society's basic constituent unit. Within the context of the nuclear family, the necessity of producing a legitimate heir is all important. Thus, female sexuality must be rigidly controlled, and is a constant source of anxiety for the males of the family. Equally significant is the suggestion that the marriage patterns implied in Hesiod and in later authors (exogamous with respect to the family[32] and andrilocal) create a situation in which a woman may be regarded as a stranger or foreigner in her husband's home. Her loyalties, therefore, might be elsewhere, while at the same time both her fertility and her contributions to the domestic economy are vitally important for the survival of the family. Arthur's analysis thus rests on a set of variables different from, although certainly not incompatible with, those I have been discussing since, as I said above, the issue is not entirely whether or not women actually did work, but the extent to which they are *perceived* as making a vital contribution to the economy.

Moreover, the difference between her interpretation and mine raises some very interesting questions about Hesiod as the basis for any kind of socio-politico-economic analysis. "We know how to tell lies like truth," say Hesiod's muses in the proem of the *Theogony,* "but we know how to speak true things also when we wish" (*Th.* 27-

28). It would be edifying to have some way of knowing when a muse is lying and when she is not; as we know, poets have many reasons for saying the things they do, and the most important of these reasons usually have little to do with any attempt to depict an "objective" or "literal" social reality. There are, of course, horrendous methodological problems that inevitably arise when artistic representations are used as a source for social history, especially when these representations are most of what we've got. But, caveats aside, if we take Hesiod at face value and assume that when he says that women are drones, he is saying that in the real world some women, at least, do not or need not work, we are, as I said, confronted by an anomaly. Why should women or any group of women be excluded from the economic community at what appears to be the time of greatest need? Or why at this point should their work be perceived as having little value? This seems totally unbelievable and attributable largely to Hesiod's lying muse, but many observable present-day societies have followed a similar pattern. Esther Boserup's more recent book *Women's Role in Economic Development*[33] examines the way in which the transition from long fallow, relatively leisurely agricultural practices to highly labor-intensive short fallow agriculture has affected the economic role and social status of women. In general, she has found that the economic contributions of women and consequently their social status has tended to be diminished with the introduction of labor-intensive modes of production. The reasons for this diminution of women's roles and the status of women's roles are complex and varied, and some of the most significant, e.g., the overwhelming impact of Western technology and attitudes have little apparent relevance for historical analysis.

Perhaps more directly relevant is Julian Pitt-Rivers[34] speculative hypothesis that the advent of the more settled form of village life (associated with short fallow agriculture) was accompanied by a shift from exogamy to endogamy, which, in turn, is to be related to the development of a whole new set of attitudes toward women and female sexuality, attitudes which have some interesting implications. Pitt-Rivers suggests that the nomadic or semi-nomadic societies of the Mediterranean practiced a form of exogamy which used their women as counters or tokens to solidify relations with neighboring societies. As these societies became less and less mobile the practice of using women as tokens of exchange decreased in significance, and, in fact, the ability to maintain control over the women in the family and to marry them as close to home as possible became an increasingly important manifestation of male "honor." It is significant that Pitt-Rivers sees one possible origin of the all-encompassing Mediterranean concept of honor[35] in relation to a shift in the economy and the social structure. He also sees in the concept of honor some explanation for precisely the kind of attitude we find expressed by Hesiod.[36]

> Feminine power is not overt, but, due to their participation in the familial honor (as the repositors of its moral and sacred aspects) women hold in their hands the power not merely to put pressure on their menfolk, but actually to 'ruin' them. The fear of female sexuality which inspires much of Europe's popular literature and beliefs runs parallel to a much more realistic fear of female sociability. It is only too easy to understand then that men, conscious and resentful of their vulnerability through the actions of their womenfolk, should be eager to credit them with the faults of character that are, however unfounded, commonplace in the literature of the Mediterranean, faults which justify their exclusion from the political sphere and the authority of their menfolk over them.

On a superficial level, the "explanation," is that a change in the basis of the economy is invariably a concomitant of other equally profound changes. If we really want to do justice to Pandora and to women's history we must begin to be aware of and learn to analyze this incredibly complex pattern. All I can do here is suggest several aspects of the situation, where investigation has already proved fruitful. One aspect is the relationship between intensive agriculture, individual ownership of land and private property, and the position of women, à la Engels.[37] Another is the trend to urbanization, to specialization of labor and the removal from the household of what had been female industries.[38] Also a population which is increasing tends to spread out and make new contacts, and perhaps comes to imitate foreign patterns in other things besides pottery.[39] Perhaps on the social-psychological level, in a society where work is so important the ability to keep an idle wife becomes a status symbol.[40] This brings us back to Semonides' mare woman, who is a suitable possession for kings and tyrants. Hesiod's "middle-class" audience (assuming he *is* in fact addressing a "middle-class" audience) may well have aspired to a status symbol of this sort, even if they really couldn't afford it. And, let's fact it, perhaps their wives, given the choice, preferred the life of an idle but decorative possession to that of a full-fledged member of the social and economic community. Women have been and often still are active collaborators in defending and maintaining their own dependence.

The inevitable rationalization, at least in our society, for the exclusion of women from economic activity (or political or religious or whatever is the high status activity under discussion) is that women's responsibilities as childbearers and nurturers prevent them from taking on too many "outside" activities. However, as Hesiod makes all too clear, in his world childbearing beyond the requisite male heir is neither wanted nor needed. His injunction to have one son (WD 376-377) obviously bears out the hypothesis that he is writing in or of a period of rapid population growth, but beyond that, it is a clear indication of how bad Pandora's situation is. Not content with depicting her as a creature of no positive value in the real world of work, Hesiod also deprives her of her biological significance and reason for existence, leaving a total non-person. Poor Pandora! Endowed with the skills of Athena, the sexuality of Aphrodite and the craftiness of Hermes, her usefulness is over when she has produced one male child, and she is otherwise good for nothing but making trouble. The will of Zeus may be inscrutable, but the workings of human societies are not. And it is in human society and human history that we might try to seek out the reasons for the degradation of Pandora.

University of Rhode Island

NOTES

[1] (New York 1970). Although Barthes is concerned primarily with contemporary mass media, I think his views might well apply to the Pandora myth. "I resented seeing Nature and History confused at every turn, and I wanted to track down, in the decorative display of *what-goes-without-saying*, the ideological abuse which, in my view is hidden there" (11).

[2] There is ample precedent for treating the Pandora stories of the *Theogony*

and the *Works and Days* as a single 'mythologem.' See, most recently, Pietro Pucci, *Hesiod and the Language of Poetry*, chapter 4, pp. 82-126 (Baltimore and London 1977) and also his bibliography and J. -P. Vernant, "Le mythe Prometheén chez Hésiode," *Mythe et Société* (Paris 1974).

3 We should note in this context the obvious resemblances between the Pandora story and the second Biblical account of human creation, *Genesis* 2.4-25 and 3.1-22, where Eve, like Pandora, is created as a kind of afterthought and is responsible for the evils of the human condition. The fact that this is one of the most familiar and universally known narratives in our culture tends to reinforce our acceptance of the Greek story as one which requires no explanation.

4 Hesiod is only the beginning in Western literature of an extensive and deepseated tradition of anti-female bias. An interesting, if somewhat apologetic, history of this kind of literary expression is Katherine Rogers, *The Troublesome Helpmate: A History of Misogyny in Literature* (Seattle 1966).

5 *Oecomomicus*, 7.17, 7.32 and elsewhere in this passage, *hē hēgemōn melitta*, clearly referring to the wife.

6 Translated by H. G. Evelyn-White, *Hesiod, the Homeric Hymns and Homerica*, Loeb Classical Library (Cambridge, Mass. 1936).

7 "Through work men grow rich in flocks and substance, and working they are much better loved by the immortals. Work is no disgrace. But if you work, the idle will soon envy you as you grow rich, for fame and renown attend on wealth. And whatever be your lot, work is best for you, if you turn your misguided mind away from other men's property to your work and attend to your livelihood as I bid you. An evil shame is the needy man's companion, shame which both greatly harms and prospers men: shame is with poverty, but confidence with wealth" (*WD* 307-318, translated by Evelyn-White, note 4).

8 M. L. West, *Iambi et Elegi Graeci* II Fr. 7 (pp. 99-104).

9 Hugh Lloyd-Jones, *Females of the Species: Semonides on Women* (London 1975).

10 *Oec*. 7.13.

11 *Oec*. 7.4-14, 8.1-23, 9.1-18.

12 See A. M. Snodgrass, "An Historical Homeric Society?", *Journal of Hellenic Studies* 94 (1974) 114-125.

13 See, for instance, *Il*. 1.31, and 9.127-130. In both cases, handiwork takes precedence over other activities and attributes. In the *Odyssey* where we see women and goddesses actually engaging in their characteristic activities, it is impossible not to notice that almost all of them weave. And I think it is safe to assume, first, that the work of women's hands is highly prized (cf. *Od*. 19.232-235 and perhaps 14.513-514) not to say essential for survival in a temperate climate and, second, that any work carried on by such personages as Helen (*Od*. 4.131-156), Calypso (*Od*. 10.220-228) and Circe (*Od*. 5.61-62) is reasonably high-status activity. "The Homeric poet focuses almost exclusively on the positive side of the

position of women; it emphasizes women's *inclusion* in society as a whole, rather than her exclu'sion from certain roles; it celebrates the importance of the functions that women do, instead of drawing attention to their handicaps or inabilities." (Marylin B. Arthur, "Origins of the Western Attitude Toward Woman," *Arethusa* 6 [Spring 1973] 14.)

[14] For a discussion of the possible role of women (most likely priestesses) as landholders during the Mycenaean period see John Chadwick, *Cambridge Ancient History*, Vol. ii, part 1 (Cambridge 1970) 618-20, *The Mycenaean World* (Cambridge 1976) 114-115. C. G. Thomas, "Matriarchy in Early Greece: the Bronze and Dark Ages," *Arethusa* 6 (Spring 1973) 173-197 draws somewhat stronger conclusions based on R. F. Willetts' *Aristocratic Society in Ancient Crete* (London 1955) and *The Law Code of Gortyn* (Berlin 1967). Willetts hypothesizes (*The Law Code of Gortyn*, p. 8 ff.) that the relatively liberal provisions of the Code relating to women are to be understood as survivals from an earlier era.

[15] WD 42-46.

[16] WD 109-126.

[17] *Transactions of the American Philogical Association*, 89 (1958) 44-65.

[18] Howe's conclusions about the composition of the Mycenaean diet are not universally accepted; see, for example, the chapter "Agriculture" in John Chadwick *The Mycenaean World* 102-133. I have also been informed by a reader that Michael Jameson in a paper read at the Princeton Conference on Kinship and Economy in Classical Greece, April 1977, remarks: "The notion that Late Bronze Age and Dark Age Greece subsisted on stock breeding is a widely held aberration that Brian MacDonald and P. R. Helm are correcting." Unfortunately, at the time of this writing I myself have seen neither the text of Jameson's paper nor his bibliography.

For the Dark Age, cf. A. M. Snodgrass, *The Dark Age of Greece* (Edinburgh 1971) 379-380: "Meat was thus an esteemed form of food and relatively widely available throughout the Dark Age; and perhaps we may tentatively conclude that the Greeks had continued to subsist by stock breeding rather than by arable farming after the fall of Mycenaean civilization. . . . But in the later Dark Age there begins to be evidence of a contrary trend, at least for Attica and Ionia; a number of Attica graves, ranging in date from about 850 and 700 have produced circular terracotta models which have been convincingly argued to represent granaries; and further the circular foundations of what are probably real granaries have been uncovered in the yards of Geometric houses at Smyrna. Perhaps we have here the early signs of a major change in course in agriculture which subsequently spread to the rest of Greece."

[19] "Origins and Ecological Effects of Early Domestication in Iran and the Near East" in *Prehistoric Argriculture*, Stuart Struever, ed. (Garden City, N.Y. 1971) 53. Flannery also cites an experiment in gathering which suggests that it is possible even in present day Turkey to gather enough wheat for sustenance (Harlan, "A Wild Wheat Harvest in Turkey," *Archaeology* 20 [1967] 197-201, and Harlan and Zohary, "Distribution of Wild

Wheats and Barley," *Science* 153 [1966] 1074-80). Flannery says that on the basis of these harvests "a family of experienced plant collectors working over a three week period when wild wheat comes ripe without working very hard could gather more grain than the family could possibly consume in a year" (54).

[20] For a detailed discussion of the relationship between method of cultivation, labor productivity and length of fallow see Esther Boserup, *The Conditions of Agricultural Growth* (Chicago 1965), especially chapters 1-4.

[21] John Chadwick, *Documents in Mycenaean Greek* (Cambridge 1973) 232-237.

[22] Lewry, "Assyro-Babylonian and Israelite Measures of Capacity and Rates of Seeding," *Journal American Oriental Society* 64 (1944) 65-73.

[23] Chester G. Starr, *The Origins of Greek Civilization* (New York 1961) 79.

[24] Note 20, above.

[25] Flannery, "Origins," (note 19, above) 54-55. See also Hole, Flannery and Neely, "Prehistory and Human Ecology of the Deh Luran Plain" in *Prehistoric Agriculture* 305.

[26] See again Boserup, and Flannery, "Origins," (note 19, above) 53: "A growing body of data supports the conclusion that starvation is not the principal factor regulating mammal populations. . . . Instead, evidence suggests that other mechanisms, including their own social behavior, homeostatically maintain mammal populations at a level *below* the point at which they would begin to deplete their own food supply."

[27] Snodgrass, *The Dark Age of Greece* (note 18, above) 365-366, Starr (note 23, above) 79.

[28] Snodgrass, *Dark Age* 366, and Starr (note 23, above) 312-313.

[29] *World Archaeology* (1972) 88-105.

[30] Angel (note 29, above) 99. E. Badian in his review of Sarah Pomeroy's *Goddesses, Whores, Wives and Slaves* in *New York Review* (October 30, 1975) 25-31 states that some of Angel's demographic speculations have been called into question. He cites the conclusions of Gilbert and McKern in *American Journal Physical Anthropology* 38 (1973) which suggest that it is not possible on the basis of skeletal analysis to determine with any degree of accuracy either how many children a woman has born or at what age she died. However, this cautionary note applies only to the causes and mechanics of population decline; it does not, I think, contradict the overall pattern of population changes outlined by Angel. This pattern, in any case, is supported by some independent archaeological evidence, notes 24 and 25.

[31] Arthur (note 13, above) 23-26.

[32] But see below, pp. 35-36.

[33] (New York 1970).

[34] *The Fate of Shechem or the Politics of Sex, Essays in the Anthropology of the Mediterranean* (Cambridge 1977) 126-171.

[35] The importance of this concept or cluster of attitudes is well documented in contemporary Mediterranean village society. See, for example, the other essays in *The Fate of Shechem;* Pitt-Rivers' earlier book, *The People of the Sierra* (Chicago 1971); Ernestine Friedl, *Vasilikia, A Village in Modern Greece* (New York 1962); and J. R. Campbell, *Honour, Family and Patronage* (Oxford 1964).

[36] *The Fate of Shechem* (note 34, above) 80.

[37] Engels, *The Origin of the Family, Private Property and the State,* With an introduction and notes by Eleanor Burke Leacock (New York 1972). A reassessment of Engels' theories in the light of modern anthropology is Karen Sacks, "Engels Revisited: Women, the Organization of Production, and Private Property," Rosaldo and Lamphere (edd.), in *Women, Culture and Society* (Stanford, Cal. 1974). Some interesting speculations about the relationship between population increase, intensive land use and labor patterns and the development of a "class" society can be found in Flannery, "Origins," (note 19, above) 77-78, and Robert Adams, "Early Civilizations, Subsistence and Environment," Kraeling and Adams (edd.), in *City Invincible* (Chicago 1960) 269-295, also reprinted in *Prehistoric Agriculture* 591-614. See also Heidi Hartmann, "Capitalism, Patriarchy and Job Segregation by Sex," *Signs* 1. 3, part 2 (Spring 1976) 137-169, especially part 1, "Anthropological Perspectives on the Division of Labor by Sex." In an entirely different vein, Marcel Detienne, *Crise agraire et attitude religieuse chez Hésiode* Collection Latomus vol. 68 (Brussels 1963) offers an analysis of the relationship between some of the specific attitudes reflected in the *Work and Days* and what we know about inequalities of land ownership and use in Hesiod's Boeotia. Unfortunately Detienne takes the fact of inequality and incipient class conflict for granted; he has little to say about their causes or possible effect on Hesiod's perception of sex roles and relationships. However this study does provide one of the few *useful* models for analyzing the specific literary and theological stance of an ancient author in relation to social and historical reality.

[38] Boserup, *Women's Role* (note 33, above) 110-118.

[39] *Ibid.,* chapters 2 and 3.

[40] *Ibid.,* chapters 2 and 3.

SAPPHO AND HELEN

PAGE DUBOIS

DENYS PAGE SEEMS UNIMPRESSED with Sappho's fragment 16 LP. He complains of line seven: "The sequence of thought might have been clearer. . . . It seems inelegant then to begin this parable, the point of which is that Helen found τὸ κάλλιστον in her lover, by stating that she herself surpassed all mortals in this very quality."[1] Of the whole: "The poem opens with a common device[2]. . . . In a phrase which rings dull in our doubtful ears, she proceeds to illustrate the truth of her preamble by calling Helen of Troy in evidence. . . . And the thought is simple as the style is artless. . . . The transition back to the principal subject was perhaps not very adroitly managed. . . ."[3] Of the end, "The idea may seem a little fanciful: but this stanza was either a little fanciful or a little dull."[4]

I will argue that the very elements with which Page finds fault, the catalogue, the example of Helen, the return to the catalogue at the poem's end, structure it firmly while permitting its center to open into a moment of radiant presence. In addition, the poem is extraordinary in its rhetorical strategy, its attempt to move from the particularity of narrative discourse to a more general, logical, philosophical language. I see also in this poem, one of the few texts which break the silence of women in antiquity, an instant in which women become more than the objects of man's desire. Sappho's fragment 16 reaches beyond the confines of the lyric structure, looks both forward and backward in time, expresses the contradictions of its moment in history.

The poem begins with a brief catalogue, a listing of horsemen, infantry, ships.[5] The ἐπὶ γᾶν μέλαιναν of line 2 is ambiguous in its position; it refers back to the catalogue and forward to the infinitive construction ἔμμεναι κάλλιστον in line 3. The dark earth is the basis for this host of warriors, and war-ships, perhaps, and recalls the diction of the Homeric poems. Sappho sets ἔγω against this background of choices, against the dark earth, and then she makes the declaration which is the logical heart of the poem, "I say it (τὸ κάλλιστον) is what one loves."

The next stanza overpowers the doubter; she asserts the ease of proof of her statement, and moves immediately into an example. The poet's strategy here is rhetorically subtle; at first the reader associates the abstract (τὸ) κάλλιστον above with Helen herself. But the epic heroine has another function within the poem; she is not herself "the most beautiful thing." She moves toward it, drawn by desire.⁶ Helen stands at first, set up by πόλυ περσκέθοισα, the hyperbole of which is echoed by τὸν πανάριστον of line 8; her name is surrounded by superlatives, masculine and feminine. In line 7, which begins with κάλλος, the quality for which she is immortal in men's memory, she is surrounded by ἀνθρώπων and ἄνδρα. She surpasses all mankind with respect to beauty. Sappho's proof is for a moment deferred, but the force of her example, the superiority of Helen to all, is stressed.

The third stanza begins with καλλίποισ'; the line ends with πλέοισα. The first letters of the first participle echo the καλλ- of κάλλος, and link the leaving behind, her act of desertion, with her beauty. The line expresses motion; we see Helen leaving, going, sailing; the ἔβα, the aorist, anchors her action in a single past moment. The participles catch her endlessly moving, taking steps, sailing away on a ship which recalls the third element of the catalogue at the poem's beginning. The following line sets her motion against the static force of that which she left behind, all those who should have been dear to her, who ought to have satisfied her. She forgets all; the μνα- of ἐμνάσθη perhaps plays on the root μαν-, μαιν- suggesting madness. (Alcaeus, in his poem about Helen, calls her ἐκμάνεισα.)⁷ The stanza ends with a sentence which is lost; someone, something, leads the heroine astray.

There follows a fragmentary passage which is legible again at με νῦν; we have moved from the world of legend back to the ἔγω of line 3, and to the present, the singer's time. The next word is 'Ανακτορίας. If the logical center of the poem is the generalizing statement of lines three and four, the moment of presence, the phenomenological center, arrives with the name of Anaktoria. We are made aware of her absence only with οὐ παρεοίσας; the participle allows us to imagine her presence as well. Sappho's memory creates her; the act of making poetry becomes the act of making here, now, the absent loved one.

The last stanza completes the process of memory and finally returns the listener to the wider world. The ἐρατόν of line 17 echoes ἔραται of line 4, makes whatever is lovely about Anaktoria partake of the general statement at the beginning. The βᾶμα is linked to ἔβα of line 9, and stresses the connection of Helen with all desire, with

Anaktoria. Sappho would rather see her way of walking, her shining face, than the Lydian chariots, than the armed foot-soldiers. The last two substantives return us to the "prooïmion," to the level of generalizing statement.

The poem works on the tension between desire, love, presence and absence, and on the threat of war outside, the drama of pursuit in love. In each of the three parts of the lyric Sappho refers to the world of war, the world of men and heroes — in the catalogue of warriors and ships, in the mention of Helen, where the Trojan War is suppressed but present behind the text, in the mention at the end of chariots and foot-soldiers. The notion of desire shimmers through the tripartite rhetorical structure, through the allusions to war; Sappho's choice of Anaktoria takes place in the context of a refusal of alternatives.

Lattimore mistranslates this poem in a way which reveals the consequences of its compactness, its far-reaching compression. He translates lines 3 and 4 thus: "but I say she whom one loves best is the loveliest."[8] In fact, the Greek κῆν᾽ ὄτ | τω τις ἔραται does not mean that; κῆν᾽ is neuter; ὄττω also does not show gender. Lattimore's translation, however, brings out an important aspect of the poem, a confusion between things and people which is essential to its logic. Lattimore makes the poem exclusively a love poem, a poem about Anaktoria. Sappho is writing something more, a sketch on the abstract notion of desire. At least as important as Anaktoria is the poet's attempt to universalize her insight, to move toward logical thought. She is defining desire with the vocabulary at hand.

Sappho wants to answer the question: what is τὸ κάλλιστον ἐπὶ γᾶν μέλαιναν? Her answer is a type of definition, a general statement — κάλλιστον is *whatever* one desires. The catalogue which precedes the general statement is not meant to be exhaustive; it is a "doublet" which includes kinds of men and ships, which transcends both these classes. Helen is a particular case, and her action proves the general statement; her beauty and fame are enlisted only to give weight to the general definition. Anaktoria is another particular, for Sappho the most beautiful thing on earth, in the poem another element in a proof. The partial listing at the end of the poem simply closes the "ring."

All the elements of the poem, which establish the oppositions love/war, men/women, men/things, work also to create a definition, a logical summary under a heading which subsumes them all. Sappho is concerned to say new things with the old vocabulary, as we see if we read the poem juxtaposed with this passage from the *Nicomachean Ethics*, where Aristotle is attempting to define τἀγαθὸν καὶ τὸ ἄριστον, the end at which human actions aim (I, v, 1-2):[9]

τὸ γὰρ ἀγαθὸν καὶ τὴν εὐδαιμονίαν οὐκ ἀλόγως ἐοίκασιν ἐκ
τῶν βίων ὑπολαμβάνειν οἱ μὲν πολλοὶ καὶ φορτικώτατοι
τὴν ἡδονήν· διὸ καὶ τὸν βίον ἀγαπῶσι τὸν ἀπολαυστικόν.

Bruno Snell says of Sappho's fragment 16, "That one man should contrast his own ideas with those of others is the theme of (this) poem by Sappho. . . ."[10] Yet elsewhere I think he comes closer to the real consequences of the type of thinking exemplified in this poem, which is not simply about personal taste. "But both of them [Archilochus and Sappho] are evidently concerned to grasp a piece of genuine reality: to find Being instead of Appearance."[11] Although she might have done so, Sappho is not saying that Anaktoria = τὸ κάλλιστον. Much of the energy of the poem comes from the force of her personal preference, her ability to make Anaktoria walk before us, but Anaktoria's presence is straining to break out of a structure which gives her existence wider meaning.

Helen is an element of the old epic vocabulary, yet she means something new here. Sappho subverts the traditional interpretation of her journey to Troy. And in so doing she speaks of desire in new terms, circling down on a definition of the abstract force. Eros as a term is insufficiently abstract; Eros is a god, Aphrodite a personification. Sappho moves toward the abstract by employing the substitutability of things, people, ships. She achieves a representation of desire by the accumulation of detail, examples, personal testimony.

The problem is very different from that which the Homeric poet sets himself, and Sappho's use of example fits into a more hypotactic structure. Homer's Phoinix tells the Meleager story as an example to persuade Achilles to return to battle. He is not concerned to describe, to define the nature of anger, or withdrawal. The story works rhetorically to put Achilles' action in a context, to convince Achilles to act further, to ensure the outcome of his wrath in terms of heroic pattern.

Homer uses this kind of example rarely; he describes more often by means of simile, sets next to some action on the battlefield an event from the pastoral world outside the poem's supposed space. The one scene seems equivalent to the other. Sappho is defining an abstraction, and she operates by citing several particulars which are logically subordinate to a whole, working by addition toward that whole.

The move from mythical to rational thought, from religion to philosophy, is caught here in a moment of transition. Sappho is progressing toward analytical language, toward the notion of definition, of logical classes, of subordination and hypotactic structure. Her ability to do so coincides in time with the invention in the eastern Mediterranean, in nearby Lydia, of coined money, a step which Aristotle sees as enabling abstract thought, as permitting the recognition of abstract value. The exchange between persons who are different but equal requires an equalizer (V, v, 10):[12]

διὸ πάντα συμβλητὰ δεῖ πως εἶναι, ὧν ἐστὶν ἀλλαγή, ἐφ᾽ ὃ τὸ νόμισμα ἐλήλυθε, καὶ γίνεταί πως μέσον· πάντα γὰρ μετρεῖ, ὥστε καὶ τὴν ὑπεροχὴν καὶ τὴν ἔλλειψιν....

The invention of money allows things, even men, to be measured by a common standard. Sappho measures men and women and things not by setting them in a hierarchy, in a situation of relative value, but against a common standard, that of "the most beautiful thing on the dark earth."

Before the invention of coined money, men exchanged valuable things. The Homeric world is characterized by an exchange of gifts; women too are exchanged, as gifts, as valuable prizes of war. The Trojan War is caused by a violation of proper exchange, since Menelaos, the recipient of Helen, loses possession of her. The *Iliad* begins with the return of Chryseis to her father and Agamemnon's seizure of Briseis. Sappho's Helen is very different from Homer's. In the *Iliad* Helen is caught within the walls of Troy; we see her weaving a web which is like the war, pointing out the Greeks heroes to Priam. She is forced by Aphrodite to go to Paris' bed when the goddess snatches him from danger on the plain below. She mourns for Hektor, and laments her coming with Paris to Troy. Because of Aphrodite's promise to the shepherd, Helen has been traded for the apple of discord; she has become a thing, passively waiting to be reclaimed.

In the *Odyssey*, Helen greets Telemachos along with Menelaos; she is a contented queen, and Homer alludes to her stay in Egypt. According to an alternate version of the story, her εἴδωλον was at Troy; she gives her guest nepenthe which she received in Egypt. We hear her story of Odysseus' spying trip within the walls, and she claims to have assisted him. In an ironic juxtaposition, her husband immediately recounts the tale of the wooden horse, and Helen's treacherous behavior, when she called to each warrior, imitating the voice of his wife. Only Odysseus kept them from crying out and betraying their mission.

Women in the Homeric world are exchanged, given as prizes, stolen, sold as slaves. The narrative structure of the *Odyssey* works on the passage of Odysseus from one woman to another, from the beautiful Kalypso to his faithful wife Penelope; he moves across the epic landscape defining himself, encountering fixed female creatures and moving beyond them. George Dimock, in a fine example of what Mary Ellmann would call "phallic criticism,"[13] says of the initial situation of the poem:[14]

> Leaving Calypso is very like leaving the perfect security
> of the womb; but, as the Cyclops reminds us, the womb is
> after all a deadly place. In the womb, one has no identity,
> no existence worthy of a name. Nonentity and identity are
> in fact the poles between which the actors in the poem
> move.

Odysseus, the only actor in sight, defines himself by leaving the womb-Kalypso, and the other boundary of his journey, from which he will depart again with his oar, is the bed of Penelope, another fixed, static place on the map of the poem, set like Kalypso's island as a landmark by which the hero marks out his direction, his existence.

The goddesses of the *Odyssey* act, but they too, except for Athena the virgin warrior, not born of woman, half-female, are static figures. In their *Dialectic of Enlightenment,* Horkheimer and Adorno speak of the sirens who tempt Odysseus, and of the circular, mythic creatures like them in the poem, figures which belong to the past which Odysseus is transcending in his *nostos*, in his trajectory through the landscape from Aia to Ithaka:[15]

> The mythic monsters whose sphere of power he enters
> always represent ossified covenants, claims from pre-
> history. Thus in the stage of development represented by
> the patriarchal age, the older folk religion appears in the
> form of its scattered relics: beneath the Olympian heavens
> they have become images of abstract fate, of immaterial

> necessity. . . . Scylla and Charybdis have a right to what-
> ever comes between them, just as Circe does to bewitch
> those unprepared with the gods' antidote. . . . Each of the
> mythic figures is programed always to do the same thing.
> Each is a figure of repetition, and would come to an end
> should the repetition fail to occur.

Odysseus moves away from Kalypso's island, away from Nausikaa and the Phaeacians, learning from Circe and leaving her, past the Sirens, past Scylla and Charybdis. The cyclical female forms mark the landscape and cannot themselves move within it; Odysseus returns to Penelope and then moves past her too, deeper inland. Women in the world of the *Odyssey* are trapped in cyclical, mythic time; except for Athena, they belong to an age which Odysseus leaves behind as he makes himself, discovers himself through his journey.

The study of narrative structure which has been a focus of recent literary criticism seems unable to see beyond the type of text exemplified by the *Odyssey*. Women appear to have a static, fixed quality in oral literatures, and structuralists generalize from oral texts to describe women as objects, things to be exchanged, markers of places, geographically, textually. Lévi-Strauss discusses women almost as words exchanged in a conversation among men.[16] In the analysis of narrative which Vladimir Propp began with his study of the folktale, woman is a princess, the object of the hero's quest, a prize.[17] A. J. Greimas, in presenting his "actantial model," applies categories appropriate to oral literature to any conceivable love story:[18]

> Par exemple, dans un récit qui ne serait qu'une banale
> histoire d'amour, finissant, sans l'intervention des parents,
> par le mariage, le sujet est à la fois le destinataire, tandis
> que l'objet est en même temps le destinateur de l'amour:

$$\frac{\text{Lui}}{\text{Elle}} \sim \frac{\text{Sujet} + \text{Destinataire}}{\text{Objet} + \text{Destinateur}}$$

The attempt to universalize models of structure denies the historicity of the models: women may be exchanged like words in some cultures, according to anthropologists, but every love story is *not* accurately represented by the narrative shapes of these cultures. Women are not always objects, sending love. Oral cultures have patterns of exchange and marriage very different from those of literate societies, and the diagram, the insistence on the subject–object duality, fail to take into account the possibility of women's status as subjects in their own right.

Sappho's poem, although not a narrative, in fact reverses the pattern of oral literature, of the Homeric poems, men trading women, men moving past women. She sees Helen as an "actant" in her own life, the subject of a choice, exemplary in her desiring. Sappho's idea of Helen is different even from that of her contemporary Alcaeus; he registers strong disapproval of Helen, in his narration of her story, by comparing her to the more virtuous Thetis.[19] Alcaeus insists on the destructive aspects of Helen's love, her responsibility for the perishing of the Trojans and their city.

Sappho does not judge Helen, and she does not make the epic heroine the victim of madness. Helen is one who acted, pursuing the thing she loved, and for that action Sappho celebrates her. Even the simple reversal of Greimas' model, which would make Helen "subject," is inadequate. Perhaps the failure of women to write narrative poetry, the silence which Sappho did not break, is linked to the invisible pressure of models like this one, patterns which insist on women's receptivity, passivity.

Sappho acts, as did Helen, in loving Anaktoria, in following her in her poem, in attempting to think beyond the terms of the epic vocabulary. Her action is possible because the world of oral culture, of a certain type of exchange, a type of marriage characteristic of such societies, is no longer dominant. The Greek world is, in the seventh century, in a stage of transition.[20] The institutions of the democratic cities have not yet evolved. The lyric age, the age of the tyrants, is a period of confusion, turbulence, and conflict; it is from the moment, this break, that Sappho speaks.

Louis Gernet, in his "Mariage des Tyrans," analyzes the anachronistic features of the marriage of the tyrants, the elements of their alliances characteristic more of the legendary past, the age of the magical kings, than of a society moving toward urbanization.[21] J. -P. Vernant's study of Greek marriage also helps to explain the peculiar situation of women in the seventh and sixth centuries:[22]

> On peut parler d'une coupure entre le mariage archaïque
> et celui qui s'instaure dans le cadre d'une cité démo-
> cratique, à la fin du VIe siècle athénien. Dans l'Athènes

post-clisthenienne les unions matrimoniales n'ont plus pour objet d'établir des relations du puissance ou de services mutuels entre de grandes familles souveraines mais de perpetuer les maisons, les foyers domestiques qui constituent la cité. . . .

The return of the tyrants to incest reveals a need, at this time, to redefine, to restructure the institution of marriage, so important in the lives of women in such cultures, to make it correspond to the new demands of urban, democratic life.

During the seventh century the old institutions which perpetuated the dominance of the aristocracy, the system of noble *oikoi*, the rural economy, pre-monetary exchange, were being challenged by growing mercantile, commercial, artisan groups which were clustering around the acropoleis.[23] The conflict which Alcaeus documents in his political poems emerged at this time, when new definitions, new loci of power were being established, and the aristocrats, the families of Sappho and Alcaeus among others, fought for survival.

The transitional nature of Sappho's society, the possible lack of definition for her class, for women, freed her from the rigidity of traditional marriage, or from the identity which arose from that fixed role. They permitted her to make poetry like the Anaktoria poem, a love poem which is at the same time an extension of the possibilities of language, and they enabled her to see Helen as an autonomous subject, the hero of her own life.

University of California at San Diego

NOTES

[1] Denys Page, *Sappho and Alcaeus* (Oxford 1959)[2] 53.
[2] *Ibid.* 55.
[3] *Ibid.* 56.
[4] *Ibid.* 57.
[5] *Ibid.* 52. Here follows the full, reconstructed text:

ο]ι μὲν ἰππήων στρότον οἰ δὲ πέσδων
οἰ δὲ νάων φαῖσ' ἐπ[ὶ] γᾶν μέλαι[ν]αν
ἔ]μμεναι κάλλιστον, ἔγω δὲ κῆν' ὄτ-
τω τις ἔραται·

5 πά]γχυ δ' εὔμαρες σύνετον πόησαι
π]άντι τ[ο]ῦτ', ἀ γὰρ πόλυ περσκέθοισα
κάλλος [ἀνθ]ρώπων 'Ελένα [τὸ]ν ἄνδρα
τὸν [πανάρ]ιστον

καλλ[ίποι]σ' ἔβα 'ς Τροΐαν πλέοι[σα
10 κωὐδ[ὲ πα]ῖδος οὐδὲ φίλων το[κ]ήων
πά[μπαν] ἐμνάσθη, ἀλλὰ παράγαγ' αὔταν
 ]σαν
 ]αμπτον γὰρ [
 ]...κούφως τ[   ]οησ[ ]ν
15 ..]με νῦν 'Ανακτορί[ας ὀ]νέμναι-
σ' οὐ] παρεοίσας·
τᾶ]ς κε βολλοίμαν ἔρατόν τε βᾶμα
κἀμάρυχμα λάμπρον ἴδην προσώπω
ἢ τὰ Λύδων ἄρματα καὶ πανόπλοις
20 πεσδομ]άχεντας.

"Some say a host of horsemen, others of infantry,
and others of ships, is the most beautiful thing
on the dark earth: but I say, it is what you love.

Full easy it is to make this understood of one and all:
for she that far surpassed all mortals in beauty,
Helen, her most noble husband

Deserted, and went sailing to Troy, with never a
thought for her daughter and dear parents. The
[Cyprian goddess] led her from the path. . .

. . . (Which) now has put me in mind of Anactoria far
away;

Her lovely way of walking, and the bright radiance
of her changing face, would I rather see than
your Lydian chariots and infantry full-armed."

---

[6] Cf. Frederic Will, "Sappho and Poetic Motion," *CJ* 61 (1966) 259-262.
[7] Page (above, note 1) 275.
[8] Richmond Lattimore, *Greek Lyrics* (Chicago 1960)² 40.
[9] Aristotle, *The Nicomachean Ethics*, trans. H. Rackham (Cambridge, Mass. [Loeb], rev. ed., 1934, rep. 1962):

"To judge from men's lives, the more or less reasoned conceptions of the good or happiness that seem to prevail among
them are the following. On the one hand the generality of men

and the most vulgar identify the good with pleasure, and accordingly are content with the life of enjoyment.''

[10] Bruno Snell, *The Discovery of the Mind*, trans. T. G. Rosenmeyer (Cambridge, Mass. 1953) 47.

[11] *Ibid.* 50. See also Garry Wills, ''The Sapphic *Umwertung aller Werte* '' *AJP* 88 (1967) 434-442.

[12] ''Hence all commodities exchanged must be able to be compared in some way. It is to meet this requirement that men have introduced money; money constitutes in a manner a middle term, for it is a measure of all things, and so of their superior or inferior value. . . .'' (Aristotle [above, note 9] 282). Cf. E. Will, ''De l'aspect éthique des origines grecques de la monnaie,'' *Revue historique* 212 (1954) 209-231.

[13] Mary Ellman, *Thinking About Women* (New York 1968).

[14] George E. Dimock, Jr., ''The Name of Odysseus,'' in G. Steiner and R. Fagles (edd.), *Homer* (Englewood Cliffs, N. J. 1962) 111.

[15] Max Horkheimer and T. Adorno, *Dialectic of Enlightenment,* trans. John Cumming, (New York 1972) 57-58.

[16] Claude Lévi-Strauss, *The Elementary Structures of Kinship*, trans. J. H. Bell, J. R. von Sturmer, and R. Needham (ed.) (Boston 1969) 496.

[17] Vladimir Propp, *Morphology of the Folktale*, trans. L. Scott; L. A. Wagner, ed. (Austin, 1968).[2]

[18] A. J. Greimas, *Sémantique structurale* (Paris 1966) 177.

[19] Page (above, note 1) 278-279.

[20] Claude Mossé, *La tyrannie dans la Grèce antique* (Paris 1969).

[21] Louis Gernet, *Anthropologie de la Grèce antique* (Paris 1968) 344-359.

[22] Jean-Pierre Vernant, ''Le mariage,'' in *Mythe et société en Grèce ancienne* (Paris 1974) 62-63.

[23] Cf. Marylin B. Arthur, ''Early Greece: The Origins of the Western Attitude Toward Women,'' *Arethusa* 6 (1973 7-58.

THE MAENAD IN EARLY GREEK ART*

Sheila McNally

T HE EXAMINATION OF WORKS of art can provide information about a culture which significantly changes what we would know from written sources alone. Examination of the role of maenads in early Greek art shows a striking development, namely the waxing and waning of hostility between themselves and their companions, the satyrs. This development is, I think, symptomatic both of strains developing in the Greeks' experience and of a growing complexity in their awareness of themselves and their universe. It reflects tensions between male and female characteristics in human nature, not necessarily tensions between men and women specifically.

We tend to think of satyrs and maenads as images of happy freedom. They first appear, dancing and carousing, in the painting of sixth century Greece, and wend their way with carefree sensuality through Western art down to the present day. There are, however, some startling early breaks in this pattern, eruptions of hostility such as that painted by the Kleophrades Painter around 500 B.C. (fig. 9). His maenad wards off the advances of a satyr with cool, even cruel effectiveness. This action sets her apart, not only from happier renditions of the same subject, but from renditions of other female figures in contemporary art. Contrary to what we might expect, no other female in Greek art defends her chastity so fiercely as the maenad. No other male figure is caught at such a disadvantage as the satyr – although he has his victories too.

Scenes of men and women in daily life, whether boldly erotic or quietly ceremonious, are invariably good-humored. In scenes from myth, most women carried off by gods or heroes are satisfied or resigned. Often they throw up both hands in despair, pleading, or simply in excitement – it is often hard to tell which. Occasionally, one may tug ineffectually at the ear or hand of her abductor. Stronger emotion is shown by the onlookers, who may rush to tell the father of his loss: the unceremonious transfer of ownership is the main source of dismay (although I will argue elsewhere that it is not so much simple transfer, as in human marriage, as it is translation from one sphere to another, union of anthropomorphic with nonanthropomorphic, which is

107

the basic subject of many of these scenes). Women attacked by centaurs are saved by their rightful husbands. Deianeira sitting on Nessos' back waits calmly for Herakles to appear, or holds out her hands trustingly toward him. The Lapith women in classical sculpture try harder, but still their salvation is not in their own hands. No one will come to the rescue of the maenad. If she is to escape, she must save herself: but why? All the other women, real or mythological, wives or hetairai or daughters-to-become-wives are playing expected parts in social contracts. The maenad is outside of those contractual relationships. We would expect her to be free of inhibitions as well.

The satyrs and maenads are the followers of Dionysos. Their images become one of the most effective expressions of the Dionysiac element in Greek culture, and freedom from ordinary restraints was certainly a vital aspect of that element. Commentators have differed about the nature of Dionysiac freedom:[1] was it innocence or liberation from pressure, naiveté or wish fulfillment, enhancing or destructive, profound or frivolous, the health of the strong, as Nietzsche would have it, or a refuge for the powerless, particularly women, as more recent commentators have claimed? No one of these alternatives is satisfactory because the freedom takes various forms. The changing relationship between satyrs and maenads is particularly revealing as to those variations. If we look at depictions of satyrs and maenads in Greek art, we see that their natures, and the implications of their natures, change. In many of the representations joy is unconfined. It may be active or contemplative, energetic or gentle, but it springs from harmony among beings completely dominated by strong, simple forces. The harmony and therefore the freedom are not, however, absolute. The desires of satyrs and maenads may come into conflict, and so the freedom of one or the other may be sharply curtailed.

In an art full of eroticism and abduction sexual conflict is rare, and Dionysiac revelry produces most of it. The supposed release gives rise to unparalleled tensions. We might conclude that the Greeks felt the most natural sexual relationship to be one of hostility, only restrained by the contracts of civilization. The depictions of conflict between satyr and maenad are not, however, ubiquitous enough to support that interpretation. They are limited to specific situations and reach a climax at one period: the end of archaic and beginning of classical art.

There are two probable reasons why the deviation has not been adequately examined. In the first place, the evidence consists solely of scenes in art. In literature hostility may be directed from outside toward Dionysos or his followers, but they do not fight among themselves. In the second place, even among works of art the scenes of conflict are the exception, not the rule. The most striking examples are a few red-figure vase paintings executed between 500 and 470 B.C. The majority of Dionysiac scenes are indeed as carefree as one could wish.

These two factors, namely the discrepancy between artistic and literary attitudes, and the change in artistic attitudes themselves, help to define the puzzle which the conflict scenes present. Most of the remainder of this paper will be an examination of Bacchic scenes before and during the outbreak of hostility to see whether tracing the development helps to explain it. First, however, the problems of evidence need to be discussed more fully. There has been a fundamental gap in the relationship between artistic and literary studies which has led to underassessment of the changing, as against the enduring manifestations of Dionysiac belief. Many of the vase paintings have been brilliantly analysed in isolation, but they have not figured in more general discussions of Dionysos. These discussions (see note 1) start from literary evidence, drawing on art to confirm or complete it. However, the emphasis in literature differs from that in art. Most of the references in poetry, history, inscriptions, etc., are to the life of Dionysos, and to the rites observed in his honor. Commentators try to determine the original, and therefore presumably most fundamental, essence of the god, and to establish what the Greeks of historical times did to honor him. Then, from knowledge of the mythical origin and the historical rite, comes assessment of what Dionysiac elements meant in Greek society. This procedure has provided a rich and many-sided picture of the Dionysiac elements, as well as penetrating, if often contradictory, insights into their meaning. Certain things, however, which were important to the Greeks are missing; perhaps most important, the satyr-maenad thiasos.

Depictions of Dionysiac themes are exceedingly popular in the Greek visual arts, but scenes either from Dionysos' life or from the rituals performed in his honor account for a very small proportion of these, especially before the mid-fifth century. From the beginning of recognizably Dionysiac scenes the dominant theme is the mixed satyr-maenad band, sometimes alone, sometimes with Dionysos, Dionysos and Ariadne, or Hephaistos. In literature, the mixed band is not mentioned until much later, and is never significant. There are obvious formal reasons why the different media choose different subjects: what is less clear, and cannot be discussed here, is the relative amount or level of significance which the pictures, as against the poems and plays, would have had in reflecting or forming the popular imagination. Still another basic problem is the degree or way in which either literature or art would have reflected contemporary social situations. Since no major literary treatments of Dionysos survive from the period under discussion here, they cannot be compared to the art as either molders or reflectors of their times. Some hypotheses about the ways in which contemporary drama or liturgy or broader social change might have affected the art will be discussed at the end.

In interpreting the art, literary references can be used only with caution, since they do not usually refer to the same subjects or reflect the same stage of development. They do not refer to the same subjects even when they use the same words. I have chosen to use the words satyr and maenad to refer to the members of Dionysos' band because those are the most commonly used words in English. Either silen or bacchante, being less common, would imply a technical precision in the nomenclature which is lacking: nymph, on the other hand, is too general a term. The Greeks used the words σάτυροι and σιληνοί, μαινάδες and βάκχαι more or less interchangeably to denote a variety of characters.[2]

The satyrs and maenads discussed here, those found in early Greek art, are most clearly characterized by their relationship to each other, and by the strictly limited set of roles which they play. Among the satyrs there are variations, notably in their hairiness, which are visually striking but do not seem to lead to differences in their activities and so do not necessitate different names. There are, on the other hand, changes, to be discussed below, in the depiction of the female figures which do seem to affect their actions. Some writers have preferred to call the earlier females nymphs, and only the later ones maenads, but since the change is less in their identity than in their characterization, I have used the same name throughout. Beyond defining the roles they play, it is not always possible to say who they are: we cannot always be sure whether we are looking at mythical figures; at contemporary female worshippers who might have been believed, or even have believed themselves to encounter satyrs at their rites; or at actors in the emerging satyr plays. In the second half of the fifth century types of Bacchic scenes multiply, and differentiations of myth from cult and drama are often clearly intended. For the period of the sixth and early fifth century, however, the period leading up to and expressing hostility, the differentiation is usually either impossible or unimportant. The similarity between most satyr-maenad groups (there are notable exceptions) shows that all are under the dominant imprint of the mythic thiasos, even if occasionally a re-enacted thiasos may be intended.

Furthermore, it is clear that the women in this thiasos should not be automatically equated with the female followers of Dionysos mentioned in literature, notably by Euripides in the *Bacchae*. Since that play is the earliest full account of maenads and of Dionysiac ὄργια in literature, the temptation to make use of it to interpret the vase paintings is great, but must be met with caution. Euripides' maenads have no acquaintance with satyrs, and perform different actions from those usually found in vase painting.[3]

This difference in subject matter is related to a difference in stage of development. Scholars dealing with the literature and religion have tended to de-emphasize development in order to isolate a basic continuum. In trying to establish the myth of Dionysos and piece together his rituals, they have assembled written evidence from various periods as relating to the same phenomena. The assessments have been historical in trying to isolate the oldest features in references from all periods, not in trying to see each reference as a manifestation of its own period. The underlying belief that the oldest is the most basic, that there is an unchanging kernel in the whole theme which provides the key to its deepest meaning may be true enough, but is certainly not the whole story. When we look at the art, we see that there are changes which are sufficiently great that they must have meant something important. Most obviously, just at the time of the *Bacchae,* the artists' image of Dionysos himself changes radically in form, a metamorphosis unique among Greek gods, and a sharp warning against transferring much later evidence to explain earlier attitudes.

For the period under discussion we must, then, depend almost entirely on the evidence supplied by the art – that is the vase painting – itself, but that presents difficulties. Gestures, facial expressions and poses are ambiguous. One scholar sees a satyr playing gently with a faun: another thinks he is about to rend it limb from limb. A maenad dancing uses the same gesture with which a woman fends off an attacking warrior: when a maenad alone uses the gesture toward a leaping satyr, we cannot be sure whether she is joyous or defensive. When a satyr creeps toward a sleeping maenad we assume he means to attack her, but when another creeps in just the same way toward the seated Dionysos his pose is dismissed as playful or meaningless. Sometimes we lack the knowledge of contemporary manners necessary to let us read what the artist has to say, but more often the confusion arises because the artist either depends on context to give significance to his forms, or uses stock figures without concern for their appropriateness in context, and because we cannot be sure which is happening. It is particularly difficult to judge the relative seriousness of a situation, or to distinguish between expressions of general excitement and those of a specific emotion.

But if depending on artistic evidence has its drawbacks, it also has its advantages. The literary evidence is sparse, and we know that most of the major works from the fifth century, perhaps about sixteen plays,[4] dealing with Dionysiac themes are lost. The art on the other hand provides a small but presumably representative sample of what was originally made, and forms a continuous record. Sculpture provides no evidence for this period. The thiasos is represented on vases, particularly on Attic vases. Although there are one or two representations on non-Attic vases which add to the permutations, they will be omitted from this discussion because they cannot be fitted into a sequence. In Athens, a basic development in the relationship between satyrs and maenads is clear. It may be divided into four parts: 580-550, tentative beginnings; 550-500, development of amicable relationships; 500-470, sporadic expressions of hostility; 470 on, decline in the proportion and strength of hostile encounters. First, around 580, an animal-tailed, -eared, and -hoofed figure makes his appearance as an image of lust, linked with a nymph or woman; a little later, on the François vase, Dionysos appears in the company of three satyrs and four nymphs. By 550 the troup of satyrs and their female companions, whom we may now call maenads, are dancing around the god. (Literary evidence may indicate that women were the first welcomers and primary worshippers of Dionysos, but in art they appear first with, and subordinate to, the satyrs.) Through the second half of the sixth century the relationship of maenads to satyrs ranges harmoniously through degrees of excitement and affection. At the same time, the female figures begin to acquire a clearer identity through the addition of characteristic attributes — things they hold or wear. On a few vases, mainly those in early red-figure technique, overtones of tension and trickery appear, culminating in the third phase. That phase begins when, around 500, the Kleophrades Painter gives dramatic expression to a new concept of the maenads, and to the hostility that concept causes between them and the satyrs. His themes echo through the work of numerous other red-figure vase painters of the early fifth century, although the amicable thiasos also continues to appear, especially in the work of late black-figure artists. The Brygos Painter, Makron and Douris are among those concerned with developing the possibilities of conflict. By mid-century the period of true hostility is over; the vehemence has largely gone out of the struggle. Hostile poses continue to be employed through the rest of the century and into the next, but without significant new developments of the theme. The execution is often limp, so that real conflict is hard to distinguish from play-acting or mindless capering.

Within this overall development a sequence of contributions by individual artists is also clear. Of course, given the accidental circumstances of the survival and recovery of the paintings, any statement that a certain artist introduced a motif, or that a subject appeared for the first time, can only be tentative; even statements of the relative popularity of certain themes at certain times never have statistical validity. The uniqueness of a total concept expressed in a major work, however, stands out undeniably.

The first satyrs who appear around 580 survive as isolated figures.[5] One plays the flute, two dart forward in great sexual excitement, each grasping a female figure, probably a nymph, by the arm. The reactions of the nymphs are less obvious than the intentions of the satyrs. The nymph on the sherd from Lindos appears at least unconcerned, if not willing: the nymph on the sherd from the Athenian Agora (fig. 1) may intend, as Young suggests (see note 5), to cast a stone at her aggressor, but her other hand seems to invite. In other words the satyr's nature is established — it is rough, aggressive, lustful and music-loving, but whether the artists feel that this nature makes him acceptably dominant, or innately threatening to the nymphs is not so clear. If there is in these first pieces a sense of innate conflict, it then all but disappears (there are one or two equivocal scenes) for about fifty years. Certainly, while the sexual excitement is a regular characteristic, and the vigorous stride a frequent occurrence, the aggressive grasp of these first satyrs is rarely repeated before the fifth century.

Fig. 1. Sherd from the Athenian agora. Courtesy of the American School of Classical Studies in Athens.

On the François vase[6] Kleitias expands the role and number of nymphs and satyrs, creating a troup parading after Dionysos. The vase marks the first certain appearance of Dionysos in Attic, and probably in Greek art.[7] He appears twice, once staring out from among the Olympian gods, and once leading Hephaistos back to Olympos. In the latter scene (fig. 2), the drunken Hephaistos is followed by three satyrs (labelled silenoi – see note 2) and four nymphs (so labelled). The first satyr labors under the sack with Hephaistos' wine: the next plays the flute, the third carries a nymph. Although she looks a little startled, her basic complacence is indicated by the fact that three more nymphs tag along behind, the last clashing cymbals. By adding wine to the two other preoccupations of the satyrs – women and music – and by allying them with Dionysos, Kleitias has created the germ of the Bacchic thiasos.

114

Fig. 2. Drawing of detail of the
François vase,
Furtwängler and Reichold,
Griechische Vasenmalerei.

Succeeding artists develop the thiasos, the dance or procession honoring Dionysos, into an independent theme. They integrate the satyrs and maenads, and exploit the various effects of wine (or divine intoxication), music, and love. During the next fifty years these effects may lead to scenes of wild physical excitement, scenes of gentle affection, and of various states in between, but while light-hearted play may develop erotic overtones, there is seldom any aggressiveness or explicit sexual activity. Among the major painters of the latter half of the sixth century, Exekias avoids the thiasos; Lydos creates one of its earliest expressions; while the Amasis painter is distinguished by the variety of interpretations which he creates.

In dances the satyrs and maenads are integrated in alignment, and often in action. Unlike the François vase, where satyrs are followed by nymphs, the later vases show them alternating with the maenads, sometimes all facing in one direction (or in two rows facing the middle), sometimes facing each other in pairs. Satyrs often dance alone, maenads less often. On Lydos' great column krater (fig. 3) done in

Fig. 3. Column krater by Lydos, detail. The Metropolitan Museum of Art. Fletcher Fund, 1931.

about 550,[8] the change is underway. Hephaistos is still present, as he continues to be in many thiasos scenes, but he is the middle of the band, not at its head: the story-telling connotation, the here-to-there progression, recedes before the endless pleasure of the dance. The alternation of maenads and satyrs is not yet completely regular. They are clearly dancing, but the dance movements are slow, and there is no relationship between the movements of the various figures. Throughout the remainder of black-figure, the dance often remains a mere shuffle, in which each figure may seem to act independently. There soon begins a parallel development, however: a crisply energetic dance in which there is more interaction. Many of the best examples of this dance fall between 530 and 510, or a little later. They include several examples by the Amasis Painter, including a cup and narrow strips on top of his amphora panels;[9] cup exteriors and interiors by the Oakeshott painter;[10] and the Nikosthenic vases by painter N.[11] On these, the dance varies from sprightly to wild, as the figures scamper, bound and lunge. As in the more sedate dance, each figure is separate: although the outlines may impinge, the figures do not deliberately touch (a rare exception is mentioned below). Each assumes something like a swastika shape by the full extension and crisp bending of limbs. There are elements of rhythmic repetition, but basically each figure creates its own configuration, and yet clearly the wilder the dance becomes, the more the patterns interlock. Each dancer improvises vigorously, but improvises in response to the steps and gestures of the dancer next in line. The action is therefore extreme but controlled, individualistic in a framework of mutual response. It is kinetic,[12] showing figures totally alive in every joint. Single pairs of energetic dancers occur on cup interiors such as that of the Siana cup in the Metropolitan[13] or the Oakeshott cup in Boston[14] (fig. 4), which shows the satyr and the maenad tightly related in a stamping and clapping dance. The satyr is as hairy as the one created by Sophilos a half-century earlier, but neither here nor on many other vases does this stress on his animal nature prevent his enthusiastic accord with the maenad.

That handclapping is the closest which the energetic dance comes to the expression of affection. This dance is an end in itself, but the action of the slower dances can easily develop into sexual foreplay. A number of vases on which satyrs lift maenads show the way in which erotic implications can come and go. The gesture seems

Fig. 4. Cup of the Oakeshott Painter, interior. Courtesy, Museum of Fine Arts, Boston.

to begin as a prelude to sex, then to become a formal dance movement, while always retaining its sexual possibilities. It occurs first, of course, on the François vase, before the procession became a dance. Between 550 and 540 it is repeated on a vase in Würzburg.[15] On each side of the vase there is a slow dance which brings the satyrs to sexual climax. In the center of one side a maenad is flourished aloft as the object, the willing object, to be penetrated by the two satyrs who hold her. Later there are a number of vases where the maenads sit on the satyr's back or shoulders, often playing the flute or the krotala. The lifting has become a jeu d'esprit, an extension of the self-fulfilling energy of the dance. That several stages in a movement (from lifting to carrying) are represented suggests that it may have formed an actual dance passage.[16] The figures on these vases slip easily from enjoyment of music and dancing for their own sakes into enjoyment of each other. For instance on a vase in Boston from the end of the century[17] there are similar symmetrical scenes on either side: on one (fig. 5), two satyrs dance on either side of a maenad; on the other (fig. 6), a satyr holds the central maenad aloft, and she continues to flourish her hands in dancing gesture, while the flanking satyrs, poised on tip-toe, reach out gently to touch her.

Both lust and affection develop still further on another vase in Boston done by the Dayton Painter around 520, where "a satyr carries a naked maenad toward a couch,...."[18] The maenad has her arms lovingly around his head and shoulders (fig. 7). This pair are on one side of Dionysos and Ariadne, while on the other a satyr and maenad kiss. The mood is quieter than on the dancing vases. On those, Dionysos may or may not be shown. The intoxication of the movements does not depend on his physical appearance. The quieter scenes of greeting or worship, however, demand the presence of the god (with or without Ariadne, whose presence or absence does not affect any other variation). The Dayton Painter's vase is an unusual example of this quiet type, which shows a satyr and maenad pair on either side of the god. They usually stand quietly, close together; and out of their closeness, as out of the slow dance, degrees of warmth may develop. The activity on this vase goes further into energetic movement and overt sexuality than in most of these scenes. Kissing is more frequent;[19] but most commonly the satyr slips his arm around the shoulder of the maenad.

The Amasis Painter is even more fond of these quiet scenes and their potential tenderness than he is of the wild dance. He is most adroit at combinations which suggest the kinship and easy passage between one moment and another, between dance and grape harvest, between common worship and mutual affection. He particularly enjoys showing figures linked by an arm around the shoulder: two lightly dancing satyrs;[20] a satyr and a clothed maenad;[21] two pairs of satyrs and nude maenads;[22] and paired maenads.[23] Fragments from Samos show warmer emotions: two satyrs carrying maenads, and perhaps (very little is left) a rare depiction of coupling.[24]

The pair of embracing maenads (see note 23) on the vase in the Cabinet des Médailles done just before 525 is significant in another

119

Fig. 5. Amphora, side A. Courtesy, Museum of Fine Arts, Boston.

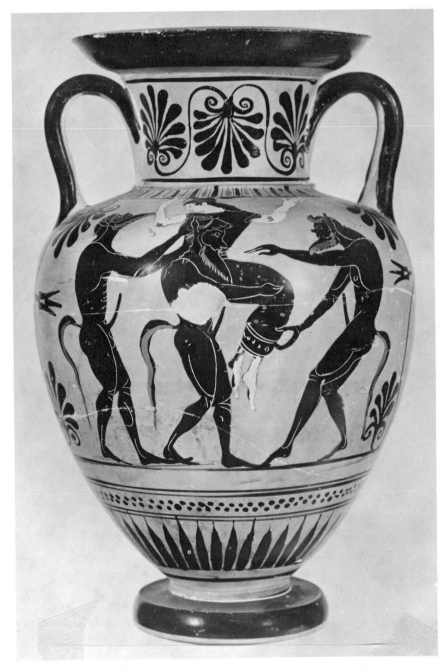

Fig. 6. Amphora, side B. Courtesy, Museum of Fine Arts, Boston.

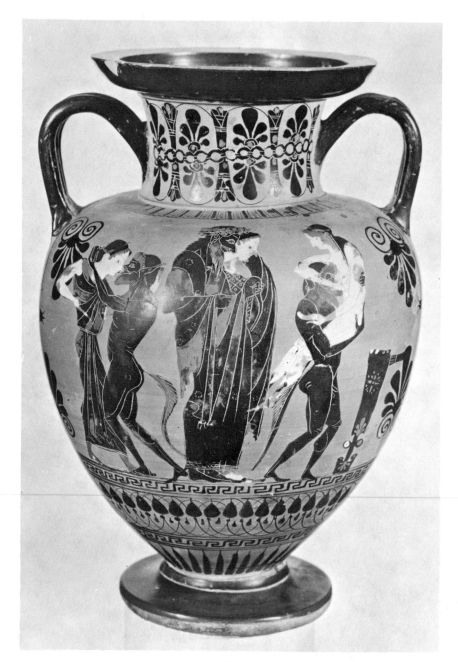

Fig. 7. Amphora by the Dayton Painter, detail. Courtesy, Museum of Fine Arts, Boston.

respect. At this period maenads appear alone less often than satyrs, presumably because satyrs have a character of their own, while maenads depend on the satyrs to make them truly Dionysian. When they are alone (with or without Dionysos, but without satyrs) they are identifiable, as here, by the vines which they hold; and, less frequently, by holding animals, or wearing animal skins. The link to the animal world is developed elegantly but with an undertone of savagery on this vase. One maenad wears the skin of a dead panther, his head prominently displayed. The other holds a hare by its ears in a manner which makes one fear for its future. Possibly the Amasis Painter is here representing either the actual women worshippers of Dionysos, the thyiades, or bacchantes in the sense of Euripides' *Bacchae,* some of the women who, often in pairs, greeted Dionysos on various of his arrivals in Greece.[25] However that may be, he is endowing the women with a richness and independence which anticipates the developments of the end of the century.

One fine example of those developments is the red-figure vase which Phintias painted about ten years later.[26] It is of the "quiet" type, showing a pair of satyrs and maenads standing close together on either side of Dionysos. One maenad holds a bird, the other is accompanied by a panther. Their relationship to the animals appears to be friendly: the panther's feet are at the maenad's throat, while its hind paws are on the thyrsos she holds — the ivy-tipped rod which is also a new element at this time. Although the maenads now have more attributes defining their personalities than do the satyrs, the relationship between the two remains close.

The interference becomes explicit on another vase done about the same time, the Chelis Painter's cup in Munich.[27] A satyr reaches out and grabs the skirt of a maenad who holds a snake and a thyrsos. Earlier maenads enthusiastically lift their skirts in invitation or acceptance of sexual advances.[28] This maenad recoils and brandishes the thyrsos like a club over her head. The moment is not complete in itself; it implies a result. All the lines are full of a spikey nervous tension.

On the black-figure vases, satyrs and maenads are preeminently engaged in having fun: "an absolutely primary category of life."[29] Their activity is an end in itself, the unfettered use of energy in the varying rhythms of worship and dance, or less often the related rhythms of the grape harvest or sexual foreplay — but not, typically, in sexual coupling, a significant distinction.[30] The distinction is certainly not due to prudery, since there are many depictions of far more erotic scenes on contemporary vases. It is due to the particular need which these scenes fill.

There is no before or after: the moment is complete in itself. That is one reason why the presence or absence of Hephaistos, or of Dionysos and Ariadne makes so little difference. Hephaistos, if present, is travelling, not setting forth or arriving: Dionysos is not discovering Ariadne, but is linked to her eternally. The actions may slip from one phase of pleasure to another, but they do not have to: fulfillment lies in each one.

Many red- and black-figure vases of the end of the century continue in this mood, but beside them appear such vases as the Chelis Painter's, Oltos' amphora in the Louvre[31] or Epiktetos' cup in Providence[32] on which trouble is beginning.[33] In that trouble the animals and the thyrsos of the maenad play an important part. Satyrs at this period seldom are shown with either attribute (although on Lydos' mid-century krater discussed above a satyr flourishes a snake which does not seem to alarm anyone, fig. 3).

A figure who does have similar attributes at this time is the sea-nymph, Thetis, often shown with a small lion and snakes or sea-serpents. Abduction scenes were growing in popularity at the end of the sixth and the beginning of the fifth centuries. Many of them involved one character who was not completely anthropomorphic – Europa and the Bull, Boreas and Oreithyia, Peleus and Thetis. The abduction of Thetis was much the most frequent of these scenes,[34] and its popularity was probably due less to the importance of the story as a whole than to the implications of the way that one moment was visualized. Its most beautiful depiction, the cup interior painted by Peithinos at the end of the sixth century,[35] shows striking similarities and dissimilarities with scenes of satyrs attacking maenads. The figure of Thetis is powerful and looks on with detached interest while her snakes and a small lion attack Peleus. As the story was later written down, she had the power to change herself into animals: certainly they here represent the expansion of her nature beyond the bounds of anthropomorphism, and it is this expansion which is inimical to Peleus. Both the expanded forces and the hostility they engender resemble those developing at the same time in Dionysiac scenes, but the outcome is different. Peleus differs in nature and aims from the satyrs, and so he achieves a union where they fail, but both situations embody the same underlying tensions.

Just a few years later the Kleophrades Painter made a dramatic summation of these tensions on his famous painted amphora in Munich.[36] In the center of the front (fig. 8) Dionysos holds vines which unfurl around him and out to either side to make a canopy over two flanking maenads. They each step toward him, and their thyrsoi impinge upon the vine, so that all three figures are linked in kinship to nature's greenness. Both maenads, however, look away from Dionysos toward satyrs tucked under the handles of the vase. The satyrs cannot

Fig. 8. Amphora by the Kleophrades Painter, side A. Courtesy of the Staatliche Antikensammlungen und Glyptothek, Munich.

125

be seen when one looks at the front picture. The typical five figure scene in which satyr-maenad pairs flank Dionysos has been spread apart so that Dionysos and the maenads have a relationship to which the satyrs are outsiders – hardly even intruders. The satyr on the right has caught the thyrsos of the maenad who moves sharply to pull – yank really seems the more accurate word – it away from him. On the left, the other satyr begins to catch at the hem of the maenad, who turns with severe grace to drive her thyrsos into his sex (fig. 9).

Fig. 9. Amphora by the Kleophrades Painter, side A, detail. Courtesy of the Staatliche Antikensammlungen und Glyptothek, Munich.

This juxtaposition makes the phallic implications of the thyrsos clear, and yet we would be wrong to identify it simply as a phallic symbol, and the expansion of the maenad's nature as simple androgeny. Phallus-tipped staffs do appear on some early red-figure Dionysiac scenes, and are used as weapons, but not by maenads. They belong to Dionysos, or the satyrs,[37] whose essentially phallic character they reinforce. Soon after the painting of this vase, painters begin to depict maenads carrying torches. Although torches might seem to us equally capable of phallic symbolism, they are seldom used as weapons. The thyrsos has a special power. It is the emblem of closeness to plant life, to growing nature and endows the maenad with a power which suggests androgeny, but is not exclusively genital. Similar expanded force is indicated by the close relationship of maenads to animals. Two maenads on this vase hold snakes. The snake has been considered as a phallic symbol or a vaginal one,[38] and could be seen as completing the maenad's specifically sexual power. I think we are safer in considering the snake, like the panther or other animals, as an indication of the breadth of vital forces which she subsumes. The satyrs do not have thyrsoi on this vase, or on most others of the early period. They are mixed beings, but the mixture appears to constitute a limitation rather than an expansion of their nature.

Since the expansion of the maenad's nature transcends the bounds of her own body, it threatens the validity of the swastika dance. There are dancers on the back of this vase (fig. 10), but they dance in a radically new way. The three-figure composition reverses the usual order of the black-figure groups. A satyr assumes the central role earlier taken by the maenad. The latent sexual magnetism with which she inspired the action is replaced by his music making. In black-figure the group would have been physically responsive, but this is hardly a group at all. The satyr concentrates vigorously on his music, and each maenad is lost in a private experience, one, snake-wreathed, in gentle revery; the other in wild abandon, with flung back head (fig. 11). It seems to have been the Kleophrades Painter who introduced this latter pose which so effectively suggests religious frenzy.[39] The figures do not express physical extension, but spiritual engrossment, which fills and at the same time isolates each maenad. This is barely a dance: it is certainly not "fun."

On several other vases, both before and after this one,[40] the Kleophrades Painter again depicts independent dancers, maenads in harmony with satyrs as long as they ignore them or only listen to their music. These paintings, especially the later ones, are powerful but more limited expressions of the new maenadism which finds its strongest and most subtle expression on the Munich amphora. "The painter's mind that day was filled with giant women...."[41]

Almost inevitably, there is another side to the Kleophrades Painter's art: he moves from high seriousness to ribaldry in decorating a hydria now in Rouen[42] which shows satyrs with a sleeping maenad.

The Amasis Painter may have employed this subject (see note 24); it had certainly appeared before this,[43] but any innocent sensuality in

Fig. 10. Amphora by the Kleophrades Painter, side B. Courtesy of the Staatliche Antikensammlungen und Glyptothek, Munich.

the earlier examples disappears in this treatment. The garment which the satyr pulls up, and the directness of his approach sharpen the irreverence. At just this time the dramatic tetralogy was coming into existence, with the satyr play forming its irreverent conclusion: a conclusion often exalting trickery, and deliberately reversing the morality expressed in the main pieces.[44] The audaciously groping fingers of the satyr in Rouen form a counterpoint to the thyrsos wielded by the Munich maenad.

While the Kleophrades Painter sharpens the joke, the Brygos Painter and Makron make it broader, inviting a snigger. Their sleeping maenads are fully clothed, and the satyrs approach them more stealthily. The delight in getting away with something, the triumph of slyness, is accented. On Makron's vase of about 480[45] the maenads are powerful forms (fig. 12): their comparative size and outstretched pose combine to suggest the quality of an earth mother. One is still fast asleep, holding her thyrsos lightly. Satyrs approach from either side, one grasping her hair, the other parting her legs. On the other side, the satyrs' actions are much the same, the maenad has begun to awake, to pull free, to wave her thyrsos – the issue is in doubt. All of these scenes demonstrate a deliberate desire to shock which indicates the

Fig. 11. Amphora by the Kleophrades Painter, side B, detail. Courtesy of the Staatliche Antikensammlungen und Glyptothek, Munich.

gulf between satyr and maenad as much or more than does the violence in other scenes. To Makron, the Brygos Painter, and others of their generation, lust as a link between satyr and maenad can only be incongruous, the basis for a joke.

Fig. 12. Kylix by Makron, side A (above), side B (below). Courtesy, Museum of Fine Arts, Boston.

Each painter also did scenes of more active hostility. Makron takes over the gesture of the thyrsos-wielding maenad from the Kleophrades Painter, but apparently winces at depicting it. Once he partially cushions the blow by reversing the thyrsos; another time (fig. 13) he lets it slip by harmlessly.[46]

Makron is also the creator of one surprisingly harmonious scene. A cup tondo in the Louvre[47] shows a maenad with her arm around a satyr in the old, affectionate gesture. He gropes under her garment with the new deviousness. Is he taking her by surprise, or is she, for once, receptive?

Certainly the sexual hostility shown in both the satyr's snigger and the maenad's thyrsos-slash does not appear in other examples of

Fig. 13. Cup by Makron, interior. The Metropolitan Museum of Art, Rogers Fund, 1906.

Makron's work. The tenderness and relative equality of the sexual relationship between a man and a hetaira on one cup,[48] the elegance of Helen escorted by Aphrodite and Eros on another[49] show him to have been happily responsive to both physical and courtly aspects of love. If, as has been claimed, there was rising tension between men and women in the Athenian society of the early fifth century, it was certainly not finding expression in most vase painting.

There is a great increase at this time in two types of scenes implying some degree of conflict: abductions and pursuits. Something has already been said about the former (p. 101 and p. 118). Although they, like the Bacchic scenes, show concern for relating non-anthropomorphic and human energies, as well as male and female, they are for the most part diagrams of union, not expressions of incompatibility. The compositions do not resemble those used in most depictions of satyrs and maenads. Pursuit scenes on the other hand can involve satyrs and maenads as well as all sorts of other couples, identifiable and unidentifiable. Pursuit was a popular artistic convention for displaying action, and only seldom provides insight into a particular relationship. We have, for instance, no way of knowing whether the satyr will catch the maenad — although it is significant that the question can be asked, that once again the moment, unlike the sixth-century ones, demands a sequel. One of the earliest Dionysiac pursuits, painted by the Brygos Painter on a rhyton[50] in Boston is an exception to these generalities. He reinterprets the convention to suit the participants. The movement of each figure is sharply characterized. A satyr bounds nimbly after a maenad whose running is enframed with crisp lines and angles conveying her desperation. Then comes the final touch which ties this to the "sleeping maenad" scene and differentiates it from conventional pursuits — the maenad looks back in terror, while there, in front of her, but out of sight, another satyr crouches to spring. It is all a trick.

Like the Kleophrades Painter, and other less important painters of the era, both Makron and the Brygos Painter can still envisage a dance which in many ways resembles those on black figure, a dance in which all is well so long as there is no physical contact between dancers. Often the row of alternating maenads and satyrs survives, although many of the most active figures no longer show any mutual responsiveness. Therefore maenads can now frequently be found dancing on their own, as for example, the Kleophrades Painter's late

132

kalpis, or the Brygos Painter's cup tondo in Munich.[51] The dancers perform the same "swastika-like" movements as before, but now the artist may stress a difference between the robust prancing of the satyrs and the lighter movement which drapery imparts to the maenads. Often, especially when the "wing-sleeve" convention is used, as on the kalpis, the drapery is startlingly successful in isolating and de-corporealizing the female figures.

The earlier dances could easily lead into sexual foreplay; while now any dance in which the dancers respond to each other seems to be on the verge of conflict. The constantly underlying sense of tension can be seen, for instance, on the cup in Cleveland which Douris painted around 480, with its "effect of continuous movement, and sense of intended violence and determined opposition."[52] Movements are ambiguous; one can hardly determine whether the maenads are dancing or striking, only that they are ready to do either. One satyr on this vase holds a thyrsos, which is unusual at the beginning of the fifth century but becomes common later. His head is thrown back: the vases discussed so far have not shown satyrs capable of ecstasy; their fulfillment had remained free extension of physical energy; only the maenads had changed.

Toward the end of his long career Douris created the last signifi-cant new version of the conflict of satyr and maenad. On the interior of cup in Boston (fig. 14)[53] he depicted an exceptional scene: the triumph of the satyrs. In the center, a satyr grasps a maenad around the body, rather than merely catching at her arm or skirt. She pulls at his ear and he does not look pleased, but his grip is firm. Two more satyrs frolic on either side, and phallic flowers thrust into the scene. The viewer might feel a momentary doubt about the satyr's success because of the maenad's size — as on many vases of this period, she is larger than the satyrs — and her upright stance. Similar power is, however, shown by female figures in many abduction scenes of the time and indicates the dignity of the forces which are being joined, rather than any doubts about their joining. The unusual determination of the satyr abductor on the Boston vase, together with the delight of his companions and the impact of the flowers (which seem to set nature itself for once on the side of the satyrs), all combine to express their victory.

This scene may be influenced by those of Peleus or Boreas grasping their brides. The total composition however, seems to come

Fig. 14. Cup by Douris, interior. Courtesy, Museum of Fine Arts, Boston.

from Douris' memories of his boyhood,[54] of the joyously uplifted maenads in late black-figure, a motif which had died out, and which he revived. When we look back at an earlier example (fig. 6), we see that the woman does not struggle, but throws up her arms in a dance gesture: she is not hostile, but open to pleasure. Douris apparently cannot any longer imagine such harmony, but he is also unwilling to accept incompatibility.

This vase brings to a close the period of major innovations on the theme of hostility. It does not usher in a new era of carefree play. After this one example, lust or affection do not again succeed in linking the satyrs and maenads. There are many amicable scenes in the second half of the century, but they are highly decorous relationships. Any time a maenad is touched, she resents it.

Sometimes she even resents being looked at: the satyr's overture is often tentative, and seems to be quelled with an icy glance. There continue to be fights and pursuits, but the tension slackens. When physical struggles occur, the poses are conventional. The artists are not trying to work out the implications of a new situation as they were in the late sixth and early fifth century. Rather they are repeating accepted patterns, which tend to drift into play-acting, so that on some vases the mixture of enticing and repulsing begins to suggest a game. Of course there are others where there can be no doubt that the maenads are in deadly earnest, and repulse the satyrs with unabated vigor.

Still, their motives may now be different. The latter part of the fifth century sees a flood of new Dionysiac subjects which involve a broad range of characterizations and activities. The simple thiasos remains important, but can no longer be studied without reference to many more specific situations which also involve the relationship of satyrs and maenads. This is a time of great change, culminating in the transformation of Dionysos himself. It will require separate consideration.

Two minor innovations which occur in old situations may serve to indicate something of the changing characterizations, and the resulting tendency to play down violence. In both situations the satyr and maenad are separate, and seem unlikely to touch. One is the moment, developing out of the dance or procession, when the satyr accosts the maenad. Often on these later vases instead of either fighting or fleeing she simply stands coldly and interposes her thyrsos as a barrier, holding it as a vertical staff which establishes her dignity and distance without further ado. The second innovation is in the scene of the ''sleeping maenad.'' On several vases[55] she is shown sitting upright, more self-possessed but less elemental than before, while the satyr creeps or capers uncertainly in front of her, not quite daring to come closer. The source of the humor shifts from his irreverence to his timidity.

Analysis of this sequence of vase paintings has shown that the relationship between satyr and maenad (or nymph) begins, about 580, with sex, and develops after 550 into exuberant play in mutual responsiveness. Then the nature of the maenad changes. By 500 that change brings about her rejection of the satyr's sexual advances, a rejection which can lead to one of three results: to isolated ecstacy, to struggles which she wins, or to the trickery in which he excels. In the latter part of the fifth century the maenad still rejects the satyr as a partner in lust or affection, but their interests are diverted into new channels.

Hostility between maenad and satyr emerges as a sudden and radical departure from earlier attitudes, related to, and I think caused by the maenad's new closeness to the world of plants and animals. Some aspects of this development, namely the greater differentiation of types of people and types of activities, are common to all of Greek art in the later archaic and early classical period, but many aspects are peculiar to this subject matter. We may look for explanations in the development of drama, liturgy, or the social structure, but we know too little about any one of them to find satisfaction. Several possible influences should be mentioned however, if only to indicate the problems they raise.

Some influence certainly came from Attic drama. The introduction of a "story line" into the thiasos suggests the requirements of the dramatist as he changes dance into theater. The juxtaposition of serious and ribald views of the same subject, the development, in fact, of the dirty joke — there had been much sex, but little or no pornography in sixth-century painting — also reflects dramatic conventions. The development of the dramatic tetralogy was a striking advance in self-consciousness, in the analysis and definition of character and action.

Developments in worship may also have been influential. Here we have no independent evidence at all. It certainly seems possible that maenads, rather than satyrs, first appear with thyrsoi and snakes because the painters had seen Athenian women with these attributes. The clinical accuracy of the head thrown back in ecstasy may indicate that painters had had opportunities to see "spontaneous outbreaks of religious hysteria"[56] or the liturgical channelling of that hysteria. Before the middle of the fifth century, however, there are very few scenes which bear a clearly liturgical interpretation, and they are not ecstatic: they show women alone (or with Dionysos, but without satyrs) engaged in solemn action.

A deeper explanation would lie in the assumption of growing tension in contemporary society. In general terms I think we must conclude that there was such tension, but not that it can be easily defined. Some commentators have claimed that a deep hostility between men and women, which resulted in the suppression (and occasional religious explosion) of women's energies, was developing at this time. The evidence is unclear. In any case, the development, if it existed, had little effect on art. Certainly the otherwise satisfactory relationships depicted between the sexes in vase painting and sculpture at this time may be due to repression, but why would the truth break through only in Dionysiac contexts?

It might seem briefly tempting to combine the last two explanations – the rise of Dionysos worship, and the growth of social tension – into one. There is no question that women played a prominent role in Dionysiac religion. The mysteries might have renewed women's sense of their own significance: a kind of "consciousness-raising." The men might then be thought to view the "raving" of the bacchante as some today do the "craziness" of liberated women: thyrsos-flourishing as equivalent to bra-burning. We might then interpret the outbreak of hostility as fear of the Dionysiac devotee losing touch with the normal, losing her place in society. This is patently ludicrous in terms of the visual evidence. The female figures are strong and successful. They are not comic; that role is reserved for the satyr. The tension here has nothing to do with any contemporary Athenian's concern about the behavior of his wife or daughter. The ecstasy envisaged is not really "consciousness-raising" – it is escape from consciousness into another sort of existence, and that may be the most significant factor.

Bruno Snell has traced the "development of the mind" in Greek civilization.[57] Man became increasingly self-aware, aware in particular of his power to reason. (I say "man" intentionally. We know very little about the experience of Greek women, and certainly we do not learn more from the vases examined here. They reflect the concerns of the people – the men – who made and used them.)

This rationality created divisions between man's mental and his physical existence, between him and the rest of the universe. A fundamental problem throughout Greek art is that of the interrelationship between humans, animals and inanimate nature. There is a continuous process of separating and recombining them in various ways. The satyr and the maenad are such combinations, the satyr from the beginning, the maenad in the course of her development. They represent two stages in the attempt to establish connectives, while the hostility between them testifies poignantly to the fissures opening in human experience.

In Jungian terms (if I may borrow them without implying a consistently Jungian outlook, supposing there to be such a thing) the development of consciousness may be characterized as the separation of *logos,* the masculine force, rational and analytic, from *eros,* the feminine force, irrational and connective. This formulation echoes the intuitions expressed in the Pythagorean Table of Opposites (of uncertain date, but certainly later than the period we are discussing) pairing ten principles: limit and unlimited; odd and even; one and plurality; right and left; male and female; resting and moving; straight and curved; light and dark; good and bad; square and oblong.[58] Whatever the Table as a whole may mean, it seems to indicate that the Greeks recognized a force which was feminine, many-sided, and boundless, and that they feared it.

The duality just expressed is too simple however, because the emerging *logos* is at the same time a degrading of the genital aspect of masculinity. By the end of the fifth century Greek writers were calling for sexual moderation or abstinence to preserve energy for higher activities.[59] Whether or not there was tension between men and women, there was certainly tension within human nature. The satyr is a mixture of animal and human which emphasizes the basically physical, especially the sexual. At first that was fine. He danced along, sometimes hairy, sometimes smooth, and the maenad liked him either way. Then she became full of her own less definably expanded powers, and firmly rejected his.

There is no single force which can be called "maenadism" in sixth- and fifth-century art. The maenad's appearance and actions change. At least in the present state of our knowledge, that change cannot be linked to any specific development in contemporary social structure. It did make a significant contribution to the struggle to understand human nature and its place in the universe. Greek self-awareness reached a crucial stage at the beginning of the fifth century. That is obvious in the transition to classical art, in the evolution of drama, and in the beginning of history writing, still another attempt to organize experience. The ecstatic dance of the maenad, and her hostility to the satyr, embody some of the richness and the strain of that awareness.

University of Minnesota

NOTES

* A preliminary version of this paper was presented at the Women's Caucus session of the Midwest Art History Society meetings, 1977. Its development owes much to the comments of students in a course on Greek Vase Painting at the University of Minnesota in 1977, especially those of Marie Friederichs.

Abbreviations:

ABV Sir John Beazley, *Attic Black-Figure Vase-Painters* (Oxford 1956).

ARV² Sir John Beazley, *Attic Red-Figure Vase-Painters,* 2nd ed. (Oxford 1963).

CVA *Corpus Vasorum Antiquorum.* Volumes are identified by city and by number in the series for that city.

Para Sir John Beazley, *Paralipomena: Additions to Attic Black-Figure Vase-Painters and to Attic Red-Figure Vase-Painters, Second Edition* (Oxford 1971).

[1] E. R. Dodds is perhaps the outstanding compiler of evidence not only from the ancient world but from comparative sources, published in several places but most extensively in this edition of Euripides' *Bacchae* (2nd ed. Oxford 1960). The most recent general interpretation is Karl Kerenyi, *Dionysos, Archetypal Symbol of Indestructible Life* (Princeton 1976). Earlier literature is cited in these books.

[2] Frank Brommer, *Satyroi* (Würzburg 1937) 2-5; Alfred Marbach, "Mainades" *Pauly's Real-Encyclopedie der Klassischen Altertumswissenschaft* 14 (1928) 561.

[3] Pentheus' death is introduced to vase painting in the late sixth century, but was not a popular subject then. Sir John Beazley, *Vase Painting in the Museum of Fine Arts, Boston,* II (London 1954) 1-2; Frank Brommer, *Vasenlisten zur Griechischen Heldensage.* 3rd ed. (Marburg 1973) 485-6.

[4] Dodds (above, note 1) xxviii-xxxiii.

[5] Frank Brommer, *Satyroi* (Würzburg 1937) 25. Cf. discussion by Christian Blinkenberg, *Lindiaka* III (Copenhagen 1926) 32; Rodney Young, *Hesperia* 4 (1935) 436.

[6] Florence 4209. *ABV* 76 #1.

[7] Ernst Langlotz identifies a figure on a Corinthian vase as the earliest Dionysos: "Dionysos" *Antike* 8 (1932) 181, fig. 14.

[8] New York 31.11.11. *ABV* 108 #5.

[9] Cup Louvre F75 *ABV* 156 #81; amphorae Berlin 3210. *ABV* 151 #21, Würzburg 265 *ABV* 151 #22.

[10] New York 17.230.5. *Para* 78 #1.

[11] *ABV* 218-219 #16-24.

[12] Cf. Lillian B. Lawler, "The Maenads," *Memoirs of the American Academy in Rome* 6 (1927). This term seems more appropriate to the sixth-century dances than to those she is analyzing.

[13] New York 12.234.3. *ABV* 69 #3.

[14] Boston 69.1052.

[15] Würzburg 252. *ABV* 315 #1.

[16] E.g., Berlin 1935. *ABV* 431 #10, Berlin 3765. *ABV* 259 #25, Boston 01.17 *ABV* 319 #2, Oxford 208. *ABV* 256 #15.

[17] Boston 12.905. *CVA* Boston 1, Pl. 51, pp. 37-38.

[18] Boston 76.40. *Para* 133 #2.

[19] As early as 550; cf. Würzburg 246. *ABV* 296 #8.

[20] Würzburg 265. *ABV* 151 #22.

[21] Basel, Antikenmuseum, *Para* 65.

[22] Berlin 3210. *ABV* 151 #21.

[23] Paris, Cabinet des Medailles 222. *ABV* 152 #25.

[24] Samos, no number. *ABV* 151 #18.

[25] Kerenyi (above, note 1) ch IV.

[26] Tarquinia Mus. Naz. RC 6843. ARV^2 32 #2.

[27] Munich 2589. ARV^2 112 #1.

[28] E.g., Bologna 1430. *CVA* 2, III H e pl. 5. Würzburg 178. Ernst Langlotz, *Griechischer Vasen in Würzburg* (Munich 1932) pl. 38.

[29] Johan Huizinga, *Homo Ludens* (New York 1950) 21. Since these figures are not human, some of Huizinga's discussion does not apply to them, but much is apropos.

[30] Huizinga (above, note 29) 63-64.

[31] Louvre G 2. ARV^2 53 #2.

[32] Providence 25.077. ARV^2 73 #34.

[33] The death of Pentheus first appears in Greek vase painting about this time (see note 3). The women who have killed him carry thyrsoi. The thyrsoi are not used as weapons against him until later.

[34] Frank Brommer (above, note 3) 321-9.

[35] Berlin 2279. ARV^2 115 #2.

[36] Munich 2344. ARV^2 182 #6.

[37] Heinrich Bulle, "Zum Pothos des Skopas," *Jahrbuch des Deutschen Archaologischen Instituts* 56 (1941) 137.

[38] Philip Slater, "The Greek Family in History and Myth" *Arethusa* 7 (1974) 16.

[39] E. R. Dodds *The Greeks and the Irrational* (Berkeley 1951) Appendix I: "Maenadism" 273-5. His argument that this gesture is a proof that maenadism arose from "spontaneous attacks of mass hysteria" seems open to question because of the date and circumstances when the trait appears.

[40] E.g., early psykter Louvre G 57. ARV^2 188 #65; early krater Harvard 1960. 236. ARV^2 185 #31; later krater Louvre G 162 ARV^2 186 #47; late kalpis Basel, Wilhelm ARV^2 189 #73.

[41] Sir John Beazley, *The Kleophrades Painter* (Mainz 1974) 4.

[42] Rouen 25. ARV^2 188 #68.

[43] Sir John Beazley, *Vase Paintings in the Museum of Fine Arts, Boston* II (London 1954) 96-99.

[44] Cf. Dana Ferris Sutton, "Satyr Plays and the *Odyssey*," *Arethusa* 7 (1974) 166-168 on trickery and reversal of values.

[45] Boston 01.8072 *ARV*² 461 #36. Cf. Brygos Painter's version, ex Goluchow, Musée Czartoyski 119. *ARV*² 382 #185.

[46] Munich 2654. *ARV*² 462 #47. New York 06.1152. *ARV*² 463 #52.

[47] Louvre G 144. *ARV*² 462 #43.

[48] Gotha 49. *ARV*² 467 #119.

[49] Boston 13.186. *ARV*² 458 #1.

[50] Boston 03.787. *ARV*² 382 #189.

[51] Maenads dancing alone, e.g., kalpis note 40; Makron's cup, Berlin 2290. *ARV*² 462 #48; Brygos Painter's cup tondo Munich 2645. *ARV*² 371 #15. Douris' cup Boston 00.499. *ARV*² 435 #89.

[52] Cleveland 508.15. *ARV*² 436 #111 (*CVA* Cleveland p. 24). Cf. two vases by Makron, Munich 2654. *ARV*² 462 #47, Brussels R 247. *ARV*² 462 #41.

[53] Boston 00.343 *ARV*² 438 #141.

[54] Sir John Beazley, *Vase Paintings in the Museum of Fine Arts, Boston* III (London 1963) 26.

[55] Sir John Beazley, *CVA* Oxford. 1, p. 34.

[56] See note 39.

[57] Bruno Snell, *The Discovery of the Mind,* trans. T. Rosenmeyer (Oxford 1953).

[58] Aristotle, *Metaphysics* I.v.6.

[59] K. J. Dover, *Greek Popular Morality in the Time of Plato and Aristotle* (Oxford 1974) 205-216; "Classical Greek Attitudes to Sexual Behavior," *Arethusa* 6 (1973) 69-73.

CLASSICAL GREEK ATTITUDES TO SEXUAL BEHAVIOUR

K. J. Dover

1. Words and Assumptions

THE GREEKS REGARDED sexual enjoyment as the area of life in which the goddess Aphrodite was interested, as Ares was interested in war and other deities in other activities. Sexual intercourse was *aphrodisia*, 'the things of Aphrodite.' Sexual desire could be denoted by general words for 'desire,' but the obsessive desire for a particular person was *eros*, 'love' in the sense which it has in our expressions 'be in love with . . .' (*eran*) and 'fall in love with . . .' (*erasthenai*). Eros, like all powerful emotional forces, but more consistently than most, was personified and deified; treated by some early poets as a cosmic force older than Aphrodite, occasionally (though not often) alleged to be her son, he was most commonly thought of as her minister or agent, to the extent that she could, when she wished (as in Euripides' *Hippolytus*), cause X to fall in love with Y.

At some time in the latter part of the fifth century Prodicus defined eros as 'desire doubled'; eros doubled, he said, was madness.[1] Both philosophical and unphilosophical Greeks treated sexual desire as a response to the stimulus of visual beauty, which is reasonable enough; rather more surprisingly, they also treated eros as a strong response to great visual beauty, a response which may be intensified by admirable or lovable qualities in the desired person but is not in the first instance evoked by those qualities. Plato finds it philosophically necessary in *Phaedrus* and *Symposium* to treat eros as a response to beauty; but even Plato shows his awareness elsewhere (*Rep.* 474DE) that superior visual stimuli from Z do not necessarily make X fall out of love with Y.[2]

Eros generates *philia*, 'love'; the same word can denote milder degrees of affection, just as 'my *philoi*' can mean my friends or my inner-most family circle, according to context. For the important question 'Do you love me?' the verb used is *philein*, whether the question is put by a youth to a girl as their kissing becomes more passionate[3] or by a father to his son as an anxious preliminary to a test of filial obedience.[4]

143

2. Inhibition

Our own culture has its myths about the remote past, and one myth that dies hard is that the 'invention' of sexual guilt, shame and fear by the Christians destroyed a golden age of free, fearless, pagan sexuality. That most pagans were in many ways less inhibited than most Christians is undeniable. Not only had they a goddess specially concerned with sexual pleasure; their other deities were portrayed in legend as enjoying fornication, adultery and sodomy. A pillar surmounted by the head of Hermes and adorned with an erect penis stood at every Athenian front-door; great models of the erect penis were borne in procession at festivals of Dionysus, and it too was personified as the tirelessly lascivious Phales.[5] The vase-painters often depicted sexual intercourse, sometimes masturbation (male or female) and fellatio, and in respect of any kind of sexual behaviour Aristophanic comedy appears to have had total license of word and act. A century ago there was a tendency to explain Aristophanic obscenity by positing a kind of dispensation for festive occasions which were once fertility-rituals, but this has no relevance to the vase-painters, nor, indeed, to the iambic poets of the archaic period, Archilochus and Hipponax, in whom no vestige of inhibition is apparent.

There is, however, another side of the coin. Sexual intercourse was not permitted in the temples or sanctuaries of deities (not even of deities whose sexual enthusiasm was conspicuous in mythology), and regulations prescribing chastity or formal purification after intercourse played a part in many Greek cults. Homeric epic, for all its unquestioning acceptance of fornication as one of the good things of life, is circumspect in vocabulary, and more than once denotes the male genitals by *aidos*, 'shame,' 'disgrace.' Serious poetry in the early classical poetry was often direct in what it said, but preserved a certain level of dignity in the ways of saying it; even when Pindar states the parentage of Castor in terms of Tyndareus' ejaculation into Leda, his style has the highest poetic credentials.[6] Poets (notably Homer) sometimes describe interesting and agreeable activities — cooking, mixing wine, stabbing an enemy through a chink in his armour — in meticulous detail, but nowhere is there a comparable description of the mechanisms of sexual activity. Prose literature, even on medical subjects, is euphemistic ('be with ...' is a common way of saying 'have sexual intercourse with ...'), and can degenerate into coyness, as when 'we all know what' is substituted for 'the genitals' in a list of the bodily organs which convey pleasurable sensations.[7] The fourth-century orators show some skill in insinuating allegations of sexual misconduct and simultaneously suggesting that both the speaker's sense of propriety and the jury's would be outraged by a plain statement of the facts; when a coarse word is unavoidable, they make a show of reluctance to utter it.[8] By the late fourth century, the obscene words which had been so lavishly used by Aristophanes and his contemporaries had been almost entirely excluded from comedy; Aristotle, commenting on this, calls the old style *aiskhrologia*, 'speaking what is shameful (disgraceful, ugly).'[9]

Linguistic inhibition, then, was observably strengthened in the course of the classical period; and at least in some art-forms, inhibition extended also to content. These are data which do not fit the popular concept of a guilt-free or shame-free sexual morality, and require explanation. Why so many human cultures use derogatory words as synonyms of 'sexual' and reproach sexual prowess while praising prowess in (e.g.) swimming and riding, is a question which would take us to a remote level of speculation. Why the Greeks did so is a question which can at least be related intelligibly to the structure of Greek society and to Greek moral schemata which have no special bearing on sex.

3. Segregation and Adultery

As far as was practicable (cf. § 7), Greek girls were segregated from boys and brought up at home in ignorance of the world outside the home; one speaker in court seeks to impress the jury with the respectability of his family by saying that his sister and nieces are 'so well brought up that they are embarrassed in the presence even of a man who is a member of the family.'[10] Married young, perhaps at fourteen[11] (and perhaps to a man twenty years or more her senior), a girl exchanged confinement in her father's house for confinement in her husband's. When he was invited out, his children might be invited with him, but not his wife;[12] and when he had friends in, she did not join the company. Shopping seems to have been a man's job, to judge from references in comedy,[13] and slaves could be sent on other errands outside the house. Upholders of the proprieties pronounced the front door to be the boundaries of a good woman's territory.[14]

Consider now the situation of an adolescent boy growing up in such a society. Every obstacle is put in the way of his speaking to the girl next door; it may not be easy for him even to get a glimpse of her. Festivals, sacrifices and funerals, for which women and girls did

145

come out in public, provided the occasion for seeing and being seen. They could hardly afford more than that, for there were too many people about, but from such an occasion (both in real life and in fiction) an intrigue could be set on foot, with a female slave of respectable age as the indispensable go-between.[15]

In a society which practices segregation of the sexes, it is likely that boys and girls should devote a good deal of time and ingenuity to defeating society, and many slaves may have co-operated with enthusiasm. But Greek laws were not lenient towards adultery, and *moikheia*, for which we have no suitable translation except 'adultery,' denoted not only the seduction of another man's wife, but also the seduction of his widowed mother, unmarried daughter, sister, niece, or any other woman whose legal guardian he was.[16] The adulterer could be prosecuted by the offended father, husband or guardian; alternatively, if caught in the act, he could be killed, maltreated, or imprisoned by force until he purchased his freedom by paying heavy compensation. A certain tendency to regard women as irresponsible and ever ready to yield to sexual temptation (see § 5) relieved a cuckolded husband of a sense of shame or inadequacy and made him willing to seek the co-operation of his friends in apprehending an adulterer,[17] just as he would seek their co-operation to defend himself against fraud, encroachment, breach of contract, or any other threat to his property. The adulterer was open to reproach in the same way, and to the same extent, as any other violator of the laws protecting the individual citizen against arbitrary treatment by other citizens. To seduce a woman of citizen status was more culpable than to rape her, not only because rape was presumed to be unpremeditated but because seduction involved the capture of her affection and loyalty;[18] it was the degree of offense against the man to whom she belonged, not her own feelings, which mattered.

It naturally follows from the state of the law and from the attitudes and values implied by segregation that an adolescent boy who showed an exceptional enthusiasm for the opposite sex could be regarded as a potential adulterer and his propensity discouraged just as one would discourage theft, lies and trickery, while an adolescent boy who blushed at the mere idea of proximity to a woman was praised as *sophron*, 'right-minded,' i.e. unlikely to do anything without reflecting first whether it might incur punishment, disapproval, dishonour or other undesirable consequences.

146

4. *Commercial Sex*

Greek society was a slave-owning society, and a female slave was not in a position to refuse the sexual demands of her owner or of anyone else to whom he granted the temporary use of her. Large cities, notably Athens, also had a big population of resident aliens, and these included women who made a living as prostitutes, on short-term relations with a succession of clients, or as *hetairai*, who endeavoured to establish long-term relations with wealthy and agreeable men. Both aliens and citizens could own brothels and stock them with slave-prostitutes. Slave-girls and alien girls who took part in men's parties as dancers or musicians could also be mauled and importuned in a manner which might cost a man his life if he attempted it with a woman of citizen status. In an instructive scene at the close of Aristophanes' *Thesmophoriazusae* (1160-1231) Euripides, disguised as an old woman, distracts the attention of a policeman with the help of a pretty dancing-girl; for a drachma, the policeman is allowed to have intercourse with the girl, but it is the 'old woman,' not the girl, who strikes the bargain, exactly as if it were a matter of paying rent for use of an inanimate object.

It was therefore easy enough to purchase sexual satisfaction, and the richer a man was the better provision he could make for himself. But money spent on sex was money not spent on other things, and there seems to have been substantial agreement on what were proper or improper items of expenditure. Throughout the work of the Attic orators, who offer us by far the best evidence on the moral standards which it was prudent to uphold in addressing large juries composed of ordinary citizens, it is regarded as virtuous to impoverish oneself by gifts and loans to friends in misfortune (for their daughters' dowries, their fathers' funerals, and the like), by ransoming Athenian citizens taken prisoner in war, and by paying out more than the required minimum in the performance of public duties (the upkeep of a warship, for example, or the dressing and training of a chorus at a festival). This kind of expenditure was boasted about and treated as a claim on the gratitude of the community.[19] On the other hand, to 'devour an inheritance' by expenditure on one's own consumption was treated as disgraceful.[20] Hence gluttony, drunkenness and purchased sexual relations were classified together as 'shameful pleasures'; Demosthenes[21] castigates one of his fellow-ambassadors for 'going round buying prostitutes and fish' with the money he had corruptly received. When a young man fell in love, he might well fall in love with

147

a hetaira or a slave, since his chances of falling in love with a girl of citizen status were so restricted, and to secure the object of his love he would need to purchase or ransom her. A close association between eros and extravagance therefore tends to be assumed, especially in comedy; a character in Menander[22] says, 'No one is so parsimonious as not to make some sacrifice of his property to Eros.' More than three centuries earlier, Archilochus[23] put the matter in characteristically violent form when he spoke of wealth accumulated by long labour 'pouring down into a whore's guts.' A fourth-century litigant[24] venomously asserts that his adversary, whose tastes were predominantly homosexual, has 'buggered away all his estate.'

We have here another reason for the discouragement and disapproval of sexual enthusiasm in the adolescent; it was seen as presenting a threat that the family's wealth would be dissipated in ways other than those which earned honour and respect from the community. The idea that one has a right to spend one's own money as one wishes (or a right to do anything which detracts from one's health and physical fitness) is not Greek, and would have seemed absurd to a Greek. He had only the rights which the law of his city explicitly gave him; no right was inalienable, and no claim superior to the city's.

5. Resistance

Living in a fragmented and predatory world, the inhabitants of a Greek city-state, who could never afford to take the survival of their community completely for granted, attached great importance to the qualities required of a soldier: not only to strength and speed, in which men are normally superior to women, but also to the endurance of hunger, thirst, pain, fatigue, discomfort and disagreeably hot or cold weather. The ability to resist and master the body's demands for nourishment and rest was normally regarded as belonging to the same moral category as the ability to resist sexual desire. Xenophon describes the chastity of King Agesilaus together with his physical toughness,[25] and elsewhere[26] summarises 'lack of self-control' as the inability to hold out against 'hunger, thirst, sexual desire and long hours without sleep.' The reasons for this association are manifold: the treatment of sex — a treatment virtually inevitable in a slave-owning society — as a commodity, and therefore as something which the toughest and most frugal men will be able to cut down to a minimum; the need for a soldier to resist the blandishments of comfort (for

148

if he does not resist, the enemy who does will win), to sacrifice himself as an individual entirely, to accept pain and death as the price to be paid for the attainment of a goal which is not easily quantified, the honour of victory; and the inveterate Greek tendency to conceive of strong desires and emotional states as forces which assail the soul from the outside. To resist is manly and 'free'; to be distracted by immediate pleasure from the pursuit of honour through toil and suffering is to be a 'slave' to the forces which 'defeat' and 'worst' one's own personality.

Here is a third reason for praise of chastity in the young, the encouragement of the capacity to resist, to go without, to become the sort of man on whom the community depends for its defence. If the segregation and legal and administrative subordination of women received their original impetus from the fragmentation of the early Greek world into small, continuously warring states, they also gave an impetus to the formation of certain beliefs about women which served as a rationalization of segregation and no doubt affected behaviour to the extent that people tend to behave in the ways expected of them. Just as it was thought masculine to resist and endure, it was thought femine to yield to fear, desire and impulse. 'Now you must be a *man*;' says Demeas to himself as he tries to make up his mind to get rid of his concubine,[27] 'Forget your desire, fall out of love;' Women in comedy are notoriously unable to keep off the bottle, and in tragedy women are regarded as naturally more prone than men to panic, uncontrollable grief, jealousy and spite. It seems to have been believed not only that women enjoyed sexual intercourse more intensely than men,[28] but also that experience of intercourse put the woman more under the man's power than it put him under hers,[29] and that if not segregated and guarded women would be insatiably promiscuous.

6. Homosexuality

It was taken for granted in the Classical period that a man was sexually attracted by a good-looking younger male,[30] and no Greek who said that he was 'in love' would have taken it amiss if his hearers assumed without further enquiry that he was in love with a boy and that he desired more than anything to ejaculate in or on the boy's body. I put the matter in these coarse and clinical terms to preclude any misapprehension arising from modern application of the expression 'Platonic love' or from Greek euphemism (see below). Xenophon[31] portrays the Syracusan tyrant Hiero as declaring that he wants from the youth Dailochus, with whom he is in love, 'what, perhaps, the nature of man compels us to want from the beautiful.' Aphrodite, despite her femininity, is not hostile to homosexual desire, and homosexual intercourse is denoted by the same term, *aphrodisia*, as heterosexual intercourse.[32] Vase-painting was noticeably affected by the homosexual ethos; painters sometimes depicted a naked woman with a male waist and hips, as if a woman's body was nothing but a young man's body plus breasts and minus external genitals,[33] and in many of their pictures of heterosexual intercourse from the rear position the penis appears (whatever the painter's intention) to be penetrating the anus, not the vagina.[34]

Why homosexuality — or, to speak more precisely, 'pseudo-homosexuality,'[35] since the Greeks saw nothing surprising in the co-existence of desire for boys and desire for girls in the same person — obtained so firm and widespread a hold on Greek society, is a difficult and speculative question.[36] Segregation alone cannot be the answer, for comparable segregation has failed to engender a comparable degree of homosexuality in other cultures. Why the Greeks of the Classical period accepted homosexual desire as natural and normal is a much easier question: they did so because previous generations had accepted it, and segregation of the sexes in adolescence fortified and sustained the acceptance and the practice.

Money may have enabled the adolescent boy to have plenty of sexual intercourse with girls of alien or servile status, but it could not give him the satisfaction which can be pursued by his counterpart in a society which does not own slaves: the satisfaction of being welcomed *for his own sake* by a sexual partner of equal status. This is what the Greek boy was offered by homosexual relations. He was probably accustomed (as often happens with boys who do not have the company of girls) to a good deal of homosexual play at the time of puberty, and he never heard from his elders the suggestion that one was destined to become *either* 'a homosexual' *or* 'a heterosexual.'[37] As he grew older, he could seek among his juniors a partner of citizen status, who could certainly not be forced and who might be totally resistant to even the most disguised kind of purchase. If he was to succeed in seducing this boy (or if later, as a mature man, he was to seduce a youth), he could do so only by *earning* hero-worship.[38]

This is why, when Greek writers 'idealize' eros and treat the physical act as the 'lowest' ingredient in a rich and complex relation-

150

ship which comprises mutual devotion, reciprocal sacrifice, emulation, and the awakening of sensibility, imagination and intellect, they look not to what most of us understand by sexual love but to the desire of an older for a younger male and the admiration felt by the younger for the older. It is noticeable also that in art and literature inhibitions operate in much the same way as in the romantic treatment of hetero-sexual love in our own tradition. When physical gratification is directly referred to, the younger partner is said to 'grant favours' or 'render services'; but a great deal is written about homosexual eros from which the innocent reader would not easily gather that any physical contact at all was involved. Aeschines, who follows Aeschylus and Classical sentiment generally in treating the relation between Achilles and Patroclus in the *Iliad* as homoerotic, commends Homer for leaving it to 'the educated among his hearers' to perceive the nature of the relation from the extravagant grief expressed by Achilles at the death of Patroclus.[39] The vase-painters very frequently depict the giving of presents by men to boys and the 'courting' of boys (a mild term for an approach which includes putting a hand on the boy's genitals), but their pursuit of the subject to the stage of erection, let alone penetra-tion, in a variety of positions, is commonplace.

We also observe in the field of homosexual relations the opera-tion of the 'dual standard of morality' which so often characterizes societies in which segregation of the sexes is minimal.[41] If a Greek admitted that he was in love with a boy, he could expect sympathy and encouragement from his friends, and if it was known that he had at-tained his goal, envy and admiration. The boy, on the other hand, was praised if he retained his chastity, and he could expect strong disap-proval if he was thought in any way to have taken the initiative in attracting a lover. The probably implication is that neither partner would actually say anything about the physical aspect of their relation-ship to anyone else,[42] nor would they expect any question about it to be put to them or any allusion to it made in their presence.

7. *Class and Status*

Once we have accepted the universality of homosexual relations in Greek society as a fact, it surprises us to learn that if a man had at any time in his life prostituted himself to another man for money he was debarred from exercising his political rights.[43] If he was an alien, he had no political rights to exercise, and was in no way penalized for

151

living as a male prostitute, so long as he paid the prostitution tax levied upon males and females alike.[44] It was therefore not the physical act *per se* which incurred penalty, but the incorporation of the act in a certain deliberately chosen role which could only be fully defined with reference to the nationality and status of the participants.

This datum illustrates an attitude which was fundamental to Greek society. They tended to believe that one's moral character is formed in the main by the circumstances in which one lives: the wealthy man is tempted to arrogance and oppression, the poor man to robbery and fraud, the slave to cowardice and petty greed. A citizen compelled by great and sudden economic misfortune to do work of a kind normally done by slaves was shamed because his assumption of a role which so closely resembled a slave's role altered his relationship to his fellow-citizens.[45] Since prostitutes were usually slaves or aliens, to play the role of a prostitute was, as it were, to remove oneself from the citizen-body, and the formal exclusion of a male prostitute from the rights of a citizen was a penalty for disloyalty to the community in his choice of role.

Prostitution is not easily defined — submission in gratitude for gifts, services or help is not so different in kind from submission in return for an agreed fee[46] — nor was it easily proved in a Greek city, unless people were willing (as they were not)[47] to come forward and testify that they had helped to cause a citizen's son to incur the penalty of disenfranchisement. A boy involved in a homosexual relationship absolutely untainted by mercenary considerations could still be called a prostitute by his family's enemies, just as the term can be recklessly applied today by unfriendly neighbours or indignant parents to a girl who sleeps with a lover. He could also be called effeminate; not always rightly, since athletic success seems to have been a a powerful stimulus to his potential lovers, but it is possible (and the visual arts do not help us much here) that positively feminine characteristics in the appearance, movements and manner of boys and youths played a larger part in the ordinary run of homosexual activity than the idealization and romanticisation of the subject in literature indicates. There were certainly circumstances in which homosexuality could be treated as a substitute for heterosexuality; a comic poet[48] says of the Greeks who besieged Troy for ten years, 'they never saw a hetaira . . . and ended up with arseholes wider than the gates of Troy.' The homosexual courting scene which becomes so common in vase-paintings of the sixth Century B.C. — the man touching the face and genitals of the boy, the boy indignantly grasping the man's wrists to push them away —

first appears in the seventh century as a youth courting a woman.[49] A sixth-century vase in which all of a group of men except one are penetrating women shows the odd man out grasping his erect penis and approaching, with a gesture of entreaty, a youth – who starts to run away.[50] In so far as the 'passive partner' in a homosexual act takes on himself the role of a woman, he was open to the suspicion, like the male prostitute, that he abjured his prescribed role as a future soldier and defender of the community.

The comic poets, like the orators, ridicule individuals for effeminacy, for participation in homosexual activity, or for both together; at the same time, the sturdy, wilful, roguish characters whom we meet in Aristophanes are not averse to handling and penetrating good-looking boys when the opportunity presents itself,[51] as a supplement to their busy and enjoyable heterosexual programmes. They represent a social class which, though in the main solidly prosperous, is below the level of most of the people we meet in reading Plato, and there is one obvious factor which we should expect to determine different sexual attitudes in different classes. The thorough-going segregation of women of citizen status was possible only in households which owned enough slaves and could afford to confine its womenfolk to a leisure enlivened only by the exercise of domestic crafts such as weaving and spinning. This degree of segregation was simply not possible in poorer families; the women who sold bread and vegetables in the market – Athenian women,[52] not resident aliens – were not segregated, and there must have been plenty of women in the demes of the Attic countryside who took a hand in work on the land and drove animals to market. No doubt convention required that they should protect each other's virtue by staying in pairs or groups as much as they could, but clearly the generalizations which I formulated in § 3 on the subject of segregation and the obstacles to love-affairs between citizens' sons and citizens' daughters lose their validity as one goes down the social scale. Where there are love-affairs, both boys and girls can have decided views – not enforceable *de jure*, but very important *de facto* – on whom they wish to marry. The girl in Aristophanes' *Ecclesiazusae* who waits impatiently for her young man's arrival while her mother is out may be much nearer the norm of Athenian life than those cloistered ladies who were 'embarrassed by the presence even of a male relative.' It would not be discordant with modern experience to believe that speakers in an Athenian law-court professed, and were careful to attribute to the jury, standards of propriety higher than the average member of the jury actually set himself.

8. *Philosophers and Others*

Much Classical Greek philosophy is characterized by contempt for sexual intercourse, which the author of the Seventh Letter of Plato,[53] offended at the traditional association of sex with a deity, calls 'the slavish and ugly pleasure wrongly called *aphrodisios*.' Xenophon's Socrates, although disposed to think it a gift of beneficent providence that humans, unlike other mammals, can enjoy sex all the year round,[54] is wary of troubling the soul over what he regards as the minimum needs of the body.[55] Virtue reproached Vice, in Prodicus' allegory of the choice of Herakles,[56] for 'forcing sexual activity before [a man] has a need of it.' Antisthenes boasted[57] of having intercourse only with the most readily available woman (and the least desired by other men) 'when my body needs it.' One logical outcome of this attitude to sex is exemplified by Diogenes the Cynic, who was alleged to have masturbated in public when his penis erected itself,[58] as if he were scratching a mosquito-bite.[59] Another outcome was the doctrine (influential in Christianity, but not of Christian origin)[60] that a wise and virtuous man will not have intercourse except for the purpose of procreating legitimate offspring, a doctrine which necessarily proscribes much heterosexual and all homosexual activity.

Although philosophical preoccupation with the contrast between 'body' and 'soul' had much to do with these developments, we can discern, as the ground from which these philosophical plants sprouted, Greek admiration for invulnerability, hostility towards the diversion of resources to the pursuit of pleasure, and disbelief in the possibility that dissimilar ways of feeling and behaving can be synthesised in the same person without detracting from his attainment of the virtues expected of a selfless defender of his city. It is also clear that the refusal of Greek law and society to treat a woman as a responsible person, while on the one hand it encouraged a complacent acceptance of prostitution and concubinage, on the other hand led to the classification of sexual activity as a male indulgence which could be reduced to a minimum by those who were not self-indulgent.[61]

Comedy presents a different picture. The speech put into the mouth of Aristophanes in Plato's *Symposium* differs from the speeches of the other characters in that work by treating eros as the individual's passionate search for the 'other half' of himself (or of herself). This view of eros is firmly rejected by Plato,[62] who presumably chose Aristophanes as its proponent because it seemed to him the view which one would expect of a comic poet; and it may have seemed so

154

to him because comedy looked at sexual behaviour through the eyes of the lower middle class (cf. § 7). Certainly in comedy of the late fourth century we find much which accords with Plato's Aristophanes, notably the remorse of a sensitive young man who realizes that he has adopted a 'dual standard' in condemning his wife and excusing himself.[63] But we have to consider also Aristophanes' *Lysistrata*, produced in 411. There is much fantasy and inconsequentiality in the play, more, indeed, than is commonly observed – and the fact that citizens denied intercourse by their wives are apparently unable to turn their attention to slaves, prostitutes or boys, or even to masturbation,[64] may be no more than inconsequentiality; Aristophanic comedy easily ignores all those aspects of reality which would be inconvenient for the development of the comic plot. Yet when every allowance is made for that important comic convention, the central idea of the play, that a sex-strike by citizens' wives against their husbands can be imagined as having so devastating an effect, implies that the marital relationship was much more important in people's actual lives than we would have inferred simply from our knowledge of the law and our acquaintance with litigation about property and inheritance; more important, too, than could ever be inferred from a comprehensive survey of the varieties of sexual experience and attitude which were possible for the Greeks.

University of St. Andrews

NOTES

[1] Prodicus fr. B7 (Diels-Kranz).
[2] See for more detailed discussion my article, "Aristophanes' Speech in Plato's *Symposium*," *Journal of Hellenic Studies* lvi (1966), 41 ff., especially 48 f.
[3] Xenophon, *Symposium* 9.6.
[4] Aristophanes, *Clouds* 82.
[5] Aristophanes, *Acharnians* 259-279.
[6] Pindar, *Nemean Odes* 10.80-82.
[7] Xenophon, *Hiero* 1.4.
[8] E.g. Aeschines i 52.
[9] Aristotle, *Nicomachean Ethics* 1128^{a}22-25.
[10] Lysias iii 6.
[11] E.g. Xenophon, *Oeconomicus* 7.5.
[12] Isaeus iii 14 (general statement); Aristophanes, *Birds* 130-132 bears it out.

155

[13] E.g. Aristophanes, *Ecclesiazusae* 818-822, *Wasps* 788-790.

[14] E.g. Menander fr. 592, Euripides fr. 521.

[15] E.g. Lysias i 8 (an adulterer's designs on a married woman), Theocritus 2.70-103.

[16] The law is cited and discussed by Demosthenes xxiii 53-55. Cf. A. R. W. Harrison, *The Law of Athens*, i (Oxford, 1968), 32-38.

[17] The speaker of Lysias i regards his wife and children as 'shamed' by the adulterer but himself as 'wronged.' However, an alternative view seems to be expressed in Callias fr. 1, 'Profit is better than shame; off with the adulterer to the inner room!'

[18] Lysias i 32f.

[19] E.g. Lysias xix 9f., 'My father, throughout his life, spent more on the city than on himself and his family....'

[20] E.g. Aeschines i 42, on Timarchus' 'devouring of his considerable estate ...because he is a slave to the most shameful pleasures.'

[21] Demosthenes xix 229.

[22] Menander fr. 198.

[23] Archilochus fr. 118 (Tarditi) = 142 (Bergk).

[24] Isaeus x 25.

[25] Xenophon, *Agesilaus* 5.

[26] Xenophon, *Memorabilia* iv 5.9.

[27] Menander, *Samia* (Austin) 349f.

[28] Hesiod fr. 275 (Merkelbach and West).

[29] Cf. Euripides, *Troades* 665 f., *Medea* 569-575, fr. 323.

[30] I have discussed the evidence more fully in "Eros and Nomos," *Bulletin of the Institute of Classical Studies* x (1964), 31-42.

[31] Xenophon, *Hiero* 1.33.

[32] E.g. Xenophon, *Oeconomicus* 12.14, *Symposium* 8.21.

[33] E.g. J. D. Beazley, *Greek Vases in Poland* (Oxford, 1928), pl. 19.1, *Corpus Vasorum Antiquorum*, Italy VIII, III Ic 1.38.

[34] E.g. B. Graef and E. Langlotz, *Die antiken Vasen von der Akropolis zu Athen* i (Berlin, 1925), pl. 85 (no. 1639), 90 (no. 1913).

[35] Cf. G. Devereux, "Greek Pseudo-Homosexuality and the 'Greek Miracle,'" *Symbolae Osloenses* xlii (1967), 69-92.

[36] The Greeks never suggested that it originated among 'decadent Asiatics'; Herodotus i 135 regards the Persians as having learned pederasty from the Greeks.

[37] That is not to say that no one was exclusively or predominantly homosexual; Pausanias and Agathon maintained a relationship that sounds rather like a homosexual 'marriage' (Plato, *Symposium* 193B).

[38] E.g. [Xenophon], *Cynegeticus* 12.20 on the efforts of the lover to excel when the eyes of his boy are on him.

[39] Aeschines i 142.

[40] *Corpus Vasorum Antiquorum*, Italy III, III He 50.13 (two youths), Italy XL, III I 3.2 (group of youths); H. Licht, *Sittengeschichte Griechenlands*, iii (Dresden and Zürich, 1928), figg. 192, 199 (boys).

[41] See, especially Plato, *Symposium* 182A-183D.

[42] No doubt an ungentlemanly lover would boast of success, as suggested by Plato, *Phaedrus* 232A.

[43] Aeschines i *passim*.

[44] Aeschines i 119 f.

[45] Cf. the embarrassment of the speaker of Demosthenes lvii 44 f. on the 'servile and humble' function to which his mother had been compelled by poverty (she was a wet-nurse).

[46] Cf. Aristophanes, *Wealth* (= '*Plutus*') 153-159.

[47] Cf. Aeschines i 45 f., on the difficulty of getting Timarchus' lover (or client) Misgolas to give evidence.

[48] Eubulus fr. 120.

[49] K. Schefold, *Myth and Legend in Early Greek Art* (English tr. London, 1966), pl. 27b.

[50] *Corpus Vasorum Antiquorum,* Germany XXXI, III Hd 143 f.

[51] Aristophanes, *Birds* 136-143, *Knights* 1384-1387, *Wasps* 578.

[52] The bread-woman of Aristophanes, *Wasps* 1388-1414 is plainly of citizen status.

[53] 335B; whether the author is Plato or not, does not matter in the present context.

[54] Xenophon, *Memorabilia* i 4.12.

[55] Ibid., i 3.14.

[56] Ibid., ii 1.30.

[57] Xenophon, *Symposium* 4.38.

[58] Plutarch, *De Stoicorum Repugnantiis* 1044B.

[59] Socrates was said to have compared Critias' eros for Euthydemus to the desire of a pig to rub its itching back against a rock (Xenophon, *Memorabilia* i 2.30). Democritus fr. B 127 (Diels-Kranz) is evidence for high valuation of scratching rather than low valuation of sex.

[60] Musonius Rufus (p. 63.17 ff., Hense) can hardly be supposed to exhibit Christian influence.

[61] Modern Christian critics of the 'permissive society' sometimes speak as if they really believed (and maybe they do) that an extra-marital sexual relationship with a person of the opposite sex is the same sort of experience as sinking one's teeth into a tender steak.

[62] Plato, *Symposium* 205DE, 212C, *Laws* 731D-732B.

[63] Charisius in Menander, *Epitrepontes* 588-612 (Körte).

[64] However inadequate a substitute for sexual intercourse masturbation may be, it is Aristophanes himself, by representing the Athenians and Spartans as creeping around in an unremitting state of erection, who forces us to ask, 'Why don't they masturbate?' Cf. also Eubulus fr. 120 on the Greeks at Troy: 'they masturbated for ten years ....'

THE DYNAMICS OF MISOGYNY: MYTH AND MYTHMAKING IN THE ORESTEIA*

T HE *Oresteia* occupies a privileged position in any examination of the Greek mind and spirit and stands as one of those monumental works of art which transcend their aesthetic values, for it gives voice and form to the social and political ideology of the period at the same time as it actively shapes the collective fantasies of its audience with its own authoritative vision. By taking as his subject a dynastic myth known to us from the very beginning of Greek literature and transforming it into a wide-ranging myth of origins, Aeschylus draws upon his mythopoetic powers in the service of world-building. The last play leads us back to a reenactment of the cosmic struggle between Olympian and chthonic forces, and the trilogy ends with two social but divinely sanctioned acts of creation: the first human court to judge cases of homicide and the new religious cult of the Eumenides. The *Oresteia*'s program is to trace the evolution of civilization by placing the *polis* at the center of its vision and endowing it with the creative power to coordinate human, natural, and divine forces.

For Aeschylus, civilization is the ultimate product of conflict between opposing forces, achieved not through a *coincidentia oppositorum* but through a hierarchization of values. The solution, therefore, places Olympian over chthonic on the divine level, Greek over barbarian on the cultural level, and male above female on the social level. But the male-female conflict subsumes the other two, for while it maintains its own emotive function in the dramatization of human concerns, it provides too the central metaphor which "sexualizes" the other issues and attracts them into its magnetic field. This schematization is especially marked in the confrontation between Apollo and the Erinyes in the *Eumenides* where juridical and theological concerns are fully identified with male-female dichotomies. Moreover, the basic issue in the trilogy is the establishment in the face of female resistance of the binding nature of patriarchal marriage where wife's subordination and patrilineal succession are reaffirmed. In the course of the drama, in fact, every permutation of the feminine is exhibited before us: goddess, queen, wife, mother, daughter, sister, bride, virgin,

159

adulteress, nurse, witch, Fury, priestess. Every issue, every action stems from the female so that she serves as the catalyst of events even as she is the main object of inquiry.[1]

Viewed as a gynecocentric document, the *Oresteia* then holds an equally privileged position in any exploration of the Greek image of the female, the definition of her social role and status, her functions and meanings. If Aeschylus is concerned with world-building, the cornerstone of his architecture is the control of woman, the social and cultural prerequisite for the construction of civilization. The *Oresteia* stands squarely within the misogynistic tradition which pervades Greek thought, a bias which both projects a combative dialogue in male-female interactions and which relates the mastery of the female to higher social goals.

But in the breadth of its scope and in the complexity of its treatment, the *Oresteia* moves out beyond the other exemplars. The diachronic sweep of the trilogic form creates a broad field in space and time for amplifying patterns and themes, while mythopoetic strata-gems lend prestigious authority to dramatic enactment. The *Oresteia* expands the paradigm by incorporating other myths and mythic elements into a comprehensive frame of reference and transforms it by an imagi-native synthesis which culminates in the creation of a definitive new myth. The trilogy looks both ways. It stands as the fullest realization of an attitude which from its first literary expression in the *Odyssey* is already associated with Clytemnestra (*Od.* 24.199-202).[2] But by integrating the issue into a coherent system of new values, by formu-lating it in new abstract terms, and by shifting to a new mode of argumentation, it provides the decisive model for the future legitimation of this attitude in Western thought. It is the purpose of this paper to examine the *Oresteia* as mythopoesis and to reveal the strategies by which it achieves its aims.

I. THE MYTH OF MATRIARCHY

The progression of events in the *Oresteia* is straightforward. Woman rises up against male authority in a patriarchal society. By slaying her husband and by choosing her own sexual partner, she shatters the social norms and brings social functioning to a standstill. Portrayed as monstrous androgyne, she demands and usurps male power and prerogatives. Son then slays mother in open alliance with the cause of father and husband, and mother's Erinyes, in turn, pursue him in retribution.

The dynamics of the process, however, are noteworthy. Clytemnestra, the female principle, in the first play is a shrewd intelligent rebel against the masculine regime, but by the last play, through her representatives, the Erinyes, female is now allied with the archaic, primitive, and regressive, while male in the person of the young god, Apollo, champions conjugality, society, and progress, and his interests are ratified by the androgynous goddess, Athena, who sides with the male and confirms his primacy. Through gradual and subtle transformations, social evolution is posed as a movement from female dominance to male dominance, or, as it is often figuratively phrased, from "matriarchy" to "patriarchy."[3]

For Bachofen, as for many who followed him, this evolution represented a true historical development, and it was no accident that for verification of his general theories of the origins of society he drew heavily on ancient classical sources, including the *Oresteia*, and gave his different phases names drawn from Greek mythology.[4] For the Greek mythic imagination is rich in projections of female autonomy and Greek religion is amply populated with powerful female deities who seem to antedate their male counterparts in the pantheon. The great Greek culture heroes, Heracles and Theseus, are aggressively misogynistic and each counts among his founding acts of civilization the confrontation and defeat of those woman warriors, the Amazons (Slater 1968: 393). Iconographically, the Amazonomachy figures on the same level of significance as those two other great victories over the giants and the centaurs. The female, the earth-born elements, and the hybrid beast share the same associative sphere.

But matriarchy in the literal meaning of the term is not provable as a historical reality whatever the differences in social structure may have been between the inhabitants of the Aegean basin and the invading Indo-Europeans.[5] Far more compelling is Bamberger's theory of the myth of matriarchy as myth, not "a memory of history, but a social charter," which "may be part of social history in providing justification for a present and perhaps permanent reality by giving an invented 'historical' explanation of how this reality was created" (Bamberger 1974: 267).

From a cross-cultural perspective, the *Oresteia* can be characterized as an intricate and fascinating variant of a widely distributed myth of matriarchy, the so-called Rule of Women, whose details differ but whose general scenario conforms to a consistent pattern. Such myths are normally found in "societies where there also exists a set of cultural rules and procedures for determining sexual dimorphism in social and cultural tasks." Women once had power, but they abused it through "trickery and unbridled sexuality," thus fostering "chaos and misrule." The men, therefore, rebelled. They assumed control and took steps to institutionalize the subordination of women. The point of the myth is not the recording of some historical or prehistorical state of affairs, but rather that women are not fit to rule, only to be ruled (Bamberger 1974: 276, 280).

While the simpler myth of matriarchy reads as a definitive masculine triumph which establishes the pattern for all time, the variations, repetitions, and frequency of the pattern in Greek myths attest to the continuing renewability of the battle between the sexes in many areas and circumstances. The conflictual nature of the encounter is consonant with the generally agonistic outlook of the Greek world, while the consistency of the portrayal of the woman reflects perhaps the deep-seated conviction that the female is basically unruly. The vigorous denial of power to the female overtly asserts her inferiority while at the same time expresses anxiety towards her persistent but normally dormant power which may always erupt into open violence. But the eruption of that force is not perceived as a purely unpredictable menace; rather it follows a discernible linear pattern that proceeds in conformity to its own particular "logic," its own dynamics, which arises directly out of this fundamental ambivalence towards women.

The central role played in mythology by male-female encounters attests to the significance and complexity of the problem even as the proliferation of versions indicates perhaps the impossibility of finding a satisfactory conclusion. In turning to Aeschylus to outline the version of this "logic" of misogyny operative in his drama – the dramatic sequence of events and the hidden assumptions that regulate this sequence – it is noteworthy that the poet must in effect invent his own solution.

The conjugal relationship is the focus of the struggle. Already assumed as the pre-existing norm, it is not accepted in its current form by the female as an absolute imperative. In the *Oresteia*, wife and mother, Clytemnestra, repudiates it from inside the society, although it may be rejected from the outside, as the Danaids, militant young virgins, do in another trilogy. The ultimate goal of both trilogies is the female's full acceptance of the marital bond as necessary, natural, and just. In each case, the prior rejection of marriage leads to the massacre of the male, the corollary of which is the threat of extinction to human society as a whole. Clytemnestra slays her husband. Danaids slay their bridegrooms on their wedding night. The polarizing imagination of Greek mythic thought not only establishes a strong dichotomy between male and female, it also posits predictable behavioral responses at either end of the spectrum where female self-assertion on her own behalf is expressed only at the cost of annihilating the Other. We might perhaps speak of an "Amazon" complex which envisions that woman's refusal of her required subordinate role must, by an inevitable sequence, lead to its opposite: total domination, gynecocracy, whose extreme form projects the enslavement or murder of men. That same polarizing imagination can only conceive of two hierarchic alternatives: Rule by Men or Rule by Women. (Cf. Eurip. *Or.* 933-37).

The portrait of Clytemnestra in the *Agamemnon* specifically links her independence of thought and action with a desire to rule (Winnington-Ingram 1948: 130-47), an emphasis which transforms a personal vendetta into a gynecocratic issue, which presents the first motive as synchronic not diachronic with the other. Husband is also king, an economy which conflates the two social statuses and erases political and domestic distinctions, and permits the merger of personal revenge and political ambition. Clytemnestra begins, in fact, as woman in charge, for, as the chorus remarks, she is entitled to rule in the absence of the husband-king (*Ag.* 258-60; cf. 84), but her intentions are to make that regency permanent and she assumes the stance of political *tyrannos*, an impression that is explicitly confirmed by both the choruses in the first two plays (Grossmann 1970: 218-26). She does not rule alone, however, in a full gynecocracy, but the principle is maintained by the delineation of her lover and later coregent Aegisthus. He is the male who has already succumbed to female domination. He occupies the female interior space (*oikouros, Ag.* 1225, 1626), renounces masculine heroic pursuits of war and glory (*Ag.* 1625). He is only an adjunct to, not an initiator of the plot against Agamemnon (*Ag.* 1633-37; 1643-45). In his erotic susceptibilities, he is not unlike his barbarian counterpart Paris who also commits adultery with a

163

daughter of Tyndareus. The subordinate male, the strengthless lion (*Ag.* 1224-25) is the only possible partner for the dominant female, and the chorus contemptuously marks this reversal of roles by calling him "woman" (*Ag.* 1625; cf. *Cho.* 304), (Vernant 1969: 107-11). And when he does assert himself by baring his own motives and flexing his new-found power, he himself conforms to the stereotypical male model of *tyrannos*.

Note too that Agamemnon must also be assimilated to the pattern before his murder at the hands of a woman. The prelude to his death is his defeat in the verbal exchange between himself and Clytemnestra, a debate which is specifically posed as a power struggle between male and female in which male eventually yields (*Ag.* 940-43). The cause of that dispute, the walking on the tapestries, is itself concerned with a clash in values, and Agamemnon's objections are based on his correct perception of the gesture as one appropriate only to women and barbarians. But he has already announced his sexual appetites by bringing back Cassandra as his concubine from Troy, while his yielding to Clytemnestra's temptation marks his secret affinity with the Trojan king Priam and with barbarian values of luxury and gratification of desires (*Ag.* 918-21; 935-39). This antithetical barbarian world is portrayed in the Greek imagination as the world of effeminacy and of sensual delights even as it is the world where, logically enough, female domination is perceived as a cultural reality and where the myths of matriarchy are most often located.

Clytemnestra fully understands this cultural dichotomy and reveals it in an oblique and subtle way. After Agamemnon has yielded to her persuasion and has entered the palace, she urges Cassandra now to come into the house and to accept her fate of slavery, and she supports her argument by allusion to a mythological precedent: even the son of Alcmene, when sold into servitude, endured his life of bondage (*Ag.* 1040-41). Heracles is identified not by name but only through his maternal genealogy, and his enslavement, of course, was to the Lydian queen Omphale who is everywhere in the tradition associated with the Rule of Women. In fact, one of the prominent features of the relationship between Heracles and Omphale is the terms of his enslavement at her hands which required him to take on the role of female, to wear women's dress, and to do women's work, as well as to serve as the male sexual object to satisfy the needs of the queen.[6]

If Omphale is an archetypal exemplar of the Rule of Women, two other paradigms point even more directly to the same mythological construct. In the *Choephoroi*, the series of monstrous women recited by the chorus culminates in a reference to the famous myth of the Lemnian women, so famous that their deed need not be recorded, but only the judgment passed upon it as proverbial for the epitome of evil (*Cho.* 631-36). The crimes of single women come first, Althaea (mother), Scylla (daughter), and Clytemnestra (wife). The Lemnian allusion completes the misogynistic progression by moving from one to all, from individual transgression to a collective menace that wipes out an entire race. Moreover, by redoubling the example of husband murder which immediately precedes, it places Clytemnestra's offense (which itself has passed into paradigm) within the larger frame of the Rule of Women where female aims to annihilate male.

If the Lemnian women serve a programmatic function in the *Choephoroi* as a justification for the murder of Clytemnestra, the Amazons assume that role in the third play where Aeschylus shifts the aetiological explanation for the name of the Areopagos from Ares' trial on that site to the battle between Theseus' Athens and the Amazons, worshippers of Ares. There the Amazons, the open rivals of men, had built their own city, had asserted their will in rival architectural and ritual structures (*Eu.* 685-90). If in the *Choephoroi*, the mythological emphasis falls both on the murderous aspect of the female in domestic relations and on her successful vanquishing of the male with its predictable results, the other exemplar shows the Rule of Women as a political issue and celebrates its decisive defeat at the hands of Theseus, champion of male interests. Clytemnestra is no longer the point of reference as Apollo points out since she did not confront the male in open combat (*Eu.* 625-28), and she is the threat from within the system not from without. The Amazonomachy in this context rather serves to demarcate the major substantive issue of Orestes' trial as a battle between the sexes. Moreover, the prior victory over the Amazons serves not only to foreshadow the outcome of the trial, but, by association, to invest the new defeat with the same symbolic significance and prestige as the earlier one. In the synchronic perspective, past, then, is paradigm, but if we shift to a diachronic view, the substitution of tribunal for warfare, of law for violence, indicates an evolutionary development and offers a new paradigm for the pacification of hostilities.

These three gynecocratic allusions, each allotted to a different play of the trilogy, and together forming a series of increasing elaboration and emphasis, mark out different aspects of the general pattern of the Rule of Women. The reference to Omphale implies role reversal and sexual bondage, that of the Lemnian women focuses on the potential outcome of the struggle as the destruction of male by female, and that of the Amazons points to the conclusion of the myth of matriarchy – the drawing of battle lines and the ultimate triumph of male over female.

In the Aeschylean version of the myth, the woman does not initiate the hostilities. She is spurred to retaliation by a prior outrage inflicted upon her by a male.[7] Clytemnestra, enraged by the treatment of her daughter as a sacrificial animal, plots revenge and is reinforced in her resolve to kill her husband by Agamemnon's intention to introduce his concubine into the domestic space of the legitimate wife.[8] The Danaids are fleeing their suitors who view marriage as acquisition, rape, and enslavement.

But the female response invariably exceeds the provocation offered by the male and creates a still more violent disequilibrium that brings society to a standstill. The havoc caused by the female in the first play of the *Oresteia* requires two further sequels to alleviate it, and the shock waves ripple out first to the city of Argos and then to the universe at large. In the *rhetorical* progression of the drama the crimes of the males of the house, Thyestes, Atreus, and Agamemnon, first fade into lesser significance and finally are mentioned no more.

In the *Choephoroi*, the uncanny power of the monumental androgynous figure of the *Agamemnon* has receded (Vickers 1973: 382-88, 393-94). Clytemnestra rules with Aegisthus over Argos, but she is now back in the interior of the house, not visible in the world of men and politics. She sends libations to the tomb of Agamemnon, but her action creates a ritual impasse since the wife who owes this duty to her husband is also his murderer (*Cho.* 84-100). This impasse is emblematic of the dysfunction of the social order under her regime, and she herself poses the problem which must be resolved if the social order is to be repaired and restored. The impasse is also manifested in the social status of the legitimate children: Electra, unwed, arrested in maidenhood, bound to the paternal hearth (Vernant 1969: 110-12), and Orestes, an exile, as yet unable to cross the boundary to adulthood, a status contingent upon his assumption of his father's name and space. The house is shrouded in darkness, literal and metaphorical, the blood is frozen in the earth (*Cho.* 51-53, 66-67), and the children have a past but no future. That past, in fact, must be recalled and recreated in the long *kommos*, even as the free flowing of pent up libations, tears, and verbal laments is the first symbolic step towards liberation from the suffocating spiritual and social deadlock of the current regime.

The only solution envisioned by the myth is the retaliatory defeat of this self-willed female principle whose potency is still a living and malignant force. And the myth proposes only one candidate for the task; the rules of blood vendetta exclude any other. Son must slay mother; father must be avenged, but in so doing, son's alliance with paternal power and interests must simultaneously be seen as repudiation of the mother. Mother must therefore be presented as hostile to both father and to son. In Clytemnestra's dream of the serpent at the breast and in his encounter with his mother, Orestes represents both himself and his father; he acts on behalf of his father but also on behalf of himself (Green 1969: 68-69, n. 14). For Orestes interprets his exile from the palace as rejection by the mother (*Cho.* 912), and mother's hostility to her children is confirmed by her treatment of Electra (*Cho.* 189-91; 418-19; 444-46), by her call for a man-slaying axe at the moment of recognition (*Cho.* 889-90), and, above all, by the nurse who exposes Clytemnestra's hypocritical grief at the report of her son's death and who herself lays claim to responsibility for the nurture he received as a child (*Cho.* 737-65).

But in the *Agamemnon* the queen's primary motive was maternal vengeance for her child, Iphigenia; her second one was the sexual alliance she contracted with Aegisthus in her husband's absence. There the two traits of mother love and conjugal chastity diverge, are, in fact, antithetical to each other. Here in the *Choephoroi* adulterous wife is now fully equated with hostile mother. The faithless wife who betrayed her husband and has taken his usurper into her bed has now betrayed her other children to gratify her own sexuality (*Cho.* 915-17; cf. 599-601).[9] The confrontation between Clytemnestra and Orestes is remarkable for the queen's mingled appeal of maternity and sexual seductiveness; the breast she bares to him (*Cho.* 894-98) has both erotic and nurturant significance. The gesture that momentarily stops him in his tracks is the source of her power over him, the source of all female power. It is the emblem of the basic dilemma posed by the female — the indispensable role of women in fertility for the continuity of the group by reason of her mysterious sexuality and the potential disruption of that group by its free exercise.

It is significant that the maternal role should be exemplified in the first place by the mother-daughter dyad, for that is a relationship from which the male is excluded, a closed circle in which his interference can only be construed as an invasion as the myth of Kore and Demeter demonstrates so well. It is essential too that the mother-daughter bond be attenuated as it is in the second play, where Electra is her mother's antagonist and her father's ally, essential too that the mother-child bond in the *Choephoroi* include both male and female offspring, although the emphasis now falls on mother and son.

The dramatic sequence of events in the trilogy suggests a linear chain of cause and effect. If the female overvalues the mother-child bond, her own unique relationship, she will, in turn, undervalue the marriage bond, which will, in turn, lead to or be accompanied by an assertion of sexual independence (free replacement of one sexual partner by another), and will be manifested politically by a desire to rule. The next step, paradoxically, will be her undervaluation, even rejection, of the mother-child bond, as in the case of Electra and Orestes. Child, in response, will undervalue and reject mother.

Orestes' victory over Clytemnestra does not, however, as in the more typical myth of matriarchy, result in the defeat of the female and in the curtailment of her power. Far from it. The murder of the mother evokes a renewed and redoubled power, exemplified now in a proliferation of negative female imagoes of supernatural origin. The chorus in the *Choephoroi* had resorted to another mythological paradigm to exhort Orestes to action: he is to be another Perseus who will slay the Gorgon (*Cho.* 835-37), the archetypal myth on another level of masculine triumph over female.[10] But the projected model is not fully applicable, first, because Orestes himself is given ophidian attributes, and secondly, because the serpent dead is deadlier still. The chorus' exulting allusion after the deed to Orestes' liberation of Argos by lopping off the heads of two serpents (*Cho.* 1046-47) is instead an ironic cue for Orestes' first glimpse of the serpentine Furies. In this play, the Erinyes by their appearance terrorize him into frenzy and flight. In the next, they would annihilate him by absorption into themselves in an exact and retaliatory inversion of the symbolism of Clytemnestra's dream.

This final stage in the developmental progression, in fact, links together the perversion of both relationships — mother-child and female-male. For the devouring voracity of the Furies, the incarnations of Clytemnestra, who would pursue and suck the blood from their living victim, represents both oral aggression against the child they should nourish and sexual predation against the male to whom they should submit.[11] Clytemnestra has banished both legitimate males from the house and blood guilt infects the earth. In the case of the Erinyes, as transformations of Clytemnestra, the result of hypersexuality is sterility and death. The virginal Erinyes are barren and sterile and create sterility in all of nature.

In the primitive portrayal of the Furies there is a regression to the deepest fantasies of buried masculine terrors. They are *paides apaides*, children who are no children because they are old and also because they are children who have no children. They are shunned and rejected by men and gods with whom they have no intercourse (*Eu.* 1033; 68-73). Daughters of Night, they inhabit the depths of the earth. Repulsive in physical appearance, they drip and ooze from every orifice; even their breath, their words, their thoughts drop poison (*Eu.* 478-79). Their virginity is negative virginity as Clytemnestra's sexuality is negative sexuality, and in each case the fertility of the land is threatened (cf. *Ag.* 1390-92).

The pacification of the Erinyes becomes the ideological effort to solve the dilemma of the inextricable connection between female fertility and female sexuality, between female beneficence and female malevolence, for the equation of the female with sterility and death creates a new impasse that spells an end not only to society but obviously to life itself. The solution moves to repair the female archetype which has been polarized at its extreme negative limit in response to its rejection and denigration. The solution also establishes marriage as the institution that controls sexuality and ensures fertility even as it serves to assert the inherent subordination of female to male. For female dominance is expressed paradigmatically by the mother-child relationship — concretely in the *Oresteia* by Iphigenia's death as the motive for the female's attack upon the male and generically by the natural dependency of the male child upon the adult female. Patriarchal marriage is paradigmatic of male dominance including the primacy of the father-son bond in patrilineal succession and the primacy of the male in political power.

II. SEPARATION FROM THE MOTHER AND THE
GENERAL PATTERN OF PUBERTY RITES

In speaking of the myth of matriarchy and the general function of myth and ritual as educational tools in pre-literate or traditional societies, Bamberger draws a parallel between the myth of matriarchy and puberty initiation rites which aim at detaching the boy from his natal household and his maternal associations and retraining him for his social and political roles. She points out that "this regrouping of adolescent boys with adult males is prefigured in some societies in myths foretelling the demise of female power and in the concomitant rise of male privilege. The myth of the Rule of Women in its many variants may be regarded as a replay of these crucial transitional stages in the life cycle of the individual male" (Bamberger 1974: 277). There is, in fact, a close correlation between myth and ritual since in the myth men often seize the sovereignty from the women by stealing their sources of power, the sacred objects (e.g., masks and sacred trumpets), and making them their own exclusive possession, while one of the important events in the rituals of initiation involves the revelation of these same sacred objects to the boys and the explication of their meaning. But in these cases myth is prior to ritual; an event of the past supports and justifies the ritual and its message.

What we find instead in the *Oresteia* is the sophisticated interweaving and transposition of traditional motifs from both the myth of matriarchy and the ritual initiation scenario. Orestes, specifically characterized as on the threshold of maturity in the *Choephoroi* (6), lives out the myth in terms that bear a remarkable resemblance to generalized and widely diffused initiatory patterns, but his own special situation now determines and directs the final outcome of the myth. Rather than following out a well-trodden path to adulthood as countless others would have done before him as we would expect of an actual cult experience, he must make his own way through an unprecedented set of procedures created expressly for him, and he himself must act as the catalyst that brings a secular non-cultic institution into being. Likewise, the myth of matriarchy reaches its predictable conclusion

170

but through a series of stratagems that combines the old and the new.

Orestes in the second play is the anomalous male, the logical counterpart of the anomalous female, Clytemnestra. Male activity is normally directed outward away from the hearth for external validation of prowess, but the domain which Orestes must enter is feminine space. If Vidal-Naquet's suggestion as to his ephebic status is correct, as I think it is, the inversion is still more precise. The boy, prior to his entry into adulthood, must separate himself from the attachments of home and childhood to serve out his military term on the wild frontiers, where he is situated temporarily in a savage state, in a liminal space as befits his liminal position.[12] But Orestes, the exile banished in childhood by his mother, *returns* at puberty to his home, that space made savage and undomesticated by his mother's action in order to undertake the most savage act of all.[13]

In fact, in order to effect that separation he must commit a crime, the crime of matricide, and far from releasing him from his mother and her influence, the Erinyes now sing a binding song over him to draw him into their domain and keep him there. Orestes' true initiatory experience begins only after his *second* expulsion from the palace in Argos and is terminated when, reincorporated into society in the third stage of the *rite de passage*, he returns to Argos now as lawful ruler and successor to his father. The overt mission of the *Eumenides* is to effect the salvation of Orestes. And that salvation is contingent upon his successful separation from his mother, in other words, upon completion of the enterprise undertaken by Orestes himself in the second play. The task now ascends to a higher level, to the level of both gods and city, even as the myth of matriarchy can only reach its prosperous conclusion in this new setting through a similar upward revision of its traditional terms. That is, the *Eumenides* must now once and for all establish and justify in abstract, theoretical, and mythopoetic terms the principles upon which the predictable sequence of the myth of matriarchy is based.

This shift to a more inclusive level of discourse is necessitated by the terms of the main preoccupation of the trilogy which reaches its fullest articulation in this third and final play. The primary issue in the *Oresteia* is, of course, justice. In its proper execution under all circumstances, matricide, the extreme transgression and the insoluble case, serves only as the means, the irresistible catalyst. Kuhns shrewdly observes that "Orestes cannot know that he is directed to act on behalf of a further purpose; he does not know that the crime is committed in order that it may be judged." (Kuhns 1962: 35).

But by posing the son's action in separating himself from his mother as a crime, the issue of justice and the issue of the female are inextricably blended, for in the offering first of justification for matricide and then in its exoneration, mother is also judged. And she is judged on two levels: first, the woman is judged as wife. The crime of Clytemnestra (mariticide) is measured against Orestes' (matricide) and found to be more opprobrious: "For it is not the same thing that a noble man die, a man honored with god-given sovereignty, and at the hands of a woman at that." (*Eu.* 625-27). Secondly, the Erinyes themselves, the first judges of Orestes, are also judged. Mother has been turned into vindictive and archetypal female. In Aeschylus' new genealogy for the Erinyes they are now daughters of Night, i.e. totally identified with the negative female principle. And they champion a justice which is judged blind, archaic, barbaric, and regressive, a justice which is to be superseded by the new institution of the law court in which they will in the future play a supporting not a starring role.

The problem of the female is posed in a new set of terms and the victory that is won is predicated on a social transformation of a higher degree. The *Eumenides* therefore is everywhere concerned with change and transformation on every level both for the son figure Orestes and for the mother. For the archaic mind, as Eliade points out, it is a characteristic belief that "a state cannot be changed without first being annihilated" and then recreated from the beginning. "Life cannot be repaired. It can only be recreated by a return to sources." (Eliade 1958: xiii; 1963: 30).

The first word of the last play of the trilogy is *"prōton,"* "first," as Burke puts it, "the final oracular beginning" (1952; 1966: 133). The *Eumenides* is a drama preoccupied with beginnings, with origins. Its *mythos* is itself a myth of origins, of aetiologies, on both the secular and cultic levels, and it supports and redeems itself by reference to the ultimate beginnings. Again to quote Eliade (1963: 21):

> Every mythical account of the origin of anything presupposes and continues the cosmogony. From the structural point of view, origin myths can be homologized with the cosmogonic myth. The creation of the World being *the* pre-

> eminent instance of creation, the cosmogony becomes the exemplary model for 'creation' of every kind. This does not mean that the origin myth imitates or copies the cosmogonic model.... But every new appearance – an animal, a plant, an institution – implies the existence of a World.... Every origin myth narrates and justifies a 'new situation' – new in the sense that it did not exist *from the beginning of the World*. Origin myths continue and complete the cosmogonic myth; they tell how the world was changed, made richer or poorer.... This is why some origin myths begin by outlining a cosmogony.

And this is precisely how the *Eumenides* begins.

The opening scene, as many critics have noted is both paradigmatic and anticipatory of the ending of the play. The Delphic succession myth (a parallel to the evolution of power in Hesiod's *Theogony*) provides a direct mythological model for the transference of power from female to male.[14] Although it would not have been inappropriate in view of the prevalence of serpent imagery in the trilogy to cite the traditional Delphic version of Apollo's acquisition of the shrine by dragon combat with the Pytho, Aeschylus has substituted an orderly and peaceful version of the succession myth in order to foreshadow the peaceful and harmonious ending of the trilogy. "For a thing to be well done, it must be done as it was *the first time*." (Eliade 1958: xiii). Here is true mythopoesis and a reversal of terms: a new civic world is in the process of creation and requires therefore as its model an alternate cosmogony, a new myth of origins.

By the terms of the revised myth, Aeschylus provides a paradigm of positive matriarchy that acknowledges the principle but relegates it to a primordial past that has been superseded. But by his other act of mythopoesis, he presents the Erinyes as daughters of Night, representatives of a negative matriarchy that must be overcome. In the Hesiodic attribution of their origin to the blood of Uranus' severed genitals, they were also associated with vengeance and retribution. In their new genealogy as parthenogenetic offspring of Night, the principle of vengeance itself is posed as wholly female and female in its blackest and most negative manifestation (Ramnoux 1959: 138-39). The new genealogy anchors them to a stage antecedent to the Uranian creativity of bisexual reproduction and the generation of regular non-monstrous forms.

173

In this juxtaposition of two matriarchal representations, the Erinyes are invested with the symbolism of the dragon-combat mythology that was displaced from Delphic myth. The Erinyes' desire to suck Orestes' blood, to engulf him, paralyze him, and draw him down into the darkness of Hades, is consonant with the general pattern of the archetype. Earlier I remarked on the failure of the Gorgon-Perseus paradigm for Orestes in the *Choephoroi*, but that failure resides not in the misnaming of the monstrous serpent female, only in Orestes' inability to play Perseus. Here the transpersonalization of the female dragon (*Eu.* 128), the archetypal encounter recurs, but will be transformed. For neither can Apollo reenact his previous victory over the Pytho, nor will Orestes himself play out the part of the typical hero and slay the dragon. Nor will the dragon truly be slain, but tamed; the act of domestication will be presented in collective, social, non-heroic terms, and violence will yield to open persuasion, *Peitho*.[15] Yet with the gods as agents, the struggle is also presented as mythic conflict between chthonic and Uranian forces, between regress and progress, that resonates with the emotive power of theogony, gigantomachy (*Eu.* 295-96), and dragon combat. The defeat of the Erinyes is already prefigured in the prologue by their temporary pacified sleep at the shrine (*Eu.* 47, 68) and by their subsequent expulsion from it by Apollo (*Eu.* 179).

In the perspective of the myth of matriarchy, the Erinyes and their characterization conform more closely to the general pattern. For they are now a collective of females rather than a single figure, and their quarrel with Apollo turns precisely on the issue of usurpation of prior female power and privilege. But it is the conflation of the myth of matriarchy and the myth of dragon combat that invests the *Oresteia* with its most persuasive rhetorical weapon. For the Erinyes on stage not only serve as concrete embodiments of the metaphorical allusions to themselves in the earlier plays, but as true primordial dragon figures, they also make visible the metaphors of female monstrosity which have been associated with Clytemnestra from the beginning. In the *Agamemnon*, Cassandra delineates her as Scylla, amphisbaena, and mother of Hades (*Ag.* 1233-36), allusions which proliferate in the second play with references to *echidna* (*Cho.* 249), *muraina* (994) and Gorgon (835). The two strands meet in the ode on monstrous women in which the mythological women who slay men are linked from the first strophe with monstrous eruptions in nature on sea, on land, and in air, in which the human Scylla, daughter of Minos, recalls her homonymous monstrous counterpart of Cassandra's accusation (*Cho.* 612-22).[16]

It is this rhetoric, in fact, which already in the first play, provides the yeast which transforms the shrewd political rebel into an archaic *daimon* that menaces the world with a renewed cosmogonic threat of total disorder and which marks the male-female conflict not as a feminine revolution but as a struggle between the new (male) and the old (female). Female is allied with the forces and values of the past not only on the mythological level, but, as the combat shifts from that of husband and wife to one of mother and son, it operates also on the personal human level. In the generational code, mother is anterior in time to son. In the juridical code, the ancient principle of the blood vendetta becomes fully identified with mother, for it was her championship of the priority of blood ties which led her first to slay the male to avenge her daughter's death and now both to pursue the slayer, the kinsman who shed kindred blood, and to refuse her son the normal passage into adulthood.

If the recitation of Delphic genealogy is a myth of beginnings, the second part of the prologue, Orestes at the shrine itself, presents another modality of beginnings directly consequent upon the first one. Orestes is seated at the *omphalos*, the navel of the world, holding suppliant emblems of white wool and covered with the purifying blood of a pig. As matricide, his condition symbolically represents his status of moral ambiguity, guilty and not guilty, polluted and purified (Jones 1962: 105-06). As neophyte, his ambiguity is emblematic of puberty rites everywhere. In a state of liminality, betwixt and between, he is separated from the world and not yet reincorporated into it. In the process of transition and change, he must go back again to beginnings, this time marked in the biological domain by the imagery of parturition. In fact, "neophytes are [commonly] likened to or treated as embryos, newborn infants, or sucklings by symbolic means which vary from culture to culture."[17] All initiations employ some nexus of death and rebirth symbolism as a mark of a transition to a new state, but the imagery in puberty rites has special relevance, since the essential aim of the rite is to dramatize the biological life cycle by indicating the death of childhood and the rebirth into adulthood, a symbolism supported by the applicability, for instance, of the cutting of hair both to rites of puberty and to rites of mourning (*Cho.* 6-7).

Delcourt, in her *Oreste et Alcméon*, inquires, why the blood of a pig in rites of purification? And she suggests that its value lies neither in its sacrificial nor its lustratory functions, but in its close association with female genitalia. The pig, as artistic representations make clear, was held over the head of the subject who sits "like a new-born under the bloody organ which gave him birth. The blood of the piglet was only symbolically purificatory. The guilty was supposed reborn, and reborn innocent, from the mystic *choiriskos*," and Varro informs us that the same treatment was applied both to homicides and to those who had been mad and were now sane (*De re rust*. 2.4.16).[18] "Just as pollution is disease and disease is death, so purification is a renewal of life" (Thomson 1946: 93).

Orestes then is ritually reborn at the *omphalos* of Delphi, the female symbol at the center of a place whose name means womb. But this symbol has been appropriated by the male hegemony of the shrine which Apollo himself received as a *birthday* gift (*Eu*. 7). The implication of the scene is of rebirth from the male, a necessary condition both for Orestes' redemption from guilt and for his passage into adulthood as son of his father. Cross-cultural ethnographical data confirms that one of the most consistent themes of puberty rites is, in fact, the notion that the first birth from the female is superseded by a second birth, this time from the male. The initiate is born again into the social world of the fathers and is thereby definitively separated from the world of his childhood and his maternal dependence.[19]

What is remarkable in the compressed symbolism of rebirth in this opening tableau is its double reference, for if Orestes' ambiguous presentation is attributable first to his liminal status as neophyte, it is also attributable to the nexus of guilt and innocence which proclaims him still attached to his mother (i.e., guilty) or separated from her (i.e., innocent). He can hardly negotiate the first set of terms until he has resolved the second. And this second issue which is, in fact, the primary focus of the trilogy, will be determined by the new Apollonic argument in the new juridical sphere that his mother is no kin to him, that he, in fact, is born from the father and only from the father.

The Apollonic argument then, is a restatement in another mode of discourse, of what has already been represented here at Delphi. Orestes himself is drawn into the Apollonic milieu and is assimilated, if obliquely, to the pattern of Apollo's own development which brought the god from Delos to Delphi, from mother to father.[20] But Orestes' position still lacks the conclusive ratification of society and its gods.

It is only a beginning, and one that must move him from Delphi to Athens, from isolation to community. And the process that will define him will be linked to the process by which society will define itself. In this double task which the drama poses for itself as a simultaneous reciprocal development, the action veers away from the sphere of myth and ritual even as it continues the impulse in a new and different way.

Orestes' experience continues to conform to the constellation of symbols and events that cluster about the pubertal initiation scenario. For in addition to the liminal situation of ambiguity and the recurrent imagery of birth, death, and rebirth, other typical features include: (1) ordeal, wakefulness, suffering, silence, isolation, wandering, and terror produced by encounter with the monstrous, (2) close connection with the deities of the group, (3) the presence of a male authority figure as guide, who dispenses the "arcane wisdom" or "gnosis" pertaining to social and political realities couched in mythic and symbolic form, especially theogonic and cosmogonic material, as well as "instruction in ethical and social obligations, in law and kinship," and (4) the passive submission and obedience to that authority (Turner 1967: *passim*). The main event of initiation rites is, of course, the revelation of the hallowed traditions and the secret lore of the group upon which that tradition is based. Here in the *Eumenides* the revelation combines both old and new to formulate the future tradition, the foundation of which is the judgment by law and the definitive hierarchical disposition of male and female statuses.

In the *Eumenides,* the power of the mother is first drastically undercut and even denied by Apollo, who, as representative of male interests, logically champions the cause of marriage, but that denial is then mitigated by a limited restoration of that power through the intervention of Athena and the transformation of Erinyes to Eumenides. But Apollo must come first, to be superseded but not fully denied.

In the short view, Apollo's argument can be regarded as a sophisticated legal maneuver designed to get his client off on a technicality, or, in a more ameliorative reading, to break the impasse caused by the disparity between the Erinyes' absolutist and rigid formulation of the issue (guilty or not guilty) and the Apollonian defense of extenuating circumstances. In the wider view, the Apollonian argument is the hub of the drama, mother right vs. father right, old justice vs. new justice.

On the one hand, his method of argumentation is fully consonant with the archaic mode of thought which can only express change in status and attitude through total annihilation or negation of the previous position. He had already demonstrated the superiority of male over female on the sociological level by proclaiming that husband-king-male is more important than wife-queen-female (*Eu.* 625-26) and by pressing the cause of conjugality over blood kinship (*Eu.* 213-18). Now he moves back to the beginning to assert the primacy of the male through appeal to the primacy of the father. This he can only do, first, by the denial of the mother's role in procreation on the biological level, and then by resort on the mythological level to the denial of the mother altogether. The mother is only necessary conditionally in the case of a uterine association; where that association is lacking, mother need not exist at all. The denial of *matriarchy* is achieved by the denial of *mater*. The tables are completely turned.

On the other hand, this archaic mode of argument is presented in the service of a new synthesis in a new environment. To break the binding force of the symbiotic link between mother and child (best expressed imagistically in the circularity of serpent symbolism), Apollo needs a new forum, namely, the law court, the city's device which admits the use of logical argument and debate even as it establishes the right of non-kin to decide disputes among kin.

In this context of a founding act, the content of the argument is concerned with beginning again, expressed biologically as embryology, mythologically as theogony. The rebirth of Orestes into innocence and the birth of the law court and civic justice are confirmed by resort to the archetypal paradigm of beginnings. But the argument itself is a new kind of argument. In proposing that the father, the one who mounts, is the only true parent of the child, while the mother is merely the stranger host to the embryo, the passive vessel during its gestation, the argument draws upon the new scientific theories of the day. But even as the argument looks forward in its advancement of new intellectual trends, it looks backward in relying for proof of this contention on the mythic concept of Athena's birth from the head of Zeus.

The mythic argument is not just an exercise in logical absurdity which poses the anomaly as paradigm. It is a sound strategy (not only for the reasons outlined above on the nature of archaic argument) within the rules of mythic thought. Athena's birth is of founding significance in the creation of the world. In the terms of Hesiod's theogonic myth of succession, Zeus, by this act, puts an end to any threat to his sovereignty, by incorporating the principle of intelligence through the swallowing of Metis and making that principle manifest in the world through the birth of a child whose sex indicates that she will be no political threat to her father and whose filial relationship proclaims her dependence on the male. The mythic form his act of creation assumes completes the trend of the *Theogony* which began with Earth's natural parthenogenetic capability and ends with the male's imitation of her. The seal is set on the finality of the transition from female dominance to male dominance by overt male usurpation of her procreative function, the basic source of her mystery and power. That usurpation is consummated in the total reversal from female as begetter of male to male as begetter of female.[21] But in the course of this transition, male generative creativity is displaced from phallos to head, or rather, put somewhat different, phallos and head are associated together.

This connection is precisely the basis that also underlines the "scientific" argument. For already in some of the pre-Socratic philosophers as well as later in Plato and Aristotle, seminal fluid is associated with spinal and cerebral fluids; the hypothesis is that semen is transmitted from the brain and the spinal column through the genitals to the womb. There is more. The major component of semen is *pneuma,* a foamlike airy substance which contains the seed of the divine. Originating in the brain, semen is responsible for endowing the offspring with the essential human capacity for reason, for *logos.* Seed of generation, of intellectual ability, and of the divine element in the human species, semen confirms the innate superiority of male over female. For Aristotle, "the male provides the form and the principle of the movement; the female provides the body, in other words, the material;... the male provides that which fashions the material into shape.... Thus the physical part, the body, comes from the female and the soul from the male since the soul is the essence of a particular body" (*De gen. an.* 1.20.729a, 738b).[22]

Here in the *Oresteia, logos* and *mythos* usually posed in two different modes, make an alliance and interact to support each other. This alliance is, in fact, a microcosmic reflection of the larger alliance between male and female, new and old, secular and sacred, on which the trilogy relies for its conclusion. Through the myth of Athena's birth, theogony is recapitulated now in the new embryology, championed by the new generation of gods in the interests of a new justice. If theogony supports embryology, it itself is reaffirmed through the authority of the other. Through this union of *mythos* and *logos*, a new mythos is engendered, one that mounts a final successful assault on the power of the female and brings a new ending to the myth of matriarchy. Bamberger points out that "from [her] cursory study... women frequently are subjected to harsh outside controls because of their putative immorality.... And so it seems from myth that less tangible forces than biology [her unique ability and her important contribution to group survival normally celebrated in female puberty ritual but overlooked in myth] were brought to bear on the subversion of the female sex role.... The case against her was made out to be a moral one, divorced from the biology that might have given her sex priority under other circumstances."[23] Here in the *Oresteia* the attack is a double one — against the adulterous wife *and* the reproductive function of the female.

As Hillman remarks, since "embryology is a *logos* of beginnings, it will be influenced by creation mythemes," and "because theories of generation reflect the differences and union of opposites, these theories will be influenced by *coniunctio* fantasies. Perhaps still more fundamental are the fantasies which afflict the male in regard to the female when the male is observer and female the datum." And he goes on to point out that "we encounter a long and incredible history of theoretical misadventures and observational errors in male science regarding the physiology of reproduction. These fantastic theories and fantastic observations are not misapprehensions, the usual and necessary mistakes on the road of scientific progress; they are recurrent deprecations of the feminine phrased in the unimpeachable, objective language of the science of the period. The mythic factor recurs disguised in the sophisticated new evidence of the age."[24] Apollo is the first to initiate this trend. "The Apollonic fantasy of reproduction and female inferiority recurs faithfully in the Western scientific tradition" (Hillman 1972: 225).

Here at its inception *mythos* still plays a determining role and the *logos* of scientific argument is still rudimentary; copulation is equated with gestation in a false analogy. But for *mythos* and for *logos* the true model is social relations, and woman's new reduced biological function is a sophisticated translation of her social function, ratified by god and science. It is the patent absurdity of Apollo's argument that offends our own fully developed scientific sensibilities,[25] not the principle itself of biology (false or true) as a justification of ideology. The issue of whether anatomy is destiny is still very much alive.

The very terms of Apollo's argument bring together phallos and head in still another way, for the ending of the trilogy is also concerned with a shift in modes of action and behavior, as it charts a progression from obscurity to clarity. Representation of symbolic signs perceived as female activity gives way to the male *logos*. Repetition and incantation yield to dialectic. Even more, "this turning away from the mother to the father," as Freud observed, "signifies a victory of intellectuality over the senses... since maternity is proved by the evidence of the senses while paternity is a hypothesis based on inferences and premises."[26] A whole series of antitheses form about the polarization of male and female roles which can be tabulated as follows (although not all of them are treated in this essay):

Male	Female
Apollo	Erinyes
Olympian	Chthonic
Unbinding (will; salvation)	Bind ("Fate"; binding song)
Marriage (non-kin)	Kinship
Father	Mother
Law (court)	Ritual (altar)
Intention	Act
Odd (three; trilogy)	Even (two, tie, *lex talionis*)
Center	Limit (frontier, interior)
Greek	Barbarian
City	House
CULTURE	NATURE
Future (young)	Past (old)
Order	Chaos
Rule	Unruly (misrule)
Above	Below
Head-Phallos	Belly-Womb
Active	Passive
Creativity	Fertility
Reason	Unreason (sexuality; passion)
Light	Dark
Life	Death
Clarity (plain speaking)	Obscurity (riddle)

Intellect (paternity, inference) Senses (maternity, representation)
Positive   Negative

If the birth of Athena is necessary for Apollo's synthesis and Orestes' reincorporation into community, her pedigree and status are necessary for reaching any workable solution to the problem of the female who resists the encroachment on her prerogatives. Androgynous compromise, Athena is the benevolent answer to her opposite and doublet, Clytemnestra. Female born of male, she can ally herself with male interests and still display positive nurturant behavior. As deified female, child of Zeus, she can initiate authoritative religious and social change. But as female herself, she can serve too as model of the female. But not alone. For Athena and the Erinyes whom she has placated are not separate entities but complements, each of them virgins, each now charged with the fostering of the group, and together representing the reconciliation of the positive and negative elements of the female archetype on the transpersonal level. Both agree that female will be subordinate to male within the family in patriarchal marriage and that the family itself will be subordinate to the city. Both in turn shower the city with blessings of prosperity and fertility. Each is content with daughter status, for the father-daughter relationship is the purest paradigm of female dependence, while the oxymoron of virginal maternity promises fertility without its dangerous corollary of sexuality. Mother is denied but not denied.

Orestes had denied his mother by the act of matricide and sought a new birth at the male-centered *omphalos* of Delphi. That new birth was just a beginning that sent him further to another altar, Athena's altar, upon which he sat, embraced her image, and held on tight. She provided him with the salvation he had sought. The positive maternal figure, in fact, restored him to his father and freed him to claim his social and political identity based on a new embryology and a traditional theogony. Like Athena, he now belongs wholly to his father.

In the double movement of this last play, Aeschylus modifies and diminishes the role of Delphic Apollo as the sole arbiter of the Orestean dilemma in favor of a larger more inclusive transaction[27] that includes the allotment of prerogatives to the Erinyes — their old negative ones of vengeance, which are now defined and limited for the city's interest, and their new positive ones of benison and fosterage. The Hesiodic theogonic model is still operative, for Athena is both

182

porte-parole of Zeus and the living incarnation of the *nature* of his sovereignty and how he secured it. Her allotting of specific roles and functions is therefore a direct continuance of her father's work which was not to create the world but to organize and classify its components (Hes. *Theog.* 885) and to make accommodations between generations. If the *Oresteia* can be viewed, as I suggested at the beginning, as a gynecocentric document, as an inquiry into the nature and limits of feminine power, this last act completes the transference of the *political* power (along the lines of the myth of matriarchy), which Clytemnestra had brazenly claimed in the first play, to the *ritual* power of the female exemplified by the role assigned to the Erinyes in Athens.

From the anthropological perspective, the solution is perfectly consistent with the observable principle of patrilineality in which the male "transmits membership in the corporate descent group," while the female transmits "mystic potentialities, powers, or attributes" through the uterine tie.[28] From this same outlook, the complementarity of positive and negative femininity is readily understandable. As Harris observes, "the double association of women as mothers with life and nurturance on the one hand and with death and destructiveness on the other is certainly widespread and may be well nigh universal.... The mother-child nexus and other ties through women always and everywhere appear both bad and good precisely because they are at the opposite end of the scale from the authority of society" (1973: 157, 158). For Harris, this double association is confined to the two poles of Erinyes-Eumenides, while I would include Athena, the other and chief custodian of Athens, as the main representative of the positive side, the one who persuades the Erinyes to modify their malevolence. But Harris' perspective enables us to understand the choice of Athena to effect the pacification of the Erinyes, for if we follow the anthropological orientation, Athena is the truly positive female figure precisely because she has neither a uterine tie of her own nor does she herself create one. Free from any but symbolic maternal associations, she thus foreswears any matriarchal projects. In this sense, the *Oresteia* also judges and justifies Athena.

Oddly enough, the androgynous woman in power does not disappear but is reasserted and reaffirmed in her divine counterpart. The displacement of the issue upwards in this last play avoids the specifically human dilemma of the female in her dual role of mother (power) and wife (deference). It also effectively removes the psy-

183

chological issue from the human dilemma of a son who has killed his own mother by defining it as a social and cosmic problem and quite literally putting it in the laps of the gods. Only they can free him (as far as it is intellectually possible) from the irrefutable and often anguished fact of human existence that man is from woman born.

In the end, this new Aeschylean myth, like all myths, as Lévi-Strauss says, "perhaps explains nothing and does no more than displace the difficulty, but by displacing it, it appears at least to mitigate any logical scandal" (1964: 13). But Lévi-Strauss is interested in defining the objective functions of myth and myth-making in a society, not in confronting the potentially dysfunctional properties of myth for legitimating social and political ideology whose mythic basis is neither recognized nor acknowledged. Psychic impulses compel the creation of the myth, but once objectified and projected outward, the myth reinforces, legitimates, and even influences the formation of those impulses by the authoritative power of that projection, especially when it is embedded in a magisterial work of art. There is a continuing reciprocity between the external and internal, between individual psyche and collective ideology, which gives myth its dynamic life far beyond the static intellectual dimension. By uncovering the apparent "logic" that informs the myth, we can both acknowledge the indispensable role of myth and myth-making for human cognition and at the same time lay bare the operations by which it organizes and manipulates reality.

Princeton University

NOTES

* A first version of this paper was given at a conference on myth sponsored by the Comparative Literature Circle of the University of Florida in Tallahassee in January 1977 and a second one was presented to the Columbia University Seminar on Women and Society in December 1977. It forms part of a larger study on the female in Aeschylean drama. A portion of it was prepared under the auspices of a National Endowment for the Humanities Fellowship for Independent Study and Research in 1975-76. My thanks for helpful suggestions to Charles Segal, Marylin Arthur, Joseph Russo, John Peradotto, and James Zetzel. References to the *Oresteia* are from D. L. Page's edition of the Oxford Classical Text.

[1] The infidelity of Helen was the cause of a vengeance that brought disastrous results; it was a goddess Artemis who blocked the fleet at Aulis and demanded a virgin as the price of the expedition. It was the hatred left by the memory of this daughter sacrificed to paternal ambition and the jealousy aroused by the concubine in the service of his royal pleasure which excited the hatred of a mother and wife. Electra arms Orestes and his persecuting divinities were female, guardians of mother right. Finally, it was a woman, the daughter of Zeus to whom the judgment fell (Green 1969: 59).

[2] "An overwhelming misogyny accompanies the appearance of Clytemnestra everywhere. Agamemnon only names her in the *Iliad* in order to reject her. In the *Nekyia* (11.400), he hardly mentions Aegisthus and he burdens all women in general with the example of Clytemnestra; Odysseus should be careful of making too many concessions to his own wife! In the second *Nekyia* (24.201), he finds some comfort in the certainty that the transgression of Clytemnestra will weigh on the reputation of all, even the most irreproachable.... It is not possible and not useful to distinguish the different layers of interpolation here. The sentiment which inspired the first poet satisfied those who later enriched the diatribe thanks to two favorite themes of popular misogyny, that which never accuses a woman of anything without immediately extending the grievance of all the others, and which concludes in recommending to husbands to keep watch over their authority" (Delcourt 1959: 84 [tr. mine]).

[3] E.g., R. Y. Hathorn, *Tragedy, Myth and Mystery* (Bloomington and London 1962) 51, R. Lattimore, *Aeschylus: Oresteia* (Chicago 1953) 30. In more general terms, Thomson (1966) 45-46, Neumann (1954) 168.

[4] Bachofen (1861; 1967) insisted on the primacy of matriarchy, or more correctly, *Mutterrecht* (the law of women) in the early stages of cultural development. He designated his two main phases of this period as Aphroditic (hetairic) and Demetrian (matrimonial) with an aberrational stage of Amazonism. *Mutterrecht* represented the telluric, the material, and the feminine which gives way gradually in the development of civilization to the higher Uranian, spiritual, and masculine values. See also Delcourt (1959) 78-79.

[5] By matriarchy is meant the actual political and economic supremacy of women in a given culture, not matriliny or matrifocality. See the remarks of Delcourt (1959) 15, 77; also G. Thomson, *Studies in Ancient Greek Society* (New York 1965) who collects a vast amount of interesting material but whose conclusions are not generally accepted. See further S. Pembroke, "The Last of the Matriarchs: a Study in the Inscriptions of Lycia," *Journal of Econ. and Soc. Hist. of the Orient* 8.3 (1965) 217-47; "Women in Charge. The Function of Alternatives in Early Greek Tradition and the Ancient Idea of Matriarchy," *Journal of the Warburg and Courtauld Institute* 30 (1967) 1-35, "Locres et Tarente: Le rôle des femmes dans la fondation de deux colonies grecques," *Annales ESC* 25 (1970) 1240-70; Vidal-

Naquet (1970); and especially the discussion of M. Arthur, Review Essay, "Classics," *Signs* 2 (1976) 383-87.

[6] For ancient testimony on Omphale see Apoll. *Bibl.* 2.6.3; 7.8; Diod. Sic. 4.31; Ov. *Her.* 9.55 ff.; Soph. *Tr.* 247 ff.; Luc. *Dial. of Gods* 13.2; Plut. *Qu. Gr.* 45; Schol. to *Od.* 21.22; Hyg. *Fab.* 32. See also Bachofen (1967) 142, 216-27 (who makes interesting connections with Tanaquil, Dido, Cleopatra and others). The importance of Omphale's name is obvious; cf. Slater (1968) 379, Fontenrose (1959) 108-10.

[7] Clearchos proposes this principle in speaking of the Lycian "matriarchy" initiated by Omphale: Cl. ap. Ath. *Deip.* 5153-5156c, Wehrli, *Klearchos*[2] (Basel/Stuttgart 1969) fr. 43a. Cf. Hes. *Theog.* on Gaia's response to Uranos (154-72). See also the discussion in Bachofen (1967) 104-05, 141-42, whose views are consonant with his idealization of pre-Hellenic womanhood. See also M. Shaw, "The Female Intruder: Women in Fifth-Century Drama," *CP* 70 (1975) 255-66, who proposes a similar scenario for Greek drama, but who does not see the massive threat to society caused by female intrusion nor the implications of the male-female hierarchy.

[8] The same principle holds true for Deianeira in Soph. *Tr.* and Medea in Euripides' play despite the vast differences in characterization.

[9] The ode on monstrous women makes universal the force of *eros* which is *thelykrates, eros* that masters the female, but it refers also to the female who, under the influence of *eros*, will master men (sons, fathers, husbands). See also Winnington-Ingram (1948) 138, n. 76.

[10] For the psychological import of dragon combat with a maternal figure, see Neumann (1954) 152-69. For him Orestes' victory over the mother and the psychological "matriarchate" of female domination "has gone a stage further.... Here, the identification with the father is so complete that the maternal principle can be killed even when it appears, not in the symbolic form of the dragon, but as the real mother — and killed precisely because this principle has sinned against the father principle" (168). But at the end of the *Choephoroi,* this liberation has not been achieved.

[11] Green (1969) 74, Slater (1968) 189-90. The alimentary and sexual appetites of the female are already important features of the Prometheus-Pandora myth in Hesiod. See the excellent structural analysis of J. -P. Vernant, "Le mythe prométhéen chez Hesiode" in *Mythe et société en Grèce ancienne* (Paris 1974) 177-94.

[12] Van Gennep (1909; 1960) was the first to identify and formulate the three main stages in *rites de passage:* separation, liminality (or *marge*), incorporation (or aggregation). Victor Turner has brilliantly elaborated the socio-cultural functions of liminality (1967, 1969, 1974).

[13] Vidal-Naquet (1969; 1973), (1968), (1974). The *ephebeia* seems to have been in origin the equivalent of male puberty initiations attached to the tribal phratry and modified later to make boys into hoplite citizens. Our evidence is late, scanty, and transmitted by a secular source (Arist. *Ath. Pol*). The Spartan *krypteia* (to which the *ephebeia* bears certain marked resemblances) and the Cretan *agelai* conform even more closely to

traditional tribal initiations. Vidal-Naquet (1974: 157) declares that in the historical period "what was true of the Athenian ephebe on the level of myth is true of the Spartan *krypteia* on the level of practice." [tr. mine]. See also the remarks of Eliade (1958) 108-09. Vidal-Naquet in "Le 'Philoctète' de Sophocle et l'éphébie" in J. -P. Vernant and P. Vidal-Naquet, *Mythe et tragédie en Grèce ancienne* (Paris 1973) 159-84 argues for the ephebic status of Neoptolemus in Sophocles' *Philoctetes* and Jeanmaire (1939) for the initiatory motifs in the myth of Theseus (227-375). With the exception of Vidal-Naquet's interest in some of Orestes' ephebic traits (hunt, ruse), Orestes' connection with puberty rites has gone unmarked by classicists, as far as I know, despite the opening statement of *Cho.* 5 which emphasizes his age and status (although Brelich [1969: 242-44] recognizes some distinctive initiatory features in Euripides' *IT*). But Meyer Fortes, the noted anthropologist, alluding to another variant in the Orestean myth, easily recognizes the frame of reference. "What is significant for us in the Orestes story is that he murdered a kinswoman, that this kinswoman was his mother, and that his expiation was to mutilate himself by biting off a finger.... The parallels that leap to mind, for an anthropologist today, are other apparently irrational mutilations of the body carried out in the context of an overt or suppressed conflict between successive generations. We think... of the very widespread association of circumcision and other forms of mutilation with the initiation of youths and maidens into adulthood" (*Oedipus and Job in Western African Religion* [Cambridge 1959] 9-10).

Thomson (1966) 46-47 and M. Tierney, "The Mysteries and the *Oresteia*," *JHS* 57 (1937) 11-21, find an initiatory pattern in the trilogy but refer it respectively to the Eleusinian and Orphic mysteries. But these recurrent mystical allusions do not form the primary pattern. In this regard, we might note the connection between the Eleusinian Mysteries and the ephebes who played an important public role in the preliminaries. But their participation might have been due to their status as civic representatives (since they were separated from their families) or to their own initiatory status in another sphere. What can be said is that the general cluster of details of which I am speaking and will discuss further below was familiar to the Greek world through the scenario of the Eleusinian Mysteries, and for ethnology, mystery initiations everywhere are secondary elaborations of tribal initiations. For the argument that the Eleusinian Mysteries were indeed derived from Athenian tribal initiations, see D. Sabbatucci, *Saggio sul misticismo greco* (Rome 1965) 153, n. 30 and 177 ff.

[14] On the *Theogony* see N. O. Brown, *Hesiod's Theogony* (Indianapolis and New York 1953) 17. On the paradigmatic function of the prologue in the *Eumenides*, see, e.g., F. Solmsen, *Hesiod and Aeschylus* (Ithaca, N. Y. 1949) 21, 23, 64, 157-66; D. Clay, "Aeschylus' *Trigeron Mythos*," *Hermes* 97 (1969) 1-9; J. H. Finley, *Pindar and Aeschylus* (Cambridge, Mass. 1955) 277; and Ramnoux (1959) 139-43.

[15] For a thorough study of the recurrent details of the combat myth, see Fontenrose (1959).

[16] See Zeitlin (1966) 645-53, especially 653. After the completion of this study, I was given access to an unpublished dissertation (1976) by N. S. Rabinowitz, *From Force to Persuasion: Dragon Battle Imagery in Aeschylus' Oresteia*, which interprets (and sometimes overinterprets) the motif of dragon combat in exhaustive detail.

[17] Turner (1967) 96. "The symbolism attached to and surrounding the liminal *persona* is complex and bizarre. Much of it is modeled on human biological processes.... They give an outward and visible form to an inward and conceptual process. The structural 'invisibility' of liminal *personae* has a twofold character. They are at once no longer classified and not yet classified. Insofar as they are no longer classified, the symbols that represent them are, in many societies, drawn from the biology of death, decomposition, catabolism, and other physical processes that have a negative tinge.... The other aspect that they are not yet classified, is often expressed in symbols modeled on processes of gestation and parturition."

[18] Delcourt (1959) 97. "All the words which in Greek and Latin designate the piglet also designate the feminine organ, *porculus* as well as *choiros* and its diminutives, *choiriskos, choiridion,* all equivalents of *kteis.* Baudo on the back of a pig holds a loom comb, the *kteis. Orthagoriskos* and *orthagoras,* other names for piglet, signify to *aidoion* [the pudenda] (*Ann. Inst. Arch.* 15, pl. E, p. 80; sch. Aristph. *Eccl.* 915; cf. e.g., *Vesp.* 1364). The womb is called *delphys*; the suckling pig is called *delphax* which is probably the same word as *vulva.* The Latins call *porca* the projecting part of a ploughed furrow, and the tracer of the furrow, in the list of the twelve gods of the *Sacrum Cereale,* is called *Imporcitor.*" [tr. mine].

Delcourt (97-98) also points to analogous rites of palingenesis. Men believed dead were not reintegrated into the community until after a simulated rebirth (washing, swaddling, nursing) on account of which they were called *Deuteropotmoi* or *Hysteropotmoi.* There was a Roman rite which obliged those thought dead in a foreign land to reenter their houses through the chimney in the roof, not through the door (Plut. *Qu. Rom.* 5).

The most famous and detailed account of a man's return home after a long absence when it was not known whether he was dead or alive is, of course, the *Odyssey.* Several scholars have pointed to the general patterning of themes of death and rebirth, notably C. P. Segal, "Transition and Ritual in Odysseus' Return," *PP* 116 (1967) 321-42, who treats the recurrent motifs of sleep, the bath/purification, and threshold. In this context, I would emphasize the way in which Odysseus' reentry into the palace (Bk. 19) recapitulates the stages of the life cycle in a scene which E. Auerbach in his well-known study (*Mimesis* [Princeton 1953]) treated merely as a digression. To reclaim his adult status on Ithaca, Odysseus must begin again from birth and reconstitute his early history: (1) Eurykleia, his nurse, who "took him in her own hands when his mother first bore him"

(19.355), washes his feet and through the recognition of his scar recalls (2) his naming on the knees of his maternal grandfather when an infant (19.399-409) and (3) his killing of the boar at the age of puberty, which included the well-known initiatory feature of a mutilation of the body (i.e., the scar) (19.410-65).

[19] "One of the most important purposes of the puberty rites is to loosen the tie between boys and their mothers and to bind the novices to the society of men. This part of primitive education... is accomplished by drastic means. The strongest tie binding the child to the mother is, of course, the fact that she gave birth to him and his dependence resulting from that. To break it, the male child is supposed to die, to be killed and to be born by man again, by his father or a father-representative. This new or newborn being begins a fresh existence as an adult and as a member of his tribe.... It is essential to recognize this most significant feature of the initiation and its purpose of breaking the tie between boys and their mothers by pretending that the initiated are born again by men. This rebirth is significant in undoing birth from the mother"(Reik 1960: 123-24; cf. Eliade 1958: 7-10). Often the women are, in fact, duped into thinking their sons have died. Often they are required to mourn for their sons who have been taken away from them by ritually aggressive means and pretend not to recognize them when they return. (*Note that Orestes reports himself dead and that Clytemnestra does not recognize him*). In extreme cases, "the initiate is allowed to insult and even manhandle his mother in token of his emancipation from her tutelage" (Hottentot), or he "walks over his mother's body, deliberately stepping on her belly, and this gesture confirms his definitive separation from her (Papua)" (Eliade 1958: 30).

On rebirth from the male or attested to by male sponsors, see also Bettelheim (1954) 113-21, and generally, see Turner's account of Ndembu circumcision ritual (1962) and Eliade (1958) 27, on the importance of blood symbolism. Vidal-Naquet's (1974) remark is eminently relevant here. "The Athenian city is constituted on the exclusion of women, even as it is constituted, in other respects, on the exclusion of strangers and slaves. The only civic role of women consists in giving birth to citizens..." (154). However, the importance of autochthony (substitution of Earth as mother) in Athenian political ideology should not be overlooked.

[20] Delcourt (1959) 103, remarks that "the Greeks unanimously saw in Apollo the natural defender of the avenging son.... It is the image of the young god assisting the young man, his double.... Apollo of Delphi is a symbol, that of Delos tenderly associated with images of birth, has a totally different value. Delphi ignores Leto and represents the maternal power in its most terrible aspects [Pytho]." [Tr. mine.]

[21] See Reik (1960) 128-31 on the creation of Eve and his remarks on the analogous but different myth of the birth of Athena. It might be pointed out that the struggle of the male to control or usurp the female reproductive function is a repetitive motif in Greek myth. Zeus himself gives birth to Dionysus, the "twice born," from his thigh. In the preceding episodes in

the *Theogony*, Uranos attempts to control creation or begrudges female productivity by refusing to allow his children to be born, and, more importantly, himself creates alone from the blood and semen of his severed genitals. The latter is particularly relevant since Aphrodite, a female, and specifically, the principle of bisexual reproduction, is born from the essence of the male. Cronos swallows his children in imitation of pregnancy, but is forced to disgorge them, while Zeus goes one step further and swallows the mother and successfully gives birth to the daughter. As Vernant (1969: 106) remarks, "ce rêve d'une hérédité purement paternelle n'a jamais cessé de hanter l'imagination grecque," and see his discussion, 106-07.

²² See the discussion of Kuhns (1962) 45-49, the remarks of Delcourt (1959) 85, n. 1, Vickers (1973) 414-15, 636-43, and A. Peretti, "La teoria della generazione patrilinea in Eschilo," *PP* 49 (1956) 241-62 on the theory of patrilineal generation in Aeschylus.

Kuhns cites the observations of R. B. Onians, *The Origins of European Thought*² (Cambridge 1954) 108-09, on the likely connection of *engkephalos* and semen in the *Iliad* as evidence of an earlier Greek belief in the primacy of the male role in procreation, but such a belief does not deny the female's role, nor does it promulgate a scientific doctrine.

²³ Bamberger (1974) 279. Embryological speculation is not, of course, limited to the Western tradition. (For some examples, see, e.g., Barnes [1973] 65, E. Leach, *Rethinking Anthropology* [London 1966] 13-14, and Vickers [1973] 637-39 with bibliography.) Nor are beliefs pertaining to procreation necessarily linked to kinship systems (i.e., matriliny, patriliny). The denial of maternity, however, is unusual, as it is for other Greek embryological speculations which follow a less drastic course. See E. Lesky, *Die Zeugungs- und Vererbungslehren der Antike und ihr Nachwirken* (Wiesbaden 1951).

²⁴ Hillman (1972) 224-25. "The Apollonic view of the feminine appears to be inherent in the same structure of consciousness as the methods by which the fantasies are supposedly proven." For instance, von Leeuwenhoek, who invented the microscope, insisted he saw *homunculi* in the spermatozoa he viewed, and Leonardo, the father of modern embryology, drew, on the basis of data from anatomical dissections, *two* urethral passages, one for the seminal fluid and a second one for the *pneuma* or *aura seminalis* (222). See also Barnes (1973) 61-87.

²⁵ Hence the tendency by modern critics to discount the argument as "rhetorical," "meaningless," "frigid," "absurd," "tongue-in-cheek," "unproved speculation," and "parody," (see citations in Kuhns [1962] 45-46 and Vickers [1973] 414, 435, n. 47).

²⁶ Sigmund Freud (1958) 145. It seems fair to point out that Freud's view of the female as a mutilated male lies squarely within the Aristotelian doctrine of the woman as a deformity in nature. Moreover, his debt to Bachofen seems evident in the following passage from *Civilization and its Discontents* (New York 1930; 1961): "Women soon come into opposition

to civilization and display their retarding and restraining influence — those very women who, in the beginning laid the foundations of civilization by the claims of their love. Women represent the interests of family and of sexual life. The work of civilization has become increasingly the business of men, it confronts them with ever more difficult tasks and compels them to carry out instinctual sublimations of which women are little capable. Since a man does not have unlimited quantities of psychical energy at his disposal, he has to accomplish his tasks by making an expedient distribution of his libido. What he employs for cultural aims he to a great extent withdraws from women and sexual life. His constant association with men, and his dependence on his relations with them, even estrange him from his duties as a husband and father. Thus the woman finds herself forced into the background by the claims of civilization and she adopts a hostile attitude towards it."

27 It is generally agreed that the connection of Orestes with the founding of the Areopagus is Aeschylus' own invention. Delcourt (1959: 27-30, 103-13) also insists that he is the originator of the link between Delphi and Orestes, although others posit another and earlier "Delphic" version against which Aeschylus is reacting.

28 Harris (1973) 157. Ortner's remarks are even more precise. "The psychic mode associated with women seems to stand at both the bottom and the top of the scale of human modes of relating. The tendency in that mode is to get involved more directly with people and individuals and not as representatives of one social category or another; this mode can be seen as either 'ignoring' (and thus subverting) or 'transcending' (and thus achieving a higher synthesis of) those social categories, depending upon the cultural view for any given purpose. Thus we can account easily for both the subversive feminine symbols (witches, evil eye, menstrual pollution, castrating mothers) and the feminine symbols of transcendence (mother goddesses, merciful dispensers of salvation, female symbols of justice, and the strong presence of feminine symbolism in the realms of art, religion, ritual, and law). Feminine symbolism, far more often than masculine symbolism, manifests this propensity toward polarized ambiguity — sometimes utterly exalted, sometimes utterly debased, rarely within the normal range of human possibilities." "Is Female to Male as Nature is to Culture?" in M. Z. Rosaldo and L. Lamphere, edd., *Woman, Culture and Society* (Stanford 1974) 85-86.

REFERENCES

BACHOFEN, J. J. 1861; 1967. *Myth, Religion, and Mother Right.* London.

BAMBERGER, J. 1974. "The Myth of Matriarchy," in M. Z. Rosaldo and L. Lamphere (edd.), *Woman, Culture, and Society.* Stanford. 263-80.

BARNES, J. A. 1973. "Genetrix : Genitor : : Nature : Culture?" in J. Goody (ed.), *The Character of Kinship.* Cambridge. 61-73.

BETTELHEIM, B. 1954. *Symbolic Wounds, Puberty Rites and the Envious Male.* New York.

BRELICH, A. 1969. *Paides e Parthenoi.* Rome.

BURKE, K. 1952; 1966. "Form and Persecution in the *Oresteia*," [*Sew. Rev.* 60, 377-96] in *Language as Symbolic Action.* Berkeley.

DELCOURT, M. 1959. *Oreste et Alcméon.* Paris.

ELIADE, M. 1958. *Rites and Symbols of Initiation.* New York.

———————. 1963. *Myth and Reality.* New York.

FONTENROSE, J. 1959. *Python.* Berkeley and Los Angeles.

FREUD, S. 1939; 1958. *Moses and Monotheism.* New York.

GENNEP, A. L. VAN. 1909; 1960. *The Rites of Passage.* Chicago.

GREEN, A. 1969. *Un oeil en trop. Le complexe d'Oedipe dans la tragédie.* Paris.

GROSSMANN, G. 1970. *Promethie und Orestie.* Heidelberg.

Harns, G. 1973. "Furies, Witches, and Mothers" in J. Goody (ed.), *The Character of Kinship.* Cambridge. 145-59.

HILLMAN, J. 1972. *The Myth of Analysis.* Evanston, Illinois.

JEANMAIRE, H. 1939. *Couroi et Courètes.* Lille.

JONES, J. 1962. *On Aristotle and Greek Tragedy.* New York.

KUHNS, R. 1962. *The House, the City and the Judge.* Indianapolis and New York.

LÉVI-STRAUSS, C. 1969. *The Raw and the Cooked.* New York.

NEUMANN, E. 1954. *The Origins of Human Consciousness.* Princeton.

RAMMOUX, C. 1959. *La Nuit et les enfants de la Nuit dans la tradition grecque.* Paris.

REIK, T. 1960. *The Creation of Woman.* New York.

SLATER, P. 1968. *The Glory of Hera.* Boston.

THOMSON, G. 1966. *The Oresteia of Aeschylus* (with notes by W. Headlam) 2d ed. Text and Commentary. 2 vols. Amsterdam.

----------. 1946. *Aeschylus and Athens.* 2nd ed. London.

TURNER, V. 1962. "Three Symbols of *Passage* in Ndembu Circumcision Ritual: An Interpretation," in M. Gluckman (ed.), *Essays on the Ritual of Social Relations.* Manchester.

-----------. 1967. *The Forest of Symbols.* Ithaca and London.

-----------. 1969. *The Ritual Process: Structure and Anti-Structure.* Chicago.

-----------. 1974. *Dramas, Fields, and Metaphors.* Ithaca and London.

VERNANT, J. -P. 1969. "Hestia-Hermès: sur l'expression religieuse de l'espace et du mouvement chez les Grecs," in *Mythe et pensée chez les Grecs.* 2d ed. Paris. 97-158.

VICKERS, B. 1973. *Towards Greek Tragedy.* London.

VIDAL-NAQUET, P. 1968. "Le chasseur noir et l'origine de l'éphébie athénienne,"*Annales ESC* 23, 947-964. [Engl. version, *PCPhS* 194 (NS 14) 49-64; rev. version in Italian in M. Detienne, ed., *Il mito* (Rome 1976) 53-72].

-----------------. 1969; 1973. "Chasse et sacrifice dans l'*Orestie* d'Eschyle," *PP* 129; 401-25 (= J. -P. Vernant and P. Vidal-Naquet, *Mythe et tragédie en Grèce ancienne* Paris. 135-158).

-----------------. 1970. "Esclavage et gynécocratie dans la tradition, le mythe, l'utopie," in C. Nicolet (ed.), *Recherches sur les structures sociales dans l'antiquité classique,* Paris. 63-80.

-----------------. 1974. "Les jeunes: le cru, l'enfant grec et le cuit," in J. Le Goff and P. Nora (edd.), *Faire l'histoire: Nouveaux objets.* Paris. 137-168.

WINNINGTON-INGRAM, R. P. 1948. "Clytemnestra and the Vote of Athena," *JHS* 68. 130-47.

ZEITLIN, F. I. 1966. "Postscript to Sacrificial Imagery in the *Oresteia* (*Ag.* 1235-37)," *TAPA* 97. 645-53.

THE MENACE OF DIONYSUS: SEX ROLES AND REVERSALS IN EURIPIDES' BACCHAE

CHARLES SEGAL

GREEK TRAGEDY, LIKE GREEK MYTH and literature generally, presents a complex and ambivalent image of woman. As the one who bears and cares for children and tends house and hearth, she is at the center of what is secure, nurturing, life-giving; but in her passionate and emotional nature and the violence of her sexual instincts which she is felt as little able to control, she is regarded as irrational, unstable, dangerous. Hence she is seen as an integral part of the civic structure on the one hand, but also regarded as a threat to that structure on the other. In this aspect she is associated also with what is hostile or threatening to the organized and formed inner space of the city. She has her place within the sheltered inner domain of the house, but also has affinities with the wild, savage world of beasts outside the limits of the city walls.[1]

The Greek poets and tragedians return to this ambiguity again and again. The *Oresteia* of Aeschylus dramatizes the horror felt toward the act whereby the woman violently overcomes the man, the queen kills the king. A whole series of animal images stresses the inversion of civilized values inherent in such an act: the lioness defeats the lion, the cow destroys the bull. The *Trachinian Women* of Sophocles develops the grim paradox that the patient Deianeira has faithfully kept the house during the years when her husband, Heracles, has been off killing monstrous Hydras and Centaurs, but she has also kept hidden in the very depths or recesses (*mychoi*) of the house – that is, in the space belonging to and symbolic of woman – the deadly poison of the monstrous Hydra, given her as a love-charm by the lustful Centaur, Nessus.[2] In the *Hippolytus* the hero, when approached by the Nurse on Phaedra's behalf, cries out that women should not have human servants, but should dwell only with the savage "biting beasts who do not speak" (*Hipp.* 645-8).

Such women in tragedy threaten the polis not only because they are associated with the irrational forces of emotion and sexuality to which they are felt to be less resistant than men,[3] and not only because of the narcissism of the Greek male in the psychological mechanisms studied by Philip Slater,[4] but also because they are seen as closer to the basic biological processes of nature, parturition, lactation, menstruation. In their greater closeness to the rhythms of the natural world, they oppose the yearning for autonomy and independence from nature, the desire for that which neither comes into being nor passes away, which permeates all Greek thought, be it Homeric epic with its ideal of immortal glory, or epinician poetry with its deathless and radiant divine world which the victor touches through his moment of brilliant achievement, or Platonic philosophy with its concern for the unchanging One or the immutable Forms which stand above and beyond the changing particulars of our transient sense-world.

In woman too the Greek desires for clarity of definition, for clearly defined limits, meets a stumbling block. Her position between culture and nature, to which a number of scholars have pointed,[5] confuses the basic antinomies with which the Greeks demarcate the human, civilized world from the savage, chaotic, violent realm of the beasts "outside."[6]

In view of these ambiguities, one can understand the affinity that exists in Greek culture between the threatening aspects of Dionysus and the threatening aspect of women. Both are associated with the release of emotional energies which are usually controlled and channeled for the benefit of the order of the polis. Both occupy an ambiguous place between the human and the bestial realms and between civic order and the potential chaos of the natural world beyond the limits of the polis. Both too are connected with the processes of nature in its vital and hence uncontrollable, mysterious aspect.

A fundamental quality of Dionysus in Greek literature is his dissolution and confusion of basic polarities.[7] He is an Olympian god, but he appears in the bestial form of bull, snake, or lion. He has a place at the center of the civic religion (the Greater Dionysia of Athens being the most familiar example); yet his worship also involves ecstatic rites on the wild mountainside, performed at night by women carrying flaming torches. He is a male god, but he has the softness, sensuality, and emotionality which the Greeks generally associate with women. He is Greek, but he comes from barbarian Asia, escorted by a band of wild Asian women. He is a local Theban divinity, but he is also a universal "god of many names," whose power, as Sophocles says in the last ode of the *Antigone*, extends

196

from Italy to the East. He is neither child nor man, but occupies a position somewhere in between as the eternal adolescent. Through his connections with wine and with the life-giving liquids and moisture that nourish life, he is also connected with the biological processes of the natural world and specifically with the growth of new vegetative life.

Rationality, clear limits between human and bestial, independence of the biological processes of the life-cycle: these implicit ideals of the male-oriented polis are all challenged and called into question both by Dionysus and by women. Women and Dionysus are closely associated in several myths which involve threats to the polis and its values. Such, for instance, are the myths of the daughters of King Proetus of Tiryns, the daughters of Minyas of Orchomenos, King Lycurgus of Thrace. *Resistance* to the god seems to be a basic component of the Dionysiac myth.[8] It is as if the very nature of the god provoked a reaction of hostility in those who represented the male-centered authority of the polis. The particular historical circumstances from which such myths may derive doubtless reflect more general, deeper attitudes and anxieties.

In Sophocles' *Antigone* the heroine's opposition to the male-oriented rationalism of Creon's *polis* in the name of the blood-ties of the family and the honor due the dead also involves Dionysus. He appears in the first ode of the play as the god of the polis to whom the Thebans pray in gratitude for the salvation of their city. But the last ode, when Creon's proud constructions are about to disintegrate, presents a very different Dionysus, a divinity connected with the maternal Demeter (1120) and with the "chorus" of "fire-breathing stars" in the vast spaces of the heavens (1146-8) beyond the citizen "choruses" (cf. 1151-4 and 152-4) within the limits of the city's theater. Associated with the vital processes of nature, with women, and with madness, answering control over nature by sympathy with nature, reason by ecstasy, Dionysus' prominence in the *Antigone* adds another dimension to its male-female conflicts.

The function of Dionysus in the sexual antagonisms of the *Bacchae* is two-fold. On the civic or political plane, he represents a threat from outside to the stable order of the polis, a threat from the wild and the alien, the ecstasy of barbarian-seeming rites. In this respect Dionysus and his women followers endanger the civilized order which is embodied in the culture-hero Cadmus, founder of Thebes, and, more ambiguously, in his grandson, Pentheus, Cadmus' successor as king of Thebes. On the personal or private plane Dionysus embodies a threat to the psychological coherence and integration necessary for the successful passage in the life-cycle from childhood to adulthood. He is a threat to the rigidly masculine value-system which the young Pentheus, standing at the critical transition between adolescence and manhood,[9] feels that he must espouse with a vehement exclusiveness, as if to maximize the differentiation between the male world to which he aspires and the female elements both in himself and outside himself. Ironically, the very vehemence of that rejection of the female leads not to a successful passage to masculine status, but to the reverse, infantile regression and domination by the female in the form of the destructive mother.

Euripides, so often the critic of his society's accepted values, reveals the paradoxical truth that male identity is achieved not by rejection or violent domination of the female and of the "feminine" forms of experience associated with Dionysus, but by a more complex process of balance and integration. It would be rash to view Pentheus as a symbol of the Greek male in general. Yet, like Creon in the *Antigone*, he seems to embody a type of overreaction to feminine modes of experience which was not uncommon in this male-dominated society. His death by dismemberment, then, is not merely a poetic justice done to one who resists the god of fusion, but also a reflection of a psychological and social reality for the society as a whole. One-sided commitment to male-oriented values involves not merely a suppression of women, but also a fragmentation of the male psyche which represses a whole area of human experience and human emotionality. This society's extreme sexual differentiation, even with its preferential treatment of the masculine, is as inimical to male as to female psychic integration. The women become mad and leave the inner space which defines them and gives them their secure, if limited, identity; yet the men too suffer dismemberment.

What is perhaps ultimately tragic in Pentheus' fate, then, lies in the implicit recognition that the narrowly masculine orientation of this society is as destructive of male as of female self-realization. Its sharp division of sexual roles, symbolically concentrated in the figure of Pentheus, can lead not to wholeness, but only to disintegration. Pentheus' insistence on (and the polis' high valuation of) maleness, for example, restricts the mode of human association to the warrior-society of the hoplite band, with its rigid discipline, its hierarchical ranking of inferior and subordinate (cf. 721, 1046), its use of intimidation as a mode of social order (cf. 668-671), its competitive rivalry or "strife" (*eris*, 715). So structured, a society is closed to the kind of communion possible in the Dionysiac *thiasos* or "holy band" (cf. the untranslatable θιασεύεται ψυχάν in 75, "mingles his spirit with the holy band" [Kirk], which denotes "the inward feeling of unity with the *thiasos* and through it with the god" [Dodds]). Unable to envisage this spontaneous fusion and communion of the total *thiasos*, Pentheus can imagine it only as the setting for isolated, individualistic sexual acts, where, incidentally, the woman still remains subordinate to the male she "serves" (221-225):

In the middle of the sacred bands (*thiasoi*) bowls of wine stand full, and one by one they go slinking off each to different places in the wilderness (ἄλλην δ' ἄλλοσ' εἰς ἐρημίαν 222) and serve the beds of men. The pretext is that they are maenads making sacrifice, but in fact they put Aphrodite before their Bacchic god.

What is true of the relation between man and man applies also to that between man and nature, for as we shall see Pentheus' male warrior code implies the rigid separation between man and nature by the barriers of gates and towers which the hoplites defend, the absolute antithesis to the Maenads' free crossing between city and wild and their open receptivity to the gentle gifts of the earth as of their god (704-711).

Pentheus' death, then, reflects not merely the triumph of Dionysus nor even the defeat of the male hoplite values, but the failure of the society as a whole, the failure of the great Athenian experiment which seemed so brilliant two or three generations before. Old and self-exiled, viewing the Greek polis from the remote and alien court of King Archelaus in Macedonia, Euripides was in a position to contemplate such a possibility even more radically than in any of his earlier works. In a world dominated by sexual (and other) dichotomization rather than complementation, neither men nor women can achieve a fully integrated identity. The city fails in one of its most basic functions, to realize the full human potential of its citizens. It can only violently reject the god whose nature it is to bypass such dichotomies; his arrival brings dismemberment, destruction, confusion of identity to *both* sides, to men and women alike.

In this respect the *Bacchae*, like the *Antigone* and the *Trachiniae*, exemplifies the capacity of tragedy to stand outside the familiar norms and the remarkable ability of Athenian culture to institutionalize a criticism of those norms, to find a socially acceptable frame which allows the anti-culture, the suppressed values and drives, to emerge and find a coherent, articulate shape. The Dionysiac myth of the *Bacchae* and the Dionysiac form of tragedy here work together to enable this "anti-culture" to come forth from unconscious into conscious knowledge. In the myth, as in the aesthetic form of tragedy which frames it and heightens its expressive possibilities, dichotomy collapses into fusion, separation yields to incorporation, and absolute division gives way to ambiguity. By uniting symbolically and analogically the various areas of Dionysus' powers (god of religious ecstasy, wine, vegetative growth, fusion with nature, illusion, tragedy) and by concentrating them upon the exaggerated masculine and civic values of Pentheus, the *Bacchae* also reveals the poet's self-conscious awareness of the radical subversiveness of his tragic form. With the repressed energies of women the tragedian also liberates the emotions, the types of religious experience, the forms of interpersonal relations and relations to external reality, the modes of verbal, gestural, and aesthetic expression which receive only limited or marginal recognition in the dominant cultural pattern.

Confusing the boundaries between youth and adult and between male and female, Dionysus embodies all that Pentheus has repressed in defining himself as the authoritarian king of Thebes: in Freudian terms, the sexual energy which now appears in prurient, perverted form – the desire to observe the Maenads secretly as they sleep; or, in Jungian terms, the *anima* or female half of his psyche which he has also denied in favor of a narrow masculine ethic of discipline, martial force, restrictive rationalism. For these reasons Pentheus cannot accept Dionysus and his rites, reacts violently against him often in terms of bitter attacks against women and what he takes to be the lechery and debauchery of his women-followers, and is destroyed – literally torn apart – by the female component of the city and of himself, rent by his mother, Agave, her sisters, and their followers, the women of Thebes in a Dionysiac rite beyond the walls of the polis on the wild mountainside.

200

The adolescent Dionysus of the *Bacchae*, as also of the vase-paintings of the latter half of the fifth century, has the force and energy of a man, but the grace, charm, soft beauty and seductiveness of a girl.[10] For Greek tragedy that combination of male and female characteristics is menacing and ominous rather than potentially helpful and harmonious.[11] Dionysus' ancestry too combines both sexes in a mysterious double birth, for he is the child of a mortal mother, but is actually born from the "male womb" of his immortal father (*Ba.* 90 f., 526 ff.). His mortal mother, Semele, also has associations with the earth and may have been the survival of a pre-Greek earth-goddess,[12] whereas his father, Zeus, is the Olympian par excellence, the god of the sky and regulator of celestial phenomena.

The play links these ambiguities within Dionysus to those within Pentheus. Pentheus too occupies an ambiguous place between the civilized world and the wild and between two "fathers." One of these, Cadmus (actually his maternal grandfather), is a founder of cities and a vanquisher of monstrous earth-born serpents.[13] The other, the "biological" as opposed to the "cultural" father, Echion, is himself an earth-born monster, an opponent of the Olympian gods (cf. 538-44).[14] For Pentheus, as for Dionysus too, as we shall see, the relation with his mother is fraught with ambivalence and violence. And finally, like Dionysus, he too stands at an ambiguous point of transition between childhood and manhood, between the softness, sensuality, and unreliability of adolescence and the firmness of the adult male warrior, disciplined, steadfast, and unmovable in his hoplite armor.

As Dionysus vacillates between Olympian and mortal birth, so Pentheus vacillates between autochthony and normal birth from a woman. As the son of Echion, Pentheus is "earth-born," γηγενής (996 f = 1015 f.). His links to autochthonous birth may be connected to an implicit denial of woman's role in birth, and hence to a denial of sexuality itself. Hence he feels that violence toward women which makes it impossible for him to achieve his adult male status and to fulfill his kingship of Thebes, for the "Earth-born Men" are notoriously violent. Elsewhere in the Theban cycle they appear as the destroyers of cities, i.e., as the threat to just that institution which Pentheus the King is supposed to protect.[15]

Taken back into his mother's arms (cf. 968-70) and into his mother's body in the rite of *omophagia*, the "raw-eating" of the hunted victim in the Dionysiac rite (cf. 139 f.), Pentheus undergoes a violent "rebirth" which contrasts with the successful "rebirth" of Dionysus, torn from his mother's body and transplanted to the "male womb" of his immortal father's thigh. Dionysus' status as a god outside of the cycles of generational passage and mortal birth reflects a deficiency of connection with the mother, at least on the biological level. It is in fact his attempt to reestablish this maternal bond by asserting his links with Thebes that produces the disaster for the human protagonists.[16] Pentheus, on the other hand, for all his defiance of woman, suffers from an excessive closeness to the mother: he never fully escapes the maternal bond. As is characteristic of Euripidean (and other) tragedy, we are left oscillating between the two extremes without a stable balance or point of rest. Being proven the son of his biological father, Echion, places Pentheus in the realm of the beasts and leaves him totally exposed to the beast-like aspect of his own mother who rends and devours him as if he were a beast. But being proven the son of his father, Zeus, establishes Dionysus in the honor within Thebes at the price of destroying the ruling family and exiling the founder of the city himself, metamorphosed into the shape of the monstrous serpent that he slew as a preliminary to the founding act itself.

Beside Pentheus' chthonic ancestry from Echion, there is also an Olympian ancestry too, namely the marriage of Cadmus and Harmonia, his maternal grandparents. But the result of this union of a goddess with a mortal is, ultimately, unhappy, as is usually the case with goddess-mortal unions.[17] Aside from Semele (whose union with Zeus can hardly be considered a success, at least from her point of view), the other three daughters of this marriage all lose their sons, two by their own hand (Ino, Agave). Even this Olympian side of Pentheus' ancestry has its sinister aspect, however, for Euripides reminds us that it has its origins in Ares, the god of war (cf. 1332) and in one tradition the father of the dangerous serpent that guards the waters of Dirce.[18]

The action of the play constitutes a kind of *rite de passage* for both god and the mortal. Here both have to come to terms with the question of birth from a woman (Semele, Agave) or birth from something else ("male womb" of Zeus, "earthborn" through Echion). The two situations have diametrically opposite results. Entering as a nameless "Stranger," Dionysus exits as a proven god, his Olympian patronymic firmly asserted (1341, 1343). Beginning as the securely ensconced king of Thebes, Pentheus exits from city to wild as the scapegoat and beast-victim, deprived of every aspect of his masculine identity, dressed as a woman and returned to his mother, a helpless and confused child who can only call out his mother's name, completely impotent before her power (1118-1121).

Because Pentheus is both an individual figure and an embodiment of the civic order of Thebes, his tragedy involves more than just a single man's crisis of identity. It implies also a vision of the political and cosmic order which centers upon him as king. Through Dionysus' dissolution of boundaries — boundaries between parts of the self as well as between parts of the social and natural order — the disintegration of personal identity is both causally parallel and typologically homologous to the disintegration of the social structures. The analogy between the internal and external or personal and social disintegration is facilitated by the fact that both the personal and the social order that Pentheus embodies have the same basis. His emotional coherence and the coherence of the civic order which he strives to defend rest upon the imposition of the sharpest possible dichotomy between male and female and upon the violent repression of the latter if it threatens to get out of control, as it does upon the arrival of Dionysus and his Maenads.

In neither the inner realm of his palace nor the outer condition of the city can he tolerate the possibility that women, bearers and symbols of free sexual instincts and uncontrolled emotion, should run around free or, quite literally, "loose" (e.g. 445). The palace is a symbol both of Pentheus' soul and Pentheus' political authority, that is, of both the internal and external dimensions of his authoritarian and repressive character. It is significant that the scene which immediately follows upon the destruction of the palace, real or illusory — the so-called "palace miracle" (576-603) — presents a microcosm of Pentheus' failure in the whole play. He attempts to fetter, control, and shut away Dionysus in the safe dark places of the palace (609-21), as he had shut him away in the dark, locked spaces of his psyche and as he would shut away in the workrooms of his palace the Maenads who would run freely on the mountains. In the parode they sang a joyful ode on leaving "the looms and shuttles" under the goad of the god's ecstasy (116-19). But Pentheus' threat is to sell them as slaves or to possess them as "servants for his looms" (ἐφ᾽ ἱστοῖς δμωΐδας κεκτήσομαι 514). In both cases, they are both enclosed as "property" (cf. *kektēsomai* 514) within the house and become part of the commercial structure of the city, which of course is in the hands of men. But in the second half of the scene with Dionysus after the "palace miracle," the god eludes him. He cannot be "bound" or "enclosed" (cf. 642-3), but "flees the bonds" (648).

The attempt and failure of Pentheus to "bind" the god encapsulated in this brief scene before the palace (604-659) are then projected on the larger screen of the civic and political order when the messenger enters with the news of the Maenads who are in fact running loose on Cithaeron (660 ff.). The link between these two dimensions of Pentheus' repressiveness toward Dionysus and his women – palace and city, self and polis – is already established in the closing exchanges of this scene: Pentheus' language of binding and enclosing, hitherto restricted to imprisoning Maenads and Dionysus within the palace, shifts to the wider spatial frame of enclosing the *city* by walls and towers against the god and his followers (653-4):

> *Penth.*: I order you to lock every tower in a circle.
> *Dionys.*: Why? Do not gods overleap walls too?[19]

Pentheus' identity-crisis, as we have suggested, revolves about the crucial passage from youth to full-fledged hoplite warrior, a passage which also involves leaving behind his mother for the totally male society of warriors. Hoplite status, however, also involves an attitude of mind, a quality of discipline and stability which stands at the opposite extreme from the female emotionality associated with Dionysus. Dionysus' rites, as old Teiresias points out at the beginning, include both young and old and potentially (as Teiresias and Cadmus' participation also implies) both men and women. But exclusiveness comes increasingly to pervade Pentheus' image of the social order: a warrior-society of obedient, disciplined male citizens in hoplite ranks who protect the enclosed, walled space of the city in which the women are safely secluded and secured.

From the very beginning of the play, however, these hoplite values are directly threatened by Dionysus. Near the end of the prologue the god warns (50-52):

> ἢν δὲ Θηβαίων πόλις
> ὀργῇ σὺν ὅπλοις ἐξ ὄρους βάκχας ἄγειν
> ζητῇ, ξυνάψω μαινάσι στρατηλατῶν.

> But if the polis of the Thebans in anger with arms seeks
> to drive the Bacchants from the mountain, I shall join
> battle leading my maenad army.

The juxtaposition of "anger" and "arms" (*orgē, hopla*) and of "maenads" and "lead an army" (*mainasin stratēlatōn*) creates two opposing, but complementary reversals. The first discordantly associates the steadiness of the hoplites, representatives of calm, firm discipline, with the passion of "anger." The second phrase confers upon the disordered "mad women" (the literal meaning of *mainades*) the military order of soldiers who follow and obey a general (*stratēlatōn* 52).

Teiresias' sophistic discourse on the powers and attributes of Dionysus develops this paradox, but in a remote, theoretical perspective. Remarking that Dionysus has "a share in Ares," god of war, he points out that the panic fear and madness (*phobos, mania*) which Dionysus can inspire "flutters an army with fright when it is under arms (*hopla*) and in its ordered ranks (*taxeis*) before it even touches the spear" (302-5). The great central narrative scene which describes the Maenads on Mount Cithaeron finally fulfills these hints. Here the men of Thebes are filled with the passion of "anger" (*orgē*) as they "rush into arms" (*hopla*) (757-8), whereas the women, initially at least, have the "moderation" or *sōphrosynē* (*sōphronōs*, 686) and "good order" (*eukosmia* 693). They proceed in ordered ranks (*tetagmenē* 723; cf. *taxeis* 303) and follow Dionysus' command to follow him "armed" (*hoplismenai*, 733) with the thyrsus, a clear echo of the god's threat to lead an "army" of Maenads in the prologue (50-2).[20] In the sequel the hoplite spear or lance (*lonchōton belos* 761) proves futile, as Teiresias, in his very different context had hinted that it would (cf. *lonchai* 304). The Maenads, "shooting forth their thyrsuses from their hands" (762, where the inverted phallic imagery is obvious) turn the male warriors "to flight" (*phygēi* 763), "women (defeating) men" 764). Pentheus' response to this news is a flurry of martial commands in elaborate language (780-4), culminating in the pointed admission of the violent sexual threat to his masculine and martial authority, "Nothing can exceed this if what we suffer we suffer from women" (785-6).

In this scene, as even more dramatically in the second long recitative in the play, the account of Pentheus' death at the hands of the Theban Maenads, women are not only warriors, but also hunters. Thus they usurp the two activities which cross-culturally are most often the prerogatives of men. In this play, moreover, they are the "hunted" who soon turn into the "hunters" (cf. 732), just as the proud and violent king becomes their helpless beast of prey.[21]

Pentheus' first response to the news of the Maenads on the mountain, as we have seen, is in terms of gates and towers, the enclosures, guarded by male warriors, which enforce the separation between the city and what lies outside. His next command, now directly after the messenger's account of the Maenads, is "Go to the Electran gates" (780-1). But of course it is in the nature of Dionysus and his followers to destroy such boundaries, both literally and metaphorically. Here Pentheus' resistance to Dionysus and his violent assertion of sexual differentiation suddenly gives way to the willingness to be dressed as a Maenad himself, a total confusion of the boundaries of the self and of sexual identities, once the god releases his repressed desire to see the Maenads.

The final destruction of Pentheus also involves both an inversion of sexual values and a destruction of gates. When he has been torn apart by his mother, Agave, a huntress and a warrior both, she, as leader of the Maenad band whom Pentheus would have kept "outside" by means of gates, towers, and bonds, now passes "within these gates" (1145) "to the palace" of the king (1149; cf. 1165), shouting to her "fellow-huntsman," Dionysus. She calls Dionysus not only "fellow-hunter," but also "victorious athlete" (*kallinikos* 1147), another inversion of exclusively male prerogatives. Pentheus, we recall, who scorned Dionysus for long hair unsuited to "wrestling" (455) admitted at his point of crucial change or confusion of sexual identities that he was "caught in a hold from which he can't escape" (800) and was brought to a "contest" where the god will be "the victor" (975).

When Agave does finally enter the palace, bearing the prey of her grisly "hunting," her first words call attention to those very civic boundaries which Dionysus and his women followers have violated and confused: "O you who dwell in the lovely-towered town (*kallipyrgon asty*) of Theban earth, come and behold this prey which we, the daughters of Cadmus have hunted..." (1202-4). She then reverses sexual values in the martial rather than the spatial sphere as she goes on to extol hunting with bare hands over the use of nets or spears (1205-8). She employs once more a compound of the word *lonchē*, spear, which was prominent in the sexual reversals in the area of war earlier (cf. 304, 762). She would affix the head of Pentheus to the palace in words that recall the attack upon a city (1213 f.), the culminating ironical destruction of the civic values of male warfare, fortifications, and boundaries that Pentheus asserted.

As Agave affixes this prey of her "hunting" as a trophy to the palace walls, so she also exhibits deeds of "daring" (*tolmē*) which properly belong to men: "Coming to the town within these walls," says Cadmus, "I learned of my daughter's deeds of daring (*tolmēmata*, 1222-3). "Daring," *tolmē*, was Pentheus' boast when, disguised as a maenad, he was going to spy on their rites (961-2): "Lead me through the middle of the Theban land, for I am the only man (*anēr*) who dares (*tolmōn*) to do this." Now, however, the male achievements which he should have won are transferred to the mother who has destroyed her son. It is she, then, who "boasts" of her "excellence" to her father in terms which, within the usual norms of the Greek family, would be appropriate to the son, not the daughter (1233-40):

> Father, you can now make the greatest boast, that you
> have sown by far the best daughter of all mortals. I mean
> them all, but me especially, who have left the shuttles
> at the loom and come to greater things, the hunt of beasts
> with my hands. And I bring this now in my arms, as you
> see, taking this prize of excellence (*aristeia*), to be hung
> up in your halls.

The coveted "prize of excellence" or *aristeia* (1239) is just what the young warrior should have obtained as the mark of his sure passage from boyhood to manhood. But now it is the daughter, not the son, who gives it to the father; and that very "prize" is the head of the son savagely killed and torn as a wild beast by the mother. Thus the differences between male and female, between kindred and enemy, between child and adult, and between beast and man are all collapsed simultaneously in this violent triumph of the Dionysiac religion.

These inversions of sexual roles go even farther in the next exchange. As Agave claims the "prize of excellence" (*aristeia*) of the successful hero-warrior and boasts to her father like a young man who has passed his first trials, so conversely she speaks as the father whose "character" the son should imitate. Still under the influence of the Dionysiac madness she utters a wish that Pentheus "might be a good hunter, resembling his mother's character (*tropoi*) when he set out hunting wild beasts with the young men of Thebes" (1252-5). "Young men," *neaniai*, reminds us again of Pentheus' adolescent status (cf. *neanias*, also at a point of crucial generational transition, in 974). But now it is the mother, who has just led "young women," *neanides* (1079), against men on the mountain and has replaced the father in forming the "character" which the young man should show in adulthood. The feast that would celebrate the boy's inscription into his fratry or male confraternity by his father is now not a feast of joyful celebration (cf. 1242, 1246 f.), but a perverted rite where the quarry to be eaten is the youth himself.

Some semblance of order is recovered when the paternal authority of Cadmus calls his daughter back to sanity.[22] The brief dialogue reestablishes Agave in the internal spaces of the house and reasserts her dependencies on its male members, husband, father, son, after the threatening autonomy of the Dionysiac release from authority (1273-6):

Cadm.: To what house did you go in marriage?
Ag.:   You gave me to one of the Sown Men, as they say, Echion.
Cadm.: What child was then born for your husband in the house?
Ag.:   Pentheus, from the union of his father and myself.

Agave still finds it hard to grasp this collapsing of inner and outer space, house and wild, Thebes and mountain, that her madness has encompassed. "Where did he die," she asks, "in the house or in what places?" (1290). Cadmus' answer, "There, where the dogs once tore apart Actaeon" (1291), associates Pentheus with another adolescent whose generational passage failed through sexual immaturity and a problematical encounter with female sexuality. Like Pentheus, Actaeon sees what he should not see and meets the death of a beast through a female figure, Artemis, whose place is in the wild, a goddess who, like Dionysus, draws women away from their role as wife and mother in the house to the wild forests.

Agave's Dionysiac experience is hardly a real liberation. At the end she is left totally bereft of any of the defining and sustaining structures of her life. Like her father Cadmus, who goes off to lead barbarian hordes against Greek cities in the form of a monstrous serpent, she is deprived of country, city, house, and its sheltering inner spaces (cf. 1366, 1367-70). She has no place in the wild either, and she feels only repugnance for Mount Cithaeron and the bacchantic rites performed there (1382-7).

As all the boundaries dissolve, Agave, not unlike Phaedra in the *Hippolytus*, is seen as both the god's instrument of vengeance and his victim. The joyful "sharing with" of the Dionysiac experience (e.g. 726 f.) becomes the sharing of exile and suffering (cf. συμφυγάδες 1382).

Speaking of the psychological functions of the cult of Dionysus Philip Slater[23] suggests that

> it provided the ultimate fantasy solution to the torment
> which sex antagonism occasioned in Greek life by elimi-
> nating the exaggerated differentiation imposed by culturally
> defined sex roles.

Yet what tragedy gives us is not the solution to these tensions, but their dramatic representation in the most extreme and uncompromising terms. The social function of myth and cult may be to mediate these polarities, as Lévi-Strauss thinks, or to provide a solution to deeply felt emotional conflicts, as Slater suggests. But the function of myth as recast in tragedy is to strip away the mediations and expose the conflict in its most absolute form.[24] The "problem of the *Bacchae*," then, has no resolution; and the power of the tragedy lies in the vehemence with which the two sides clash and in the unmitigated horror of the wreckage that emerges from that encounter. Neither young nor old, neither men nor women, neither the yielding nor the recalcitrant are spared. However useful Slater's formulation may be for understanding the social and psychological function of the cult of Dionysus, it does not do justice to the suffering and violence of Euripides' play. Here equilibrium is not restored; we are left with a sense of total disorientation: exile, suffering meted out far beyond what the offense seemed to merit, cruel and distant gods who liberate men and women from the limitations of their ordinary consciousness, but at the price of also releasing their most destructive impulses.

Euripides vividly dramatizes the conflicts created by Dionysus' presence in the polis, the release of the emotional and irrational forces so closely associated with women. In Bacchylides' account of the myth of the maddened daughters of Proetus, the paternal figure can appease the angry goddesses with sacrifices and temples, and the girls can be brought back within the framework of house and city not much the worse for their wanderings in the Arcadian wilderness.[25] But in the tragedy even the paternal figure is exiled and brutalized; and the irrational forces which woman is felt to embody and contain have to run their fearful course until house and city and the women themselves are overwhelmed by the disaster.[26]

Brown University

NOTES

[1] See Jean-Pierre Vernant, "Hestia-Hermès: sur l'expression religieuse de l'espace et du mouvement chez les Grecs," *Mythe et pensée chez les Grecs*[3] (Paris 1974) 1.131 ff. See also Froma I. Zeitlin, "Ritual, Symbolic, and Expressive Behavior in the Women of Aeschylus," sections I and IV (forthcoming).

[2] See Charles Segal, "Mariage et sacrifice dans les *Trachiniennes* de Sophocle," *AC* 44 (1975) 35-36 and "Sophocles' *Trachiniae*: Myth, Poetry, and Heroic Values," *YCS* 25 (1976) 126 ff.

[3] Male lust, of course, also receives its due share of responsibility in Greek tragedy: cf. Euripides, *Hippol.* 966 ff.

[4] Philip Slater, *The Glory of Hera* (Boston 1968) and "The Greek Family in History and Myth," *Arethusa* 7 (1974) 9-44, with the useful caveat in Helene P. Foley's review, *Diacritics* 5.4 (1975) 31-36 and Marilyn B. Arthur's critique, "Review Essay: Classics," *Signs* 2.2 (Winter 1976) 395-397.

[5] For example Sherry B. Ortner, "Is Female to Male as Nature is to Culture?" in M. Z. Rosaldo and L. Lamphere, *Woman, Culture, and Society* (Stanford, Calif. 1974) 67-88, especially 73 ff.; also M. Z. Rosaldo, "Woman, Culture, and Society: A Theoretical Overview," *ibid.*, 30 ff.

[6] See Charles Segal, "The Raw and the Cooked in Greek Literature: Structure, Values, Metaphor," *CJ* 69 (1974) 289-308, especially 296 ff.

[7] See, *inter alia,* Walter F. Otto, *Dionysus, Myth and Cult* (1933), transl. R. B. Palmer (Bloomington, Ind. 1965) 110 ff. and 120 ff.; R. P. Winnington-Ingram, *Euripides and Dionysus* (Cambridge 1948) 176-177; René Girard, *La violence et le sacré* (Paris 1972) 181 ff.; P. Vicaire, "Place et figure de Dionysos dans la tragédie de Sophocle," *REG* 81 (1968) 355-356; L. Gernet, *REG* 66 (1953) 392-393.

[8] See Otto (preceding note) 71 ff.; Girard (preceding note) 197-200; Henri Jeanmaire, *Dionysos* (Paris 1951) 139, 142 ff. (on the *Bacchae*), 201 ff.

[9] Pentheus is repeatedly called a "young man," *neanias* (274, 975, 1254), and his passage from youth to adulthood is stressed throughout the play,

a point which I hope to develop elsewhere. See also A. J. Podlecki, "Individual and Group in Euripides' *Bacchae*," *AC* 43 (1974) 155. Though Pentheus is not literally an adolescent, he reenacts the emotional and archetypal experience of the passage from adolescence to maturity. In psychological terms, he is fixated at the adolescent stage of personal development.

[10] For the change from the virile bearded Dionysus of black-figure vase-paintings to the more youthful, softer god of the latter half of the fifth century, see Jeanmaire (above, note 8) 155.

[11] Clytaemnestra's "man-counseling heart" is the most familiar example: Aeschylus, *Agam.* 11; see also Zeitlin (above, note 1) section IV. For the reverse see Euripides, *Electra*, 932 ff. and 948 ff.

[12] See Otto (above, note 7) 59 ff. for this theory and its uncertainties.

[13] Pentheus calls Cadmus "father" (*pater*, 251, 1322), as Cadmus calls him "child" (*pais* or *teknon*: 330, 1308, 1317). As culture-hero, Cadmus slays the serpent that guards the spring of Dirce and makes possible the founding of the city: see J. Fontenrose, *Python* (Berkeley and Los Angeles 1959) 306-320 and Francis Vian, *Les origines de Thèbes: Cadmos et les Spartes* (Paris 1963), 94-113, especially 105 ff.

[14] For the sinister significance of Echion and Pentheus' "earth-born" ancestry see Fontenrose (preceding note) 316-317, Winnington-Ingram (above, note 7) 79 and 181, Marilyn Arthur, "The Choral Odes of the *Bacchae* of Euripides," *YCS* 22 (1972) 171-175. The dangerous serpent, from whose teeth the "earth-born Sown Men" are born, is also earth-born or *gēgenēs*: see Fontenrose, 308 and Vian (preceding note) 29 and 106-109.

[15] See Aeschylus, *Septem* 424 ff.; Euripides, *Phoenissae* 128-130, 1131.

[16] In the prologue (line 41) Dionysus gives his desire to vindicate his mother's name as one of his reasons for coming to Thebes.

[17] See, for example, Sarah Pomeroy, *Goddesses, Whores, Wives, and Slaves* (New York 1975) 9 ff.

[18] See Vian (above, note 13) 106-109; Arthur (above, note 14) 173-174.

[19] For the importance of architectural motifs in the play see William C. Scott, "Two Suns over Thebes: Imagery and Stage Effects in the *Bacchae*," *TAPA* 105 (1975) 339 ff., especially 341.

[20] See Richard Hamilton, "*Bacchae* 47-52: Dionysus' Plan," *TAPA* 104 (1974) 139-149; Podlecki (above, note 9) 150-151.

[21] For hunting and its reversals see Winnington-Ingram (above, note 7) 94 ff. and 106 ff.; Otto (above, note 7) 108-109; Scott (above, note 19) 339 with the further literature cited there in note 9; G. S. Kirk, *The Bacchae by Euripides* (Englewood Cliffs, N.J. 1970) 13-14.

[22] For other aspects of the awakening scene see Winnington-Ingram (above, note 7) Chapter 10.

[23] Slater (above, note 3) 283-284.

[24] See, for instance, Girard (above, note 7) 196: "La tragédie ne parvient à

trouver son équilibre nulle part, elle n'a pas de lieu où elle puisse s'installer. De là son incohérence féconde, face à la cohérence stérile de tant de schèmes intellectuels et esthétiques irréprochables."

[25] Bacchylides 11.95-112. In Bacchylides' version the madness is sent by Hera, but elsewhere it comes from Dionysus: see Apollodorus 2.2.2, and the remarks of A. Henrichs, *ZPE* 15 (1974) 300 f., à propos of Hesiod, frag. 37.15 M-W.

[26] A version of this paper was presented at the "Berkshire Conference on Women's Studies" at Bryn Mawr College in June, 1976. I thank especially Professor Froma Zeitlin and Professor Joseph Russo for friendly and helpful discussion. Some of the preliminary research for this study was done during my tenure of an American Council of Learned Society's Fellowship (1974-1975), which I gratefully acknowledge. I have also benefited from the seminar which I offered at the École des Hautes Études, VI Section, Paris, in the winter of 1975-76, where some of this material was presented. It is a pleasure to record my warm thanks to Mmes. Nicole Loraux and Suzanne Roy-Said and MM. Jean-Pierre Vernant, Marcel Detienne, and Pierre Vidal-Naquet for stimulating discussion and valuable criticism as well as cordial hospitality.

PLATO: MISOGYNIST, PAEDOPHILE, AND FEMINIST

DOROTHEA WENDER

HENRY THE EIGHTH, says Alistair Cooke,[1] was genuinely fond of women. The forms that fondness took are well known: let it be said that about the only thing Henry did for the status of women was to father the bastard Elizabeth.

A fondness for women, then, is no guarantee of an enlightened attitude toward the sex. To be sure, John Stuart Mill liked women; in fact he liked them to the extent of a rather maudlin uxoriousness. And quite a number of 19th and 20th century male supporters of feminism have first been drawn into the movement because they liked their wives. But Plato, the nearest thing to a systematic feminist produced by the ancient world, cannot be put into this category of philogynists. He was a bachelor and a paedophile; moreover, as I shall try to demonstrate, he disliked women as a class. In this essay, I shall discuss, first, Plato's feminism, next his homosexuality and misogyny. Finally I will offer some possible explanations for his attitude, in an attempt to resolve the apparent paradox of the woman-hater who championed women.[2]

First, a few words about words: when I say "feminist," I mean a man or women who believes that women should be given a "better" place in society (legally, politically, professionally, etc.) or one which more closely approximates that held by men of the same class. I do not mean by "feminist" a person who simply likes women, or pities them, or who necessarily believes that they are equal to men in any way. By "homosexual" I mean a person whose sexual and romantic preference is for members of the same sex, whether or not he/she carries this preference to its full physical expression. By "Plato" I mean Plato; by "Socrates" I mean Socrates.

The *locus classicus* for Plato's feminism is Book V of the *Republic*. He proposes the same education for girls as for boys, freedom from housework and child care for guardian-class women so that they can serve the state, and an equal opportunity to become rulers. Except in their ability to bear children, he says, women are no different from men in kind: what is virtuous for a woman is virtuous for a man, and and vice versa. Women may be weaker than men, and the average woman may be inferior to the average man, but superior women are better than inferior men, and we would not want our ideal state deprived of their services. To the objection that women are fundamentally different from men and, therefore, should do "specialized" jobs in our specialized state, Socrates replies that it is a non-essential difference, like that between bald men and men with hair. We do not separate male and female dogs, he says, and consider raising puppies to be sufficient occupation for the females; they may be somewhat weaker, but they hunt, keep watch and guard flocks with the males.

The dog is a continually recurring figure in the *Republic*. In II 375-376, Plato considers at length the qualities of the well-bred watchdog, with his sharp vision, speed, strength, courage, and high spirits, the very qualities we want in our guardians. Then, too, and more important, our guardians must be fierce to enemies, but gentle with friends — another quality to be found in dogs, and one which Socrates says requires discrimination, which requires knowledge. Therefore, he jokes, the dog has a 'philosophic nature,' which our guardians must also have. In III 416, the auxiliaries must be watchdogs, not wolves. In IV 422, he compares the Republic's warriors to lean and wiry dogs, fighting against soft, fat sheep. In VII 537, young children are to be given a taste of warfare, as young hunting dogs are given a taste of blood. In fact, Plato seems to have had so much admiration for well-bred dogs that one might almost guess he came to some part of his feminism simply from observing how slight the difference is between male and female dogs. Bitches are fed and trained in the same way that male dogs are: you would not expect an underfed, ill-trained dog to perform well, he says (451); and the unspoken corollary, of course, is that human females do not at present receive the same τροφή as males, so we cannot really predict how well they would perform if well-trained.

Our ideal polis, then, will give women for the first time the opportunity to perform as well as they can. Any woman who can compete successfully in the weeding-out process may become a guardian, and all women of the guardian class will be freed from domestic work, child-rearing, and the tyranny of husbands, for there will be no husbands.

These proposals, especially when compared with the actual situation of women in Athens at the time,[3] are delightfully radical. He does not promise that women are equal to men — he cannot; it seems to him they are not. But he proposes complete equality of opportunity; indeed, with the abolition of all domestic work he goes further in this direction than many feminists even today would go.

The *Laws*, which describes what Plato calls the second-best state, weakens the feminist program to some extent, but even so, the treatment of women remains the most radical part of the proposed constitution. In II 658, he classes "educated women" with young men, in their preference for tragedy (one step above older children, who prefer comedy; one step below older men, who would vote for epic.) In III 680, he says that in primitive society the father *and mother* ruled. In III 690, he quotes what is apparently supposed to be an exhaustive list of the natural dominance relationships, which hold for states as well as families. This is highly interesting: it is proper, he says, for parents to rule over children, the noble (or well-bred) over the ignoble, older over younger, masters over slaves, the stronger over the weaker, most important, the wise over the ignorant, and finally, the winner of the lot over the loser. We are reminded of the three basic dominance relationships which form the basis of society in Aristotle's *Politics* (Book I). They are 1. father over child; 2. man over woman; 3. master over slave. Notice, first, that in Aristotle it is the father who rules the child; in Plato, the parents. In Aristotle man-woman is one of the three basic natural pairs; in Plato there are seven pairs, but man-woman does not appear. The Athenian stranger goes on to advocate the same education for girls as for boys, public common tables for women (but segregated from the men's), public nurseries, military training for women, and public praise of outstanding women as well as men. Marriage is not only reinstated in the *Laws*, it is to be compulsory and publicly supervised, but with fairly liberal divorce laws, dowries abolished, and strict Puritan standards of premarital chastity and marital fidelity for both sexes. Up till now, one-half the talent in the state has been wasted; if only one-half the state is happy, the legislator has not done his job (VII 806).

Evidence for feminism in the other dialogues is present but not overwhelming. The *Meno* is the most striking: Gorgias is reported as saying that the virtue of a woman is different from that of a man. The virtue of the man is to order the state and avoid harm, that of the woman to keep house and obey her husband. (72) Socrates counters that health and strength are the same in man and woman, and so too must virtue be the same, whether exercised in the state or in the house. If it is virtuous for a man to be moderate or just, it cannot be virtuous for a woman to be immoderate or unjust. (This argument is still alive: Dr. Spock and others maintain that it is man's "nature" or "contribution" − i.e. *virtue* − to be aggressive and creative; woman's to be gentle and receptive. The opponents maintain that there may indeed be these differences between men and women, but if gentleness, say, is a desirable quality in woman, it should also be desirable in a man.)

The *Menexenus* gives us a parody of an epideictic oration, which Socrates says he learned from Aspasia. Menexenus indicates that he thinks Socrates wrote it himself; Socrates insists that Aspasia has composed many other political speeches as good as this one.

In the *Critias* (110), Plato tells us that men and women had common pursuits in the good old days of Athens, before the war with Atlantis. They had a statue of Athene fully armed, he says, to signify that the virtue appropriate to each species of animal belongs to both the male and the female of that species.

The *Politicus* tells us that the golden age knew no private property nor families. (This may not be evidence for feminism, but it is consistent with the feminist program of the *Republic*, and this tends to indicate that that program was not just a product of casual whimsy. And indeed, as Engels, de Beauvoir, and others have pointed out, there *is* a connection between private property and the suppression of women, although I am not sure that the standard Marxist interpretation of this connection is correct.)

The evidence for Plato's feminism, then, rests chiefly on the *Republic* and the *Laws*, but is fairly substantial.

Now let us proceed to the other side of the picture. That Plato's sexual or romantic preference was exclusively for men seems clear, in spite of an occasional denial in the Victorian scholars. Even if we regard the love poems as spurious (and I do not so regard all of them), the dialogues themselves are filled with homosexual banter, with flirting of a sort that would be considered charming today – and clearly, harmlessly sexual – if the participants were adolescent boys and girls. I shall give only one example from the many available, and to make my point clearer, I will change the name of the beloved object, Charmides, to a feminine one, Carol.[4] Critias is telling Socrates about his cousin Carol. *Charmides* 154:

> "As for the good-looking girls, Socrates, you'll be able to judge for yourself; the young men who are just coming in are the advance guard and admirers of the girl they consider the prettiest one around, and she herself can't be too far away."

She enters, and Socrates reports:

> "I'm no judge of beauty – all girls that age look beautiful to me – but when I saw her coming in, I admit I was aston-

216

ished at her looks and her figure. All the young men seemed
to be in love with her, all of them bashful and awkward,
and a whole other gang of suitors came following behind
her.... Chaerophon asked me 'What do you think of her?
Doesn't she have a lovely face?' 'Breathtaking,' I said.
'You ought to see her in a bikini,' he said. 'You wouldn't
even remember she *had* a face.'

Critias asks Carol to join them, on a flimsy pretext.
Everyone pushes so hard trying to sit next to her that the
fellows on the ends of the bench get knocked off, and
everyone has a good laugh. Finally, Carol sits between
Critias and Socrates, who is at first unaccountably bashful. "Then," says Socrates, "Oh, what a sight! I caught
a glimpse down inside her dress, and I caught on fire....
but I controlled myself, and said..."

This sort of byplay always takes place between or among men;
no women take part in the dialogues. Throughout the dialogues, various
boys and young men are called good-looking; to my knowledge, no
woman's beauty is ever praised by Plato. To be sure, this state of
affairs was probably typical among men of Plato's class; but while
not unique, his attitude is also not universal, as a quick glance through
the writings of Xenophon will show.[5] However, it also seems clear
that Plato was repelled by the full physical expression of passion.
The *Phaedrus* indicates that he quite understood the temptations of
the lover, and was prepared to accept the lover's yielding to that
temptation as a permissible but second-best sort of behavior, but his
almost worshipful admiration for Socrates' indifference to sexual
temptation (clearest in the *Symposium*) is evident. It is one of the
magical things about Socrates, like his *daimonion*, his eloquence, his
catalepsy, and his ability to hold liquor. Socrates survived the supreme
test – to be in bed with a willing Alcibiades; such a man is 'above'
other men, fit to be priest and ruler. Ability to remain chaste – like
the ability to enter a trance state – has from early times marked out
the 'born' priest. And Plato's guardians, like the priests of the Roman
Catholic church, are to be singled out from the masses of followers
for this very quality, among others. We cannot know whether Plato had
this ability to withstand sexual temptation (we can guess that he
didn't, but it's only a guess); we do know that he admired it and we
see in the *Republic* and the *Laws* that he wishes all men, as far as
possible, to acquire it. For procreation, sex is necessary; for pleasure,
he nowhere encourages it.

In one respect, Plato's paedophilia seems to have gone beyond that of the typical Athenian aristocrat of his day (who was bisexual): he never married. Shorey calls him "an Athenian old bachelor,"[6] which makes him sound like somebody's dear old courtly uncle, and Levinson imagines that he very much wanted to marry, but refrained partly because the Athens that killed Socrates was no fit place in which to raise children.[7] But I think we can find in Plato's writings, without going into his personal life, about which we know almost nothing, two reasons for his rejection of marriage, in spite of his own edict in the *Laws* that marriage and procreation should be compulsory: his antipathy to sex and his dislike of women. Why he disliked women is an unanswerable question (unless we are willing to fantasize about his mother, à la Kelsen).[8] Women were, no doubt, not very likeable in Plato's day, and there was certainly a long tradition of Greek misogyny before him, but why Plato should follow the Hesiodic tradition while Xenophon, for example, did not is not so obvious. *That* he disliked women seems apparent from examples like the following:

The treatment of Xanthippe and 'the women' in the *Phaedo* is strikingly unsympathetic. She wails that it is the last time Socrates and his friends will ever see each other; Socrates has her taken away, and later rebukes his friends for lamenting like the women. "I had the women taken away," he says, "because it is necessary for a man to die among auspicious words." (117) (Implication: women are silly and weepy, and have no self-control. They aren't capable of letting a man die in peace.)

Gorgias: (502) "Even women and children and slaves hear the tragic poets." (Implication: women are to be classed with the two other impressionable, inferior groups.)

Alcibiades: (121) "The son of the king of Persia is not raised by a woman nurse, worth nothing." (Implication: women should not be entrusted with the important function of education of the young, as they are in Athens.)

Republic: In III 395, he says that our future guardians should not imitate women acting 'womanish' nor slaves acting 'slavish.' (Implication: the typical behavior of women, like that of the other major class of inferiors, slaves, is bad. Free-born men do not form a 'class' as slaves and women do; they are mankind; they are the species. Slaves and women are peculiar varieties, deviant from the norm.) Again, 398: "Even to women with a sense of propriety Lydian laments are harmful, more so to men." (Implication: "good women" form a subcategory of the class 'woman'; they are somewhat similar to 'man,'

in that they can be corrupted by music. Most women, presumably, are
so "low" they cannot be so harmed. Men, the species, can be corrupted to a greater degree, since they start out on a higher plane.)

In VIII 548, he says that timocratic men (i.e. Spartans) spend
too much money on their wives. (Implication: women misuse freedom
and luxury. But I am not certain that Plato would not feel the same
way about men, so I include this quotation with some hesitancy. It does
assume, though, that it is, of course, the male's prerogative to spend
or not spend on the female.)

In VIII 549 we find the really unpleasant and rather gratuitous
picture of the wife of the good man in a bad state, who makes her
son into a timocrat. She is greedy and ambitious, and wholly mis-
understands her husband's high-minded abstention from public life; she
raised her son to despise his gentle father by accusing him of a lack
of virility, and adding "all the other sorts of complaints which women
love to hymn." (Implication: the woman, being inferior to her husband
in wisdom, cannot share his lofty goals. She corrupts her son. Also,
women enjoy complaining.)

In 557 he says that democracy is like a many-colored cloak; as
women and children like many-colored things best, so some men prefer
democracy. (Implication: women have crude, poor 'taste,' like children.)

In 563, one of the worst features of licentious democracy is the
'equality' and 'freedom' of the sexes. (The meaning of this statement
is somewhat unclear. Plato may only be talking about sexual promis-
cuity. But when he goes on to complain about slaves and *animals*
getting 'uppity' in this democracy, we get the impression that his
complaint against women, too, is that they don't know their *place*.)

In 605, we learn that poets bring out the 'womanish' in their
hearers. (Implication: any normal man is repelled by the 'womanish'
qualities – emotionalism, irrationality – and is ashamed if he exhibits them.)

The *Timaeus* is a real treasure-trove of classic male chauvinism:
we learn in 42 that woman was created inferior to man, and that a sin-
ful man in his second incarnation would become a woman. In 76, we
learn even more: "Our creators know that some day woman *and the
other beasts* would be formed out of man." And in 90, "Whatever men
were cowardly (δειλοί) and lived unjustly (ἀδίκως) quite logically
(κατὰ λόγον τὸν εἰκότα) became women in the second generation."

In the *Theatetus* (176) there is a contemptuous reference to
"old wives' fables."

In the *Laws*, we hear more about the license of Spartan women

(637), the bad practice of imitating women, slaves, or animals (669), and the bad temper of women (731). We learn that women educated Cyrus' sons badly (694), and that it would be nice if cowards were turned into women (944). In 774, we hear that dowries make wives insolent and men subservient (presumably, the reverse is desirable); in the middle of a defense of the emancipation of woman (781), Plato tells us that women are inferior and inclined to stealth and secretiveness. In 796 comes the unkindest cut: women are responsible for the fact that many people believe themselves to be right-handed, whereas any fool knows that everyone is naturally ambidexterous.

I have omitted a fair number of minor examples, and have undoubtedly missed some. I have not included in this list any of the misogynistic remarks in the *Symposium* because it seems to me doubtful that any speaker in that dialogue (including Socrates-Diotima but perhaps excluding Alcibiades) wholly represents Plato's view.

Occasionally Plato offers or implies praise to a woman as an individual (e.g. Aspasia in the *Menexenus*, Diotima in the *Symposium*, Socrates' midwife mother in the *Theatetus*.) As a class, he praises them only once, to my knowledge: *Laws* 803, where he advocates a blending of courage (the manly virtue) with moderation (the womanly virtue).

The apparent paradox should now be clear: Plato both despised women as a class, and advocated more liberation and privilege for them than any man in history had ever done, so far as we know. If I may borrow Patin's marvelous *mot* about Lucretius, we have here a striking example of *l'Anti-Platon chez Platon*.

This point is worth some discussion in itself. Plato is extraordinarily full of the tension of ambivalence, even more than Lucretius is, more, I think, than almost any other classical writer or thinker. He would censor poetry, would legislate it almost out of existence; yet he loves and honors Homer and many another poet exceedingly, and is himself a poet. He believes that imitation of an inferior is a major corrupting evil, to be avoided at all costs; yet he himself is a master parodist, a superb dramatist because he can so skillfully put on the mask and garb of others. He is an elitist, a despiser of the opinions of the many; yet he constantly recurs to common experience and belief ("if you were sick, would you go to a doctor or a sculptor?"). The masses are the belly, the lowest, most despicable part of the state; yet his elite would find their happiness in giving up all worldly pleasures to serve that belly and make it comfortable.

It is no surprise that Plato is full of contradiction and tension; only such a man would choose to write philosophy in dialogue form. It was always characteristic of the Greeks – and the major source of their greatness in several areas of writing – that they could see two sides of a question. Homer has sympathy for Greeks *and* Trojans; Herodotus for barbarians as well as Greeks; Thucydides for Spartans as well as Athenians. Tragedy, too, depends on valid conflict between worthy opponents, whether they are men or ideas. Melodrama, the conflict of hero with villain, is rare in classical Greece. But this characteristic, so admirable in writers of epic, of drama, of history, had an unfortunate corollary in real life: does any other national group have in so brief a history so many distinguished traitors, so many instances of bad faith and disloyalty? The list of deserters and traitors begins with Achilles and Ajax, and passing into real history culminates in Ephialtes, Themistocles, Pausanias, Lysander, and πάντων δεινότα- τος, Alcibiades.

Let us leave the gloomy subject of Greek treachery, and return to the sunnier topic of philosophy. The dialogue genre seems the perfect expression, in philosophy, of the Greek passion for seeing both sides (which is certainly related to the more frequently noticed Greek love of contests, athletic or verbal). And Plato, the master of the dialogue is extremely Greek in his love of a good argument, and in his ability both to state one position and to generate sympathy for its opposite. This, I think, he has done with regard to women.

But before returning to the anti-Plato, I must digress, briefly, on the historical origins of Plato's feminist program. Clearly, something about women was going on in the last part of the fifth century. The *Trachiniae*, the *Medea* and the *Alcestis* all touch on the mistreatment of women; the *Lysistrata* and *Ecclesiazusae* give even stronger indications that the "woman question" was in the wind. Who started it? Was it spontaneously generated in many minds at once, all engaged in questioning traditional assumptions? Did Herodotus start something by pointing out that in other cultures people do things differently, and did the Athenians suddenly start to take notice of their Dorian neighbors and their freer women? Or can the movement (or better, the question) be traced to a more specific source? In the pitifully small fragments of the pre-Socratics and major Sophists, I can find only one who mentions women with any frequency: that is Democritus,[9] and he is distinctly hostile to them. Gorgias, too, is reported by Plato (in the *Meno*, as we have seen) to have taken a misogynist position. In our search for possible feminist forerunners of Plato, we must now consider the

221

claims of Aspasia and Socrates. Aspasia seems a good possibility because a) existing ancient sources are unanimous in praising her brains and political shrewdness, b) being a 'foreign' hetaira, she was not hampered by the stifling upbringing of an Athenian Lady, c) she apparently had plenty of opportunity to talk with and influence philosophers, poets, and other intellectuals of the day, d) there is a tradition that she 'taught' Socrates (we find it in the *Aspasia* of Aeschines of Sphettus, Plato's *Menexenus*, and Plutarch's life of Pericles), and e) it would be so nice if a woman had started the movement. This last, of course, is really a major reason for being suspicious about her role; in addition, Pericles' position on women (if we are to believe Thucydides) seems pretty uncompromising. If she had so much influence on Euripides, could she have failed so miserably with her lover? Perhaps, of course, he feigned an orthodox attitude in order to protect her, or to demonstrate to the masses that no foreign woman had any influence over *him*. But still, there is no real evidence for Aspasia's playing any part in feminist thinking; her 'speech' in the *Menexenus* never touches on the question; the most we can confidently say is that her mere existence, as a competent person who was female, provided an example, for those who wanted one, that not all women were "womanish."

For Socrates we have better evidence. In fact A. E. Taylor says:[10] "It is important to remember that...the general principles which underlie the treatment of the position of women in *Republic* V are no personal 'development' of Plato's; they belong to the actual Socrates." For this conclusion he relies on the fragments of the *Aspasia*, an apparently feminist dialogue by Aeschines of Sphettus (not the orator, but the follower of Socrates), in which Socrates discusses the political acumen of Aspasia and the military prowess of the Persian Rhodogyne. This *does* look like good independent evidence, but of course Taylor neglects to consider the possibility that Aeschines got his feminist Socrates right out of the *Meno*, or the possibility that the dialogue is a later forgery. Diogenes Laertius (in the Life of Aeschines) records considerable doubt in antiquity about the genuineness of Aeschines' dialogues, and also reports that on at least one occasion Aeschines was accused of plagiarism. Still, Aeschines and Plato were apparently not friends, and as far as we can gather from the titles and fragments of Aeschines' dialogues and Laertius' statement that their style was Gorgianic, they seem more or less independent of Platonic influence.

Taylor also says (p. 278): "Aeschines, in the remains of his

Aspasia, agrees with Plato in representing the philosopher as insisting that 'the goodness of a woman is the same as that of a man.' " But Taylor has blundered badly here. Aeschines' *Aspasia* does seem to deal with feminism, or at least with several noteworthy women, like Aspasia and Rhodogyne, but the fragments nowhere say "the goodness of a woman is the same as that of a man." Taylor carelessly copied his statement out of Heinrich Dittmar's *Aeschines von Sphettos* (1912), p. 13, but Dittmar was there referring to *Antisthenes*, not Aeschines. Antisthenes did also write an *Aspasia*, and he did write Socratic dialogues, and he did say (not necessarily in his *Aspasia*) "Virtue is the same for women as for men" (ἀνδρὸς καὶ γυναικὸς ἡ αὐτὴ ἀρετή) (Diogenes Laertius, Life of Antisthenes, 12.), so he presents us with another bit of evidence for a feminist Socrates.

Further evidence (not used by Taylor) can be found in Xenophon. In the *Memorabilia*, Socrates quotes Aspasia (II, 36); he visits and has a long friendly conversation with a hetaira, Theodote. In the *Oeconomicus*, he mentions Aspasia again, and in the *Symposium* (II, 9) Xenophon's Socrates, on seeing a skillful female juggler, says "In what this girl does, and many other instances, it is clear that the nature of woman is not inferior to that of man, except in intelligence (γνώμη) and strength (ἰσχύς)." This last wonderful quotation seems significant, for it illustrates perfectly how the noblest Socratic ideas are misunderstood and trivialized by Xenophon until he feels comfortable with them. If Socrates really was fond of saying "Virtue in a woman is the same as virtue in a man" it seems quite in character for each of his three successors, Plato, Aeschines and Xenophon, to have transmitted the message precisely as we receive it from them: Plato uses the idea as a philosopher and political theorist, with his analogy to bald cobblers and cobblers with hair, followed by a practical program for putting the principle into effect. Aeschines responds like a rhetorician, with historical examples to prove his point. And Xenophon treats the idea as material for one more anecdote with the silly example of juggling, and the damning qualification," "except in intelligence and strength," which all but annihilates the original statement. It would seem, then, that Plato, like Xenophon, got his feminism, or a push in that direction, from Socrates.

And what does that make of our *anti-Platon chez Platon*? Is the anti-Plato in Plato's boots merely Socrates? And does the misogynistic side of Plato represent the "real" Plato? Taylor thinks so: ... "hence the thought that the duties of statesmanship and warfare should be extended to women must be regarded as strictly Socratic, and the rest of the proposals of Republic V are no more than necessary conse-quences of this position."[11]

I cannot accept that. Taylor goes too far in his Socratism. D. J. Allan says in his appendix to "Greek Philosophy" in *Fifty years (And Twelve) of Classical Scholarship*,[12] "The thesis of Burnet re-garding the historical Socrates is now defunct." Taylor was a champion of that thesis, which would make the historical Socrates responsible even for the theory of forms. Even if we believe with Taylor that it was Socrates (perhaps inspired by the personality of Aspasia) who first impelled the Athenian intellectuals to give some thought to the neglected half of their citizenry – and Socrates who convinced Plato (and Xenophon and Aeschines) that women were worth taking seriously, it is almost impossible to believe that Plato would have devised – against his own inclinations – a program of emancipation for women, and would have been still advocating it when he wrote the *Laws*, so long after the death of Socrates. After all, Plato had other important views (for example, the doctrine of recollection) which apparently he did not hesitate to abandon altogether. No. Even if the idea was Socrates' to begin with, Plato didn't take it up merely out of reverence for his dead master; he adopted it voluntarily, justified it, filled it out, and gave it a central place in his ideal state. Even without Socrates, the Plato and the anti-Plato must have been there in Plato all along.

In contrast, Xenophon's heart – softer though it was for the ladies – was relatively stony ground for the scattered feminist seed. For what are his proposals for women?

Memorabilia VII: Xenophon's 'Socrates' saves a friend from poverty by suggesting that he put his female dependents to work making clothes. This makes the women happier and the man prosperous. If they complain that you do not work, explain to them, says 'Socrates,' that you are like a sheep dog: you don't work but you protect them. (To be sure, this *is* a step in the direction of emancipation: Xenophon rec-ognizes that women are not wholly useless, and he sets up what for him is a highly satisfactory "separate but equal" arrangement.) Again in III, 11, he refers to the principle of 'equality' again: "in wool-spinning, women 'govern' men, because they know how to work the wool and men do not." In others words, women have their sphere (wool-working) in which they govern; men have theirs (everything else *except* wool-working and kindred subjects) in which *they* govern. Therefore, women should have no complaint; they are queens in their own realm. (For Plato's attitude toward that wonderful realm, see Republic V 455: "Do we need to waste time talking about weaving,

224

and the tending of flatcakes and puddings, in which women *do* seem to be superior, and in which 'being victorious' or 'losing' is too ridiculous to mention?'')

In the *Oeconomicus*, Xenophon is equally 'modern' and 'liberated'; his Ischomachus instructs his child bride in domestic management, pointing out that they are equals and partners. The woman has her sphere (indoors) and he his (outdoors). He has reached the full Victorian position of a Ruskin here; his tone throughout the essay is affectionate, but patronizing and smug, most pleased with himself for his daringly Socratic kindness to the little woman. Of course, his bride's lot undoubtedly *was* a happier one than most of her Athenian predecessors' or contemporaries': "equal rule" was an illusion, but at least the words were kind; affection and communication were part of the new domestic scene, and the wife could feel she had at least some degree of importance and status in her husband's eyes. Her gratitude in the dialogue is fulsome. At one point, (x, 1) Socrates comments on her progress: "By Hera, your wife has a masculine mind!" "Yes," says Ischomachus, "and I'll show you other examples of her high-mindedness: times when she obeyed me instantly when I had only spoken to her once!" Her great 'male' mind then, is chiefly proved by her ability to understand a simple command without its being repeated, and in instant *obedience*. So much for equality in Xenophon!

Why then, should Plato, who disliked women and denied that they had *any* 'sphere' of superiority, champion their emancipation, while Xenophon, who liked them, consigned them to a premanently subservient position? I would suggest several possible explanations. First, the well-adjusted heterosexual man (or bisexual, in Greek society) is more apt to be contented with the status quo, with women the way they are and the family the way it is. He likes women; they serve his physical needs, his desire to reproduce himself, and his desire to feel superior. He doesn't want his mother or wife or daughter to be unhappy, so he tells them they *are* as good and important as men *in their own way*; he tells them that Nature intended them to do just what they are doing. He praises their wool-working and cooking and child-rearing; good heavens, who would do it if the women refused? The misogynist-homosexual, on the other hand, is more apt to come from a disturbed family background; he chooses not to marry because his experience of family life has not been good. If women are emancipated, he has less to lose than the married man; he does not depend on the little woman at home to boost his ego and provide his comforts. Since he does not like women as they are, he would think it a small loss if they changed;

if they should lose their feminity and become more like men, he might actually *like* them.

There is a second possible explanation: the heterosexual male is more afraid of the power of women. He isn't, god knows, jealous of their wool-working ability, but he knows how women can 'get around him' with their crying, and can have their own way by exploiting his sexual desire for them. The sexual desirability of a beautiful woman is a dangerous trap: Pandora was responsible for the introduction of evil into the world; Epimetheus couldn't control her (any more than Adam could stop Eve) because of her sexuality. Circe turned men into animals. Helen started a war. It is not necessary (though it may be valid) to invoke any tribal memory of matriarchy; men who like women can find that attraction frightening and unfair in any society. To even things up, women must be suppressed. If women are not kept in their place, these men calculate, women will walk all over them. If women are ever given a really equal chance, then they might become *superior*, because of the unfair advantage of their sex. (This type of 'masculine' man is particularly well portrayed in the Heracles of the *Trachiniae*, with his violent and self-destructive philandering.) On the other hand, the man who is more or less indifferent to the sexuality of women can presumably face competition from them with greater equanimity. He may believe that they are 'inferior'; he may not like them or be physically attracted to them, but by the same token, they offer no threat; there is nothing to get hysterical about if their status improves.

To the two possible explanations I have given, I will now, rather hesitantly, add a third. Is it possible that the homosexual male, because of the way he makes love, is less convinced than the heterosexual that the "natural" is the "good?" I am afraid that this hypothesis will at first appear trivial or far fetched or possibly offensive to a good many readers, but I beg them to consider it seriously for a moment. The chief complaint against homosexual intercourse, since it produces no babies and is not favored by the rest of the animal world, has always been that it is contrary to nature, or sometimes 'offensive' or 'repulsive' to the 'laws' of Nature (or of God). One of the chief arguments against any change in the status of women has *also* been the teleological one: Nature (or God) made the sexes different — made women physically desirable to men but smaller and weaker than they are — for a purpose. The biologically oriented thinker (from Aristotle to Dr. Spock) has traditionally assumed that "Nature's way" is more or less identical with the state of affairs he sees in his culture. This leads Aristotle to approve of slavery, as a 'natural'

226

institution; it leads Xenophon and Aristotle and Dr. Spock (and Dr. Freud and many of his latter-day followers) to assume that woman is now in a subservient position because her nature makes her happiest — and serves society best — when she is dominated. Women, say the orthodox psychoanalysts, are fundamentally masochistic. As a homosexual, however, (and, perhaps, as a mathematically rather than a biologically oriented thinker) Plato is not so concerned to preserve the natural at all costs. The 'real' world is not to be found in the observable phenomena of nature or the society he lives in. Thus, if he is unhappy with government as he knows it, Plato will smash the current one and invent a better. If he dislikes the religion and mythology he finds around him, he will invent better gods and myths out of whole cloth. If he feels the mass of mankind are unhappy and behave like brutes, he will bring every possible cultural influence to bear on molding, curbing and changing their 'natural' instincts. If he dislikes women as he finds them, he is willing to try changing them.

It might be objected here that I am being inconsistent, having already expressed the view that Plato was opposed to homosexual intercourse. I believe he was opposed to it (clearly in later life, probably earlier as well), whether or not he actually practiced it. His objection, however, was not that it was unnatural, but that it was *carnal*, an objection which holds equally well against heterosexual coitus. The important point is that the *desire* for homosexual intercourse is more appealing to Plato than heterosexual desire, and thus we find in him no particular worship of 'natural' (i.e. typically mammalian) behavior. The artificially bred and carefully trained dog is superior in every way to the wolf-like canine "Nature" produces; so, too, there might be hope for women, if we will pay some attention to them.

I think it should now be clear that there is nothing so very surprising in Plato's "self-contradictory" attitude toward women. It was important for his *Republic* to break up the family and property and direct the citizens' loyalty and affection toward the whole state, toward "all their brothers." This would also break the destructive chain of nepotism, in which able fathers virtually bequeath political power to their incompetent sons. The emancipation of women fits in with this plan nicely, and would also add a fresh supply of potential talent to the states reserves. Although he gave up, in the *Laws*, on the idea of abolishing the family, he still wanted to free that wasted half of the populace. He assumed that the women themselves would object

227

to being dragged out "into the light," and he was right. Many women do object to it, even now.

He did not like or admire us. But he felt it would be just and expedient to give us a chance. Xenophon liked us, and felt that it was important to keep us just the way he liked us. It is a difficult choice for many women. It is hard to give up being liked.

Wheaton College

NOTES

[1] In his introduction to an episode of the National Educational Television production of the "Six Wives of Henry the VIIIth."

[2] The fullest treatments I have found are in Ronald B. Levinson, *In Defense of Plato* (Cambridge, Harvard, 1953), pp. 125-138 (and elsewhere) and Jowett's five-volume *Plato*, which has a delightful discussion of Plato's attitude toward women, in the introduction on the *Republic* (volume III). Interesting relevant material can be found also in A. E. Taylor, *Plato: the Man and his Work* (N. Y., Meridian, 1956), pp. 277-278 (and elsewhere), A. D. Winspear, *The Genesis of Plato's Thought* (New York, Dryden, 1940), pp. 241 ff., Rupert Lodge, *The Philosophy of Plato* (London, Routledge and Kegan Paul, 1956), pp. 270-271, and Paul Shorey, *What Plato Said* (Chicago, U. of Chicago Press, 1933) *passim*. But it is surprising how many major books on Plato hardly consider the topic at all; for example Paul Friedländer, *Plato* (Princeton, Bollingen, 1969).

[3] See, for example, Alfred Zimmern, *The Greek Commonwealth* (Oxford, Clarendon, 1924) Part II chapters 2 and 12.

[4] After I wrote this I discovered that Warner Fite (*The Platonic Legend*, New York, Scribners, 1934, p. 178) had used precisely the same example to make precisely the same point. Generally, I find Fite's tone unfair and his scholarship deplorable.

[5] For example at the end of Xenophon's *Symposium*, a pair of dancers (boy and girl) portray the passionate love of Dionysus and Ariadne so effectively that "the unmarried spectators vowed that they would marry, and the already married mounted their horses and galloped home to their wives." (IX, 7).

[6] *Op. cit.,* p. 632.

[7] *Op. cit.,* pp. 116-118.

[8] Hans Kelsen, "Platonic Love," in *American Imago* 3 (April 1942), 3-110.

[9] Fragments 110, 111, 214, 273, 274.

[10] Taylor, *op. cit.*, p. 278.

[11] *Ibid.*

[12] *Fifty Years (And Twelve) of Classical Scholarship* (Oxford, Basil Blackwell 1968), p. 170.

THE WOMEN OF ETRURIA

Larissa Bonfante Warren

OVER A HUNDRED YEARS AGO, J. J. Bachofen published his book on "Mother-right," and *The Myth of Tanaquil*,[1] with which, like his friend Nietzsche, he revolutionized the world of classical scholarship. The case was overstated – the "tyranny of women" never happened. Bachofen's "matriarchy" must be carefully distinguished from equality. Yet he understood and described a historical fact: that the status of Etruscan women, in the archaic period at least – seventh to fifth century B.C. – was surprisingly high in comparison to that of Greek and Roman women.

Since then archaeology, by studying direct material evidence, such as tomb paintings and inscriptions, has told us more of the Etruscans' luxurious style of life, and the considerable role played by the women.[2] Accounts of Greek and Roman writers give further evidence for these facts – more importantly, they show how the Etruscan way of life differed from their own, and how this difference frightened them. They experienced it as a conflict in civilization, and expressed it in terms of relations between men and women, and different attitudes to sex.

Bachofen saw the great difference between the early Roman system of the *pater familias* with legal powers of life and death, and the type of society implied by tales of the Etruscan queens. I would like to suggest that Rome's contact with the civilization which confronted her across the Tiber, from whom she took so much external culture – letters, the arts, symbols of royalty, so that eventually Rome looked like an Etruscan city too – represented Rome's first "cultural shock." Making her conscious of her own "moral" identity – Rome never gave up her language, religion or customs – it perhaps foreshadowed, on a vastly different scale, the later Hellenistic explosion, when two different cultures met, and long continued to live in an uneasy proximity. The Etruscans were for the Romans from the first, and always remained, "the others." The foreignness of their language encouraged, true or not, the story of their Oriental origin.

What we know best about them is their art, and the importance of the women in society. The art puts us in direct contact with this rich and cultured people, who brought art and letters to Italy and to

Rome. Literary evidence, as we shall see, speaks of the freedom and power of Etruscan women. How much of this is true? And how are the wealth and women's freedom connected?

Roman sources, chief among them Livy, mostly belong to the Augustan period, which had its own concerns and ideals,[3] and for whom Etruscan contacts with early Rome lay in a distant past, re-created rather than remembered. For the facts of the archaic period and contemporary reactions we must start with the Greeks.

Differences between Etruscan and Greek women were striking. Theopompus, the Greek historian of the fourth century B.C., was startled by them, and drew the worst possible conclusion from what he saw and heard about Etruscan women.[4] According to his report, they took great care of their bodies, often exercising in the nude with men and with each other; it was not considered shameful for women to show themselves naked. They were very beautiful. At dinner, he tells us, they reclined publicly with men other than their husbands. They even took part in the toasting — traditionally reserved for men and regulated by strict formalities at Greek *symposia*. Etruscan women liked to drink (so, by the way, did Greek women, according to Aristophanes and others; this is the most familiar accusation of immorality). Most shocking of all, they raised all their children, according to Theopompus, whether or not they knew who the fathers were.

Theopompus' misunderstanding of the real situation is comparable to the misconceptions regarding Swedish girls current among men in Italy today. His account of Etruscan society, with what seems to us today to be sexual freedom for women — incomprehensible, according to Greek standards, as anything other than immorality — resembles Herodotus' description of the Lydians (I, 93-94), among whom, we are told, women give themselves up to prostitution before marriage. Even more striking is the resemblance to the account Herodotus gives of the Lycians, whose family structure was different from that of the Greeks. There, descent was reckoned through the female line, the matronymic took the place of the patronymic, and free women married to slaves could pass their status on to their children.[5]

Yet, although Theopompus' account distorts the truth, much of what he says is in fact confirmed by archaeological evidence. He is right in saying that women reclined at dinner together with men. We see them so on tomb paintings at Tarquinia.[6] We are not sensitive, however, to the shock and distaste this information produced in a Greek of Theopompus' time. While it is normal in Etruscan art to see women reclining together with men on banquet couches, on the contemporary Greek vase paintings of *symposia* which served as models for pictures of Etruscan banquets, wives are conspicuous by their absence.[7] Men recline with men, or with pretty flute girls whose nakedness shows them to be slave girls, not respectable women.

A sensational recent discovery, the painted tomb from Paestum with scenes from a *symposium*, imitating Etruscan tomb paintings in technique, but with Greek subject matter, points out this contrast. The South Italian scene shows men courting a handsome young boy with bright red lips and cheeks. No women appear, not even as dancers or attendants. In striking contrast, Etruscan art seems to show a world of married couples: see for example the justly famous and aptly named sarcophagus of the Bride and Groom — "Sposi" is a better word — in the Villa Giulia Museum in Rome.[8]

To Theopompus, seeing husbands and wives so unexpectedly together must have seemed a serious breach of culture and good taste, leading him to draw further conclusions of lasciviousness. He imagines that women joined men in another traditionally male place, the gymnasium, where Greek men, by definition, exercised naked. That women exercised together with men in the nude, in either Athens or in any Etruscan city, is patently untrue. Etruscan women did join men publicly in watching sports, a custom most un-Greek[9] — they are so represented on funerary paintings and reliefs.[10] They apparently were not, however, particularly fond of such strenuous exercise as Spartan women practiced; nor do they ever appear naked. As for exercising in the nude, even Etruscan men normally wore shorts, heroic nudity being a peculiarly Greek invention in the ancient Mediterranean world. It was practiced by Greeks alone — and even then only after Homeric times — constituting, as much as language did, the chief distinction between Greeks and barbarians, including Etruscans.[11]

Other observations of Theopompus, after due allowance has been made for his difficulty in understanding something foreign to him and threatening, are supported by evidence. Etruscan funerary inscriptions identifying the deceased by means of the matronymic as well as the patronymic show the greater legal and social importance of women, though they deny, at the same time, Bachofen's theory of the survival of a real matriarchy in the sense of rule by women.[12] Then, too, if Etruscan women, unlike Greek women — but like Herodotus' Lycian women — had the right to raise their children without their husbands' formal recognition — this would probably be connected with their right to own property — Theopompus would translate this situation, in terms of Greek law, as ignorance of the father's identity, or illegitimacy.

Furthermore, if Theopompus was correct in stating that Etruscans
– men and women, one would suppose – raised *all* their children, this
might mean that they did not need or depend on infanticide, child exposure, as a population control. Perhaps, then, their greater wealth
allowed them more freedom in this respect, unlike the Greeks, who
were faced with the constant threat of overpopulation and poverty.[13]

Proof of the high status of Etruscan women is also their literacy,
implied by the many decorated bronze mirrors, regularly inscribed with
names of divinities and mythological figures, buried with them in
cistae or toilet boxes after death.[14] Women's graves were marked, like
those of men, with symbols of boxes or houses – instead of the phallos
of the men – at Etruscan Cerveteri; and in the rock-cut tombs their
death beds are more luxurious than the men's.[15]

In dress, too, there was less distinction between men and women.
An outsider could easily think that Etruscan women dressed like men.
In the late sixth century, for example, they wore mantles and high
shoes elsewhere reserved for men and later used by Romans as special
symbols of citizenship and rank.[16] All these marks of equality shocked
the Greeks, who took them as signs of immorality.

Roman sources of a much later period, Livy and other writers of
the period of Augustus, show a similar picture of Etruscan women –
and condemn it. In their characterization of Lucretia as the model
Roman wife, they contrast her to the wives of the Etruscan Tarquins.[17]
But the Roman woman of the sixth century played a far more important
part than her Greek contemporaries.[18] A Greek wife of the classical period could never properly have been allowed to appear in such a story. According to Greek sources it was the tyrant's lust, not for a woman, but
for a beautiful Athenian boy, Harmodius, that precipitated the Tyran-
nicides' action in the Athens of 514 B.C.[19] It would be interesting to
study further the contrasting treatment of this particular motif of
Athenian and Roman history. What is the relation between sex and
revolution, rape and violence and moral indignation? The victim's honor
is attacked, Athenian lover, or Roman father and husband defend it,
a private feud becomes public and political; and the city gains its
freedom.

In the Roman story a moral contest takes place between Lucretia
and the Etruscan princesses. It is pictured visually in Livy's vivid
prose, as the writer contrasts two artistic motifs, one from Greek and
Roman funerary stelai and the other known to us from paintings of
Etruscan tombs. The first shows the classical matron seated on a
chair, working at her wool;[20] the second, as we saw, the Etruscan

lady reclining on her banquet couch. The contest takes place when the young Etruscan princes, excited by wine during a pause between battles, in wartime leisure in their camp come to talk of women and boast about their wives. To prove their women's worth they ride into the night "to find Lucretia – quite unlike the king's daughters-in-law they had seen at a luxurious dinner party, passing the time with others of their set – seated hard at work at her spinning, though it was very late. She was surrounded by her servants, all of them working well into the night."[21] It is a Roman contest, and Lucretia wins it. The contrast is obvious. Lucretia is the *mater familias* seated at her work, caring for home and household, surrounded by the Roman *familia*, her slaves. The Etruscan princesses recline, "passing the time away," in drinking and sophisticated frivolity in the company of other rich aristocrats, as young and charming as those eternalized in the tomb paintings of Tarquinia and slandered by Theopompus. A serious Roman matron, the moral superior of an Etruscan princess, precipitated the fall of the dynasty of the Tarquins.

The indulgence of Etruscan fathers towards their sons is similarly contrasted, in Livy's pages, with the strict, heroic rule of the Roman *pater familias*. The permissive Tarquins, for example, are thus felt to be diminished as men. There is a nice exchange in which Tarquin justifies his lateness with the excuse that he had been judging a case between father and son – evidently appealing to the Roman sentiment of *pietas*. The retort, prompt and contemptuous, is that there was nothing to judge – the son must obey the father, or pay for it.[22]

According to Roman tradition, too, each of the last three (Etruscan) kings of Rome owed his throne to an Etruscan woman. Tanaquil and Tullia, the wives and daughters of Etruscan kings in the first book of Livy's history of Rome, rank among the great queens of antiquity; it is not the least part of their influence that they inspired Bachofen's work. Their characterization owes something to Cleopatra, the Oriental queen whom Livy in his own time had seen hated, feared and admired in Rome, and something also to Roman Republican desire to downgrade the kings by exalting their queens.[23] Even so, they are Etruscan, and many details fit into a tradition we can recognize.

The individual names of Etruscan women indicate also their different legal and social status. Etruscan inscriptions confirm Livy's simple use of the name Tanaquil without reference to father or husband. In contrast, a Roman woman bore no name of her own.[24] She was known first as her father's daughter and later as her husband's wife, when she came into his *manus*, or legal power; hence the legal formula of

233

marriage, *ubi tu Gaius, ego Gaia*. Augustus, Julius Caesar by adoption, had a daughter named Julia, roughly "Julius' daughter." Lucretia meant the daughter of Lucretius. This system is not unlike the English and American custom of covering up a married woman's maiden name with the full name of her husband in formal address, a custom originally designed to protect the privacy of the woman's first name, a sign of intimacy to be kept from any but close friends and relations.[25] In the instance of Servius Tullius the Etruscan king, a naturalized Roman in the tradition, Livy calls his daughters in Roman fashion, Tullia (Maior and Minor).[26] In other ways quite Etruscan, actually each daughter would have borne her own name, unhappily unrecorded.

The story of all these Etruscan queens seems to preserve genuine Etruscan elements. Married to Lucumo Tarquinius, son of a Greek *émigré*, Tanaquil urged her husband to move from Tarquinia to Rome. An expanding city – as she saw – would afford his talents larger scope. At his side in the carriage approaching Rome, she foresees, in the tradition of the *Etrusca disciplina* of augury, his royal destiny. Together they work toward his election as king. In time she chooses the heir to the throne, Servius Tullius, her son-in-law.[27]

The story of Tullia, the younger daughter of Servius Tullius, indicates the energetic Tanaquil was the rule rather than the exception. Married, and notoriously mismatched, to the less ambitious of two young Tarquins, Tullia arranges to marry instead Lucius Tarquinius, her brother-in-law. She characteristically despises her less forceful sister for her lack of *muliebris audacia* (a term so un-Roman it was rejected by several editors of Livy's text![28]), finally realizes the wished-for union through the double murder of the weaker pair, and pushes Lucius Tarquin into taking over the throne. She is as anxious to have this testimonial of her power as Tarquin, later, is to have his name and reign remembered by the great temple of Jupiter Capitoline. But as it turns out, Tullia's crime becomes her *monumentum*, memorialized by the *Sceleratus Vicus*, where she drove her chariot over her father's body.[29] Freedom of action has turned to crime, justifying, perhaps, Roman order. Were the Roman historians saying that freedom had turned to license, which had to be suppressed?

Another question, previously implied but not yet asked directly, is whether we can connect the earlier freedom of action for women with the ease reflected in the art of the archaic period in Etruria, so full of movement for all its occasional awkwardness. At what point do literary tradition and art agree? Theopompus' account of the daily life of the Etruscans includes tales of orgies and homosexual love.

But Etruscan art, with its few scenes of men making love together, or with prostitutes or naked women – there are the two strange little erotic scenes in the Tomba dei Tori, one homosexual, the other hetero-sexual – does not confirm Theopompus' emphasis on orgies or homosexuality, a frequent literary motif.[30] (Compare the prominent place Herodotus gives to prostitutes in his description of the Lydians.) Actually the Etruscan paintings, with their representation of wives, suggest nothing illicit, rather simple domestic scenes. After dinner, Theopompus says, prostitutes and young boys and "even wives" enter, and the lights are left on. Again his wonder points to different customs and a stricter moral code sharply distinguishing wives from prostitutes, as in Victorian days, when the lights were not left burning (Horace, *Odes*, 3, 6, 28). Another passage of Theopompus which has the ring of truth also seems to reflect this surprise – almost nostalgia – for a wonderful simplicity of manners. "And so far are they from regarding it as a disgrace that they actually say, when the master of the house is making love, and someone asks for him, that he is involved in such and such, shamelessly announcing what he is doing."[31]

Etruscan luxury, proverbial in Greek and Roman eyes, accompanies all such scenes, in Theopompus, in Livy, and in art. Rich gold treasures from Cerveteri are proof of the actual wealth as well as the love of ostentation of the South Etruscan cities.[32] Wealth was used for private luxury. Recent excavations show private houses of the archaic period as richly decorated as temples, a thing unheard of in Greece in the fifth century or in Rome in early times.[33] The Etruscans loved Greek luxury. There are more Greek vases from the sixth century in Etruria than in Greece. So, too, rich Americans bought up the art of Europe.

We already remarked, in connection with children, the relation between this wealth and the status of women. Wealth and luxury also apparently affected the place of slaves. Etruscans are so rich, says Posidonius, that in Etruria slaves dress more luxuriously than their status warrants.[34] Conspicuous consumption for private rather than religious use fits in with the love of pleasure we see in archaic Etruscan art and sense through Theopompus' anxious condemnation.

In the archaic period, then, the Etruscans' wealth and freedom brought home to the Romans their first experience of civilization and threatened their own vastly different culture, rigorous country life and Puritanical ideals. Rome herself looked like an Etruscan city. For centuries after the Etruscan monarchy, the art of Rome was still nearly all Etruscan. The great temple of Jupiter Capitoline and innumerable statues of the gods of terracotta and bronze, all in Etruscan style, served to remind the Romans of the artistic superiority of their rich neighbors. The Etruscans had represented the first challenge to the Romans, forcing them to assert themselves to defend their beliefs. In the confrontation between two such different societies, the poorer one, with its belief in its own moral superiority, won.

Etruscan art from the fourth century on perhaps reflects some of the psychological results of the Roman conquest of Etruria. At this point in their history, the cruelty so often popularly attributed to the Etruscans first appeared. At Tarquinia and Orvieto the world of the dead replaces the world of the living in the Tomba dell'Orco and the Tomba Golini, where the Etruscan Hades and Persephone reign. The style changes as well. A brooding quality and a melancholy never there before appear. Yet the customs of the living still continue beyond death: clothes, jewelry, household furniture, whole kitchen staffs. Here the woman's place has definitely changed. No longer does she lie next to her husband, but sits by him primly in Roman style as he reclines.[35] The moralists have won. Now Roman citizens, the Etruscans changed in more than name and title. The Tullias and Tanaquils had in fact become Lucretias, a father's daughter, a husband's wife. Rome's patriarchal society had won out, not over "matriarchy" as Bachofen saw it, but over what seems to have been a far different society, more open, more able to experience the luxury of life.

New York University

NOTES

Abbreviations used are those of the *American Journal of Archaeology.*

[1] J. J. Bachofen, *Myth, Religion, and Mother Right,* Bollingen Series 84 (Princeton 1967). *Das Mutterrecht* (Basel 1948, orig. publ. 1861); *Die Sage von Tanaquil* (Heidelberg 1870). E. S. McCartney, review in *CP* 45 (1950) 123-125. *Contra*: L. Euing, *Die Sage von Tanaquil. Frankfurter Studien zur Religion und Kultur der Antike* 2 (1933); cf. F. Altheim, *A History of Roman Religion* (revised ed., translated by H. Mattingly, London 1938) 50-51. A. Momigliano, "Tre figure mitiche, Tanaquilla, Gaia Cecilia, Acca Larenzia," *Misc. Fac. Lettere e Filosofia, Torino* (1938) 3-10.

[2] J. Heurgon, *La vie quotidienne chez les Étrusques* (Paris 1961; translated as *Daily Life of the Etruscans,* London 1964) 95-122; "Valeurs féminines

et masculines dans la civilization étrusque," *MEFR* 73 (1961) 138-160; "Tite-Live et les Tarquins," *L'Information Littéraire* 7 (1955) 56-64; and A. J. Pfiffig, "Zur Sittengeschichte der Etrusker," *Gymnasium* 71 (1964) 17-36, provide full references, as well as the most important discussion and interpretation of the material treated in the present essay. Pfiffig stresses the "foreignness" of the Etruscans, an island in the Indo-European world of the seventh century in the Mediterranean. Cf. Altheim, *op. cit.*, 50-64.

[3] D. Musti, *Tendenze nella storiografia romana e greca su Roma arcaica. Studi su Livio e Dionigi d'Alicarnasso. Quaderni Urbinati di Cultura Classica* 10 (1970), especially 30-37.

[4] Theopompus, quoted in Athenaeus, *Deipnosophistae*, 12, 517 D – 518 B. *Fr. Gr. Hist.* 2, fr. 204. W. R. Connor, *Theopompus and Fifth Century Athens* (Washington 1968).

[5] Herodotus 1, 173. Heurgon, *La vie quotidienne* 107-108.

[6] E.g. Tomb of Hunting of Fishing, Tomb of the Leopards, M. Pallottino, *Etruscan Painting* (Geneva 1951) pl. 67 f., pls. on 67-71; and *passim*. S. de Martinis, *La tipologia del banchetto nell'arte etrusca arcaica* (Rome 1961).

[7] O. Brendel, "The Scope and Temperament of Erotic Art in the Greco-Roman World," *Studies in Erotic Art* (New York-London 1970) 19-25; 29-30, on the "banquet type"; on the status of women in Greece, 32-33.

[8] M. Napoli, *La Tomba del Tuffatore* (Bari 1970). Sarcophagus in Villa Giulia Museum, W. Helbig, *Führer durch die öffentlichen Sammlungen Klassischer Altertümer in Rom* III (Tübingen[4] 1969, ed. by H. Speier) No. 2582.

[9] On the controversy concerning women's attendance at the theater in Athens, see K. J. Dover, *Aristophanic Comedy* (Berkeley and L. A. 1971) 17; Menander's *Samia, ad fin.*, refers only to men. On the Olympiads, Paus. 5.6.7; 6.20.9 (doubted).

[10] Tomb of the Bigas, Tarquinia, L. Banti, *Il Mondo degli Etruschi* (Rome 1969[2]) 110. E. Richardson, *The Etruscans* (Chicago 1964) 228: "the Etruscans, like the Romans, preferred spectator sports."

[11] Thuc. 1. 6. 8; Paus. 1. 44. 1.

[12] Heurgon, *La vie quotidienne*, 97, with refs. A. J. Pfiffig, *Die etruskische Sprache* (Graz 1969) 88-89, 119-120, 189. J. Heurgon, "L'État étrusque," *Historia* 6 (1957) 75, on the title *tamera*, which could be held also by a woman; cf. also A. Neppi Modona, in *Studi in onore di G. Grosso*, III (Turin 1969) 70.

[13] W. K. Lacey, *The Family in Classical Greece* (London 1968) 164-167. W. W. Tarn, *Hellenistic Civilization* (Originally published 1927; revised ed. 1952, reprinted, Meridien Books, Cleveland-N.Y. 1967) 100-102. G. Glotz. Dar.-Saglio, *s.v. expositio, infanticidium*.

[14] E. Gerhard, *Etruskische Spiegel* (Berlin 1840-1897). A corpus of these Praenestine mirrors and cistae is being prepared by Gabriella Bordenache and Maria Teresa Falconi Amorelli, under the direction of M. Pallottino and the Istituto di Etruscologia e Antichità Italiche of the University of Rome.

[15] J. Heurgon, *MEFR* 73 (1961) 138-160, with refs.

[16] L. Bonfante Warren, *AJA* 75 (1971) 281; and forthcoming book on Etruscan dress.

[17] M. Durry, review of E. Burck, *Die Frau in der griechisch-römischen Antike* (Munich 1967), in *Gnomon* 43 (1971) 303. Heurgon, *La vie quotidienne*, 101-102.

[18] Dionysius of Halicarnassus' interpretation, from a Greek point of view, of the reason for Horatius' initial anger against his sister is instructive (3, 21, 2): "he was distressed that a virgin ripe for marriage should have deserted her household tasks at her mother's side and joined a crowd of strangers." (Translation by E. Cary, E. Spelman, Loeb Classical Library, 1961).

[19] The purpose of the "digression" on Harmodius and Aristogeiton in Thucydides is difficult to understand (6, 54-59; cf. 1, 20; Hdt. 5, 55; 6, 123; Aristotle, *Ath. Pol.* 17 f.) It is connected with Alcibiades, and with the idea of *eros*. A. Momigliano, *"L'excursus* di Tucidide in VI, 54-59," *Studi di storiografia antica in memoria di Leonardo Ferrero* (Turin 1971) 31-35.

[20] M. Durry, *Éloge funèbre d'une matrone romaine (Éloge dit de Turia)* (Paris 1950), which contains important observations on the status of Roman women. They received, but did not present, *laudationes*, for example (XXI). *Domum seruauit, lanam fecit* (XXVIII; Bücheler, *Carm. Lat. Epigr.* 52, 8). Heurgon, *La vie quotidienne*, 102. Cf. Tibullus, 1, 3, 83 ff.

[21] Livy 1, 57, 4-58. *Cum aequalibus* can mean both men and women their age (Heurgon, *La vie quotidienne* 102: their sex is not specified); or, as I have translated, other rich young people their own class, in contrast to Lucretia, who oversees the slaves at work.

[22] Livy 1, 50, 9: *infortunium*, "punishment," or "there will be hell to pay," is a word used in comedy, J. Bayet, *Tite-Live, Histoires, I* (Paris 1963) *ad loc.* G. Dumézil, " 'Pères' et 'Fils' dans la légende de Tarquin le Superbe," *Hommages à F. Bidez et à F. Cumont* Collection Latomus II (Bruxelles 1949) 77-84.

[23] Livy uses the technical word *appello* only for the Etruscan kings, and puts it in the mouth of an Etruscan queen: 1, 48, 5, *regemque prima appellauit*. Cf. 1, 34; 1, 39; 1, 47, 3; 1, 47, 5; and 1, 47, 10, *muliebri dono regnum occupasse*. Earlier kings received only the *salutatio*: Numitor, 1, 6, 2; Romulus (and Remus) 1, 7, 1.

On Cleopatra in Horace's Ode 1, 37, M. Putnam, forthcoming article in *Ramus*.

[24] E. Peruzzi, *Origini di Roma I. La Famiglia* (Florence 1970) 49-66.

[25] Cf. Peruzzi, *op. cit.* 67: "conoscere il nome della donna sarebbe equivalso a *cognoscere mulierem*"; therefore only the *nomen* (patronymic) was used, not the *praenomen*.

[26] But see the tradition that Tarquin changed his *praenomen*, from *Lucumo* to *Lucius*, thus becoming "naturalized," with the normal Roman three names, L. Tarquinius Priscus (Livy 1, 34, 10: *domicilioque ibi comparato L. Tarquinium, Priscum edidere nomen*).

[27] Livy 1, 34; 1, 39.

[28] Heurgon, *La vie quotidienne*, 110-111.

[29] Livy 1, 46-48. The whole passage is carefully worked out as a Greek

tragedy (*tulit enim et Romana regia sceleris tragici exemplum*), with the strong figure of the queen, leading finally to the Republic and to *libertas* (*...ut taedio regum maturior ueniret libertas ultimumque regnum esset quod scelere partum foret*); cf. above, Lucretia and Harmodius and Aristogeiton. The *monumentum* set up to this crime by Tullia is the Vicus Sceleratus, made impure by the blood of her father scattered on the chariot wheels. The reading *monumentum* in 1, 47, 6, where Tullia complains that she, unlike Tanaquil, *nullum monumentum in dando adimendoque regno faceret*, makes more sense within this whole context than the reading, *momentum*, adopted by most modern editors; though the majority of the mss. and the best ones, have *monumentum*. The edition of W. Weissenborn and H. J. Müller (Berlin 1885) has *monumentum* in the text, but refers to 4.12.9, *nullum momentum,* in the notes. Cf. *ut Iouis templum in monte Tarpeio monumentum regni sui nominisque relinqueret*, of Tarquinius Superbus (1, 55, 1; cf. 1. 36. 3, where Tarquinius Priscus eventually leaves a *monumentum* to his defeat by Attus Navius).

[30] Athenaeus, 517F. Homosexual love seems to be a standard literary rather than an artistic (realistic?) motif, even in Greece, Brendel, *op.cit.* 25. Perhaps what seemed most shocking to a Greek was the unseemly presence of the wives.

[31] Athenaeus 517E-F: ζητῆ δέ τις αὐτόν, ὅτι πάσχει τὸ καὶ τό, προσαγορεύοντες αἰσχρῶς τὸ πρᾶγμα. Cf. Tacitus' account of Nero's outrageous conduct: what really horrifies the aristocratic Roman historian, even more than incest and murders, are the unsuitable artistic, Greek — therefore foreign — ideals of the emperor. G. Charles-Picard, *Augustus and Nero* (New York 1965; translated from the French, originally published in Paris, 1962) 86 ff.

[32] Banti, *op.cit.* 65, on Caere's great wealth and foreign contacts, and the baroque, exaggerated taste of her gold jewelry (74-75). It was Rome's fate to be next door to the most cosmopolitan city of the richest people in the Mediterranean, when she herself was still only a village. It has been supposed that pieces of silver plate in the Regolini-Galassi and Bernardini tombs were inscribed with the names of their owners, who were women: *Vetusia*, and *Larthia* (or *Larthi*) — Heurgon, *La vie quotidienne* 112f.; *MEFR* 73 (1961) 142-145; A. Alföldi, *Early Rome and the Latins* (Ann Arbor 1965) 192 — but the ending may be the masculine genitive, the names then being masculine, *Vetus, Larth*: M. Pallottino, *StEtr* 34 (1966) 427. See H. Jucker, *Gnomon* 37 (1965) 298, for discussion and bibliography.

[33] K. Oestenberg, "Excavations of the Swedish School at Acqua Rossa," paper presented at the V Congresso Naz. di Studi Etruschi e Italici, Orvieto, June 28 - 30, 1972.

[34] Posidonius, in Diodorus Siculus, *Bibl.*, 5-40. L. Bonfante Warren, *JRS* 60 (1970) 60, on Livy 2, 12. Slaves and freedmen in Etruria: W. V. Harris, *Rome in Etruria and Umbria* (Oxford 1971) 121-129, with previous bibliography, and Pfiffig, *Gymnasium* 75 (1968) 111.

[35] Banti, *op.cit.* 112-114, pl. 38.

THE ROLE OF WOMEN IN ROMAN ELEGY:
COUNTER-CULTURAL FEMINISM

JUDITH P. HALLETT

DOMUM SERVAVIT. LANAM FECIT: "She kept up her household; she made wool." This was the ideal Roman woman – in the eyes and words of what was doubtless a male obituary writer, late second century B.C. vintage.[1] Our information on the role traditionally assigned Roman women – and by *role*, as distinct from social position and rank, I mean the socially prescribed pattern of behavior manifested by females when dealing with people who are not females – suggests that it involved little more than submissiveness, supportiveness, and stability. By the end of the Roman Republic and the beginning of the Empire, the men empowered to determine how women could and could not comport themselves apparently modified certain inconvenient regulations; nevertheless, they remained remarkably faithful to the spirit, if not the letter, of earlier laws reducing women to chattel status. While Roman society undeniably acknowledged the existence of women's physical charms and mental endowments, for the most part it merely "patronized" females, accepting them only when they adhered to rigidly (and externally) delimited norms of conduct. Women were not as a rule admired for their individual qualities, much less permitted to function autonomously or esteemed for so doing.

But very few rules want for exceptions. In Latin love elegy, and the particular upper and upper-middle class social environment in which it flourished, we directly encounter a violation of the general behavioral principles outlined above. The women featured therein managed to attain a singularly exalted stature, to be appreciated as people in their own right. Their admirers, moreover, not only glorified them out of genuine adoration, they were also motivated by a powerful, often mischievously subversive desire to differentiate themselves and their own system of values from existing forms of conduct. Consequently, the amatory elegists do not restrict themselves to venerating their beloved. They even cast her in the active, masterful role customarily played by men. They do not simply conceive of their emotionally-absorbing romantic liaisons as acceptable activities; they consider them, and the poetry emanating from them, no less strenuous and praiseworthy pursuits than conventional Roman careers in

241

business, the military and the law. What is more, they are not satisfied with justifying their behavior; the Augustan elegists even recommend it wholeheartedly to others! By utilizing a new form of art to portray this role-inversion and achieve their sought-after moral conversion, they seem also to characterize themselves as a veritable "counter-culture," a modern term whose applicability to the love elegists deserves further exploration. We should, however, first ascertain the exact role of women in the elegists' Rome so that we can comprehend precisely what they reject and redefine. Then we may redefine. Then we may examine more closely the perversity and proselytism in the elegiac poetry of Catullus, Tibullus, Propertius and Ovid.

I. *Mores*

We can marshal abundant and varied evidence to substantiate our initial assertion that Roman society relegated women to a subservient, confined role. Tomb inscriptions, for instance, affirm that wifely obedience (the technical Latin term is *obsequi*),[2] domesticity, chastity and fidelity to one man brought their occupants earthly fulfillment and will qualify them for eternal acclaim.[3] Literary works also portray "nice women" as submissive and docile. Capitalizing upon the permissive, "holiday," mood granted comic performances, the playwright Plautus parodies the conventional Roman marriage formula, which consigns the bride to her husband's tutelage (*Cas.* 815-824). There a male slave, masquerading as a blushing bride, receives instruction from a slave woman on a Roman wife's duties and rights. Like everything else in the scene, however, the advice reverses reality: it depicts the *wife* as the dominant, forceful marriage partner.[4] Of equally great interest is the account which the Augustan historian Livy gives of the first protest demonstration over women's rights (or lack thereof), the insurrection against the *Lex Oppia* in 193 B.C. (34.1-8.3). Even the story's most outspoken liberal, the tribune who successfully agitated for the law's repeal, believes that women are by nature passive and retiring. He seasons his complaints over Roman women's lack of privileges and his demands for their equitable treatment with pious homilies on how women prefer dependence on males to emancipation of any sort (34.7.12-13). In this passage, moreover, we may discern the much-touted Augustan attitude toward women, a crucial component of the emperor's moral rearmament programme. This effort (promoted by wool-spinning among the socially invisible women of the imperial household and repeated claims of the empress' virtue) provides further, historical, corroboration for a view of Roman women as quiet, submissive creatures.[5]

But contradictory evidence confronts us as well. Scholars are quick to point out that, by the first century B.C., Roman women enjoyed considerable power and freedom, particularly when one compares them to their counterparts in fifth century Athens and in the early Roman Republic.[6] Marriage no longer required that a husband possess absolute ownership, *manus*, of his wife. Under the conditions of what was called marriage *sine manu*, wedded women could for all intents and purposes control property they had acquired from their male relatives and thereby retain some sort of individual identity; this arrangement also entitled either party to a divorce if he, *or she*, so wished.[7] And upper class Roman women could lead morally relaxed, independent lives without having to resort to *divortium*. One modern scholar notes that they began emulating the conduct of the exotic émigrées, largely Greek freedwomen, who flooded Rome from the eastern cities of her newly-obtained Mediterranean empire.[8] We can probably attribute such consciously loose behavior to a combination of envy and delayed emotional development: married by their fathers at the onset of puberty, Roman women faced the responsibilities of matronhood before they could cope with the romantic and sexual fantasies of adolescence.[9] Whatever the explanation, some *matronae* from illustrious Roman families so completely adopted the freedwoman's dissolute mode of conduct that students of Latin poetry have never been also to determine the marital status and social class of the Augustan elegists' mistresses with any certainty.[10]

How, then, can we reconcile these two sets of facts? First, by recognizing that Roman society offered its women only a limited and illusory brand of liberation – visible independence, yes; autonomy, no. Limitations first. For one thing, whatever possibilities for emancipation *did* exist only affected a small minority of Roman women, the wealthy and the rootless. For another, even the most emancipated and self-assertive Roman woman lived in a state of bondage if we compare her to the most retiring Roman male. Historians who deal with first century B.C. Republican Rome are prone to talk about the political sway exercised by the ladies of Rome's leading houses.[11] Women with the right connections – such as Fulvia, wife successively of Clodius, Curio, and Antony, or Brutus' mother Servilia – no doubt constituted a political force in their own right.[12] But to wax enthusiastic over the *total impact women as a group* had on the Roman political scene is in many ways tantamount to marvelling over the extent to which house pets influence their owners' living habits. *Quanta erit infelicitas urbis illius, in qua virorum officia mulieres occupabunt*, Cicero is reported to have said – stating unreservedly that woman's place is *not* in the forum.[13] Forbidden to vote or hold political office, women could not have possibly exerted an influence on political affairs that even vaguely approximated their representation in the general population. We should not, moreover, cling to any false notions about Roman women's freedom to come and go as they liked, or imagine that they cast off all sexual restraints. Before the civil wars women invariably stayed at home while their husbands travelled abroad to fight and engage in provincial adminis- tration; even after Augustus formally instituted the practice of taking his wife along on journeys, respectable women practically never left Italy without a male escort.[14] And, as Saara Lilja points out, while husbands had the right to philander as they chose – as long as they respected the chastity of a virgin or of another man's wife – wives were legally bound to uphold *fides marita*.[15]

Moving on to the grand illusions, we must not lose sight of the fact that a woman's social class and social acceptability were deter- mined by the men in her life, her "patrons" as it were. The upper class matron owed her eminence – and probably her blueblooded husband – to the wealth, contacts and maneuverings of her father and other male kinsmen; by the end of the Republic, the very survival of a marriage like hers depended upon her attractiveness as a symbol of success.[16] In addition, she was as strongly compelled to gratify men's whims and yield to their demands as was a freedwoman like Volumnia/ Cytheris, an actress whose coquetteries gained her the affections of Rome's leading men (among them Antony and the love elegist Cornelius Gallus). A major historical study of the late first century B.C. relates how some women of the upper classes took selfish advantage of existing social opportunities – involving themselves in politics and the arts, managing their own financial affairs – and paid dearly. Such "uppityness" lost them the ability to attract their male peers. "The emancipation of women had its reaction upon the men, who, instead of a partner from their own class, preferred alliance with a freedwoman, or none at all."[17]

This brings us to the second major *trompe-l'oeil* of Roman women's so-called liberation: the fact that women's new freedoms had really evolved in order to render them more serviceable to men and male political ambitions. As marriage without *manus* deprived a wife of claims to her husband's estate, one scholar on Roman law conjectures that it was originally devised by the prospective bridegrooms' families to obtain for their sons the advantage of a marital alliance without the usual obligations.[18] Easy divorce had similar benefits. It permitted fathers and brothers as well as spouses to discard politically useless in-laws in favor of more useful ones. Furthermore, in this world of constantly changing ententes and enmities, where women functioned as temporary cement, the power-hungry males who selected a kinswoman's marital partners often viewed women as things, not sentient, sensitive human beings. They tended to value women *as* mere political assets and not *for* redeeming personal qualities, evincing no concern for any feelings they might have. Witness Julius Caesar's behavior: how he cold-heartedly broke his daughter's engagement so that he might marry her to Pompey, or how he later contemplated shedding his own loyal wife in order to wed Pompey's daughter.[19] Or how his nephew Augustus forced a match between his daughter Julia and stepson Tiberius, at great emotional pain to them both.[20] Or how their legendary ancestor Aeneas abandons Creusa and Dido, two women who deeply love him, the first basically out of loyalty to male relatives, the second so that he may continue upon a political quest. When Aeneas finally decides to commit himself to a lasting relationship with a woman, he selects as his mate a king's daughter who cares nothing for him; he must also destroy much that is beautiful in primitive Italy to achieve this aim.[21] Hot political properties to be sure, but properties nonetheless, women of the late Republic and early Empire essentially reverted to their acquiescent, 'non-person' status under early Roman law. *Plus ça change, plus c'est la même chose*. No wonder women "over-availed" themselves of what freedoms they did have, indulging in clandestine sex or engaging in challenging activities at the risk of losing male approbation!

But we must reconcile the *ideal* of Roman women's seclusion and obsequiousness with the *fact* that many proper Roman women could and did mingle freely in public and have legally sanctioned carnal knowledge of more than one man. We must also come to grips with the patently licentious behavior of freedwomen and with the openly acknowledged demand for unrestrained, free-wheeling women of their type voiced by the men of the propertied classes. The frequent claims of uxorial rectitude on funeral inscriptions, Augustus' efforts to re-affirm the "old" Roman morality — such insistent self-righteousness suggests that its eulogizers are trying to combat a trend in the other direction, to contrast examples of "what should be" to "what actually is." The *princeps'* moral programme — lest we forget — included not only propaganda and financial rewards for child production. Its architect designed it for the express purpose of replenishing the depleted senatorial and equestrian ranks, Rome's ruling élite; it also featured laws requiring intra-class marriage of upper class males and forbidding adultery.[22] Clearly Augustus, notorious exploiter of the new moral freedom though he was, found the conduct of certain upper class men, and the effect that it had upon the females whose lives they controlled, downright subversive.

Suetonius and Cassius Dio tell us that the "new, moneyed" aristocracy, the equestrian rank, opposed Augustus' marriage and moral legislation.[23] We have, in addition, a far more eloquent and extensive protest against the sanctimonious moral assumptions and abusive social conventions of the late Republic and early Empire than ever could have echoed in the halls of the Roman Senate. It is, moreover, readily available and well-known to all students of ancient Roman culture. I refer to Latin love elegy, a form of self-revelation and indirect social criticism created and developed by members of the dissident equestrian class.[24] To be sure, the elegists' personal dissatisfaction with standard *mores* extended far beyond simple disenchantment with women's role – idealized and actual – in contemporary society. Yet Catullus, Tibullus, Propertius and Ovid all reveal discontent with both the traditional Roman view of women as demure, submissive chattels and the current Roman practices which allowed women an ostensible increase in freedom so as to exploit them more fully. They write of a social milieu which pays no heed to common social expectations about female – and, conversely, about male – behavior. The amatory elegists, or at least their literary *personae*,[25] speak on behalf of the people whose iconoclastic actions ultimately struck Augustus as threatening. They constitute what present-day social historians would call a "counter-culture," a movement which seeks to "discover new types of community, new family patterns, new sexual *mores*, new kinds of livelihood, new esthetic forms, new personal identities on the far side of power politics."[26]

I do not employ this current phrase, "counter-culture," simply to sound chic and *au courant*. If the wisdom of the past has anything to teach the present (certainly a belief cherished by all self-aware classicists), then the insights of contemporary man should bear on previous human experience as well. Furthermore, the label I am applying to the Latin love elegists and their coterie could not be more *à propos*. Like the counter-culture which sprang up in the industrialized Western nations during the late 1960's and early 1970's, this particular group was both young and conscious of youth's special privileges,[27]

246

advantaged in terms of social and educational background, and relatively affluent.[28] Their youthful self-assurance, well-placed connections, high degree of intellectual attainment, and financial security enabled them to disdain accepted social practices. While more humble, unschooled and impecunious Romans deemed the "nuclear" family arrangement an economic necessity, the elegists could reject the idea of a subservient, supportive wife who bears multitudinous potentially useful offspring in favor of an exciting, attractive and spiritually inspiring female companion. These same personal advantages also permitted the amatory elegists to display a certain cynicism about politics; Propertius, for example, actually appears to question whether he or *any* individual can influence the governmental processes in what latter-day terminology would call a totalitarian state.[29] Instead, they invested their hopes and energies into maintaining romantic attachments, replacing the loyalty they were expected to pledge their *patria* with undying allegiance to their *puellae*. In addition, the Latin love elegists, like the counter-culturists of today, tried to forge a new, more meaningful set of values, embody them in actions which substituted for conventional social practices, and glorify them through art, the most exalted and effective means of human communication. Their redefinition of female and male roles, our concern here, nicely exemplifies their arch contrariness and wistful inventiveness in all matters; the attractive way in which they generally depict their relationships with women helps recommend their *vitae novae* to others.

II. *Amores*

From the very first, the Latin amatory elegists indicated both their non-compliance with widely-accepted behavioral norms and their bent toward social innovation by consciously and deliberately (if sometimes ironically) inverting conventional sex roles in their poetry. Catullus draws on the language of Roman politics in describing his relationship with Lesbia. He thereby infuses his avowals of love and devotion with a peculiar immediacy for the Roman reader; at the same time he indirectly attempts to question current social assumptions about upper-class male conduct and re-tailor them to accommodate his own emotional needs. Thrice in his elegiac poems, most notably in the closing lines of 109 with *aeternum hoc sanctae foedus amicitiae*, Catullus terms his association with his beloved a *foedus*. The word *foedus* means a bond, a treaty, a political pact made by two equally powerful − in other words, *male* − parties;[30] *amicitia*, moreover, does not only signify friendship in our modern sense, but the political alliance in Catullus' day which substituted for party affiliation and demanded unswerving loyalty.[31] The poet depict this *foedus* as a hallowed pledge of mutual devotion, requiring efforts of a religious nature to sustain. Thus he attests to his own *pietas* and labels his commitment to his mistress *sancta fides, fides* being the late Republican word for "the bond of shared trust making possible political *amicitiae* between equals" (72.2-3).[32] Catullus, then — in direct contrast to many contemporary Roman males who regarded their womenfolk as insensate political pawns — conceives of his Lesbia as a full equal deserving of the deepest trust. What is more, we have no evidence to indicate that Catullus ever revered or deeply involved himself in the late Republican political scene or adopted its underlying values; consequently, we might further conjecture that he is also expressing some doubts as to the ultimate validity of a system in which men's feelings about their personal associates are often respected while women's just as frequently pass unacknowledged. Such an interpretation of Catullus' purpose in utilizing political imagery can also apply to lines 3-4 of poem 72, where Catullus swears that he loves Lesbia *non tantum ut vulgus amicam / sed pater ut gnatos diligit et generos*, "not only as most men love their girlfriends, but as a father loves his sons and sons-in-law."[33] A recent study of Catullan poetic language argues that these lines are also employing the metaphor of political alliance; Roman aristocrats of the late Republic chose sons-in-law (and their own sons' fathers-in-law) with great care.[34] They deemed a suitor's political connections and influence far more important than their daughter's feelings about him, since marriage would join their house with his.[35] In this passage, therefore, Catullus would be comparing his special affection for Lesbia to that which men hold for their closest political allies and "public representatives." His juxtaposition of *gnatos* and *generos* may well, furthermore, imply that while politically ambitious men tend to prize their hand-picked supporters as highly as their natural male offspring, they accord a lesser degree of esteem to their female children, whom they force to function in an adhesive capacity. Whatever Catullus' poetic and social intents, by likening his fondness for Lesbia to paternal pride and support, he distinguishes himself quite trenchantly from most Roman men.

Catullus' poetic vocabulary in his love elegies abounds with other politically-charged words and expressions: *officium, iniuria, bene velle, benefacta*.[36] Inasmuch as the end of the Republic also brought down the curtain on the large-scale political maneuverings by ambitious aristocrats (what Lily Ross Taylor calls "party politics"), we should not be surprised that the Augustan elegists never employ the word *amicitia* for the relationship between poet and mistress and invest the words *foedus* and *fides* with far more imprecise connotations.[37] Yet Catullus delineated his emotions and unusual social behavior through non-political language as well, by inverting an aspect of Roman social reality which endured for far longer than the political machinations of the late Republic. I have already mentioned the obligation imposed upon a Roman wife to remain faithful to her husband alone, though no such pressures impinged upon a male's sexual freedom. In Catullus, and later in Propertius, we find the males adopting the loyal, trustworthy, conventionally female role and even trying to come to terms with their mistresses' real and potential infidelities. The former compares himself – in lines 138-140 of poem 68 – to Juno, who was constantly deceived by her philandering spouse (140 *omnivoli plurima furta Iovis*), just as he is by Lesbia (136 *furta feremus erae*). The latter assumes a traditionally female stance in 2.7, when recounting his beloved Cynthia's joy at the repeal of a law which would have forced him to marry a woman of his own social standing and produce children to increase Rome's triumphs. In lines 7-10 he expresses utter revulsion at the now-remote possibility of marrying another woman. Even more significantly, he does not entertain the idea of adultery, of continuing his liaison with Cynthia despite his change in marital status; he in fact labels his legal involvement with a woman other than Cynthia betrayal (10 *prodita*) of their love. Further on in the same poem Propertius reaffirms his monogamous intentions (19 *tu mihi sola places*) and begs, in the subjunctive, that Cynthia feel the same way about him (*placeam tibi . . solus*). One can cite other instances in Propertius' elegies where a male in love assumes the traditional female role of devoted, dependent passivity and imputes masterful, active conduct to his beloved. Most notable is 2.13a.35-36 where the poet asks that his tombstone claim that he was *unius . . servus amoris*, the male equivalent of such well-utilized terms for wifely virtue as *univira*.[38] Of greatest importance, however, remains the fact that Propertius, like Catullus, expects faithfulness from men as well as, if not more than from, women and thereby spurns the double standard characterizing Roman male-female relationships.

We now come to the most-commented upon inversion of Roman love elegy, that depicting the mistress as enslaver, *domina*, and the lover as slave. Giving vent to one's darkest, most radically misandrous impulses, one could attempt to trace the source of such an elegiac convention solely to the love elegists' rightful anger at the way Roman men virtually shackled their women; after all, feminist doctrine maintains that patriarchal societies such as that of ancient Rome treat females no better than they do their lowest, most despised slaves. But such does not turn out to be the case. Catullus, Tibullus, Propertius and Ovid do not appear to posit any analogy between the social position of women and that of slaves. Nonetheless, the love elegists' use of the *topos* characterizing a lover as his mistress' slave should not for that reason strike us as any less remarkable or revolutionary. The idea of love-as-servitude, it is true, had circulated for centuries prior to the brief efflorescence of Roman elegy.[39] Yet the specific literary convention portraying one's lover as enslaver has an altogether different history. Formally originating in Alexandrian erotic poetry, it there invariably casts a *male* in the role of enslaver, whether the enslaved be a male, as happens most often, or a woman.[40] By transforming the archetypal erotic slave master into a slave mistress, then, by ascribing so much importance to a woman, the amatory elegists are displaying intellectual courage and originality as well as sheer infatuation. One critic calls this sort of transmutation a "radical break with Alexandrian poetic tradition," suggesting that the elegists were making a conscious rupture with literary as well as social and political orthodoxy.[41] But let us examine the development of this particular idea in the elegists themselves.

One tends to think of the Latin word *domina* as nothing more than a fancy term for "woman" or "lady." Such is the sense conveyed by the word's Romance descendants such as *dame* or *donna; domina* already has such a diluted connotation in the later books of Propertius[42] and in the love poetry of Ovid, who employs it in such places as *Amores* 1.4.60 and 3.2.80 as synonymous with *puella*. Its primal meaning, however, is that of "woman in command of household slaves," "the wife of the *dominus* in her capacity as overseer of the operations of the *domus* and its slaves."[43] *Domina* makes its début in Latin love elegy at lines 68 and 158 of Catullus 68. In each of its occurrences it appears in close connection with a *domus* which the lady inhabits, an indication of both its etymological parentage and Catullus' own connection of the word with residence in an impressive abode. But only by extension can we interpret the poet's use of it to describe the enslaving power a *domina* has over her combination lover / house mate. Catullus is, more likely than not, reverting to a socio-political frame of reference, as is his wont: characterizing the *domus* as a woman's particular sphere of influence, an area in which men prove powerless outsiders. Nevertheless, when he *does* talk about his helpless sub-servience to Lesbia, he calls her an *era* (68.136, in a passage dis-cussed earlier), a word which also means mistress of slaves.[44] *Domina*, then, does not come into its own as a term for "enslaving, tyrannical controller of man's fate as a result of man's adoration for her" until Tibullus and Propertius begin to use it — and then quickly deteriorates into an amatory commonplace.

Tibullus delineates his subjection to a *domina* as, figuratively speaking, a painful, physical state linked with chains and lashings. At 2.3.79-80 he speaks of doing his mistress Nemesis' bidding (*ad imperium dominae*) and thereby accepting *vinclis verberibusque*. He opens the succeeding poem by yielding to *servitium* and his *domina*, here again Nemesis, and bidding farewell to his inherited freedom (*libertas paterna*); he depicts this *servitium* as involving *catenae* and *vincla* (2.4.1-4). *Vincla puellae* also figure in poems referring to Delia: at 1.1.55 and (along with *verbera* and *slavery*) at 1.6.37-38. In the twenty-odd times that *domina* is applied, in the elegies of Pro-pertius, to the poet's mistress, the word lacks Tibullus' characteristic implements of physical torture as escorts. Only five occurences of *domina*, all in the Monobiblos, even portray Cynthia as imperious.[45] Yet Propertius also views his emotional state as a form of *servitium* (cf. 1.4.4, 1.5.19, 1.12.18; 2.20.20; 3.17.41). At lines 21-30 of 1.10, moreover, he dilates upon what this *servitium* entails: complete role reversal with a dollop of masochism. He himself must constantly en-dure Cynthia's faithlessness, but can only expect cruel punishment from her if he gives the least sign of infidelity on his own part. None-theless, he equates great self-humiliation with deep self-fulfillment in love; in 23-24 of the next poem he proudly attributes his moods to her treatment of him. Although Tibullus' and Propertius' modification of this particular "beloved-as-enslaver" convention serves primarily as a poetic, and not a social, protest, the two poets certainly must have taken cognizance of the extent to which men in Roman society decided the fate and feelings of women. At any event, by having women control them, they are sharply reversing social reality.

A post-script on Ovid and *servitium*. As stated previously, the word *domina* has shed its original connotations of "powerful, absolute rule" in Propertius' later books and in Ovid. What is more, when Ovid does speak of love's slavery in such passages as *Amores* 1.3.5 and 3.11a.12, he never bothers to define his interpretation of the concept; in his elegies it has become a hollow cliché for the idea of a lover's dependency. We can best explain the literal enervation of this once daring, vivid metaphor by saying that as its newness wore off, so did the zeal of its employers to legitimatize it. But there may be more to it than that. A point Ovid stresses in both the *Amores* (1.10.29-36) and the *Ars Amatoria* (2.682 and 727-728) is that both male and female should derive *equal* pleasure from love; in fact, he rejects homosexual practices (*A.A.*2.683-684) for their ''undemocratic'' nature, in that both parties are not equally gratified by lovemaking. Equal rights to erotic satisfaction — recalling Catullus' use of political imagery to elevate women's status in love to equal that of men — strike him as far preferable to inequality of any sort, regardless of the more powerful individual's sex. Could it be that Ovid is here trying to correct what he sees as emotional and moral imbalance in the attitudes of his Augustan predecessors? Not that he criticizes them outright — far from it. Propertius and Tibullus, especially the former, had to battle fiercely in order to establish the validity of love poetry and its practitioners' devotion to it (a point to which I want to return later); overstatement and exaggeration of the beloved's power apparently helped gain love elegy popular acceptance. But, after the battle had been waged and won, Ovid could tone down amatory elegy's polemic excesses and re-think its assumptions. To me, at least, it seems likely that he both recognizes and resents the ability of either sex to control or exploit the other *and* wants to resolve all sexual rivalries and tensions through equality in sex.

Finally, the most important inversion of all, one greatly facilitated by the love elegists' comfortable backgrounds and, in the case of the Augustans, by their feeling that they were not vitally needed in the Roman governing and expanding process. I am referring to the elegists' substitution of their mistresses and the pleasures derived from celebrating them for traditional Roman careers and their rewards. Their poetry describes *otium*, love and elegy (free time, women and song?) as activities which in importance rival accepted pursuits: the law and politics, financial acquisition, and the military, all pursuits which, in addition, supplied the elegists' male peers with livelihood, challenge, glory and security. To most Roman men of the elegists' station, women served as a means to one or several of the above ends. To the elegists, their mistresses and the satisfactions — sensual, artistic and emotional — they provided were end enough.[46] Catullus concludes 68 with the remark that Lesbia makes his life sweet, even though his adored brother is dead (159-160).[47] Tibullus proclaims at 1.1.57-58 that he does not care about praise; as long as he is with Delia, he can be labelled sluggish and lazy by ambitious men. What is more, at 2.5.111 he maintains that he could not write at all, were it not for Nemesis. Propertius, who at 2.1.4 calls his mistress his very *ingenium*, at 1.7.9-12 insists, like today's proud-to-be-unliberated suburban housewife, that he only desires identity through his beloved. Ovid ascribes his poetic talent to his mistress' inspiration (*Am.* 1.3.19; 2.17.34; 3.12.16); at *Amores* 1.15.1-6 he maintains that his poetry will grant him as much renown as military, legal and political careers do others.

What is more, all of the elegists use the language of "establishment practices," i.e. politics, law, finance and warfare, to portray their love affairs. Catullus, of course, speaks about his liaison as if it were a political alliance. Tibullus, Propertius and Ovid also employ political and juridical imagery:[48] Tibullus with *leges* at 1.6.69 and *lege* at 2.4.52; Propertius in such elegies as 3.20 (15-16 *foedera . . iura / lex*, 21 *foedere*, 25 *foedera*) and 4.8 (71 *foedera*, 74 *formula legis*, 81 *legibus*); Ovid with *Amores* 2.4.48 (*noster in has omnis ambitiosus amor*), 2.7, and 2.17.23-24 (*in quaslibet accipe leges; / te deceat medio iura dedisse foro*). We find the Augustan elegists all defending their love life as a respectable replacement for rank and wealth: Tibullus at 1.1.51ff., Propertius in 1.8a and at 2.34.55-58, Ovid petulantly in *Amores* 3.8. Most common of all, however, is the time-honored depiction of love as an equivalent of military service.[49] One calls to mind Tibullus 1.1.75; Propertius 1.6.30, 2.7.15-18, 2.14.24, 4.1b.135-138, 4.8.63-70; Ovid *Amores* 2.12.1, 2.18.2 and especially 1.9 (*Militat omnis amans*).

By using the "mainstream" language of conventional Roman careers to represent the devotion they bestow upon and the rewards which accrue to them from their mistresses, the amatory elegists are trying to make their feelings understandable to "straight" readers, those who have not undergone the same experiences that they have. They aim for comprehensibility, chiefly so that they can justify their life styles to individuals (and possibly even to portions of their own psyches) who subscribe to conventional assumptions, believing love and love elegy something worthless, *"nequitia."* Yet the Augustan elegists also appear to be struggling toward a greater goal: the conversion of others to their beliefs and behavior. Ovid's attempts to turn potential lovers into practicing ones need no lengthy documentation; his self-styled tenure as *praeceptor amoris* managed to terminate both his stay in Rome and the Latin love elegy. Tibullus soft-pedals his approach in such elegies as 1.1, 1.5, and 1.6: he simply paints his rural idylls with Delia so attractively as to entice his audience away from their tawdry existences. One immediately thinks of Charles Reich's lyrical, though often infantile and over-simplified, evocations of Consciousness III in *The Greening of America*.

But it is Propertius that should concern us here, since he, more than any of the elegists, fought to convince and succeeded in convincing the Roman literary public of love poetry's worth (without Propertius' victory, we should never have had an Ovid).[50] Furthermore, Propertius' efforts to justify his life style and recommend it to others deal to a large extent with specifying what personal qualities and traits he admires in the woman he loves. In further clarification of these ideals, he wrote his most spirited defense of and exhortation to his *raison de vivre*, the fourth and final book of his elegies. There, the poet devotes considerable attention to women who are *not* his love objects — something heretofore rather unusual in Latin love elegy. There, through contrasting the behavioral roles and personal values of these various women, both legendary and contemporary figures, with those of his mistress Cynthia, Propertius voices his general discontent with Augustan beliefs and reaffirms the validity of his own.

A word on the special character of Book 4, which in many ways represents a new phase in Propertius' poetic development. Cynthia, omnipresent in Book 1, highly visible in Books 2 and 3, is offstage more than on in Book 4. If any one figure can be said to hold center stage it is Rome — featured in aetiological elegies about her holy shrines, festivals, topography and in love elegies about her inhabitants, past and present. Yet, as stated above, Book 4 introduces several "other women," all in some way Roman, all quite different from Cynthia. Elegy 3 stars the contemporary *nupta relicta*, Arethusa, who bemoans the fact that her husband has left her to fight Augustus' campaigns. 4 is about the fabled traitress Tarpeia, depicted by Propertius as betraying the Roman citadel to the Sabines out of love for their commander, and not, as most accounts do, out of avarice for Sabine golden ornaments. In 5 and 11 Propertius delineates, through speeches delivered in the first person, two newly-dead women: the greedy procuress Acanthis and the idealized noble matron Cornelia. Cynthia's rivals (her successor Chloris in 7, the courtesans Phyllis and Teia in 8) and the Bona Dea worshippers barring Hercules from their shrine in 9 also play substantial parts within the book, not to mention such cameo roles as Arria and Cinara in 1b, Cleopatra in 6.

Cynthia, however, is still very much a presence in Book 4. Elegy 7, in the fashion of elegies 5 and 11, features a *post-mortem* on her; it largely consists of her own words to Propertius when her ghost appears to him in a dream. She is also dealt with explicitly in 8, implicitly in 1 and probably in 5. Furthermore, Propertius' characterization of Cynthia in Book 4 is perfectly consistent with that presented in Books 1, 2 and 3: a *dura puella*, masterful, assertive and ultimately successful in her attempts to maintain complete control of Propertius. On the contrary, none of Book 4's other leading ladies — Arethusa, Tarpeia, Acanthis, Cornelia — are shown to be truly vigorous, strong-minded individuals who in the last analysis succeed in their endeavors. All pale in comparison beside the incandescent Cynthia: Acanthis and Tarpeia are described as utter failures (5.66-74; 4.89-92), Arethusa and Cornelia as self-obsessed and dependent (cf. 3.11-16, 29-62; 11.29ff., esp. 61-72). And, most important of all, while Cynthia represents the very kind of woman Augustus — judging from the purport of his moral legislation — would have liked to eliminate, the other, "inadequate," females in Book 4 in one way or another embrace or even embody conventional Roman, that is to say Augustan, beliefs about woman's role. Her triumph implies their defeat, or at least casts considerable doubt on the worth of their conduct and their values.

III. *Clamores*

The plight of the young bride Arethusa in 4.3 poignantly illustrates the dire consequences of war, particularly Augustus' expansionistic campaigns and the enforced estrangements between men and their loved ones that they wrought. An off-and-on nine-year separation from her husband Lycotas[51] has rendered Arethusa querulous, hyper-emotional and neurotic; although she gives evidence throughout the poem that she is basically a stable, self-reliant and resourceful individual (17, 18, 33-40, 57-62), she melodramatically describes herself in a letter to her husband as a weak, minimally functioning creature who is perishing from loneliness (2, 3, 41-42, 55-56). Propertius paints Arethusa with love and sympathy. He intends, I think, that his readers laugh indulgently at Arethusa's efforts to bring her husband home through arousing his pity. Yet Propertius also wants to bring home to his audience the basic incompatibility between the demands placed upon women — to live in seclusion, faithful all the while to one man — and those placed upon men — to abandon the women they love and prove their virility through dangerous warfare abroad. Women in Arethusa's situation have every good reason to become unrealistic about themselves, purposely childlike, ultimately ridiculous. Elegy 9, moreover, serves as a structural and contentual counterpart of 3; it shows how men's adoption of brutal, warlike postures can alienate them from women of sensitivity and principles: Hercules' testimony to his past conquests avails him not in obtaining access to the spring of the Bona Dea worshippers.

Tarpeia in 4.4 also possesses qualities commonly found in respectable Roman women. By profession a Vestal Virgin, she is basically a passive, sheltered girl who values herself solely in terms of the material advantages she can give her prospective bridegroom: Propertius'/Tarpeia's exact word is *dos*, dowry (56); this dowry is Rome betrayed. Propertius does not, moreover, blame her tragic end on her moral impropriety, her defiling her vows of chastity. In fact, he portrays her compassionately, even to the point of assigning her guardian goddess Vesta and ruler Romulus complicity in her crime (69-70, 79-80). What he does see as responsible for her undoing are her materialistic, altogether inadequate, definition of her worth as a person *and* her total miscalculation of her idolized Tatius' nature resulting from her abysmal self-ignorance. In lines 55-60, when listing her qualifications for marriage to Tatius, she never bothers to document her all-consuming love for him. She blindly assumes that her *dos* alone can win him; in lines 57-60 she even claims that ravishing her alone would revenge the rape of the Sabine women — clearly deeming herself an invaluable political asset. Tatius, so noble that he would not honor crime (89), kills her as a traitress. The word employed for his punishment of her is again *dos* (92); Propertius thus stresses the potentially disastrous consequences of women's naive reliance upon connections rather than internal strengths for social acceptance.

In elegy 5, the poet represents the bawd Acanthis as a woman who prizes the conventional, outward signs of manly — and, in his day, Roman — valor .. material acquisition and military glory. What is more, not only does Acanthis consider material rewards the sole worthwhile incentives in life (21-26) and encourage a client, probably Cynthia, to accept the advances of well-paying soldiers and sailors and slaves (49-53); not only does Acanthis conceive of women's beauty and charms as highly marketable qualities (59-62), valuable only if lucratively capitalized upon, she also views the events customarily comprising a love affair, those which frequently serve as subjects for amatory elegists' poems — quarrels (31-32), observance of Isis' rites (34), involvements with other men (29, 39-40) and one's birthday (36) — as opportunities for a girl to squeeze money out of her admirer. She also tells her client to be dishonest at any, and for every, price, beginning with advice to *sperne fidem* in 27 (cf. also 28, 29, 34, 41-42, 45). Predictably, she also disdains poetry and its practitioners because they lack material rewards (54-58). Acanthis, then, epitomizes the attitudes Propertius and his fellow elegists opposed: esteem for money and the external indications of "manliness" (in the word's narrowest sense); "reification" of women as potentially profitable items; acceptance of unfaithfulness and mutual exploitation as part and parcel of male-female relationships; scorn for poetry and its spiritual benefits. At the close of 5, Propertius and his ideals are vindicated: Acanthis dies penniless and unmourned. Like other women in Book 4 who care inordinately for money — Arria in 1, even Cynthia's rival Chloris in 7 — or war — Cleopatra in 6 — she has been doomed to failure, punished for her faulty appraisal of what really matters in life.

Propertius no doubt admires Cornelia, the noble matron featured in the closing elegy of Book 4, for strictly adhering to the behavioral code prescribed for women of her class. But her portrait, a defense of her life which she herself delivers from the grave, is not, upon close inspection and after comparison with the similar posthumous address given by Cynthia in 7, altogether flattering. Although Cornelia makes much of her lifelong fidelity to one man (11, 35-36), although she has virtuously followed the rigid patterns of conduct set forth for "nice" Roman women (cf. especially 33-34, 45-46, 60-64), although she takes great pride in the fact that her male relatives have done all the right things in war and politics (29-32, 37-42, 65-66), although she can congratulate herself on the moral rectitude of her female ancestors (51-54), nevertheless Cornelia is totally devoid of real personality and utterly lacking in substance. In 7.53 and 70 Cynthia speaks openly of her faithfulness to and love for Propertius, a surprising avowal for a a *demi-mondaine*; yet we never hear Cornelia say what one might expect from a devoted wife and mother, that she *loved* her husband or her children. One gets the impression, in fact, that Cornelia has no true emotions, just acquisitive impulses. She imagines the events and people in her life as material possessions, describing them either by the physical objects connected with them (11 *currus*, 29 *tropaea*, 32 *titulis*, 33 *praetexta*, 34 *vitta*, 61 *generosos vestis* etc.) or, in the case of her children (12, 73), as financial entities, *pignora*. She herself does not want to be judged as a person; instead, she derives her entire sense of self-worth from her ancestry (11, 23-32, 37-40), the accomplishments of her living relatives — including her mother's brief and unhappy marriage to Augustus (55-60, 65-66), and her own possession of a socially prominent husband and the three requisite children (61-64, 64-70). Furthermore, she carries this materialistic evaluation of herself and her colorless behavior to unrealistic extremes: she demands privileged treatment in the underworld (19-26), predicts that her family will be beset with unendurable grief over her loss (77-84), and expects special status in the afterlife (101-102). Propertius has portrayed Cornelia as the ideal wife of both longstanding Roman tradition and contemporary political reality: chaste, fecund, retiring, loyal; rich in political connections and associations with Republican Rome. Yet, when one compares her to Cynthia as she is depicted in Book 4, one understands quite clearly that, and why, Cornelia is not Propertius' kind of woman.

And what is Propertius' kind of woman? Self-sufficient, forthright, unmaterialistic in her desires and self-image. Within the confines of Book 4, we encounter Cynthia rejecting wealthy admirers in favor of Propertius, criticizing the greed of her successor Chloris, expressing her own wants as plain ones, and forcing Propertius himself to abandon luxurious habits (8.51-52, 7.39-40, 7.73-76 and 79-86, 8.75-78). She wants to be cherished for her own personal qualities, notably her honesty and deep affection – not purchased as one would a material commodity. Appearing in Propertius' dreams after her demise, she recalls how she remained faithful to him *in her fashion* (7.52 *me servasse fidem*), thereby winning an ultimate resting place beside Andromede and Hypermestre, both wronged, *sine fraude maritae* (7.62ff.). Yet she does not hesitate to chide Propertius for his ungrateful and unfaithful conduct (7.13-32, 8.73-80). Furthermore, her unabashed frankness extends beyond her displays of passion and temper to her realization that mere complaining does no good in effecting reconciliations with a wayward lover. In 8, while alive, she singlehandedly stages an actual military siege to expel rivals (51-66); in 7, posthumously, she coolly declares that death will soon reunite the temporarily errant Propertius with her (93-94). Cynthia may be willful, unpredictable, domineering; to Propertius she seems sensuous, unaffected, exciting. What better advertisement for his unconventional life style could he have selected than his portraits of her in 4.7 and 4.8, surrounded as they are by pictures of more conventional, far less interesting, female types? What better cause for living counter to standard *mores* than a female companion who defies the expectations of what is ultimately an inequitable, hypocritical society and affords inspiration for a simple, honest and rewarding life?[52]

Clark University

NOTES

[1] *ILS* 8403; cf. also M. I. Finley, "The Silent Women of Rome," collected in his *Aspects of Antiquity* (London 1968) 130-131.

[2] See G. Williams, *JRS* 48 (1958) 25, for instances of *obsequi* on the gravestones of Roman women from varied social backgrounds and historical periods.

[3] Cf. *CIL* 6. 1527=31670, the so-called *Laudatio Turiae*; cf. also *CE* 81 and 968 and the inscriptions quoted by Williams (above, n.2) 21 n.20.

[4] So Williams (above, n.2) 17-18.

[5] See R. Syme, *The Roman Revolution* (Oxford 1939) 335, 443-445; cf. also Horace, *Odes* 3.14.5.

[6] For example, Syme (above, n.5) 445; G. Luck, *The Latin Love Elegy,* 2nd edition (London 1969) 22-24; S. Lilja, *The Roman Love Elegists' Attitude to Women* (Helsinki 1965) 31-42.

[7] On the difference between *manus*-marriage and marriage *sine manu*, see Cicero, *Topica* 3.14 and, *inter alios*, P. E. Corbett, *The Roman Law of Marriage* (Oxford 1930) 68-106, 113.

[8] So Luck (above, n.6) 23-24. In dissuading his (male) readers from sexual intrigues with respectable married women, Horace (*Satires* 1.2) implies that adultery, often of a promiscuous variety, on the part of matrons from the best families was a well-acknowledged fact of Roman life in the late first century B.C. Horace condemns such intrigues as dangerous and inconvenient for the men involved — not as immoral in themselves!

[9] On the standard age of marriage for Roman women, see J. A. Crook, *Law and Life of Rome* (Ithaca 1967) 100 n.9, who cites M. K. Hopkins, *Population Studies* 1965, 309 ff.

[10] See the discussion of Lilja (above, n.6) 37-41, from which one may choose to conclude that the Augustan love elegists deliberately left the social status of their mistresses vague.

[11] Cf. Syme (above, n.5) 12, 384 ff., 414.

[12] For their political wheeling and dealing, see, *inter alios*, Cicero, *ad Att.* 2.11.2; Velleius Paterculus 74.2.3.

[13] The remark is quoted by Lactantius, *Epit.* 33(38)5. See K. Ziegler's fifth Teubner edition of the *De Republica* (1960).

[14] See J. P. V. D. Balsdon, *Life and Leisure in Ancient Rome* (New York 1969) 237.

[15] See Lilja (above, n.6) 176-177, who in turn cites T. Mommsen, *Römische Staatsrecht* (Leipzig 1899) 22 f., 688 f. and 691. See also Balsdon, *Roman Women* (London 1962) 214, who calls attention to the elder Cato's dogged championship of a double standard already codified in law, and Cato's own remarks on the topic given by Aulus Gellius (*Noct. Att.* 10.23.5).

[16] See C. L. Babcock, *AJP* 81 (1965) 1-32, on Fulvia, the aforementioned female "politico"; he ascribes her ability to attract three prominent and powerful spouses to her consular stepfather and considerable wealth.

[17] Syme (above, n.5) 445.

[18] Crook (above, n.9) 104. Marriage without *manus* also enabled the male members of a woman's own family to retain control of her property after her

marriage. Admittedly, such an arrangement benefitted women in certain respects. Their husbands no longer held complete sway over them; they could appeal to their fathers against their husbands and vice-versa. But it also permitted and in fact encouraged male relatives to interfere in "personal," conjugal relationships whenever they felt it in their interest.

[19] Plutarch, *Caesar* 14.4-5; Suetonius, *Julius* 27.1.

[20] Suetonius, *Augustus* 63.2 and 65; *Tiberius* 7.2-3.

[21] See K. Rogers, *The Troublesome Helpmate. A History of Misogyny in Literature* (Seattle 1968) 44, who notes Aeneas' imperviousness to female charms, "male chauvinism," and Lavinia's utter vacuity. In all fairness to Vergil's Aeneas. however, it should be said that Creusa's ghost justifies — *ex post facto* — Aeneas' abandonment of her as divinely ordained (*Aen.* 2.776 ff.).

[22] Cf. Suetonius, *Augustus* 34.1; Cassius Dio 54.16; Horace, *Carm. Saec.* 17-20; also the review of Balsdon (above, n.14) by T. J. Cadoux, *JRS* 52 (1963) 207.

[23] Suetonius, *Augustus* 34.2; Cassius Dio 56.1.2.

[24] For a summary of the evidence for the elegists' social standing, see Lilja (above, n.6) 10-16.

[25] On the issue of sincerity in the Roman elegists, see A. W. Allen, *CPh* 25 (1950) 145-160. While the elegists' allegedly autobiographical poetry may not be telling the exact truth about their personal lives, it at least presents an internally consistent picture of the "characters" which the elegists assume *gratia artis*. Latin love poetry also must have purposely contained enough general social realism to strike a chord of recognition in readers' hearts; i.e. the Roman literary public must have known other men who acted as Tibullus, Propertius and Ovid claimed to behave. See also Lilja (above, n.6) 23-30.

[26] T. Roszak, *The Making of a Counter Culture* (Garden City 1969) 66; cf. also C. Reich's similar descriptions of Consciousness III in *The Greening of America* (New York 1971) 233-285. Counter cultures have blossomed in other historical eras too — recall the medieval Goliards and their revolt against ecclesiastical moral strictures.

[27] So Propertius at 2.10.7 ff., Ovid at *Amores* 3.1.26 and 68 label love poetry an art form for young artists.

[28] See again the evidence assembled by Lilja (above, n.6) 10-16 about the backgrounds of the Latin love elegists; see Roszak (above, n.26) 26-41 on those of the 1970-style counter-culturists. From what the elegists tell us about their origins and imply about their education and social contacts, we should, I think, infer that the "poverty" of which they speak (e.g. Tibullus 1.1.19-22; Propertius 4.1b. 128-130, 4.5.54-58) is either fictitious or a voluntary form of social protest against the materialistic occupations and preoccupations of the equestrian class.

[29] See, for example, his unwillingness to participate in the emperor's military campaigns and the national military spirit in 3.4.15-22. Cf. also two recent studies: J. P. Hallett, *Book IV: Propertius' Recusatio to Augustus and Augustan Ideals* (unpublished dissertation, Harvard 1971) 98-102, on 4.2, which details Vertumnus' futile pleas for continued forum residence in the

face of the emperor's projected expansion of the Basilica Julia; J. P. Sullivan, *Arethusa* 5 (1972) 17-25.

[30] See D. Ross, *Style and Tradition in Catullus* (Cambridge, Mass. 1969) 85.

[31] So L. R. Taylor, *Party Politics in the Age of Caesar* (Berkeley 1949) 7-8.

[32] Ross (above, n.30) 85, who cites M. Gelzer, *Die Nobilität der Römischen Republik* (*Kl. Schr.* 1.71-73).

[33] *gnatos* can, of course, mean both male and female children, but its juxtaposition with *generos*, which can only signify husband of a daughter or female relative, strongly suggests that it here refers to sons.

[34] Ross (above, n.30) 89.

[35] See discussion in Taylor (above, n.31) 33-34; see also the evidence regarding Caesar cited in n.19 above.

[36] See discussion in Ross (above, n.30) 86-88.

[37] At 1.11.23, in fact, Propertius calls Cynthia his *domus* and *parentes*; at 2.18b.34 he expresses a desire to be her *filius* or *frater*. In so doing he recalls the words of Andromache at *Iliad* 6.429-430 and of Tecmessa at 518ff. of Sophocles' *Ajax*, both of whom liken their relationship with their husbands to that a child enjoys with his parents. Yet Propertius is here assuming the dependent, helpless role of these defenseless women and not the protective one of their heroic spouses. Instead of seeking in Cynthia an equal with whom he can carry on an adult relationship of mutual respect, he looks to her for nurturance and protection, roots and direction. See the discussion below on the mistress as *domina* and as a replacement for worldly satisfactions as the logical extention of Propertius' submissive yearnings.

[38] Cf., for example, 2.27.13-16, where the mythical plight of Eurydice is assigned to a male lover, the behavior of Orpheus to his *puella* — an observation made by Luck (above, n.6) 128-129; cf. also 1.11.23 and 2.18b.34, discussed in the preceding note.

[39] Cf., for example, Euripides, fr. 132; Plato, *Symposium* 183a.

[40] See F. O. Copley, *TAPA* 78 (1947) 285ff.; A. La Penna, *Maia* 4 (1951) 187ff.; Lilja (above, n.6) 76ff.

[41] Luck (above, n.6) 129.

[42] 2.3.42; 2.9.45; 2.17.17 are good examples.

[43] Cf. A. Ernout and E. Meillet, *Dictionnaire étymologique de la langue latine*, 3rd edition (Paris 1951) I 326ff. s.v. *"dominus."* Lilja (above, n.6) 81 notes that we have no Republican examples of the word *domina* to describe a *dominus'* relationship with his wife — the word only refers to relationships between slaves and their mistresses.

[44] Cf., for example, Ennius, 287 Vahl. (Medea described by her household staff); Plautus, *Cas.* 311.

[45] 1.21, 3.17, 4.2, 7.6, 17.15.

[46] Cf. also J. E. Fontenrose, *CPCP* 13 (1949) 371-388.

[47] The interpretation of these lines given by K. Quinn in his commentary on Catullus (London and Basingstoke 1970) 396.

[48] For a fuller discussion of "establishment imagery" in the Augustan elegists, see Lilja (above, n.6) 63-73.

[49] The earliest occurrence of the theme is *Anacreonta* 26 A. For the tradition of *militia amoris*, cf. A. Spies, *Militat omnis amans* (Diss. Tubingen, 1930).

[50] On Propertius as "ur-Ovid" (so L. A. Richardson and K. Quinn) or on Ovid as "Propertius vulgarized" (so J. P. Sullivan), see the *entretiens* of the American Philological Association-Propertius colloquium, December 29, 1971, recorded by D. N. Levin, 422 and 426 respectively.

[51] 29-20 B.C. Line 9 refers to the war against the Getae waged by M. Crassus in 29 B.C. and to Augustus' planned invasion of Britain in 25 B.C.; lines 7 and 63 describe a proposed campaign against the Parthians, just prior to Augustus' recovery of long lost Roman standards from them in 20 B.C.

[52] I would like to thank the following for assistance and encouragement: Sheila Dickison, Katherine Geffcken, Carol Kline, Donald N. Levin, Mary Lefkowitz, Jane Loeffler, John Sullivan and Dorothea Wender.

RAPE AND RAPE VICTIMS IN THE METAMORPHOSES

Leo C. Curran

O VID'S ATTITUDE TOWARDS women may appear paradoxical. Although some of his work may give the impression of extravagant, if elegant, sexism, at other times he exhibits a sympathy for women and an effort to understand, as well as a man can, women's intellectual and emotional life rivaled by no male author of antiquity other than Euripides.[1] Ovid was a keen student of female behavior and his painstaking observation of women finally led him in the *Metamorphoses* to a recognition of aspects of their condition that have only in very recent years become common currency.

In the *Metamorphoses*, Ovid's fascination with the experience of women and their behavior and his passion for infinite variation on a theme combine to produce a survey of women and rape from manifold points of view.[2] These predilections, so often misapplied by the poet elsewhere, here lead to much more than the collection of techniques for manipulating women that constitutes so much of the *Amores* and the *Ars*.

The *Metamorphoses* is not a treatise on rape, any more than it is merely a handbook of mythology, an analysis of love and desire in all their manifestations, a critique of Roman values, traditional and Augustan, an enquiry into the nature of personal identity, an affectionate parody of the *Aeneid,* or a survey of the varieties of the universal phenomenon of metamorphosis. It is more and less than any of these. Ovid has many irons in the fire and in a given story the relative emphasis on any one of these themes varies in accordance with the economy and requirements of that story and of the poem as a whole. When one stands back to look at the *Metamorphoses* from the perspective of rape (of course other perspectives are appropriate in other circumstances), one can see that by sketching a detail here and a detail there, Ovid has produced a coherent and consistent vision of rape. No single story exhibits all the elements, although some, for example the Daphne, come close; but when the tales are taken together, a unified picture emerges.

Although there are some fifty or so occurrences of forcible rape, attempted rape, or sexual extortion hardly distinguishable from rape, one would scarcely guess the fact from reading most of the commentaries on the *Metamorphoses*, Ovidian scholarship in general, or the retellings of Ovid's stories in the mythological handbooks. Traditional scholarship, systematically ignoring this fact and refusing to take rape seriously, glosses over unpleasant reality and prefers eumphemism to the word rape.[3]

Rape is the dirty little secret of Ovidian scholarship. It is true that the language of ancient myth is full of euphemism (usually transparent, however) and Ovid himself may give some encouragement to obscurantism since his own language is often less than explicit. However, he had as justification of his practice the artistic principles of decorum and of variety and indirection of expression. Modern scholars have no such excuse. Once we accept the fact that Ovid's subject is frequently rape, the commentators' elegant variation of nomenclature becomes either evasion or condonation.

When commentators discuss or annotate the sexual exploitation of women by, for example, Jupiter, they prettify the ugly facts of serial rape with such coy euphemisms as "amours," "loves," "courtship," or even "marriage" (the latter term may seem to betray an eccentric understanding of the institution of marriage, but is actually bowdlerism carried to the point of dishonesty), although there is occasionally a closer approximation to the truth and we may hear of a woman being "ravished." When scholars can bring themselves to utter the word "rape," it is employed as a noun and in a most imprecise sense, with connotations suggesting anything from a love affair to seduction to abduction; thus we find "the rape of Europa," rather than "Europa's rape by Jupiter" or "Jupiter raped Europa," wording which would carry some intimation that rape is a most intimate violation of a woman's person. "The rape of Europa" is as vague and figurative as the Nazis' "rape of Czechoslovakia." In fact, the second phrase conveys a greater impression of shockingness and atrocity, since the language of the literature on Ovid has made us so used to phrases like the first where the word "rape" has been thoroughly sanitized.

The commentators' arabesques of euphemism are the verbal manifestation of certain underlying prejudices and habits of mind. In the commentaries, as in society, it has not been the practice of men lightly to accuse another male of rape even if, as it turns out, the rapist is a figure in a myth thousands of years old. Classical scholars apparently require the same stringent proof of rape as do our least enlightened rape laws, police, and courts. When such proof is lacking, the reaction is disbelief or amusement.[4] Whether it be motivated by by timidity or prudery, their own sexual anxieties, or a misguided and fundamentally hypocritical reverence for the innocence of their younger readers, the conventional reticence concerning sexual matters is a badge of our profession and I will not concern myself here with what contribution it may make to the preservation of our society's patriarchal mythology of rape. However, such reticence has obstructed a full ventilation of what Ovid has to tell us about rape in the *Metamorphoses*.

Many of the best known stories are of rape and their victims' less well known sisters are also numerous. In addition Ovid will insert rape into a myth where other versions omit it; for example, Tereus in other sources *marries* Philomela after tricking her into believing that her sister has died. Book I establishes the centrality of the theme very quickly. After the Chaos, the Creation, the Flood, and the Deucalion and Pyrrha, the latter half of the book is devoted to three tales of attempted rape, the successful rape of Io and the failed attempts upon Daphne and Syrinx. With these rape stories, comparable in length with the introductory ones, the poem has in its first book settled down into one of its dominant themes.

The varieties and strategies of violation to be found in the *Metamorphoses* are many. In the discussion that follows it will not always be necessary to distinguish between successful attempts and failures, since Ovid, as we shall see, seems to regard failure, in its consequences for the woman, almost as seriously as success.

The act of rape itself, i.e., penetration and the manner of its accomplishment, usually takes very little time to relate. This holds true both in those stories which are told at length and deal at leisure with things other than the act itself, e.g., preliminaries, concomitants such as flight of the victim, a transformation of shape, or other consequences, and in those instances which constitute little more than a mention of the occurrence of rape. Ovid is not writing pornography but a kind of epic and does not have a lickerish interest in clinical and anatomical details.

Brevity, however, is often less a concession to decorum than a means of illustrating some significant aspect of rape. The various quick rapes have different causes and effects and, although there may be violence, actual, threatened, or implied, it is not dwelt upon in such stories.

The casualness may be on Ovid's part. He simply does not take time to stop for details in the rape of Liriope (3.342-344), Medusa (4.798-799), and Dryope (9.331-332). Offhand allusions to rapes are reminders that, in the world of the *Metamorphoses*, whatever else is going on in the foreground, rape is always present or potential in the background. Arachne's catalog of divine lechery in which most of the rapes take less than a line, depicts a universe infested by rapists dressed like Disney characters. The brevity and the need for variety of expression make it difficult here to separate rape from seduction, but Ovid calls them all *caelestia crimina* (6.131). Moreover, as I shall argue later, seduction can be so grossly deceptive or unfair as to be the equivalent of rape.

At other times the casualness may not be Ovid's but the rapist's: he impulsively takes a woman who momentarily catches his fancy. Syrinx is an example, although her rapist fails. Her story follows the Daphne, whose encounter with Apollo was her first and only one with a potential rapist. Syrinx is in contrast a seasoned veteran, who seems to have made a career out of evading rapists. In all previous encounters, she escapes with both virginity and humanity intact; with Pan she salvages virginity only at the cost of human nature. Pan seems to have no more than the most fleeting interest in her; Ovid does not bother to mention the god's physical arousal or emotional state.

One type of quick and easy rape is rare in the *Metamorphoses*, although it is commoner among the few rapes in the *Fasti*: the sleeping victim. In the *Metamorphoses* this happens only to Chione, whom Mercury puts to sleep with his wand before raping her, and Thetis, who is asleep when Peleus begins his assault, although she soon awakes and the assailant is denied his swift conquest after all.

At other times rape is instantaneous in order to demonstrate the helplessness of woman in the face of overwhelming male superiority. The suddenness speaks to the familiar men's fantasy of instant and effortless conquest of women (to which are directed the advertisements in men's magazines for aids guaranteeing to make women fall at the user's feet as soon as they see him). For the god in such stories it is lust at first sight, followed by immediate gratification, or

266

gratification slightly delayed by pro forma preliminaries. In the Io verbal seduction and flight are merely a brief prelude to the swiftly accomplished act:

> terras
> occuluit tenuitque fugam rapuitque pudorem.   (1.599 f.)

The speed of the rape of Persephone is breathtaking:

> paene simul visa est dilectaque raptaque Diti.   (5.395)

Similar instantaneous rapes occur in the Caenis (12.189 ff.) and the Perimele (8.592).

Violence is more prominent in the longer rape stories, where it ranges from wrestling (in the Thetis) to overt sadism and killing. The rape of Orithyia is over quickly and the force of the assault itself pales before what might be called rhetorical or pictorial violence in the long and impressive portrayal of the raging fury of Boreas after the failure of his polite and proper courtship (6.685 ff.). As Ovid merges the anthropomorphic features of Boreas with a more naturalistic representation of the irresistible force of wind and storm, he creates such a vigorous poetic image of virility as aggressive potency on the scale of the forces of external nature that the actual rape becomes almost anticlimactic. At the same time there is a large measure of burlesque, although Ovid is not making a joke out of rape. For him it is no contradiction to present rape simultaneously as both an outrage committed upon a woman and as a grotesque caricature of masculinity.

In the Semele, although the act is not technically rape, the violence of male sexuality is so enormous that it annihilates the woman.[5] This myth and, to a lesser extent, the Orithyia illustrate some of the darkest shadows not only of rape but of certain other aggressive and sadistic forms of male sexuality. We are confronted with an especially disagreeable fantasy and one that, if modern pornography from de Sade on is a reliable guide, has an appeal to no small proportion of "normal" men: virility of such spectacular potency that it can seriously hurt, wound, or even destroy a woman in the very act of intercourse.

It was not of course Jupiter's own wish that Semele be immolated. However, there is deliberate and undisguised sadism in the Tereus where, after having raped Philomela the first time, her brother-in-law tears out her tongue and goes on raping her. In what is probably the most repellant passage in all of Ovid, Tereus is represented as repeatedly deriving sexual pleasure from Philomela's mutilated body and the language implies that the mutilation was itself a further sexual stimulant (6.549 ff.). Ovid understands male sexuality at its most savage.

Rape can be prefaced by attempted seduction. Jupiter approaches Io with a speech which, although it is short, manages to combine flattery, an invitation to enjoy the cool of the woods, an offer of protection against any dangers there, and a boast of his distinction as a lover; when all fails, he is ruthlessly direct and efficient in taking what he wants (1.589-600). Peleus makes a very brief effort of this kind (11.239). Apollo's very long seduction speech to Daphne is so absurd that he makes a fool of himself, but after its failure, he proves to be as ruthless as his father (1.504-552). The Pomona is one of the longest versions of this theme (14.623 ff.). Vertumnus, having tried many disguises, finally subjects the woman to a long speech of seduction. When this method fails, he resumes his true form and prepares to rape her.

The longest version of the theme of the seducer who is ready to turn to rape if persuasion fails is the Polyphemus and Galatea (13. 749 ff.). In a literary equivalent of the archaeologist's Cyclopean walls, Polyphemus sings an interminable love song of ludicrously overstated rhetoric (782 ff.). The frustration of his suit drives him to kill his rival Acis and would obviously have driven him to rape Galatea had she not already plunged into the sea (870 ff.). The monstrous scale of the Cyclops' rhetoric and violence is a reductio ad absurdum of, respectively, the overweening confidence of some seducers and, like the fury of Boreas, an image of the headlong ferocity of exaggerated male sexuality.

There is another kind of seduction. Germaine Greer makes the useful distinction between "grand rape" and "petit rape." The former is what is usually defined legally as forcible rape. Petit rape she proposes as the proper label for certain conduct which is conventionally called seduction, but in which the seducer in fact has some disproportionately unfair advantage over the woman. He need not threaten her, but it is his superior power which induces her to acquiesce against her will. Susan Brownmiller speaks of "unpleasant but not quite criminal sexual extortion." Examples are the employer and secretary or the professor and student, both matters to which the attention of the courts is currently being drawn in civil rights violation cases. A good specimen in Ovid is Leucothoe, who has excited the lust of the god Sol. After gaining entry to her room disguised as her mother, it takes the god less than three lines to reveal his identity in grandiloquent and self-laudatory terms and simply to announce that he finds her desirable, an indeed smug and perfunctory way to proposition a woman (4.226-228). Although absolutely no force is used or threatened and even the proposition is left unspoken, Leucothoe is seized with fear. Yet it is not so much her fear that makes her submit as it is the awesome appearance and power of the god after he has resumed his own form. Ovid makes clear the distinction between the two: "*Although* she was terrified, she was overwhelmed by the god's radiance and endured his assault without protest" (4.232-233). The Latin conveys her emotional state with exquisite accuracy: *posita vim passa querella est.* Although the phrase *vim passa* and its variants verge on the formulaic in the *Metamorphoses,* Ovid here uses it with extreme precision. No force or threat of force is present, but the effect is the same. She recognizes that resistance or demurrer would be futile. To many jurors in a trial today this would not constitute rape at all. Ovid knows better; and so does the woman, if one were to try to imagine a modern parallel to Leucothoe's situation, who is alone in her house when a powerfully built man of supreme self-confidence enters her bedroom and announces to her that he wants her.

There are in the *Metamorphoses* what may be called truncated or elliptical rape stories, in which the act itself is not mentioned and which, although longer, resemble the casual allusions to rape discussed above. Sometimes we are told only of events after the rape, as in the Latona and the Alcmena, in which Ovid relates the wandering of the pregnant Latona and the difficulties both women endure in giving birth of the fruit of their rape. At other times we are given only the preliminaries and the story is never finished. Such is the case in the Europa, which begins with a leisurely description of Jupiter in the guise of a bull, the growing passion of the deceived Europa, and then the gradual and literal fading into the distance (and out of the poem) of the girl on the back of the swimming bull. Since we all know the story or can easily guess how it will end, Ovid does not have to tell it all.

Along with actual rape, we sometimes find rape fantasy or metaphorical rape in which the man's "conquest" is characterized by the language and imagery of rape. The Tereus, in addition to actual rape, also includes a large section which is an extended rape fantasy in the mind of the rapist (6.455 ff.). As for metaphorical rape, the language used of Hippomanes' race with Atalanta has clear sexual implications and the implications are often those of conquest (10.560-685).[6] Pluto's violent entry into the earth by splitting the pool of Cyane to its depths and the effects upon Cyane herself (5.492) are cast in the language of rape and shortly thereafter Arethusa speaks of the penetration of Cyane as rape: *patuitque invita rapinae* (5.492).

*   *   *

Of much greater moment throughout the *Metamorphoses* than the mechanics and strategies of the act of rape is the matter of the intellectual and emotional experience of the woman and her suffering. It is this aspect of rape that most deeply engages Ovid's acute observation and sympathetic imagination.

The stereotype of woman as victim, frequently with the corollary of masochism, is nowadays such a commonplace in life and so much a staple of the news and entertainment media that we may be conditioned to accept it unthinkingly as perfectly "natural." In soft- and hardcore pornography and in both popular as well as in much professional psychology, women are supposed to enjoy being victims, to prefer masochistic fantasies, and to want to be raped. (The degree of consciousness with which the idea of woman as victim is entertained or the degree of explicitness with which it is portrayed on a given occasion is of course variable.) We may be predisposed therefore to overlook the significance of the fact that a major function of woman in the *Metamorphoses* is to be a victim, usually, although not exclusively, of rape. The victims are not always female, and when they are, it is not always rape that they suffer; nor are the persecutors by any means always male. Victimizers are frequently female and often the stories in which they figure have to do with divine jealousy and other subjects unrelated to rape. In spite of these qualifications, those victims who are raped females constitute a large proportion.

Ovid does not simply take the role of woman as victim for granted and get on with the story at hand; rather he draws out its implications.

He shows that there are few from whom the victim can expect sympathy or comfort. She and not the rapist is the one who must bear the injury, the guilt, society's blame, and the punishment.[7]

Damage, physical or psychological, done to the raped woman is ignored or taken lightly by society. Jupiter dismisses Pluto's rape of Persephone as *amor* rather than *injuria* (5.525-6). The suffering of the victim is deemed by others to be secondary to that done to father or husband, since traditionally in Western and other societies, rape is perceived primarily as an offense against the property or honor of men. The rivers of Thessaly, instead of lamenting the fate of Daphne, are worried about her father and whether he should be congratulated or consoled (1.578). Perimele's father found her rape so unendurable that he cast her from a cliff to her death (8.593 f.). When the Centaurs begin raping the women at Pirithous' wedding, Theseus protests that this is an offense to the groom and to himself as a friend of the groom, not to the women being raped (12.227-229). Guilt is perhaps the most unjust burden the victim must bear. Women have been so brought up that the victim may be quite ready to believe that *she* is somehow guilty and that she must have done something to provoke or to cooperate with the rape. Daphne curses her beauty because it has made her too desirable (1.547). The raped Philomela speaks of her own *crimen* (6.541) and cannot look her sister in the eye (605 f.); she twice gives vent to her shame by using of herself the highly pejorative term *paelex* (537 and 606). In the *Fasti*, the husband and father of Lucretia *forgive* her (2.819 ff.). Society's blame is the external counterpart of guilt. A portion of society has always believed that unless a woman is beaten senseless or bound helpless, what she calls rape must always require at least minimal consent on her part. Leucothoe pleads that she was raped against her will, in vain, since no force was used and she did not cry out for assistance (4.225 ff.). Callisto's pregnancy, when it becomes known, is called *crimen* (2.462) and she is guilty of *culpa* (452). Ovid is here speaking from the point of view of society; earlier it is Jupiter to whom he ascribes *crimen* (433). Philomela realizes that if she tells others of her rape, it will be at the cost of her own *pudor* (6.544-545).

In addition to blame, punishment is the lot of the victim, while the rapist normally suffers nothing worse than occasional embarrassment. Leucothoe's father buries her alive. Vengeance may be exacted by a deity of the victim's own sex. Minerva takes vengeance on Medusa for having the presumption to be raped in the goddess' temple with her version of a punishment fit the crime: defilement of what was most beautiful in her, her hair. Harshest of all in her persecution of rape victims is Juno. It is Juno who destroys Semele and chooses a means which, since she is at the same time delivered of her fetus, is also a travesty of childbirth, a mordant irony on the part of the deity to whom women in labor pray for easy delivery. It is Juno who torments the parturient Latona (6.232 ff.) and Alcmena (9.284 ff.). In such stories which link woman's reproductive functions so closely with extreme suffering or death and in which the expected protector of women is instead a cruel personification of the horrendous dangers of childbirth, Ovid display a sensitivity to the enormous risk women faced in exercising their sexuality in a period long before the advances in gynecology of the past century. In addition, most of his rape victims are very young virgins (a subject to be discussed below in another context) and the considerably higher incidence of complications in childbirth in the case of primiparas in their early teens cannot have escaped the notice of the Romans. It is against this grim background of medical helplessness, in which intercourse, pregnancy, and childbirth mean potential destruction for the women, that the poet sets his band of light-hearted rapists.

The punishment of the victim is not limited to her body. Ovid subordinates the physical discomforts of Io's new life as a heifer to her psychological suffering and to the indignity and degradation of her new state.[8] Her ludicrous appearance expresses the humiliation and mortification to which the raped are subject. She has no privacy under the constant gaze of the many eyes of Argus, like a woman in a small town who must endure the stares of all in their knowledge that she has been raped. (One is reminded of the look in the eyes of the villagers who surround the widow in *Zorba the Greek*.) She is so terrified by the sight of herself in a reflection that she tries to flee from herself. That rape has robbed her of her very humanity is shown less eloquently in her external bovine shape than in her terrible isolation and inarticulateness. In the strange transformation rape has forced upon her, she is unable to plead with her captor by either voice or gesture; she cannot at first communicate with her father and sisters nor can they recognize her. When she does succeed in making her identity known, the reunion is short-lived since Argus soon drives her off. The psychological torture worsens when Argus is replaced by the Fury Juno sends to drive her in madness and terror all over the world. When her sanity and humanity are finally restored it is only with timidity that she can resume speech.

Callisto, before any physical punishment, must undergo the anguish of rejection by Diana, who pitilessly exiles from her company the nymph who had once been her special favorite by reason of the very virginity robbed from her by a Jupiter who had played the cruel trick of assuming Diana's own appearance. When Juno subsequently transforms Callisto's grace into the shambling awkwardness of a bear, the grotesqueness of the elaboration of the details of metamorphosis again expresses mental as much as bodily suffering in a dehumanization the victim lasting long after the rape itself.

The role of Juno requires special discussion, since it may seem anomalous for a female so often to be the one who punishes other females. One obvious reason why we find her victimizing women is that she happens to be the very jealous wife of the greatest womanizer in ancient mythology. She has, however, a much larger significance. However unhappy Juno's own experience with marriage, she was in myth and, much more importantly, in cult, the divine patroness of the social institution of marriage. In the *Metamorphoses* she is the embodiment, on the level of myth, of society's attitudes toward marriage and such related matters as virginity and adultery. As Virgil is in the *Aeneid*, Ovid is dealing with social realities not in discursive terms but through symbolic objectification of them in the figures of myth. Juno is the villain of the *Aeneid* and, as Pöschl has shown, represents certain historical, political, and social phenomena.[9] Much of the *Metamorphoses* is devoted to playful, yet respectful, parody of the *Aeneid*, as Ovid merrily stands many of its characters and incidents on their heads. In his hands, the Virgilian Jupiter, that champion of order and the values of civilized society, becomes an anarchic rapist; Virgil's Juno, the embodiment of anarchy and the breakdown of society, becomes the defender of society's rules regulating marriage and extramarital sexuality. As such, it is altogether fitting that dehumanization be so often her way of punishing the rape victim: expulsion from the human race is the ultimate excommunication from society. That her motives are very personal and even small-minded does not diminish her credibility as an objectification of society's sexual mores. On the contrary, her character, especially her jealousy and vindictiveness, provides the handy, natural, and thoroughly human (in the sense in which the gods of ancient myth behave like humans) motivation for her behavior. Juno was appropriate because her husband's rapes constantly put her into situations in which it was natural and plausible for her to punish rape victims and thus be the agent of society in enforcing its rules.

For Ovid to take the Homeric Hera of sometimes comic jealousy and the Virgilian Juno of antisocial anarchy and turn the goddess into society's police is no harder to accept than Virgil's elevation of the rather disreputable Aphrodite of Greek myth and literature into the patroness of the loftiest of Roman and Augustan ideals. Indeed, the union of the all-too-human character of the deity as a mythological figure with a larger social reality is much more convincing in the case of Ovid's Juno than in that of Virgil's Venus. Although Ovid can hardly have conceived of it in such explicit terms, the treatment of Juno as such a prominent victimizer of women shows how a patriarchal society conditions women to punish their own sisters.

Beauty is dangerous. The victim's beauty (and, as in sensational newspaper accounts today, the victim is always beautiful) is an invitation to and a justification for rape, as in the case of Herse (2. 723 ff.), Philomela (6.451 ff.), Caenis (12.189 ff.), or Daphne. Since Daphne does not want to be raped, she is turned into a tree. One way of reading this story is to conclude that a woman who is unwilling to accept what is the potential threat faced by every woman might as well be a tree. That way she can never be dressed in the wrong way or in the wrong place at the wrong time. Since being the inhabitant of a beautiful young female body seems to some a standing invitation to rape, Daphne is emitting misleading signals. Transforming her into a tree prevents further misunderstanding. Daphne is the kind of woman about whom a certain sort of man says, "All she needs to straighten her out is one good rape." Or as Ovid himself says to Daphne in apostrophe:

te decor iste, quod optas,
esse vetat, votoque tuo tua forma repugnat.   (1.488 f.)

Compare the daughter of Coroneus, who prefaces the account of her rape with the words: *forma mihi nocuit* (2.572). Cephalus pays a compliment, very odd in a context other than the *Metamorphoses*, to his wife's beauty: alluding to the rape of Orithyia, he calls his wife "more worthy of raping" than her sister (7.697).

274

Beauty and sexual desirability are enhanced by disarray of clothing or hair, by discomfort and embarrassment, or by fear. For the rapist these are all aphrodisiacs. Daphne's hair and dress are attractively disordered by the breezes as she flees Apollo and Leucothoe's "terror was becoming to her" (4.230). Of Europa we are told in the *Fasti*: "and her very fear was a source of additional beauty" (5.608). Below I will discuss the theme as the subjective, internal experience of the victim; here terror is an external attribute that further goads her attacker on.

In age the typical rape victim in Ovid is quite young, although only once does he speak of child rape as such; in the Persephone he conveys the pathos of a situation in which the girl is too young even to realize what rape is: she grieves more for the damage done to her clothing than to her person. Most of the other victims are also very young and would today be considered virtually children or what many would call Lolitas (although this is to ignore the fact that Nabokov's heroine was only pubescent and in the event was no innocent virgin). In Ovid's society a girl was an appropriate sex object from her earliest teens, i.e., as soon as she was actually nubile.

The premium placed on the extreme youth of the victim is closely related to, but by no means the same thing as, the exaggerated value given to virginity. The obsession with being the first man to possess a woman is dramatized sharply in the story of Chione, who is simultaneously spotted by both Phoebus and Mercury (11.301 ff.). Both desire her at once, but Apollo has at least the patience and decency to wait until nightfall. Mercury rapes her on the spot and forces Apollo to reap *praerepta gaudia* (310). It is clear that Mercury's priority by a few hours is a major feather in his cap.

What are the implications of the fact that the victims are rarely married and almost always barely nubile virgins? We have seen that the price of beauty is rape. So too is the price of childish innocence and virginity. It is all in the nature of things, the normal.

Girls have always been taught to be passive rather than assertive and that training, along with relatively lesser size and weight, makes women physically vulnerable to rape.[10] Although Ovid creates some notably forceful female characters elsewhere in the *Metamorphoses*, his rape stories exhibit women's weakness. As he puts it succinctly in the *Fasti*, "When a woman fights, she loses" (2.801), and in the Callisto he asks, "Whom can a girl overpower?" (2.436).[11] The theme is stated over and over again in the constantly recurring similes likening women to the hapless prey of ferocious beasts and birds. Furthermore, the youth and the innocence of the typical victims enhance their weakness, as in the case of Philomela; she is exceptional, however, in her transition from helplessness at the time of her rape to immense strength in her vengeance at the end of the story.

The story of Caenis is especially instructive for an understanding of Ovid's awareness of the implications of the physical vulnerability of women. The story shows that the only totally sure way for a woman to avoid rape is to give up her own sex and become a man. Neptune, having raped Caenis, offers her a reward. The crime just committed against her determines her greatest desire, that she lose her womanhood: *tale pati nil posse; mihi da, femina ne sim; / omnia praestiteris* (12.202-203). Ovid makes clear the aggressive nature of rape and its intention to harm or hurt by having Caenis call it an *injuria* and, much more explicitly a few lines later, by identifying sexual penetration with a wound: changed from woman to man, Caeneus is now to be immune from any kind of penetration (12.206-207). The other sorts of penetration the speaker here (Nestor) has in mind are those of warfare, but the deliberate vagueness of language also includes vaginal and anal rape (which latter may be what Fränkel has in mind when he sees "a touch of dry masculine humor" in 12.201-203).[12] But it may not be a joke. It may be further emphasis on the vulnerability and passivity of women. Caenis' *tale pati nil posse* reminds one of the common Latin expression for the act of the passive male homosexual: *pati muliebria*. So far from womanhood is Caeneus now that he is impregnable to even that one kind of rape that makes a man like a woman. When the story of Caeneus is resumed later, Ovid again sounds the theme of the physical inferiority and timidity of women by having a Centaur taunt Caeneus with his once having been a woman (12.407 ff.). In Hermaphroditus' prayer that every man who enters Salmacis' pool, as he did, *exeat inde / semivir...ut mollescat*, there is a measure of anatomical accuracy in *semivir*; but this word and *mollescat* imply in a more general way that a woman is only an incomplete and softened (not just softer) man (4.385 f.).

Rape poses a devastating threat to personal integrity and identity and can destroy a woman's sense of self and of her relationship to others. A recognition of the severe emotional damage rape can inflict upon the personality of the victim is not surprising in a poem so con-

276

cerned with the nature of personal identity. Frequently the victim becomes confused as to who she is. Daphne can no longer live with her own body (a sharp distinction between self and body which is characteristic of schizophrenia). The raped Callisto has "forgotten who she is" (2.493).[13] Philomela suffers a confusion in her relation to her sister/rival and to her rapist/brother-in-law of exactly the kind being reported today by those who work with young incest victims (6.537 ff.). Io, so bewildered over her identity after her rape when she saw herself reflected in a pool as a cow-woman, "in terror fled from herself" (1.641).[14]

Rape does worse than undermine a woman's identity; it can rob her of her humanity. Change from human to non-human is a constant occurrence in the *Metamorphoses*, and the majority of instances of course has nothing to do with rape. However, transformation into the non-human is uniquely appropriate in the case of rape, for the process of dehumanization begins long before any subsequent metamorphosis of the woman's body. The transition from human to sex object and then to object pure and simple proceeds by swift and easy stages, its onset being simultaneous with the decision to commit rape. The final physical transformation of so many rape victims is only the outward ratification of an earlier metamorphosis of the woman into a mere thing in the mind of the attacker and in his treatment of her.[15] The identification of rape and dehumanization is intimate and virtually immediate in the Daphne, where the heroine begins to lose her humanity as soon as the chase begins. As Daphne runs from Apollo, the effect of the wind on her fluttering clothing and streaming hair corresponds closely to what the wind will do to the branches and leaves of the tree she is to become. After her transformation, Daphne as tree is an exact analog of a victim so profoundly traumatized by her experience that she has taken refuge in a catatonic withdrawal from all human involvement, passively acted upon by her environment and by other persons, but cut off from any response that could be called human. Ovid's language describing what he and Apollo choose to take as the laurel's "reactions" (1.556 and 566-567) has an eerie but psychologically correct ring to it.

The two elements perhaps paramount in Ovid's understanding of the psychology of rape are the victim's unwillingness and her terror. The women of the *Metamorphoses* do not secretly wish to be raped nor, when faced with rape, do they turn into more or less eager accomplices in their own violation, contrary to ancient and modern cliche and to the glib assumptions of the poet in his earlier works. The facile cynicism of the Ovid, where a woman's "no" means "yes," gives way to a new empathy with women and their real wishes. It is significant that he resists any temptation to exploit Tiresias' notorious appraisal of the pleasure women derive from sex (3.316 ff.).

The unwillingness of the victim is explicit or implicit in Ovid's telling of the stories I have dealt with so far. Here I wish to restate the point by way of calling attention of a special category of reluctant women. A great many of his heroines are nymphs and his seemingly eccentric treatment of them is a testimony to the significance he attached to his somewhat late discovery that women do not like to be raped. He takes such pains to make the resistance of these women unmistakable that he endows some of them with a deep-seated abhorrence of sexuality that would seem to border on the pathological. These are very special nymphs indeed.

Nymphs after all were young women who had a reputation for very active sexual lives (or "amorous propensities" as one of the handbooks discreetly puts it). Normally they did not have to be raped; nymphs played a role in myth not unlike that played in the male imagination today by the mention of airline stewardesses or cocktail waitresses.[16] But some of Ovid's nymphs are very different; they are totally dedicated virgins, much to the bewilderment of the satyrs they live among, who are used to more typical nymphs.[17] When the nymphs of the *Metamorphoses* resist, they are not being coy; they mean it. They will more readily endure the loss of anything rather than virginity, including womanhood, humanity, or life. We do not find that favorite modern male fantasy, the reluctant virgin who learns during or after rape that she actually enjoys it in spite of herself and becomes what is usually but illogically called a nymphomaniac. (One would expect *nymphiasis* on the analogy of *satyriasis*; it is the satyrs who were nymphomaniacs.)

With his penchant for ironic reversal, what Ovid has in fact done is to treat these nymphs as if they were those paragons of female virtue, the heroines of Roman legendary history, or the daughters of traditional, respectable Roman families, whose most precious possession was premarital virginity, a notion which, in his earlier works he had ridiculed as uncouth *rusticitas*. To state his case in the strongest and most paradoxical terms, he shows that *even nymphs* can be unwilling rape victims and chooses them as his heroines over and over again;

278

an analogy today would be a feminist who maintained the right of even a prostitute not to be raped as an a fortiori argument in defense of all women.

Callisto and Pomona are good instances of this extraordinary hostility to sexuality, but it is conspicuous from the first book of the poem, beginning with the programmatic Daphne, where Ovid has Cupid invent for use on the heroine a novel anaphrodisiacal arrowhead, as if she had to be inoculated against her normal proclivities as a nymph. The result is to make her reject all men and not simply resist Apollo's advances (1.471 ff.). Arethusa blushes because of her unwanted beauty and thinks it a *crimen* to be desired by men (5.584).

Ovid's emphasis on the violation of unwilling young women deeply committed to the protection of their sexual integrity illuminates the psychology of rape. The victims can apparently be ranked in a hierarchy of desirability. The married or sexually mature victim, almost entirely absent from the *Metamorphoses*, ranks lower than the young, inexperienced virgin, because her innocence means that what the rapist is forcing her to undergo is totally new to her and he is the first to have her. If she is not only inexperienced and simply reluctant, but also has a positive aversion to sex and wants desperately to keep her virginity, she is an even better victim because the rapist can then enjoy his mastery over her futile resistance against what she finds detestable and degrading. The three tiers in the hierarchy of rape might be likened to: the theft of used goods; the conquest of virgin territory, to change the metaphor to one of the many identifying woman with the land; and the rape of the will, which for many real-life rapists is much more important than anything done to the woman's body. The third type of victim is also more likely to have still another desirable feature lacking in the other two: timidity and fear, to which we shall now turn.

Perhaps the most impressive element of Ovid's treatment of rape is his understanding of the sheer horror of the experience for the woman and his ability to empathize with her and thereby to portray her terror with compelling authenticity. I shall for the most part be concerned with fear at the time of the rape, but it should be noted that it can last long after the actual danger has passed: the Muses must live on in a state of dread with the memory of their narrow escape and Persephone remains fearful even as Queen of the Underworld.

Ovid may simply state that the woman is terrified. He also has techniques for dramatizing the horror for us by casting it in the form of some common dread or anxiety we are all familiar with. Arethusa is especially threatened because she is naked. Nudity makes both men and women feel more vulnerable, even when there is no overtly sexual danger. Totalitarian police are well aware of its value as intimidation in enhancing the effects of actual physical torture and the famous shower scene in Hitchcock's "Psycho" owes much of the profound effect it has on audiences, male and female, to the fact that the defenseless heroine not only faces an armed psychopath but is in addition nude.

The terror can take the form of the suffocating dread of being overwhelmed, enshrouded, engulfed, or trapped. The victim may be surrounded or caught up in some embracing substance, as Arethusa is (5.621 ff.). In the Io, in the space of a little over a line, Ovid depicts the blinding, suffocating embrace with which Jupiter encloses the girl in order to rape her (1.599 f.). This kind of fear resembles the infantile dread of the dark, and we must remember that the victims in the *Metamorphoses* are young. When Boreas comes to rape Orithyia, the poet stresses the all-embracing dark cloud and the terror it inspires in the girl. Peleus twice *binds* Thetis. In the Tereus Ovid deals with the same fear so well evoked in Fowles' *The Collector*, that of being abducted and imprisoned far from home with no idea of where one is.

Unquestionably the most effective of Ovid's techniques for conveying the traumatizing horror of rape and to which he resorts throughout the poem is the recurring motif of flight and pursuit, of chase and the attempt to escape.[18] Pursuit is so frequent an incident that it may strike us at times as gratuitous or automatic; in some cases, he does not even indicate why the rapist, who at least some of the time is standing close to his victim, cannot simply reach out and seize her, but must instead resort to a chase. Far from gratuitous, flight was for Ovid the consummate means for the expression of the terror of the rape victim, the predatory appetite of the rapist, and the dehumanizing reduction of a woman to the level of a hunted animal.[19] It is also an excellent poetic method for putting the reader in the position of the victim, since we have all experienced similar dread in our nightmares and there is a distinctly nightmarish quality in the flight scenes of the *Metamorphoses*. We know this fear not only from our dreams but also from its evocation in so many films; indeed, our familiarity with it

280

derived from this source may lead us to underestimate the originality and perceptiveness of Ovid's choice of the motif.[20]

I have chosen to discuss the two salient instances of the use of the flight motif to express the terror of the victim, the Daphne and the Arethusa, although the peculiar horror evoked in these stories can be experienced only by reading Ovid's text and not the critic's paraphrase, analysis, and excerpting. That in one story the rapist fails entirely and in the other succeeds only in a qualified, i.e., metaphorical, sense can be no accident on Ovid's part. If actual penetration had been achieved it would have obscured the true import of these stories: the psychological effect on the victim's mind of the ordeal of being hunted down like prey can be more damaging than any physical invasion of her body. Of course there are other stories in which the pursuer does succeed in catching and raping his prey. In such cases flight, in addition to portraying the emotional state of the victim, illustrates other aspects of rape, such as the vulnerability of woman, who must flee instead of fighting back, and rape as an exercise by men of the aggression and violent physical activity they are trained in from boyhood.

In the case of Daphne, if we wish to be generous, we may say that Apollo's actions at first are closer to seduction than to rape, for he refrains from running as fast as he can and tries to persuade her as he pursues her. Ovid makes fun of Apollo and his overblown rhetoric. For example, he has the god resort in his excess to no fewer than four similes of animal predators chasing their prey only to claim, with transparent hypocrisy, that they do not apply to him (1.504 ff.). But the situation is no joke for Daphne and Ovid makes the frivolous Apollo spout his ridiculous similes only to lend a contrasting gravity to his own similar comparison a few lines later when Apollo abandons his slower pace and the chase begins in earnest. Now he employs the single, extended simile of a hunting hound chasing a hare (532-539). Its deadly seriousness is enhanced by language strongly reminiscent of Aeneas' final pursuit of Turnus (*Aen.* 12.749-765). Like its Virgilian model, the simile has a haunting quality. The direct description, resuming after the simile, contains two terrifying touches: the god is so close to the girl that he looms over her and breathes on her neck (541-542).

As for the Arethusa, the initial question of the story at once determines the tenor of all that follows: the terror of flight.[21] Ceres' *quae tibi causa fugae...?* ostensibly asks why Arethusa has taken refuge in Sicily and left her home (5.573). By the choice of *fuga* to designate her exile Ovid has at once established the act of fleeing (the basic meaning of *fuga*) as the dominant motif in the story and the feeling of being a hunted animal as a central element in the emotional experience of the rape victim. The tale proceeds at a leisurely pace until, from the depths of the water in which she is innocently and nakedly bathing, Arethusa hears a strange murmuring sound. At once the tempo quickens (5.598). In the two words *territa insisto* we are swiftly given the emotional reaction (terror) and the immediate defensive action (flight to the river bank: *insisto* is frequently used of the alighting of birds). Her would-be rapist's brief question, insidious in its simplicity and sinister in its repetition, again speaks of fleeing:

> 'quo properas, Arethusa?' suis Alpheus ab undis,
> 'quo properas, Arethusa?' iterum rauco mihi dixerat ore.
>
> (599-600)

Her flight is now described at some length, with similes (including the dove and the hawk), with catalogs of geographical names and varieties of terrain, and with constant reiteration of words for flight, pursuit, and physical exhaustion (605 ff.). Such elaboration may be self-indulgent and may suffer by comparison with the chilling economy of Alpheus' succinct question, but it is simply another technique, this time perhaps a shade too mechanical, to convey the feelings of the rape victim as prey in flight.

Two motifs first used in the pursuit of Daphne appear again, now with greater elaboration: her attacker's shadow looms threateningly before her and behind her she hears the sound of his feet and feels his panting breath on her hair. Diana comes to her aid by engulfing her in darkness, a form of assistance which, as I have argued above, illustrates another, but related, side of the terror of the rape victim. Hidden and trapped in a mist around which her attacker skulks, she is in her fear turned into water. Recognizing her in her new form, Alpheus resumes his own aqueous state. She loses her identity in his in a commingling of their waters that is described in sexual terms: *se mihi misceat* (638).

"Flight" in English has an ambiguity Ovid would have relished had it been available to him: flight is flying as well as fleeing. Despite the impossibility of the word play in Latin, the flight of the rape victim in the *Metamorphoses* can take the form of flying. In this manner the Muses thwart their attempted rape (5.288). As the daughter of Coroneus runs from Neptune, she is turned into a bird (2.580 ff.). The motif of flying is displaced in the Tereus until the end of the story (6.665 ff.), long after the rape, so that the pursuit of Procne and Philomela becomes an eternal reenactment of the original violation, as if the rape victim were to have a constantly recurring dream of her terrifying experience.

Terror, whether it be manifested by flight or in other ways, is thus placed by Ovid at the heart of the experience of the victim, which has been the major subject of my discussion. In the course of it, I have had occasion to comment on various aspects of the poet's treatment of the rapist as well. I would like to link these observations together by way of summary in order to argue that Ovid's habit of reverting to certain themes and motifs suggests that he was on the verge of a realization that rape is less an act of sexual passion than of aggression and that erotic gratification is secondary to the rapist's desire to dominate physically, to humiliate, and to degrade. Among these themes the most significant are: the violation of youth, the defilement of beauty, the exploitation of vulnerability, the representation of the rapist as a predatory beast, the predilection for violence, and the pleasure taken in the victim's terror and in the mastery of her will. Finally, Ovid's rapists are on the whole not the depraved or abnormal monsters who are the inaccurate stereotypes of the popular notion of the typical rapist today, but ordinary males, with the exception that, since most of them are devine, they enjoy greater ease and less restraint in obtaining what they desire. Jupiter and Apollo are no drooling psychopaths.

Although Ovid may not always have shown great respect for women as a sex, his fascination with them led him to an insight into their plight as rape victims almost unique in ancient literature. There are other major implications of my subject, but they cannot be discussed in this paper: 1) What role can we presume his rape stories to have played in the fantasy lives of his audience of upperclass Roman women[22] and men (the latter of whom had such ready accessibility to the bodies of women that any interest in rape must be explained)? 2) To what extent is Ovid himself, in the manner of a scientific analyst of society rather than an artist portraying society, consciously aware in the fullest sense of all that his stories reveal about rape? 3) Is his attitude sympathetic, indifferent, amused, or a sadistic? As for the last issue, it has not been possible to conceal my own belief, although I have not defended it, that Ovid exhibits a sympathy which, if sometimes patronizing or obscured by a lightness of surface or tone and by his love of burlesque and exaggeration, is fundamentally genuine and well conceived.

State University of New York at Buffalo

NOTES

[1] I wish to thank Ms. Margaret M. Tarajos for assistance in research for this paper and for advice and comments on matter of substance and style. I have also profited from discussions with Ms. Teri Ellen Marsh and Ms. Judy Godfrey. My female students, especially those in undergraduate courses on women in antiquity I have taught over the past few years, (some of whom have had direct or indirect experience with rape and rape victims) have also provided me with insights from perspectives far closer to those of Ovid's heroines than are personally accessible to me and with some knowledge of how women feel about rape. See also note 2 below.

The text used is Haupt-Ehwald-von Albrecht, *P. Ovidius Naso: Metamorphosen* 11th ed. (Zurich 1969), with one minor orthographic change: I will use the letter *j*.

This is an abridgement of the original essay in *Arethusa* 11 (1978). A still shorter version of it was read at the Women's Classical Caucus at the annual AIA-APA meeting in Atlanta in December, 1977.

[2] The most accessible and useful contemporary study of rape is Susan Brownmiller, *Against Our Will: Men, Women and Rape* (New York 1975), which has also been published in a paperback edition. Some of her argument is anticipated in briefer compass by Susan Griffin, "Rape: The All-American Crime," *Ramparts* 10 (September 1971) 26-35, reprinted in Jo Freeman, ed., *Women: A Feminist Perspective* (Stanford 1975) 24-39. Other recent works are Nancy Gager and Cathleen Schurr, *Sexual Assault: Confronting Rape in America* (New York 1976) and Carolyn J. Hursch, *The Trouble With Rape* (Chicago 1977). To those who are familiar with it, it will be obvious that contemporary literature on rape has very much influenced my approach, but this paper is about Ovid and to rehearse the evidence and parallels from such literature, except for an occasional reference, would add undue length.

[3] Recently there has been an encouraging tendency to replace reticence with

candor and to call a rape a rape. Some examples: Hugh Parry, "Ovid's *Metamorphoses:* Violence in a Pastoral Landscape," *TAPA* 95 (1964) 268-282 deals frankly with forcible rape; C. P. Segal, *Landscape in Ovid's Metamorphoses: A Study in the Transformation of a Literary Symbol* = *Hermes Einzelschr.* 23 (Wiesbaden 1969) which has some excellent remarks on such serious issues in the *Metamorphoses* as violence, suffering, brutality, and the violation of innocence and recognizes rape as such; W. S. Anderson, *Ovid's* Metamorphoses: *Books 6-10* (Norman 1972) which is candid and sensitive on the subject of rape and the victimization of women; Eleanor Winsor Leach, "*Ekphrasis* and the Theme of Artistic Failure in Ovid's *Metamorphoses*," *Ramus* 3 (1975) 102-142.

[4] For a specimen of one contemporary classical scholar's treatment of rape as a matter of innocent merriment, see *Classical News and Views* 21 (1977) 63, with its translation into elegant Latin verse of a joke about rape which is most insulting to women.

[5] Ovid's language is explicit in indicating that Semele's immolation takes place *during* the act of intercourse and not merely when Jupiter approaches her (3.284-286 and 308-309).

[6] Cf. Anderson's note *ad locc.* in his commentary (see note 3 above).

[7] On guilt and society's blame, see Adrienne Rich, *Of Woman Born* (New York 1976) 244.

[8] Cf. Fränkel 80. W. S. Anderson, in his article, "Multiple Changes in the *Metamorphoses*," *TAPA* 94 (1963) 1-27, and in his commentary, cited in note 3 above, is acutely sensitive to *psychological* metamorphosis.

[9] V. Pöschl, *Die Dichtkunst Virgils: Bild und Symbol in der Aeneis* (Innsbruck-Wien 1950) 31 ff.

[10] It is more than a matter of upbringing, size, and weight. Adrienne Rich (see note 7 above) 14 quotes an apparently anonymous review of Brownmiller: "...rape is the crime that can be committed because women are vulnerable in a special way; the opposite of 'vulnerable' is 'impregnable.' Pregnability, to coin a word, has been the basis of female identity, the limit of freedom, the futility of education, the denial of growth." For another supposed biological reason for vulnerability, menstruation, see Janice Delaney, Mary Jane Lupton, and Emily Toth, *The Curse: A Cultural History of Menstruation* (New York 1976).

[11] Many instances in the category of quick rape discussed above also illustrate female vulnerability.

[12] Fränkel 222 n82.

[13] Cf. Fränkel 80.

[14] Fränkel 79-80.

[15] For an analysis of the importance and meaning of other than physical transformation, see the works of W. S. Anderson cited in note 8 above. I have discussed two of the best examples of the dehumanization inherent in rape, the Io and the Callisto, above in another context.

[16] For the robust sexuality of the typical nymph, cf. Paully-Wissowa 17.2, col. 1547, *s.v. nymphai* (e.g., the preferred epithets for them of Roman poets were *salaces, improbae,* and *procaces*).

[17] Both kinds of nymph are represented in ancient sculpture and painting. Generally, they are the willing partners of the satyrs, but satyrs are occasionally depicted as resorting to rape.

[18] For the chase motif, cf. Otis 78f. As Parry (see note 3 above) puts it: "In the majority of instances, then, heterosexual relationships in the *Metamorphoses*, particularly when one party is divine, suggest violence, a chase, ultimate rape...." (273)

[19] Flight during or just after rape attempt resembles the *punishment* of wandering that often *follows* rape, e.g., Io, Callisto, and Latona. It should also be noted that some women who are not rape victims but who are driven to sexual acts against their will (like incest) by inner psychological compulsion, pay for their deeds by the same punishment of wandering. Myrrha wanders for nine months after her father discovers the identity of his mysterious mistress. The language of 10.475-476 is sexually loaded and suggests a further connection in Ovid's mind with rape:

> pendenti nitidum vagina deripit ensem;
> Myrrha fugit.

Byblis wanders after her incestuous lust is revealed and so does the object of that lust, her brother, who behaves here in a manner analogous to the female rape victim. Wandering is an endless repetition of the fearful experience of rape or an objectification of the guilt felt by the unwilling subject of incestuous desires.

[20] Ovid anticipates Hollywood, which has long capitalized on the profound psychological resonances of the theme, and film is perhaps a medium better suited to the realistic representation of the chase than is verbal narrative. The chase has become a cliche of the film, its comic variant going back beyond the Keystone Kops and what may be called its mechanical variant having become almost obligatory in so many recent films in which the spectator is more often expected to identify with the pursuer or to experience vicariously the exhilaration of controlling powerful machines at very high speeds. But the movies also have a long tradition in which the chase is chosen as the supreme expression of the terror of the victim, whether the pursuer be rapist, murderer, spy, vampire or other monster, or wild animal. Ovid was trying to do something similar in a much less tractible medium.

[21] Cf. L. P. Wilkinson, *Ovid Recalled* (Cambridge 1955) 176 on the motif of flight in the Arethusa.

[22] Research, which I have recently started, is beginning to shed some interesting light on the reaction to Ovid's rape stories on the part of contemporary young women.

THEODORA AND ANTONINA IN THE HISTORIA ARCANA: HISTORY AND/OR FICTION?[1]

Elizabeth A. Fisher

The Historia Arcana of Procopius is a puzzling work. The historian himself describes it as a continuation and correction of his eight-book de Bellis,[2] but its tone seems remarkably different from that of the earlier work – polemical, slanderous, even obscene.[3] Nevertheless, the Historia Arcana is useful as a record of opposition to Justinian's reign, and it is the longest and most detailed source for the life of his Empress, Theodora, and for that of General Belisarius' wife, Antonina. Historians discussing Theodora and/or Antonina must turn to the Historia Arcana, and they must adopt some working assumptions about the accuracy of Procopius' black picture of these women, since it contrasts with a few more favorable references to them elsewhere.[4] Scholars do not agree on this question, although it is important in reconstructing the lives of Theodora and Antonina and in assessing Procopius' historical methods. Gibbon, Holmes, and Ure, for example, accept Procopius' biographical statements as essentially accurate; Mallett rejects them as entirely false.[5] Recent opinion,[6] however, tends to regard the Historia Arcana as a mixture of fact and fiction, cautioning that the polemical and scandalous tone of the Historia Arcana compromises its accuracy, but conceding that some truth lies behind its slander. (A problem arises, of course, in separating basic truth from decorative lies; Diehl and Rubin,[7] for instance, credit the Historia Arcana with what they term "psychological reality" in Theodora's portrait). Once noted, it is not uncommon to account for the deceptive mixture of truth and exaggeration in the Historia Arcana by labeling it a reflection of gossip about the court current in Procopius' time.[8] The gossip theory is attractive, for it explains why Procopius' statements, outrageous and inaccurate as they may be, might have been widely believed by his contemporaries. Gossip as Procopius' source is difficult to prove, however, and no one has really tried to do so, beyond Diehl's observation that adultery of famous women was a communis opinio of the times and may be a topos in the biographies of Theodora and Antonina.[9]

287

A second and related problem is that Theodora and Antonina should appear at all in a work devoted to discrediting the Emperor and his general, Belisarius. Evans has noted the unusual prominence of these women in the *Historia Arcana* without really explaining the phenomenon except for an observation that Procopius apparently hated domineering women and therefore attacked Antonina;[10] presumably, a similar explanation could be offered to explain Theodora's appearance in the *Historia Arcana*. Ure, Schubart, Diehl, and Rubin[11] regard Theodora as a necessary object of the *Historia Arcana* and its slanders because of the great influence she wielded in the Empire; Rubin[12] (with Comparetti) also detects a literary purpose in the portrayals of Theodora and Antonina, observing that they effectively blacken the reputations of their husbands by association.

Procopius' purpose in including Theodora and Antonina prominently in the *Historia Arcana* cannot be determined with certainty, nor can it be separated from the question of the accuracy and/or credibility of the character portraits of Theodora and Antonina in the *Historia Arcana*. Evans' explanation depends upon the assumption that Antonina was either in fact – or in then-current opinions – as domineering as Procopius says she was, and therefore earned the historian's ill will and a place in the *Historia Arcana*. The other two explanations – that Procopius intended to discredit either the women or their husbands with his portrayals of them – persuade only if these biographies actually would discredit their subjects in the eyes of contemporaries; in such a case, the characterizations may be influenced by contemporary gossip and need not be true to be credible in the eyes of a contemporary audience. Modern readers assume that the portraits of Theodora and Antonina in the *Historia Arcana* were as scandalous and offensive to a Byzantine audience as they are to us. As Diehl suggests, however, this may be an unwarranted assumption;[13] what shocks us may have only amused or titillated Procopius' contemporaries, and portrayals which seem to us slanderous may have been relatively unremarkable to a sixth-century audience.

In evaluating Procopius' portraits of Theodora and Antonina, I propose first to examine what sorts of behavior were considered offensive and unacceptable for women in Procopius' time, and then to assess his characterization of Theodora and Antonina according to the standards of their own age. If the portraits are found to be *inoffensive* in sixth-century terms, I assume that Procopius did not include them in order to discredit either the women or their husbands, but rather to present a comprehensive and accurate picture of Justinian's court. If, on the other hand, the portraits are found to be *offensive*, I assume that Procopius included them in order to discredit the women and their husbands for contemporary readers.

Once the purpose of these portraits has been deduced from their effect on a Byzantine audience, it will be possible to draw some tentative conclusions about the historical accuracy of Theodora and Antonina as they appear in the *Historia Arcana*. If the characterizations are *inoffensive* in terms of sixth-century standards, it seems to me very likely that they are also accurate, because I see no reason why Procopius would fabricate inoffensive characterizations which would serve no discernible purpose in the *Historia Arcana* and which might cause well-informed contemporary readers to doubt the reliability of the whole work (cf. *Arc.* 1.4-5). On the other hand, if the portraits are *offensive* by contemporary standards, the degree to which they correspond with sixth-century ideas of unacceptable female behavior will be instructive and relevant to the question of accuracy vs. credibility in these characterizations. Portrayals which appear to offend sixth-century norms of behavior need not satisfy modern standards of accuracy in order to be credible in their time, so long as the misdeeds described fit contemporary notions of offensive conduct. Such portraits of reputedly offensive persons would be credible to a contemporary audience whether these portrayals were based on fact or on gossip and fiction. The modern historian, therefore, must approach such portraits with extreme caution, because they are not necessarily accurate in the modern sense of the word.

Little work has been done on the subject of Byzantine attitudes toward women. Bréhier and Lambros[14] have made brief general surveys and come to opposite conclusions; Bréhier detects a subservient position and low general regard for women in Byzantine society, while Lambros finds an attitude of reverence and respect towards them. Downey[15] describes the position of women in sixth-century Constantinople as independent and respected; Evans[16] suggests that Procopius reflects the values of a "traditional 'male vanity culture'" which relegated women to a passive role. However, no systematic study of the question has been attempted. In the scope of this article, it is possible to offer only partial evidence and tentative conclusions on the attitudes and expectations about women operating in Procopius' society. These tentative conclusions may be compared with Procopius' portrayal of Theodora and Antonina in order to determine whether the portraits were offensive to a sixth-century audience, and whether they are likely to be accurate as well as credible.

In outlining sixth-century attitudes towards women, it is necessary to examine not only the opportunities theoretically open to them, but also the concurrent definition of the "good woman." What women are allowed to do and what women gain approval for doing may be entirely different; the limits of approved behavior indicate attitudes and stereotypes about women's capacities and nature much more clearly than tolerated behavior. Traces of society's view of women may be drawn from evidence of their position before the law, in the Church, and in daily life.

Although Byzantine law recognized women as persons and protected their rights, marriage legislation traditionally treated them as inferior to men and placed them in a disadvantaged position if they sought divorce. From the time of Constantine, the law designated different standards of marital conduct for women and for men and applied different punishments for women and for men who divorced without sufficient grounds. For instance, under Constantine[17] a wife was entitled to divorce her husband, but only if he was a murderer, poisoner, or tomb robber; a woman claiming other grounds such as drunkenness or sexual offenses was deported without dowry or privilege of remarriage. On the other hand, a man had grounds for divorce if his wife was an adulteress, procuress, or poisoner; a man divorcing his wife for "light conduct" had only to forfeit her dowry and refrain from remarriage for two years. Legislation enacted by Theodosius and Valentinian ameliorated these penalties somewhat, but the inequality between the positions of husband and wife before the law remained.[18] The marriage legislation of Justinian attempted to equalize the penalties meted out to women and to men for similar misconduct; for instance, according to legislation of 542 and 548 A.D., both women and men repudiating their mates without grounds could be confined to a nunnery or monastery for life.[19] Justinian also enacted legislation which afforded protection to women in the family and placed them in a more advantageous legal position than they had previously enjoyed. Women could demand divorce if their husbands capriciously beat them or indulged in flagrant adultery,[20] but wives were protected from divorce on false adultery charges by more stringent requirements of proof of

290

misconduct.[21] In addition, a woman who married without dowry was protected from repudiation on that account.[22] Finally, even women outside respectable family life benefited from Justinian's legislative attention; for instance, it was prohibited to require an actress to swear an oath to remain in her profession.[23] We must not assume, however, that the innovative regard for women's position and rights in Justinian's legislation necessarily reflected a new and egalitarian attitude towards women in society at large; rather, as Diehl has suggested, Justinian alone may have entertained an unusual respect and consideration for the position of women, perhaps because of the influence of Theodora.[24]

Women received a certain amount of status in the Church. Bury has observed that the increasing prominence of the Church in Greek life had an ameliorating effect upon the position of women and upon social attitudes towards them, for they were conceded the dignity of an immortal soul, welcomed into the Faith, and allowed to take religious orders.[25] The early Christian writers, however, displayed a distinctly unfavorable attitude toward the nature of women and their effect upon men. As Katharine M. Rogers observes in a study of literary views of women, "Every one of the major Christian writers from the first century through the sixth assumed the mental and moral frailty of women, dwelt upon the vexations of marriage, and reviled the body and sexual desire. This attitude was to pervade the medieval Church and persists into religious writings even today."[26] Evidence for the inferior and even dangerous nature of some women could be drawn from both the Old Testament (e.g. Samson and Delilah, *Judges* 16:4-22; Job's wife, *Job* 2:9-10; Lot's wife, *Gen.* 19:17-26) and the New (e.g. *Cor.* i 11:1-15);[27] Rogers traces this derogatory view of women in scripture back to the "Yahwist" version of the creation of woman from man (*Gen.* 2:18-23; cf. *Gen.* 1:27) which suggests woman's more distant relationship to the Creator and her greater susceptibility to vice and folly.[28] In spite of the low regard accorded women in the eyes of the Church, the Theotokos enjoyed great reverence and prominence; as a special and divinely favored woman, Mary's position was apparently quite different from that of her fallible and mortal sisters. This is clear from Procopius' references in the *de Aedificiis* to women honored by the Church. Many churches mentioned bear the names of female saints and martyrs, some renowed (as St. Anne, i 3.11), some obscure (as St. Prima at Carthage, vi 5.9), but the most prominent female figure in terms of the Church and its buildings is, predictably enough, the Theotokos. Procopius begins his discussion of imperial churches by enumerating the churches honoring Mary in Constantinople; it is reasonable, he observes, to proceed from God to His mother (i 3.1). The *de Aedificiis* closes with a description of the fortress and church dedicated to Mary at Septem, which symbolized her protection of the entire Empire and its invulnerability (vi 7.16).

The everyday life of Byzantine women, what they typically did in sixth-century society, is an important but elusive element in assessing society's attitudes towards them. Saints' lives provide some information on the role of women, especially among the lower classes, and deserve to be examined in a separate study. The prestige and power of various assertive empresses (such as Ariadne, widow of Zeno) is well known. The experiences and position of women of the middle and upper class, however, cannot be assumed to be identical either with the exceptional life style and position of the Empress[29] or with the experiences of very poor women. Elusive as these more privileged women may be in their daily lives, they are important for this study because it was through them that the upper class formed its opinions of the nature and capabilities of women. It is presumably among the upper class that the audience of the *Historia Arcana* was to be found, and to upper class attitudes towards women that it would appeal.

Some information on the lives of upper class women can be derived from the works of Procopius himself, who moved in aristocratic circles[30] and who mentions women of this class incidentally in the course of his narrative. Women apparently could be expected to marry at a fairly early age, for Procopius notes with surprise one young woman still unwed at eighteen (*Arc.* 5.9) and incidentally describes another as a former child bride (*Bell.* vii 31.11). It is plain from marriage negotiations described in the *Historia Arcana* (*Arc.* 5.9; 5.18) that families often arranged beneficial unions between their offspring; these marriages were sometimes within the extended family (*Bell.* vii 31.11). Married or not, women apparently led somewhat restricted and segregated lives. They could not go to the theater (*Bell.* i 24.6); they were assigned to a separate stoa in St. Sophia (*Aed.* i 1.56) and accommodated in separate hospitals and travellers' hostels (*Aed.* ii 10.25). Women encountered slights and rebuffs within the family because of their sex. Procopius refers to a will overturned by Justinian in which the testator's brother and nephews received a greater inheritance than his daughter (*Bell.* vii 31.17-18), and he cites an ancient law which assigned part of the property of a deceased senator to the state should no *male* offspring survive him (*Arc.* 29.19). Also, certain appeals to public morality mentioned by Procopius reflect a general distrust of female sexuality throughout society. Intercourse with a holy woman (but not with a holy man) is specified in a list of opprobrious crimes (*Arc.* 19.11), and illicit relations with a woman justified executing an envoy (*Bell.* v 7.15). (The latter opinion, although enunciated by a barbarian, is accepted in substance by his Roman interlocutors.) Procopius also implies that society developed protective taboos concerning women. In his description of prostitutes at Amida, he observes that "they displayed naked the parts of a woman which it is not right (οὐ θέμις) to show men" (*Bell.* i 7.18). Fear of women and the effect of their sexuality on men appears to have motivated this attitude toward displaying the female genitalia, and the generalized form of its expression suggests that society acknowledged and respected the taboo.

To judge from Procopius' observations on women, the Empress did indeed occupy a special place in society and enjoy unique prestige among women, not unlike the case of the special woman in the Church, the Theotokos. The Empress possessed a public stature otherwise accorded only to men; statues were dedicated to her (*Aed.* i 11.8), foundations established bearing her name (*Aed.* iv 7.5; vi 5.10; vi 5.14), and her tomb placed with her husband's in the Church of the Holy Apostles (*Aed.* i 4.19). Other imperial or royal women could receive similar honors; for instance, Constantine enlarged and renamed a Bithynian city for his mother (*Aed.* v 2.1) and the town of Zenobia was named by and for the queen who founded it (*Bell.* ii 5.4; *Aed.* ii 8.8). These, however, are the honors accorded royalty and, in the case of the Empress or the Queen Mother, the honors accorded a close female connection of the Emperor. The position of typical women, even of the upper class, need not be affected in the least by the prestige of these exceptional women.[31]

Fragmentary as it is, this picture of daily life among upperclass Byzantine women agrees in several respects with the situation of women in classical Athens as described by Sarah B. Pomeroy.[32] Early marriage and restricted contacts outside the family circle contributed, in Pomeroy's opinion, to a "patriarchal" stereotype of women as dependent and intellectually inferior to men. The combined data from the law, the Church, and daily life in sixth-century Byzantium suggests that this stereotype survived in upper class attitudes from classical into Byzantine times and was additionally justified through the Christian theme of woman as a creature dangerous by nature. Such a patriarchal attitude finds full development in the non-polemical writings of Procopius, namely in the *de Bellis* and *de Aedificiis*, where his attention focuses upon the deeds of men, but where the demands of vivid historical writing dictate the inclusion of a certain number of female characters. Procopius subscribes to the practices of the so-called "tragic historians" of classical literature to the extent that he often concentrates on the dramatic aspects of a historical event and animates his narrative by focusing on the characters involved.[33] These characters are often female, and frequently incidental to the main progress of historical events. Procopius has chosen to include them for artistic reasons; in describing them, he reveals his assumptions about women through the roles which they act out.

In the *de Bellis* women are frequently mentioned as passive members in marriage or family relationships. The story of the noble Roman lady Prejecta, related at some length in Books Four (27.19-28. 43) and Seven (31.2-15), typifies the situation of many women described by Procopius. She is helpless and dependent upon the men who cross her path; imprisoned by the murderer of her husband, Prejecta was forced to misrepresent the situation to her uncle, Justinian, for her captor hoped to marry her and enjoy the benefits of an imperial connection and a large dowry. An assassin came to Prejecta's rescue, however, and was rewarded both by Justinian and by Prejecta as the avenger of her husband's murder. In Book Seven, Procopius explains that the lady's gratitude impelled her to marry her deliverer, a prospect which pleased his ambitious nature. The appearance of a long-neglected wife foiled these marriage plans, however, for the claims of the wife were championed by Theodora and Prejecta married another man.

Contemporary ideas of the character and motivation of a well-behaved woman probably affect the presentation of Prejecta's story, for the *de Bellis* was the official history of Justinian's reign, and Prejecta's position as the Emperor's niece would dictate that all delicacy and regard for her reputation be observed. In carefully explaining Prejecta's desire to remarry as an act of gratitude, not of passion (*Bell.* vii 31.3), Procopius suggests that reverence for the marriage bond and passionless devotion are proper female attributes.[34] By stressing the fact that Prejecta was never interfered with during her captivity (οὔτε τι ὑβρίσας λόγῳ ἢ ἔργῳ ὁτῳοῦν ἐς αὐτὰς iv 27.20), Procopius appears to reflect society's high regard for female chastity. The story of Prejecta also introduces several themes frequent in the *de Bellis* when women's activities are described: their typically passive role in society, the importance of the marriage connection for a woman, and the benefits to a man's career and finances which an expedient marriage might bring.

The theme of the marriage devised to profit a man recurs frequently in discussions of Roman (vii 12.11) and barbarian unions (v 11.27); v 12.22; v 12.50; v 13.4; vii 39.14). The ability of women to transmit power and influence to their male connections, if not actually to wield it themselves, is apparent in various ways. A Roman wife may enable a barbarian to establish himself as friendly and "Romanized" (viii 26.13; viii 9.7-8), or a woman may serve as a link of power and influence between important men. Prejecta, for instance, first appears in the *de Bellis* to explain the prestige which her husband gained through marriage into Justinian's family (iv 24.3), and even Placidia, notable as regent of the Western Empire (iii 3.16), is first mentioned only to establish the important relatives whom her husband gained by marriage (iii 3.4). It is rare indeed that a woman achieves sufficient prestige to be cited as a powerful and recognizable figure in her own right. The Gothic queen Amalasuntha is such a figure (v 11.27), as is Antonina, wife of Belisarius (vi 7.15). In fact, the roles which these two women play in the *de Bellis* are extraordinary in numerous respects and warrant fuller attention later in this paper.

Procopius follows the practice of the "tragic historians" particularly in his descriptions of war scenes,[35] where women are portrayed as helpless victims to heighten the pathos of the narrative (*Bell.* vii 26.11-12; v 10.15-19; vi 17.2-3; ii 9.9-10). They are sometimes described as the potential or actual victims of rape, a particularly horrible crime in a society which valued chastity highly. The plight of the women at the fall of Antioch (ii 8.35) and Rome (vii 20.30-31) is dramatized in this way. In the Roman episode, the Goth Totila saves the daughter of Symmachus from rape and also takes a firm moral stand against his own nobles when they intervene on behalf of a rapist (vii 8.12ff); he describes rape as "sin" (ἁμαρτάδα) and "pollution" (μίασμα *Bell.* vii 8.18). The excellent moral character of Totila is thus established in terms of his behavior and attitudes as judged by Procopius under a strict code of female chastity; it contrasts sharply with the laxity and licentiousness of the Roman commanders described in a juxtaposed passage (vii 9.1).

Women considered "good" according to a strict code of chastity may nevertheless occasion lustful and intemperate behavior in men. An anonymous woman described by Procopius in Book Eight provides an excellent example of this situation, which recurs through the *de Bellis* (*cf.* also i 6.1-9; iii 4.17-24). The lady's beauty inflamed a Persian commander, who failed to persuade her to his will and tried to force her; enraged, her husband killed the Persian and his soldiers, men described by Procopius as "lost uselessly because of the commander's lust" (παρανάλωμα τῆς τοῦ ἄρχοντος ἐπιθυμίας viii 10.6). It is sobering to reflect that in the narrative of Procopius a man is typically drawn to a woman because of her beauty (e.g. ii 5.28; v 11. 7-8), but her beauty is also potentially dangerous. These stories leave the impression that women are the passive objects of men's inevitable lust and cannot avert the disaster thus occasioned by any good or moral action on their own part. This viewpoint is articulated by the tyrant Maximus when he claims that passionate love for the Emperor's wife motivated all his own evil deeds (iii 4.36); Maximus is an unsympathetic character, but the explanation which he offers is consistent with the viewpoint underlying the *de Bellis*. Procopius himself reflects the same assessment of male-female interaction when he catalogues "self-restraint" (σωφροσύνη) among the virtues of the general Belisarius and illustrates it by explaining that Belisarius generally avoided contact with women (vii 1.11-12); he touched only his wife, and he refused even to view the beautiful women captives available to him. The famous passage on prostitution in the *de Aedificiis* (i 9.2-9) reflects and elaborates the same view of male lust as a destructive and aggressive element in society. Procopius explains the prostitution trade in Constantinople in terms of lust victimizing poverty; he emphasizes the prostitute's helplessness before male demands, thus rousing pity and indignation in the audience.[36] Although this passage describes whores as the passive and passionless victims of male lust, like "good women" they are not considered guiltless when men desire them. Procopius explains that Justinian and Theodora established a convent expressly for reforming ex-prostitutes and called it "Repentance" (Μετάνοια).

Although the female characters examined so far are typically passive and dependent upon men, there are a number of episodes in the *de Bellis* where women initiate and carry out a plan of action. The conditions and outcome of such action are noteworthy.

In a number of cases, women act independently because they are overwhelmed by emotion; Proba opens the gates of Rome to the enemy out of pity for her starving neighbors (iii 2.27), Matasuntha so resents her forced marriage that she betrays her people (vi 10.11; vi 28.26), and Eudoxia seeks revenge on her husband by appealing to the Vandal Gizeric, who plunders Rome and takes the women (including Eudoxia) captive (iii 4.36 = iii 5.3). Each of these influential and highborn women is driven by emotion to act contrary to the best interests of her own people and of herself. Undeterred by higher considerations such as loyalty and patriotism, they act with poor judgment and suspect morality to indulge their own emotions.[37]

Poor judgment is also the hallmark of the reign of Placidia, who held imperial power in the West as regent for her son Valentinian. Procopius attributes the vicious character of Valentinian, his occult and adulterous interests, to the "womanish" education given him by his mother (θηλυνομένην παιδείαν τε καὶ τροφὴν iii 3.10) and traces the loss of Libya, the great disaster of his reign, to her ineptitude when confronted with the court intrigues which resulted in a Vandal takeover (iii 3.14-36). Finally recognizing the situation, Placidia appealed to men for help (iii 3.29), thus typifying both the characteristic bad judgment of women and the familiar theme of female helplessness.

In several situations, women act independently to persuade their male connections to some novel course of action, which almost invariably proves ill-advised and/or disastrous. Particularly noteworthy among these episodes (*cf.* also i 23.8-21; iii 6.26; vii 1.37-42) is the bloody military rebellion in Africa attributed by Procopius to a number of causes, including the pressure of Vandal wives upon their Roman husbands (iv 14.8-21). Significantly, Procopius concludes his account of the revolt with the reminder that these women caused it; the other factors (i.e., Arian discontent, arrival of other mutineers) were apparently less shocking to Procopius and are not reiterated (iv 15.47). When women initiate and carry out a course of action in the *de Bellis,* the outcome is disastrous because they typically act emotionally and with limited foresight; when men follow the initiatives and suggestions

of women, Procopius implies that their compliance is not only dangerous but also particularly outrageous. An atypical variation on the
theme of a woman's influence over her husband is the tragic encounter
between the doomed pretender to Justinian's throne, Hypatius, and
his wife Mary, "a woman of intelligence, renowned for her prudence"
(ξυνετή τε οὖσα καὶ δόξαν ἐπὶ σωφροσύνῃ μεγίστην ἔχουσα i 24.23).
In a hysterical parting scene, Mary fails to restrain her husband from
disaster during the Nika riots; her reputation for intelligence and
prudence does not earn this woman a hearing. In Procopius' narrative
the incident seems to heighten the pathos of her husband's fate.

The theme of women who act independently receives its most
startling expression in an anecdote used by Procopius to illustrate
the horrors of famine at Ariminum. Two women, the only survivors in
their neighborhood, killed and devoured passing travelers until their
eighteenth victim surprised and overpowered them (vi 20.27-30). The
story, more folktale than history, is especially interesting because it
capitalizes upon the viability of female monster figures in the contemporary imagination. "Bogeymen" in Greek were, after all, "bogey-
women" (Μορμώ, Λάμια).

The women encountered so far in Procopius' narrative were
depicted either as helpless and dependent or as independent and
dangerous (with the exception of Hypatius' wife). Because Procopius
does not label their behavior as unusual, it was apparently congenial
with the expectations of women entertained by Procopius and his
audience. Such expectations complement an assumption on the part of
society that women were in fact inferior to men. This attitude seems
to underlie an incident in which the Romans refused a prisoner exchange involving a Goth of quaestor rank and a Roman woman of high
status because they deemed the exchange of a noble woman for an
influential man in no way proper (vii 40.23).

Particularly interesting among the women of the *de Bellis* is
Amalasuntha, queen of the Goths, and the only prominent woman who
earns Procopius' obvious approval for her good character and active
role as a ruler. Amalasuntha's career recapitulates a number of familiar
themes: she is typically identified in terms of her relationship to
an important man ("mother of Athalaric," iii 14.5; iv 5.18; v 2.1-2), and
she depends for her power upon the good will of men (of Justinian,
iii 14.6; v 2.23; v 3.28; of the Goth lords, v 3.11). Although clearly
acting in a man's world, Amalasuntha is atypical in her behavior to-

wards men. She is never described as beautiful or said to influence a man through her feminine appeal;[38] instead, Procopius praises her for virtues rare in the women he portrays, sagacity and justice (ξύνεσις καὶ δικαιοσύνη v 2.3), and summarizes her admirable character as "extremely masculine" (ἐς ἄγαν τὸ ἀρρενωπὸν v 2.3).[39] Procopius further observes that she neither feared the Goth lords whose intrigues threatened her position nor bent "in womanly fashion" (οὔτε οἷα γυνὴ ἐμαλθακίσθη) to them, but maintained regal conduct (v 2.21) by banishing (v 2.21) and murdering (v 2.29; v 4.13) her enemies. However masculine her virtues might have been, Amalasuntha could not finally escape the weaknesses of her sex. Fear led her to compromise her plans for her son's education (v 2.18) and to undertake the betrayal of her people to Justinian (v 3.28); poor judgment led her to an inaccurate assessment of her chief rival's character and strength (v 4.4). The victim of this mistake, Amalasuntha died as the helpless captive of her rival (v 4.13-27), thus dramatizing the dependence and poor judgment typical in Procopius' view of women. Although she appears as a woman of great ability who merits admiration and approval (cf. v 4.28-29; vii 9.10), Amalasuntha is also a comforting witness to male superiority, for she appeals to Justinian's superior strength for protection and falls victim to her male rival's greater skill at intrigue.

In two other passages Procopius labels women who act independently and effectively as "masculine," and also illustrates the ultimate subservience of these superlative women to men. A tale developed in some detail (viii 20.11-41) focuses upon an unnamed princess of Brittia who wages war "in the manner of a man" (τὸ ἀρρενωπὸν ἀνελομένη viii 20.25) to avenge her honor and to punish the prince who jilted her. In a climactic scene the unfortunate prince appears in chains before the warrior princess and finds, to his relief and surprise, that she wishes only to complain of her dishonor and to demand marriage. Procopius develops this drama with particular attention to the prince's terror before his powerful female opponent and his relief at her submission (viii 20.37-41); it seems that these features of the tale pleased Procopius and his audience by dramatizing the subservience of a strong and threatening woman to a man. A similar motif underlies Procopius' explanation of the legendary Amazons (viii 3.5-9). Procopius denies that an entire race of manly women (γένος γυναικῶν ἀνδρείων) could have existed, because such would defy human nature (viii 3.7). He suggests instead that a historical accident fostered the

Amazon legend; women traveling in a nomadic tribe were left on their own at the death of their men and were forced by fear and hunger to adopt the manly arts of war until they were destroyed by their neighbors. In this passage Procopius disarms the threatening legend of a female warrior society by extrapolating back from societies known to him (viii 3.8-9). He capitalizes upon contemporary ideas about women when he explains that the Amazons did not choose to live apart from men, that they only fought because they were afraid and hungry, and that they could not defend themselves against the normal societies around them.

Such an interpretation of the Amazons is entirely consistent with the patriarchal stereotype of women inferred from Procopius' society (as typified by law, the Church, and daily life) and from his non-polemical writings. This stereotype implies that women were rightly subject to the control and protection of men because of their naturally disruptive influence upon men and upon society. Women who avoided control by men would be distrusted by their contemporaries, for such women affronted God and society by rejecting the domination generally considered beneficial to all. In the context of sixth-century attitudes toward the independent woman, it is extremely significant that independence of action and influence over men are characteristic of Theodora and Antonina as portrayed in the *de Bellis*. Viewed in detail from a contemporary perspective, these portrayals inspire apprehension rather than admiration and suggest a link to the biographies of Theodora and Antonina in the *Historia Arcana*.

Theodora and Antonina make frequent but sporadic appearances through the *de Bellis*. They are mentioned numerous times as the companions or co-agents of their husbands in official business; Procopius frequently notes Antonina traveling on campaign with Belisarius (*Bell.* i 25.11; iii 12.2; iii 19.11; v 18.43; vi 4.6; vii 28.4; vii 30.2) and Theodora acting in co-operation with Justinian (*Bell.* iv 9.13; *Aed.* i 2.17; i 9.5; i 11.27; v 3.14). An impression of equality or at least shared influence between husband and wife thus emerges in these two marriages. In the case of Theodora, it is reinforced by Procopius' description of the palace mosaic which portrayed Justinian and Theodora celebrating victory over the Vandals and Goths while the Senate looks on (*Aed.* i 10.16-18). More important, episodes in the *de Bellis* suggest that Theodora exercised independent power, sometimes opposing or directing the will of her husband. The Empress begins her famous speech to the royal council at the time of the Nika riots by citing the opinion that she should not, as a woman, speak at all (*Bell.* i 24.33); the fact that she does so, and that she claims for herself lust for imperial power (i 24.36), establishes her among those unusual women who do not adopt a helpless, submissive role among men. Because Justinian follows her advice and events establish its soundness, she is an additionally atypical female. Thus Theodora shares with Amalasuntha the independent exercise of royal power and the ability to deal with men on their own terms. Unlike Amalasuntha, however, she is not said to fear men and is not portrayed as inferior to them. Indeed, the conclusion of Prejecta's story indicates that Theodora was capable of enforcing her will upon a man (vii 31.12-16); that men also feared Theodora's power is apparent from the excruciating terror of her which Procopius attributes to John the Cappadocian (i 25.4-7), a powerful member of Justinian's retinue. The story of John also illustrates the one respect in which Procopius describes Theodora as a typical woman; she could influence men through her sex appeal. Procopius remarks that John misjudged Justinian's tremendous devotion to his wife and thus acknowledges the influence which she wielded over her husband; in the general context of the *de Bellis,* the typically female capacity to influence men appears dangerous and makes Theodora an additionally threatening character. When Procopius celebrates her great beauty in the *de Aedificiis*, his words are ominous as well as fawning (i 11.8-9), given his view that female beauty is dangerous.

In many ways, Antonina reflects and extends the characterization of Theodora. Like the Empress, Antonina acts in concert with her husband, inspires his devotion (*Bell.* vii 1.11), and can influence his decisions (v 18.43). She is also a woman of initiative and independent action among men (iii 13.24; vii 30.25). Procopius describes Antonina as "most capable among mankind of doing the impossible" (ἦν γὰρ ἱκανωτάτη ἀνθρώπων ἁπάντων μηχανᾶσθαι τὰ ἀμήχανα i 25.13) and proceeds to illustrate his judgment by recounting her successful plot against John of Cappadocia (i 25.13 ff), an adventure demanding masterful deception and engineered with the help and encouragement of Theodora. Like Theodora, Antonina displays no need to depend upon men. It is Theodora who provides her with motivation for her deeds (i 25.13 and 22) and with financial resources for her ambitions regarding Belisarius (vii 30.3). Together, these women are extremely threatening, for they demonstrate the dangerous and typically female ability to influence men through their sex appeal, but they also possess the typically male opportunity and inclination for independent action.

Antonina and Theodora are portrayed as independent women capable of influencing men both in the *de Bellis* and in the *Historia Arcana*. Because Procopius' tone in the *de Bellis* is not polemical and his character observations are surely not intended to misrepresent and displease his imperial patrons, these portraits were probably accurate and acceptable to their subjects. Evidence supporting the accuracy of the portrait of Theodora in the *de Bellis* comes from statements in Justinian's own legislation which indicate her independence and power and his devotion to her.[40] Antonina may well have been a powerful figure as well; the anecdote from the *Liber Pontificalis* regarding her complicity in the destruction of Silverius,[41] true or false, at least implies that she was active and recognizable at court. In terms of their independence and influence over their husbands, the earlier and apparently accurate portraits of Antonina and Theodora in the *de Bellis* forecast their later ones in the *Historia Arcana* and provide a consistency of characterization between the two works which has been denied by Rubin.[42] The actual personalities of Antonina and Theodora, as far as they can be assessed from Procopius' report in the *de Bellis,* would have offended Procopius and his contemporaries deeply and would have predisposed them to believe that these were offensive women who were very likely to demonstrate all the negative attributes applied to women in the sixth century. A careful examination of Antonina and Theodora as portrayed in the *Historia Arcana* indicates that Procopius presents them as women who would offend sixth-century sensibilities in almost every particular. At this point, I propose to compare Theodora and Antonina as they are portrayed in the *Historia Arcana* with sixth-century ideas of offensive women in order to suggest (1) what part of the portrayals is consistent with a contemporary stereotype and need not be true in order to be credible to a contemporary audience, and (2) what parts are not consistent with the stereotype and may be historical.

Procopius describes Antonina before Theodora in the *Historia Arcana*, and in many respects his treatment of Antonina forecasts his famous portrait of the Empress. The portrayal of Antonina centers on the observation, already expressed in the *de Bellis*, that she was the close companion of her husband's career and exerted influence over him. In the *Historia Arcana,* Antonina's companionship and influence over her husband are presented as evidence of a relationship between husband and wife which violated contemporary standards of proper behavior. Procopius attributes Antonina's unusual influence over her husband to dark and supernatural causes; he claims that she practiced magic to control Belisarius. By portraying her as much older than her husband (4.41) and by comparing her to a deadly scorpion (1.26), Procopius presents Antonina as a sort of predatory witch figure. Following the view expressed in the *de Bellis*, that a woman's control over her husband is dangerous and offensive, Procopius illustrates the humiliating consequences of uxoriousness with a vivid scene perhaps created especially for the *Historia Arcana* (4.20-31). In a supposedly private interview, Belisarius is shown as terrified, submissive, and slavishly grateful to his wife for intervening with the Empress on his behalf; Antonina is cold and haughty, accepting her husband's servile devotion by allowing him to kiss her feet. Procopius traces various misdeeds of Belisarius to the dangerous control exerted over him by this woman. Because of his insane love for her, he neglects his military duties (2.18-21), condones embezzlement of booty due to the Emperor (1.19), forswears his solemn oaths (1.21, 1.26; 3.30), and accepts the role of cuckold (1.19-20).

Because Antonina has wilfully inverted the normal relationship of control by husband over wife, she appears to be unaffected by the normal restraints placed upon women by natural inclination and social convention. She has no respect for social contracts, breaking her solemn oath (2.16), revoking the betrothal of Belisarius' daughter (5.23-24), and, in the central anecdote concerning her, indulging in flagrant adultery. In this, the tale of Theodosius, Procopius claims that Antonina deliberately rejected the proper attitudes of a wife; she intended adultery from the time of her marriage and was deterred from it neither by shame nor by fear of her husband (1.13). She also appears as an unnatural mother, for Theodosius is first introduced as her Christian "foster son" by baptism (1.16), and Antonina's passion for him leads her to undertake the destruction of her real son (1.34; 2.3-4). Since Procopius has described Antonina as an unrestrained woman, he is free to amplify her character in the directions in which contemporary attitudes regarded women as most dangerous and excessive. He builds upon the assumption that women are overly emotional by describing

Antonina's hysteria at the loss of Theodosius (1.38) and her savage punishments of her enemies (e.g. 1.27). He exploits society's concern for the effect of female sexuality by portraying Antonina as an untrammeled libertine.[43] The account of her early life forcefully establishes shameless and lustful associations; Antonina is said to be the daughter of a prostitute, the mother of many bastards, and a generally lewd person (1.11-12). Her adulterous alliance with Theodosius is marked by shameless exhibitionism (1.17-19) and insatiable lust; Procopius stresses this aspect of her passion by asserting that Theodosius wished to escape from her and felt terror and guilt at their misdeeds (1.36).

Like Antonina, Theodora is said to exert influence over her husband because of his love for her (9.30-32) and because of her skill in manipulating him (13.19). To explain Theodora's control of her husband, Procopius asserts that she practiced magic (22.27-28) and emphasizes her continuous program to cultivate her beauty, which would increase Justinian's vulnerability to her (15.6-8). Belisarius' insane love for his wife supposedly diminished his effectiveness in military affairs, the chief area of his fame; similarly, Justinian's passion for Theodora supposedly corrupted law and foreign relations, two areas of his special concern. Procopius complains that Justinian's desire to marry Theodora motivated him to allow senators to marry courtesans (9.51); Procopius considers this legislation harmfully innovative and conducive to a lower standard of public morality. (The possibility that Justinian intended a genuine improvement in the condition of women before the law is conveniently ignored by Procopius.[44]) Justinian's reputation among foreign powers is ruined by Theodora's supposedly secret assurance to the Persian king that she controlled her husband's judgment absolutely; the king declares that a state controlled by a woman is no state at all (2.33-36). In ordinary men excessive devotion to a woman appeared to be a prelude to disaster; in Justinian's case, the disaster is expressed in superlative terms: "His love burned up the Roman state" (ἡ πολιτεία τοῦ ἔρωτος τοῦδε ὑπέκκαυμα 9.32). Having asserted Theodora's influence over her husband, Procopius extends the theme of domination to other men because of Theodora's position as Empress. She is depicted as exercising control over men by demeaning male officials and dignitaries of the court (15.13-16; 15.24-35), by pursuing and torturing her enemies

(3.9-12; 16.23-28; 17.38-45), and by advancing the careers of her favorites (3.19; 17.13; 22.5; 22.22).

Like Antonina, Theodora is portrayed as a woman subject to none of the controls imposed by nature or society on her sex. She betrays none of the normal feminine concern for her children, practicing numerous abortions during her early career (9.19) and allegedly murdering her embarrassing and only son (17.17-23). She does not respect the behavior considered typical of women in the family sphere, for Procopius remarks that she undertook the matchmaking functions normally performed in the family throughout the whole Empire, but discharged the office in a heartless and wilful manner (17.28-32). Although Theodora is described as an unrestrained female, she was apparently known to be a chaste wife, and Procopius makes no accusations of infidelity against her.[45] Apart from citing a weak tale that she favored a palace slave and tortured him in order to discount rumors of her interest (16.11), Procopius prefers to use indirect methods to attack her reputation as a wife. First, he attributes much of Antonina's success as an adulteress to Theodora's help and encouragement (3.6-18). Then Procopius declares that Theodora used her position to force impure behavior on the part of other women, compelling unwilling cohabitation (5.21). In this way, she is portrayed as destroying marriage on a large scale in society; she also forces socially inappropriate (17.7-9) or degrading (17.32-37) unions, and encourages and supports adultery among wives (17.24-26). Thus she appears to inflict further insults upon men of a particularly odious sort (17.26).

As an unrestrained woman, Theodora indulges her whims and emotions in a typically female fashion. She is capricious, causing inconvenience to her retinue (15.36-38) and unmerited financial distress to her subjects (25.18-19); the tortures which she inflicts on her enemies show her to be savage in her wrath; and, as in the *de Bellis,* she is capable of terrifying men (3.26). Theodora's determination to carry out her will (15.2-3) makes her emotional motivations all the more formidable.[46] In establishing Theodora's sexual liberation, an indispensable component of slander to his audience, Procopius concentrates on her early life, probably exploiting the generally known rumor of Theodora's early career in the circus[47] by attaching to it a string of tales consistent with the taboos and fears related to women. Thus Theodora's sexual aggressiveness and voracity are emphasized by anecdotes of her early life (9.15; 9.16; 9.18), and she is said to prefer younger men (9.15). Exhibitionism (9.17; 9.20; 9.23) is attributed to her in words recalling the anecdote of the prostitutes at Amida (γυμνὰ ἐπιδεῖξαι, ἃ τοῖς ἀνδράσι θέμις ἄδηλά τε καὶ ἀφανῆ εἶναι 9.14). The taboo against viewing female genitals lies behind a particularly notable insult contributed by Procopius: Theodora seemed to wear her genitals on her face, where all must see them (9.24)! The charge of irregular sexual practices, a slur favored by Procopius (9.15; 9.25), is extended to Theodora's childhood in an unusual way, for Procopius claims that she acted as a pederast's partner before reaching maturity (9.10). Here Procopius apparently exploits another social taboo current in his time, for there are references in the *Historia Arcana* to prosecution of suspected homosexuals (11.34; 16.19; 16.23; 19.11; 20.9).

Procopius' sexual profile of Theodora is not only shocking, it is monstrous. An incident in which Theodora actually castrates a young man (16.18-21) suggests that Procopius intends to portray her as a woman whose sexual misdeeds surpass the violation of regular taboos. Sexual slanders against her are intensified by associating her sexuality with the supernatural: Theodora is credited with a dream foretelling her marriage to the King of Demons (12.31-32) and demons supposedly banished several of her lovers from her chambers (12.28).

The excessive and shocking behavior attributed by Procopius to Theodora and Antonina is emphasized by the presence of several inoffensive women in the *Historia Arcana*, who act in conformity with the high standards of female behavior implicit in the *de Bellis*. One such lady dies to preserve her chastity (7.37-38), a figure of reproof when contrasted with the sexual excesses attributed to both Theodora and Antonina. Three other "good" women mentioned and approved in the course of the *Historia Arcana* are of royal status and seem to offer specific contrasts with aspects of Theodora's character which Procopius considered especially offensive. As noted above, royal women apparently occupied a special position in Byzantine society and received special respect and privileges. Privilege, however, is not to be equated with license. To judge from the story of Domitian's unnamed wife (8.16-18), a royal wife was approved for respecting and honoring her deceased husband publicly, even if he was patently immoral and unworthy. Theodora's declaration to the Persian king that she controlled her husband, for example, contrasts starkly with this example of good regal conduct. Procopius' treatment of Lupicina/

Euphemia, the wife of Justin, offers a number of interesting parallels and contrasts to the portrayal of Theodora. Like Theodora, Euphemia came from a humble and not completely respectable background (slave, barbarian, and concubine of Justin, 6.17). Unlike Theodora, however, she was retiring and self-effacing as Empress, totally incapable and unwilling to participate in government; her character is approved by Procopius as "very far from wicked" (πονηρίας μὲν γὰρ ἡ γυνὴ ἀποτάτω οὖσα 9.48). Procopius emphasizes the fact that this modest and good woman entered public affairs only to oppose Theodora as future Empress (9.47); her disapproval apparently interested Procopius because he could represent it as the moral outrage felt by a "good" woman towards an "evil" one of similar background. The possibility that Euphemia was simply jealous of an upstart is of no use to Procopius and he does not mention it. Finally, the figure of Amalasuntha reappears briefly in the *Historia Arcana* (16.1-5) as a queenly paradigm who contrasts sharply with Theodora. Amalasuntha's regal qualities are retained from her earlier portrait in the *de Bellis* (*Bell.* v 2.3) but are described somewhat differently in order to suggest Theodora's impression of her: a woman rivaling the Empress in position, beauty, and ingenuity, but also possessing the advantages of noble birth and "magnificent, masculine bearing" (*Arc.* 16.1). Theodora's reaction to this rival is expressed in terms of her desire to maintain control over Justinian. In one of the most controversial passages in the *Historia Arcana*, Procopius claims that she murdered Amalasuntha (16.2-5; *cf.* 24.23) for fear of losing control over the Emperor.[48]

We may now assess the likelihood that Procopius relied upon lies and slanderous gossip current in Constantinople for his statements regarding Theodora and Antonina in the *Historia Arcana*. As stated above (p. 268), Theodora apparently *was* a very independent woman, and her husband *was* devoted to her; these same things may well have been true of Antonina and Belisarius. The *Historia Arcana* is apparently accurate in this respect. The most striking features remaining in Procopius' portrayal of Theodora and Antonina, however, are consistent with the sixth-century stereotype of areas in which independent (or uncontrolled) women would be expected to misbehave. As Procopius depicts them in the *Historia Arcana*, Theodora and Antonina are sexual libertines, emotional volcanoes, and savage, unscrupulous manipulators of the men around them. We would expect sixth-century gossip to concentrate upon exactly such topics.

Procopius' methods in the *Historia Arcana* are admirably suited to presenting rumor and gossip about Theodora and Antonina in such a way that it appears to be historical evidence. Procopius suggests by innuendo crimes which he cannot actually prove, such as Theodora's supposed murder of her mysterious son John (17.22-23) and describes crimes perpetrated by her against unnamed persons (15.25; 17.43-44; 17.7); he also claims detailed knowledge of private interviews (4.21-23) and secret documents (2.32-36), for which a reliable source is difficult to envision. Occasionally Procopius assumes an extravagant and hyperbolic tone in describing Theodora's activities, for instance in claiming that she inflicted many abortions upon herself (9.19) and enjoyed at least forty men in one evening (9.16). All these allegations are basically unprovable and could well be outright fabrications; their veracity is especially suspect because Procopius complains that it was virtually impossible to gain any information about the Empress which she did not wish to be noised abroad (16.12).[49] These allegations are effective, however, because they create an impression of her guilt in the mind of the reader. Similarly, damaging editorial comments intruded by Procopius on the character and motivations of his subjects create an impression of knowledge and authority where none need exist (e.g. Antonina intended to commit adultery from the time of her marriage, 1.13; Theodora took special care lest her appointees be good men, 17.27). Procopius also employs the technique of the tragic historian, the dramatic scene, to create a vivid impression of an event which may never have occurred (e.g. the above mentioned "private" interview between Belisarius and Antonina). These methods of distortion — innuendo, hyperbole, editorial intrusion, and perhaps outright fabrication — allow Procopius to transform his subjects as he deems appropriate to then-current expectations and his own purposes.

Both Procopius' methods and the stereotyped quality of his material argue that his portrayals of Theodora and Antonina in the *Historia Arcana* cannot be used to reconstruct their biographies, but only to indicate the sort of slander and gossip which was directed against them in Procopius' time. In my opinion, the apparently historical details of these two portrayals, although not necessarily false, cannot be regarded as certainly factual unless they fall into one of two categories.[50] (1) Details which do not contribute to the picture of Antonina or Theodora as typical sixth-century female villains. Two examples of such details are Procopius' statements that Theodora was short (10.11) and that she founded the Metanoia convent for re-formed prostitutes (17.5). On the other hand, the story that Theodora had a prostitute sister (9.9) contributes to the impression of her as a person of disreputable connections; her son John and his mysterious fate establish her savage and anti-maternal character (17.16-23). Such details lend an air of truth to a stereotyped picture of Theodora as an offensive woman in sixth-century terms and are not necessarily bio-graphical. (2) Details which contribute to the stereotype of a bad woman in the *Historia Arcana* but which are also confirmed by other sources in a neutral tone. John of Ephesus' story that Antonina had a son, Photius, who was once a monk is such a detail, for it occurs without any reflection on the character of Antonina (*Hist. Eccl.* i 32). On the other hand, the passages in Cassiodorus which Bury considers corroboration of Theodora's complicity in the murder of Amalasuntha (*Var.* x 20; 21)[51] are so neutral and vague that they prove nothing about Theodora unless the reader already assumes her guilt.

Procopius' portraits of Theodora and Antonina in the *Historia Arcana*, although shocking and not necessarily factual, were not likely to damage Procopius' credibility with contemporary readers. His methods preclude direct contradiction of so-called biographical evi-dence. The data is often so vague (e.g. regarding anonymous victims of torture) or of such a nature (e.g. private interviews) that no con-firmation – or contradiction – could exist. It would be as difficult for a sixth-century reader as for later historians to prove Procopius false.[52] Also, I believe that Theodora and Antonina were actually the sort of independent, strong women whom Procopius and his contemporaries would find extremely threatening to their concept of how women should behave, and whom they would therefore label offensive. It seems to me that Procopius and his contemporaries *wanted* to believe that Theodora and Antonina did the sort of things attributed to them in the *Historia Arcana* because such portraits agreed with the then-current stereotype of independent or offensive women.[53] Whether these portrayals were based on fact or on gossip and fiction did not affect their credibility with a contemporary audience.

The characterizations of Theodora and Antonina in the *Historia Arcana* were extremely offensive to contemporary readers and probably believable as well; these portraits would discredit Justinian and Belisarius, the primary targets of the *Historia Arcana*, with a force impossible to achieve by simply attacking the two men.[54] Procopius apparently recognized what an effective weapon he had against Justinian and Belisarius in his portraits of their wives and therefore gave great prominence to Antonina and Theodora in the *Historia Arcana*. Procopius' attack on Belisarius relies entirely upon describing Antonina's misdeeds and Belisarius' submission to her; Antonina was apparently the only aspect of Belisarius' upright life (cf. *Bell.* vii 1.4-22) in which he was vulnerable to disapproval.

In his attack on Justinian Procopius has utilized and extended the technique of defaming the wife in order to insult her husband. Although Justinian is portrayed as fully capable of independent mischief, much of the evil in his character is traced to Theodora's influence and encouragement. Moreover, Procopius treats Justinian and Theodora as two aspects of a single evil being, with the result that he can slander one and blacken both. The identification between husband and wife is accomplished and reinforced in a number of ways. Procopius first mentions the name of Justinian in the *Historia Arcana* together with Theodora (1.4); they are cited as co-rulers frequently in the work (4.33; 6.1; 9.53 etc.). Procopius claims that the two rulers were perfectly united and coordinated in their activities (13.9), differing only in non-essential respects of personality (13.9; 15.19) and sharing the unique characteristics of demons incarnate, bent on destruction of the world (12.14). Thus official misdeeds of one ruler cast odium equally upon both; accusations made against Theodora damage Justinian as well. Procopius also manages to turn defamation of Theodora's private life into slander of Justinian. He asserts that Justinian proved his utter depravity by rejecting all manner of chaste, noble, beautiful and proper candidates for marriage and by marrying Theodora instead (10.2). Thus any evil imputed to Theodora before her marriage to Justinian becomes his crime as well (10.4-5).

The portrayals of Theodora and Antonina in the *Historia Arcana* are thus essential to its purpose. Procopius was himself subject to and conscious of the attitudes toward women typical of his times; in skillfully exploiting these attitudes to destroy the reputations of Justinian and Belisarius, he has created an extraordinarily effective work of slander. Procopius has gone beyond the methods normally connected with modern historical method and modern historians, taking for his sources what is likely to be gossip and rumor, and appealing to his readers' prurience and spitefulness. His ingenuity as a historian, if not his integrity, is admirable.

Georgetown University

NOTES

[1] This study developed from a paper presented at the Ninth Conference on Medieval Studies, Western Michigan University (May 1974). I would like to thank Catherine Reid Rubincam, Robert Hadley, Angeliki Laiou-Thomadakis, Janet Martin and Christopher Rowe for their helpful suggestions. I am grateful to the Center for Hellenic Studies, Washington, D.C., for the leisure and resources with which to pursue this study.

[2] *Arc.* 1.1-3.

[3] Cf. John W. Barker, *Justinian and the Later Roman Empire* (Madison 1966) 68, 78. J. B. Bury, *History of the Later Roman Empire* (London 1923) ii 424.

[4] See Charles Diehl, *Justinien et la civilisation byzantine au vi^e siècle* (Paris 1901) 42 n. 2.

[5] Edward Gibbon, *History of the Decline and Fall of the Roman Empire*[3] (London 1908) iv 335 n. 128, p. 211; William Gordon Holmes, *The Age of Justinian and Theodora* (London 1912) i 337 f.; Percy Neville Ure, *Justinian and his Age* (Harmondsworth, Middlesex 1951) 198-199, 216-217. C. E. Mallett, "The Empress Theodora," *The English Historical Review* 2 (1887) 1-20.

[6] Bury ii 426-427; Wilhelm Schubart, *Justinian und Theodora* (Munich 1943) 51; Ernest Stein, *Histoire du Bas-Empire* (Paris 1949) ii 236; Berthold Rubin, *Das Zeitalter Iustinians* (Berlin 1960) i 106; Barker 68-70; Robert Browning, *Justinian and Theodora* (London 1971) 67; J. A. S. Evans, *Procopius* (New York 1972) 88-90.

[7] Charles Diehl, *Theodora, Empress of Byzantium* trans. by Samuel Rosenbaum (New York 1972) 3, 38; Diehl, *Justinien* 45; Rubin i 116.

[8] Diehl, *Theodora* 68; *Bury* ii 427; H. B. Dewing *Procopius* (Cambridge, Mass. 1935) vi p. vii; Barker 68; Rubin 202; Evans 89-90.

[9] Diehl, *Theodora* 70-71.

[10] Evans 93, 91; *cf.* 97.

[11] Ure 198; Schubart 52; Diehl, *Theodora* 78; Rubin 216.

[12] Domenico Comparetti, *Le inedite Libro Nono delle Istorie di Procopio di Cesarea* (Rome 1928) 203; Rubin 215.

[13] Diehl, *Justinien* 45; *Theodora* 38.

[14] Louis Bréhier, *Le monde byzantin: la civilisation byzantine* (Paris 1950) 10-12; Spiro Lambros, " Ἡ Γυνὴ παρὰ τοῖς Βυζαντινοῖς" in *Neos Hellenomnemon* xvii (1923) 259-260.

[15] Glanville Downey, *Constantinople in the Age of Justinian* (Norman, Okla. 1960) 29.

[16] Evans 97.

[17] *Codex Theodosianus* 3.16.1 (331 A.D.), 2 (421 A.D.). For a discussion of late imperial marriage legislation, see A. H. M. Jones, *The Later Roman Empire 284-602* (Norman, Oklahoma 1964) ii 974-75.

[18] *Codex Iustinianus* 5.17.8 (449 A.D.), 9 (497 A.D.).

[19] *Novella* 117.13 (542 A.D.); *Novella* 127.4 (548 A.D.) specifies that "no difference" in penalty for men and women must exist.

[20] Beating: *Novella* 117.14. Adultery: *Novella* 117.9.5.

[21] *Novella* 117.15.

[22] *Novella* 22.18. For a discussion of dowry practice, see Stein ii 414.

[23] *Novella* 51.

[24] Charles Diehl, *Justinien et la civilisation byzantine au vi^e siècle* (Paris 1901) 63.

[25] Bury i 20.

[26] Katharine M. Rogers, *The Troublesome Helpmate: A History of Misogyny in Literature* (London 1966) 21.

[27] For additional passages, see Rogers 3, 8-9.

[28] Rogers 3.

[29] For a colorful description of the Empress' way of life, see Charles Diehl, *Byzantine Empresses,* trans. by Harold Bell and Theresa deKerpely (New York 1973) 7-17.

[30] Evans 17.

[31] For a development of this theme, see Simone de Beauvior, *Le Deuxième Sexe* (Paris 1949) 121.

[32] Sarah B. Pomeroy, *Goddesses, Wives, Whores, and Slaves: Women in Classical Antiquity* (New York 1975) chapters 4 and 5.

[33] F. W. Walbank, "Tragic History: A Reconsideration," *Bulletin of the Institute of Classical Studies* 2 (1955) 4.

[34] The general impression that marriage is important for a woman is incidentally reinforced by descriptions of barbarian customs and legends illustrating a woman's dependence on her husband. Cf. *Bell.* vi 14.6-7 and viii 20.57.

[35] Walbank 4.

[36] This passage recalls Justinian's use of similar themes in his legislation. The greed of the procurers, the poverty of their female victims, and the disgust felt by prostitutes for their profession are cited in *Novella* 14 (535 A.D.).

[37] These women are in the tradition of the Tarpeia figure, who betrays her country for love. See F. Mielentz, "Tarpeia," *RE* iv A (1932) 2337-38 for a discussion of this *topos* in ancient literature. Also Alexander Krappe, "Die Sage von der Tarpeja," *RhM* 78 (1929) 249-267 for a discussion of the figure in world literature. I am indebted to Peter Siewert for this reference.

[38] Although Amalasuntha was not unattractive physically, to judge from *Arc.* 16.1.

[39] For approval of a woman expressed in similar terms, cf. Socrates' exclamation, ἀνδρικήν... τὴν διάνοιαν τῆς γυναικός, Xen. *Oec.* 10.1; Xerxes' comment on Artemisia, οἱ μὲν ἄνδρες γεγόνασί μοι γυναῖκες, αἱ δὲ γυναῖκες ἄνδρες Hdt. viii 88; the Hellenistic essay "Periktione," where a woman is advised to be δικαίη καὶ ἀνδρηίη καὶ φρονέουσα καὶ αὐταρκείη Stob. iv 28. 19: and the Roman orator Maesia Sentia, *quam, quia sub specie feminae virilem animum gerebat, Androgynem appellabant* Val, Max. viii 3.1. For women disapproved as "manly," *cf.* Sall. *Cat.* 25.1; Tac. *Ann.* xii 7.

[40] Theodora's financial independence: *Novella* 28.5.1; 29.4; 30.6. Her power in government: *Novella* 8.1. Justinian's devotion to Theodora: *Novella* 8.1. Discussed by Bury ii 30-31 and by Diehl *Justinien* 52.

[41] "Vita Silverii," *Liber Pontificalis* ed. L. Duchesne (Paris 1886) i 292-293. Discussed by Evans 89-90, and by Bury ii 378-9.

[42] Rubin states that the *de Bellis* forecasts the calumnies of the *Historia Arcana* in the case of Justinian but not of Theodora (p. 441 n. 542).

[43] It is not surprising that sexual slanders of women were not uncommon in classical literature, for they effectively complement a patriarchal stereotype. *Cf.* Semon. *fr.* 7.48-54 (Diehl); Sall. *Cat.* 25.3; Tac. *Ann.* xi 12; xi 26; xii 3; Juvenal, *Sat.* 6.

[44] David Daube, "The Marriage of Justinian and Theodora. Legal and Theological Reflections," *Catholic University Law Review* 16 (1967) 391.

[45] Diehl *Theodora* 38, 70-76; Barker 70; Rubin 106.

[46] In this respect Theodora resembles the wrathful and powerful Hera/Juno figure familiar from the epic tradition (e.g. *Il.* 4.20-36, *Aen.* 1.4-75).

[47] Rubin 101-2.

[48] For a selection of views on the murder of Amalasuntha, see Diehl *Theodora* 98; Barker 151; Evans 11; and Bury ii 426.

[49] Diehl *Theodora* 62.

[50] It would be extremely interesting to isolate all the details of Theodora's and Antonina's biographies which fall into these two categories and which are therefore likely to be accurate. I include only a few illustrative examples of each category, for I feel the task of considering them all requires a separate article.

[51] Bury ii 166-167.

[52] *Cf.* Evans, 87 quoting Bury, ii 426-427; "in no instance can we convict him [Procopius] of a statement which has no basis in fact."

[53] Similarly, the biographies of ancient authors were affected by invective topoi and "typical" anecdotes, as shown by J. Fairweather, "Fiction in the Biographies of Ancient Writers," *Ancient Society* 5 (1974) 231-275 (esp. 244-247, 270-272).

[54] The reputation of a man is similarly damaged through association with a powerful woman in the cases of Antony and Cleopatra (Plut. *Vit. Ant.*) and Claudius and Messalina (Tac. *Ann.* xi 25-38) and Agrippina (Tac. *Ann.* xii 3-7).

SELECTED BIBLIOGRAPHY

ON WOMEN IN CLASSICAL ANTIQUITY

SARAH B. POMEROY

Index

Introduction

The women of Greece and Rome have never been the subject of a modern bibliographical survey of scholarship. The present bibliography attempts to provide a general introduction to the material and to some of the controversies.

Because women pervade nearly every aspect of antiquity, the bibliography will be immensely selective, and much material will be left unconsidered. The emphasis will be sociological rather than literary – not necessarily out of agreement with those who believe that literature does not portray real or normal women, but rather because usable bibliographies already exist for most major classical authors. On the other hand, an effort will be made to introduce the viewpoints of scholars in disciplines other than classical studies.

The bibliography has been designed primarily for use by classicists intending to introduce undergraduate courses on women in antiquity, or to include more material on women in existing classical civilization curricula. Only work written in languages commonly read by classicists will be cited. Availability of texts will be considered, and where differences are not crucial, a modern work will usually be cited in preference to an earlier work covering the same material. An effort will be made to mention paperback reprints. Citations of articles in standard classical encylopedias, references, and other surveys, and editions of classical authors have been omitted, with a few exceptions, since these works will be known to classicists. Scholars in other disciplines using this bibliography would be well advised to begin by consulting the articles pertinent to women in the standard classical reference books to be found in the reference rooms of college libraries, as well as scholarly editions of the classical texts mentioned in the suggested reading list for the undergraduate course on "Women in Antiquity," which follows this bibliography.

I GENERAL WORKS ON THE WOMEN OF BOTH GREECE AND ROME

1. *Works by classical scholars*

Although there are a number of books by classicists which may serve as an introduction to the subject, the survey recommended for both the lay reader and professional scholar is *Histoire mondiale de la femme I: Préhistoire et antiquité* (Paris: Nouv. Libr. de France, 1965). This volume includes slightly more than 100 pages on the women of Crete and Greece written by Robert Flacelière, and an article of similar length on Roman women by Pierre Grimal. The work is selected not only for its readability, relevant illustrations, and attention to a variety of ancient sources, but especially for the sober and impartial attitude of the authors. On controversial topics, both sides are presented, and evidence evaluated. Other survey books include E. Burck, *Die Frau in der griechisch-römischen Antike* (Tusculum Schriften; Munich: Heimeran, 1969); C. Seltman, *Women in Antiquity* (London and New York: Thames and Hudson, 1956); J. Leipoldt, *Die Frau in der antiken Welt und im Urchristentum*, 2nd ed. (Leipzig: Köhler and Ameland, 1955); and T. Birt, *Frauen der Antike* (Leipzig: Quelle and Meyer, 1932). A word of caution must be entered here against the Seltman book, inasmuch as it is probably the general work most readily available to *Arethusa* readers. This book appears to be directed to the non-scholarly reader, and in his attempt to make the Greeks attractive, Seltman skirts scholarly arguments. He praises the relationship between the sexes in Sparta, claiming that in that wholesome atmosphere there was an absence of adultery, prostitution, and homosexuality. Seltman also exaggerates the freedom of women in classical Greece in order to culminate in a subtle polemic against St. Paul, whose influence caused a decline in the status of women.

2. Works by non-classicists

The women of Greece and Rome have not been the subject of detailed study by scholars approaching from the viewpoint of the "History of Women" rather than from classical studies. Nevertheless there are some commendable, though brief, chapters on antiquity in Simone de Beauvoir, *Le deuxième Sexe* (Paris: Gallimard, 1949; Eng. tr. *The Second Sex* New York: Knopf, 1953; paperback reprint, Bantam, 1961). The contents of the entire book could be used by the classical scholar; for example, de Beauvoir's comments on "The Married Woman" illuminate the problems of such heroines as Alcestis, Medea, and Phaedra. Emily James Putnam, who lectured on Greek literature while serving as Barnard College's first dean, wrote chapters on The Greek Lady and The Roman Lady in *The Lady* (New York: G. P. Putnam, 1910; reissued Chicago; University of Chicago Press, 1970). Elizabeth G. Davis, *The First Sex* (New York: G. P. Putnam, 1971) is crammed with misinformation about antiquity cited pell-mell to support the thesis of the primacy of women in early societies. Davis is a librarian, and her book is listed here merely for the sake of her wide-ranging footnotes which may seduce the classicist into considering the viewpoints of modern anthropology, sociology, and psychology on women in antiquity. A standard reference work to be recommended to college students is Norma Olin Ireland, *Index to Women of the World from Ancient to Modern Times; Biographies and Portraits* (Westwood, Massachusetts: Faxon, 1970). The biographies actually refer the reader to an article in a standard secondary source, while the portraits include depictions of famous ancient women throughout the course of western art.

3. Literary studies

Among the numerous studies of women in Greek and Latin literature several approaches have particular relevance for the study of the actual women who lived in antiquity. Katharine M. Rogers, *The Trouble-some Helpmate: A History of Misogyny in Literature* (Seattle: University of Washington Press, 1966) gives a careful, though brief, survey of the attitudes towards women expressed by most major classical authors. In the Jungian tradition Maud Bodkin, *Archetypal Patterns in Poetry: Psychological Studies of Imagination* (London: Oxford University Press, 1934; paperback reprint, London: Oxford University Press, 1963), explores the symbolic function of female images including goddesses of Greek tragedy and Vergil's Dido and Eurydice. A sensitive evaluation of attitudes toward women expressed in sepulchral inscriptions may be found in Richmond Lattimore, *Themes in Greek and Latin Epitaphs* (Illinois Studies in Language and Literature 28, 1 and 2; Urbana: University of Illinois Press, 1943; paperback reprint, Urbana: University of Illinois Press, 1962).

II THE BRONZE AGE, MATRIARCHY, MATRILINY, HOMERIC SOCIETY

Few topics in ancient history have occasioned as extended a debate as the question of the role of Bronze Age women. As far back as the fifth century B.C., Herodotus and Thucydides considered whether the seduction of Helen could have been the true cause of the Trojan War;

nor has later scholarship resolved the controversy. Some of the major questions at issue are: whether Bronze Age society was matriarchal; whether descent was matrilineal (possible even in a non-matriarchal society); whether matriarchy or matriliny can be posited for all strata of society, even if found to exist among the upper class, such as those whose exploits were later related by Homer; and whether the classifications "matrilineal" and "matriarchal" are relevant.

1. *Historical survey of scholarship including Anthropology and Classics*

Our retrospect of scholarly opinion on the status of Bronze Age women can begin with the influential work of J. J. Bachofen, *Das Mutterrecht: Eine Untersuchung über die Gynaikokratie der alten Welt nach ihrer religiosen und rechtlichen Natur* (Stuttgart: Krais and Hoffmann, 1861). Bachofen, although not a professional classical scholar, formulated his concept of the priority of mother-right and matriliny on classical data, beginning by classifying as matrilineal the Lycians described in Herodotus I, 173. Selections from his writings have been translated into English by Ralph Manheim as *Myth, Religion, and Mother Right: Selected Writings of J. J. Bachofen* (Bollingen Series 84; Princeton: Princeton University Press, 1967), with the important additions of a preface by the anthropologist George Boas and an introduction by Joseph Campbell.

The American, Lewis Henry Morgan, a lawyer who became an anthropologist, also determined that the matriarchy was a basic principle of prehistoric social organization in his work *Ancient Society* (Cleveland and New York: World, 1877; paperback reprint, Cleveland and New York: Meridian, 1963). The work of Morgan became a decisive influence in the Marxist interpretation of pre-history. The concept that matriarchy preceded patriarchy and was, in many respects, a superior form of society, is basic to Friedrich Engels, *Der Ursprung der Familie, des Privateigentums und des Staats* (4th ed. 1892); reissued in *Karl Marx Friedrich Engels Werke,* 21 (Berlin: Dietz, 1962), pp. 25-173. The book appears in English as *The Origin of the Family, Private Property and the State*, introd. E. Leacock (New York: International, 1972; also paperback). Robert Briffault, *The Mothers: A Study of the Origin of Sentiments and Institutions* (New York: Macmillan, 1927; paperback abridgement, introd. G. R. Taylor; New York: Universal, 1963), likewise found abundant evidence for the existence of matriarchal and matrilineal usages in the pre-historic Aegean.

A more detailed historical account of scholarship combining the viewpoints of classics and anthropology especially in the 19th and 20th centuries is given by C. Kluckhorn, *Anthropology and the Classics* (Colver Lectures 1960; Providence: Brown University Press, 1961). A highly critical evaluation of the schemes of Bachofen, Morgan, and their followers from the viewpoint of the mainstream of contemporary anthropology can be found in Marvin Harris, *The Rise of Anthropological Theory* (New York: Thomas Crowell, 1968), 180-189. Harris fails to comment on the divergent opinion of the British anthropologists Jacquetta Hawkes and Sir Leonard Woolley, *Prehistory and the Beginning of Civilization* (New York: Harper and Row, 1963), p. 122, who discovered evidence of matrilineal descent in "Homeric society, while among the Cretans the position of women seems to have remained exceptionally high."

A creative and non-polemical approach to the question has emerged in the articles of Simon Pembroke, "Last of the matriarchs. A Study in the inscriptions of Lycia," *Journal of the Eco. and Soc. Hist. of the Orient*, 8, 3 (1965), 217-247, and "Women in charge. The function of alternatives in early Greek tradition and the ancient idea of matriarchy," *Journal of the Warburg and Courtauld Inst.*, 1, 30 (1967), 1-35. Pembroke re-evaluates the evidence from Herodotus concerning Lycian society which had been seminal in Bachofen's formulation of the theory of *Mutterrecht*, and determines that evidence from Lycian inscriptions does not confirm the report of Herodotus nor the interpretation of Bachofen. Rather, Pembroke suggests that it is erroneous to try to subsume those ancient societies described by Herodotus in terms of modern anthropological categories such as "matrilineal" and "matriarchal." Inspired by the work of Simon Pembroke, Pierre Vidal-Naquet, "Esclavage et gynécocratie dans la tradition, le mythe, l'utopie," *Recherches sur les structures sociales dans l'antiquité classique* (*Actes du Colloque de Caen* 25-26 avril 1969; Paris: Centre national de la recherche scientifique, 1970), 63-80, investigates the myths surrounding female power and the connection between slaves and women. This essay is extremely provocative and iconoclastic.

In the face of so much uncertainty, the classical scholar who wishes to compare the Greek and Roman data with evidence from the 20th century "primitive" societies should consult the works of the anthropologist Bronislaw Malinowski, e.g. *Sex and Repression in Savage Society* (Cleveland: World, 1927; paperback reprint, Cleveland: Meridian, 1955); and Margaret Mead, e.g. *Male and Female, a study of the sexes in a changing world* (New York: W. Morrow, 1949; paperback reprint, New York: Dell, 1970).

2. *Viewpoint of contemporary classical scholarship*

Nowadays among classicists, as among anthropologists, there is a diversity of opinion regarding the status of women in prehistoric society. Yet M. I. Finley, *The World of Odysseus* (London: Chatto and Windus, 1954; paperback revision, New York: Viking, 1965), p. 93, gives the majority verdict when he writes: "that a repressed memory of ancient matriarchy is reflected in some of the [Homeric] verses seems a fragile argument." W. K. Lacey, *The Family in Classical Greece* (Ithaca: Cornell University Press, 1968), p. 11, refuses to discuss the theory of matriarchy since it is "based on wholly false premises." The most extensive recent argument in support of matriarchy as well as matriliny by a classical scholar is George Derwent Thomson, *Studies in Ancient Greek Society I: The Prehistoric Aegean* (New York: International, 1949). Thomson adopts the Marxist anthropology, illustrating the 19th century arguments with a profusion of details from classical sources. The scholar who rejects Thomson's politics will nevertheless find much useful material on such topics as "the formation of a goddess," or "female taboos." Likewise evidence supporting the existence of matriarchy and matriliny is presented by Kaarle Hirvonen, *Matriarchal Survivals and Certain Trends in Homer's Female Characters* (*Annales Academiae Scientiarum Fennicae*, Ser. B, 152; Helsinki: Suomalainen Tiedeakatemia, 1968). Her book is a valuable collection of citations relevant to women in Homer, and contains a twelve page bibliography. Hirvonen has been criticized for postulating the existence of matriarchy on the basis of inconclusive evidence, and for relying unduly upon the controversial opinions of Robert Graves (e.g. *The White Goddess: a Historical Grammar of Poetic Myth*, New York: Farrar, Straus and Giroux, 1966) concerning the importance of woman in pre-history. Hirvonen's arguments for matriliny have, however, received a better reception by reviewers. Likewise A. R. Burn, *The Pelican History of Greece* (Harmondsworth, Middlesex: Penguin, 1968), p. 33, finds evidence of matrilineal practices in heroic times. Most recently Sarah B. Pomeroy, "Andromache, and the Question of Matriarchy," *REG* (1973), sees some evidence for the high status of women in the birthplace of Andromache.

A number of French scholars remain open-minded toward the theories of matriarchy and matriliny. In reviews of Thomson's *Studies*

in the Prehistoric Aegean, Ch. Delvoye (*AC* 18 [1949], 479-82) and
Paul Cloché (*RH* 209 [1953],100-02) did not challenge the conclusions
concerning matriarchal and matrilineal customs. More recently, Robert
Flacelière (cited above, I, 1) concluded his discussion of the Minoan
culture with a statement that he lacked sufficient evidence to comment on the status of women in aspects of Minoan culture other than
religious.

The preceding surveys of anthropological and classical scholarship have indicated the wide range of scholarly opinion concerning the
status of women in the Bronze Age. However, the viewpoint tending to
prevail in both disciplines is that there is some evidence for matrilineal
usage, but far less to support a belief in matriarchy.

3. *Opinion of Marxists, psychologists, and feminists*

Belief in the historical reality of the matriarchy is still maintained by some orthodox Marxists following the doctrine of Engels —
especially in some Communist countries; by some schools of psychoanalytic thought; and by some members of the contemporary
movement for women's liberation. A number of the authors named in
the following section fall into two of the three categories mentioned.

The theory of the matriarchy is upheld by the psychoanalyst
Erich Fromm, *The Forgotten Language* (New York: Grove Press, 1951),
196-231, who interprets the struggle between Antigone and Creon
according to the principles established by Bachofen. Likewise, the
historical priority of matriarchy is basic to the psychological writings
of Wilhelm Reich, e.g., *The Invasion of Compulsory Sex-Morality*
(paperback translation, New York: Farrar, Straus and Giroux, 1971).

It is appropriate to comment here that the majority of psychoanalytic writing which touches on the question of matriarchy at all
deals with it in terms of the psychic development of the individual
rather than the objective history of the human race. Among the many
interpretations of the matriarchy as a psychic image, some are of
particular relevance to classical scholars. A Jungian interpretation of
the "feminine" element may be found in Erich Neumann, *The Great
Mother: An Analysis of the Archetype*, tr. R. Manheim (Bollingen
Series 47; New York: Pantheon, 1955). The universality of the
archetype is demonstrated by illustrations from a variety of cultures,
including those of the pre-historic Aegean. Neumann does not see any
necessary connection between the primacy of the woman in religious
cult and her actual political or social status. The psychological con-

notations of femininity and masculinity in the *Iliad* and other epics are outlined by Paul Zweig, "Man on the Run," *Columbia Forum* (Winter, 1971), 54-55, and "Man on the Run - II," *Columbia Forum* (Spring, 1972), 40-43.

Modern feminists comprise a third category of believers in the historical existence of the matriarchy. Among popular writers the theory is expressed by Evelyn Reed, *Problems of Women's Liberation* (New York: Pathfinder Press, 1970), 16-19; by Jill Johnston, "Who is the father of her child?" *The Village Voice* (June 24, 1971), 28, 29, 48; and, less assertively, by Eva Figes, *Patriarchal Attitudes* (New York: Fawcett, 1970), p. 32. Among more scholarly feminists may be noted the cautious approach to the problem by Kate Millett, *Sexual Politics* (New York: Doubleday, 1969; paperback reprint, New York: Avon, 1971, 108-111), and the total rejection of the theory by Simone de Beauvoir (cited above, 1, 2, pp. 64-65), following Lévi-Strauss. Some feminist scholars have enthusiastically greeted the evidence in James Mellaart, *Çatal Hüyük: A Neolithic Town in Anatolia* (New York: McGraw-Hill, 1967). Although Mellaart himself does not discuss matriliny or matriarchy, he does write (p. 60): "The woman's bed never changed its place, nor did the arrangement of the kitchen, but the man's bed did. The sociological implications to be drawn from this are fairly obvious. Children were buried either with the women or under the remaining platforms, but they never accompany the master of the house."

4. *Digression on scholarly attitudes toward the matriarchy*

Few areas of scholarship are filled with more uncertainty than ancient history, and few periods of ancient history provide less opportunity for incontrovertible proof than the Bronze Age. A case in point is the question of the social organization of Minoan Crete. Reviewers of Kaarle Hirvonen's recent book (cited above, II, 2) criticized her deduction that Minoan Crete was a matriarchy from the evidence of a few fresco paintings. For example, a reviewer (*CW* 63, 2, 55) wrote: "clear evidence must be presented to support the hypothesis that matriarchies existed in the pre-Homeric Mediterranean world ..." and condemned the notion that "the well-known peculiarity of Minoan female dress is a reflex of 'matriarchy.'" There is, to be sure, a dearth of clear evidence establishing the matriarchy, but there is equally, as no reviewer pointed out, a lack of conclusive evidence proving the existence of patriarchy in Minoan Crete. There is no reason to refer, as did Mellaart to the father as the "master of the house."

Nevertheless, the assumption is usually made that patriarchy existed, and the burden of proof is put on those who would believe otherwise, and then the "evidence" is ridiculed.

The virulence with which the theory of Bronze Age matriarchy has been attacked is remarkable. The theory may have attracted hostility due to its association with Marxism and militant feminism. There may also be some truth in the analysis of Erich Fromm (cited above, II, 3, p. 210) that this hostility derives from "an emotionally founded prejudice against an assumption so foreign to the thinking and feeling of our patriarchal culture." That some scholars are so influenced by their prejudices concerning women that they misread the text of Homer is the contention of Sarah B. Pomeroy (cited above, II, 2).

Modern anthropology has described so large a variety of social structures that further evidence may reveal that Minoan Crete cannot be labelled either matriarchy or patriarchy. For the time being, it would seem best to scrutinize the available evidence without sexist bias, and to withhold final judgment.

III WOMEN IN CLASSICAL GREECE

The women of Classical Greece have long been a topic of essays and dissertations. Some readers may be interested in the quaint discussions of Greek women in Castiglione, *The Book of the Courtier*, tr. George Bull (Harmondsworth, Middlesex: Penguin, 1967), Book 3; or in Friedrich Nietzsche, "The Greek Woman," *The Complete Works of Friedrich Nietzsche*, ed. Oscar Levy, 2 (New York: Russell, 1964), 19-27; or in the attitude of a Yale Professor of Political and Social Science in 1911, W. G. Sumner, *War and Other Essays* (Freeport, New York: Books for Libraries Press, 1970), 65-102. The present bibliography will, however, cite those works most useful to the contemporary scholar.

1. *General works*

The books on ancient women cited above in section I of this bibliography include discussions of many of the subtopics treated in the following sections. Also worth mentioning among recent general studies specifically of Greek women is U. E. Paoli, *La donna greca nell' antichità* (Florence: Le Monnier, 1953), a prime source for the realities of daily life, including facts about clothing, toilette, and the like, abundantly illustrated. The text is 98 pages, with an additional

76 pages of footnotes indicative of the highest quality of research. This scholarly book is marred, however, by the tone of levity giving rise to such sentiments as "La donna sarà sempre una donna, e l'eterno femminino trova anche il modo di disarmare Solone" (p. 81). A survey in a popular style, first published in 1923, is F. A. Wright, *Feminism in Greek Literature* (Port Washington, New York: Kennikat, 1969). Wright believed that the principal cause of the downfall of Greek civilization was the degradation of women, and that Greek women should be classified with slaves.

2. *Daily life*

While this subject has been adequately covered in the multitude of works giving a general picture of the daily life of both sexes, of particular value for women's life are Victor Ehrenberg, *The People of Aristophanes* (Oxford: Blackwell, 1943; paperback revision, New York: Schocken, 1962), and R. Flacelière, *La vie quotidienne en Grèce au siècle de Pericles* (Paris: Hachette, 1959; Eng. tr., *Daily Life in Greece at the Time of Pericles*, New York: Macmillan, 1964).

The importance of archaeological evidence cannot be overstressed. Utensils commonly handled by women – pots and pans, looms, mirrors, and the like – as well as the depiction of women in the visual arts including vase painting, sculpture, gems, and coins can tell much about the life of women. In the field of art history, a useful study of attitudes toward women is D. and E. Panofsky, *Pandora's Box; the changing aspects of a mythical symbol* (Bollingen Series 52; New York: Panetheon, 1956). Archaeological publications such as G. M. A. Richter, *Korai: archaic Greek maidens; a study of the development of the kore type in Greek sculpture* (London: Phaidon, 1968) and D. von Bothmer, *Amazons in Greek Art* (Oxford: Clarendon, 1957), tend to be more descriptive than interpretive. The history of the female nude in Greek art has not been extensively studied, and questions such as why the kouros was nude while the korē remained draped have scarcely been raised.

Epigraphical material is also potentially valuable, but has not been exhaustively studied. Some work has been done by Helen McClees, *A Study of Women in Attic Inscriptions* (New York: Columbia University Press, 1920), and the comments of Richmond Lattimore (cited above, I, 3), on the epitaphs of young maidens and wives are illuminating.

3. *The family*

This subject has been well studied by W. K. Lacey (cited above, II, 2). The book concentrates on the family in classical Athens, but also treats the family in Homeric Society, Sparta, Crete, and other Greek states. While detailing women's lack of freedom deriving from wide-ranging familial obligations, Lacey calls attention to the positive aspects of her position – that she "had protection against unscrupulous males" (p. 176), as well as "an economic security not enjoyed even by the modern married woman" (p. 174). Lacey's work will be considered again below, in sections III, 6, 7, and 8. Useful still for defining the relationship between the city, the family, and the individual is Fustel de Coulanges, *La Cité Antique: Etude sur le culte, le droit, les institutions de la Grèce et de Rome* (Paris: Hachette, 1864; Eng. tr., *The Ancient City*, paperback reprint, New York: Doubleday, 1956).

Although classicists either ignore or postulate the non-existence of mature, never-married women among the Athenian citizen class, there are some interesting ideas in the essay of Philip Weissman, a psychoanalyst, "Sophocles' *Antigone*; the Psychology of the Old Maid," in his book *Creativity in the Theater: A Psychoanalytic Study* (New York: Dell, 1965).

Greek family patterns are extensively analyzed from a psychological viewpoint by Philip E. Slater, *The Glory of Hera: Greek Mythology and the Greek Family* (Boston: Beacon Press, 1968; paperback reprint, Boston: Beacon, 1971). Although its publication was virtually ignored by classical journals, the book has attained an "underground" reputation. Slater's irreverent treatment of the classics and of classical scholarship has produced some fascinating and original ideas including an explanation of how female characters can be dominant in Greek drama while being severely repressed in true life.

Slater's studies of the modern family are highly regarded in his own discipline, but his venture into the field of classics could have been vastly improved by collaboration with a classical scholar. As the book is written, a teacher may well hesitate to recommend it to a college student, for Slater barges through the centuries with such abandon that the unknowledgeable reader could suppose that Achilles lived in Periclean Athens. One of many specific examples of Slater's failure to use the resources of classical scholarship (p. 162): "...while Oedipus is the concern of only three surviving Greek tragedies, Orestes is in seven, and is treated by all three of the great dramatists. It could in fact be said that the Orestes myth was the most popular subject in Greek drama, and that the theme of matricide was one with which the Greeks were peculiarly preoccupied." Is Slater aware that the Oedipus legend appears in Euripides' *Phoenissae* and *Suppliant Women*? Would not a classicist have combed lists of all titles of tragedies, not only surviving plays, and have turned up a Theban trilogy by Aeschylus? A more rigorous weeding out of "proofs" which are irrelevant because of date or source would have produced a shorter but sounder book. Despite its many defects, however, *The Glory of Hera* should be read by anyone who is interested in Greek women.

4. Erotic *

The erotic life of Greece in all its aspects has received a thorough treatment by "Hans Licht" [P. Brandt] in his *Sittengeschichte Griechenlands* (Dresden and Zurich: P. Aretz, 1925-26; Eng. tr., *Sexual Life in Ancient Greece*, New York: Am. Anthropological Society, 1934). A scholar dealing with any aspect of Greek erotica will be well advised to consult this book, which is the most exhaustive assemblage of the relevant sources. R. Flacelière, *L'amour en Grèce* (Paris: Hachette, 1960; Eng. tr., *Love in Ancient Greece,* New York: Crown, 1962; paperback reprint, New York: MacFadden-Bartell, 1964) pays less attention to clinical details, and is much shorter. A new interpretation of an old problem is given in G. Devereux, "Greek pseudo-homosexuality and the 'Greek Miracle,'" *Symbolae Osloenses* 42 (1967), 69-92.

The most important secondary source on ancient prostitution is H. Herter, "Die Soziologie der antiken Prostitution im Lichte des heidnischen und christlichen Schrifttums," *Jahrbuch für Antike und Christentum* 3 (1960), 70-111.

5. Law

The chief sources for all of Greek private law are the private orations of Demosthenes (nos. XXVII-LIX; the pseudo-Demosthenic speeches are of no less value than the authentic ones) and those of Isaeus. For the latter the commentary of Wyse (W. Wyse, *The Speeches of Isaeus*, Cambridge: Cambridge University Press, 1904; reissued

---

* Sections 4, 5, and 6 covering erotic, legal, and economic aspects were written by David Schaps, Tel Aviv University.

Hildesheim: Georg Olms, 1967) is indispensible, though it has been criticized as overly skeptical of Isaeus' veracity. The most important non-Athenian document is the Gortynian Code, most easily accessible either in the edition of Willetts (R. F. Willetts, *The Law Code of Gortyn, Kadmos* Supplement 1, 1967, with a commentary closely following the controversial theories of George Derwent Thomson), or in that of Guarducci (*Inscriptiones Creticae*, ed. M. Guarducci [Rome: Libreria dello stato, 1935-50], 4, no. 72).

Since the sources are so overwhelmingly Athenian, there is little practical difference between studies that purport to examine Greek law and those that restrict themselves to Athens. The most accessible general study is the first volume of A. R. W. Harrison, *The Law of Athens: The Family and Property* (Oxford: Clarendon Press, 1968), a competent work with extensive citations of ancient sources and secondary interpretations. A scholar will also avail himself of J. H. Lipsius, *Das attische Recht und Rechtsverfahren* (Leipzig: Reisland, 1905-15; reissued Hildesheim: Georg Olms, 1966), and of L. Beauchet, *Histoire du droit privé de la république athénienne* (Paris: Chevalier-Marescq, 1897; reissued Amsterdam: Rodopi, 1969). The latter must be used with caution (cf. Harrison's remarks, p. viii), although it is a standard resource for French scholarship.

The most important legal study of marriage is H. J. Wolff, ''Marriage Law and Family Organization in Ancient Athens,'' *Traditio* 2 (1944),43-95, including a summary of the distinction between ''free'' marriage in Athens and marriage without *manus* in Rome. Now out of date, but of value for its broader scope is W. Erdmann, *Die Ehe im alten Griechenland (Münchener Beiträge zur Papyrusforschung und antiken Rechtsgeschichte*, 20 [Munich: C. H. Beck, 1934]). In this, as in all fields touching on law, the works of Harrison, Lipsius, and Beauchet cited above should also be consulted.

Three more institutions dominate the legal problems involved with Greek women: the dowry, the laws of *epikleroi* (heiresses whose hand could be claimed by the nearest male relative), and the powers of the woman's *kyrios* over her property. The first of these has been treated by H. J. Wolff, προίξ RE, 23, A (1957), 133-170. The second has been treated by L. H. Gernet, ''Sur l'épiclérat,'' *REG* 34 (1921), 337-79, as well as by Harrison, Lipsius, and Beauchet. An unorthodox and highly questionable interpretation of the myth of the Danaids in Aeschylus' *Suppliants*, as dramatizing a rebellion against the Athenian law of the *epikleros* has been aired by G. D. Thomson, *Aeschylus and Athens: A study in the social origins of drama*, 3rd ed.

(London: Lawrence and Wishart, 1966; paperback reprint, New York: Grosset and Dunlap, 1968), 289-292. For the powers of the *kyrios* see the general works cited, as well as L. J. Th. Kuenen-Jansens, "Some Notes upon the Competence of the Athenian Woman to Conduct a Transaction," *Mnemosyne* ser. 3, 9 (1941), 199-241. Some very important questions relating to these subjects and to the larger problem of women's property rights have been raised by G. E. M. de Ste. Croix, "Some Observations on the Property Rights of Athenian Women," *CR* 20 (1970), 273-78.

Consideration of marriages and informal liaisons between Greeks and barbarians in the pre-classical period, in contrast to the restrictions on such unions in the classical period may be found in Jean Rougé, "La colonisation grecque et les femmes," *CH* 15 (1970), 307-17.

6. *Economics*

The only important item dealing solely with the economic activity of women is P. Herfst, *Le travail de la femme dans la Grèce ancienne* (Utrecht: Oosthoek, 1922). Herfst reviews the various types of work which women pursued, as well as the social status of working women and their reasons for working outside the home. The importance of women in domestic economy is also dealt with in the works on the life of women mentioned above, in III, 2, while works discussing the legal aspects of women's property are considered in III, 5. Lacey's book (cited above, II, 2) gives a good general background of the economic life of women in Sparta and Crete as well as in Athens.

7. *The status of women in classical Athens*

While there is general agreement that politically and legally the condition of women in classical Athens was inferior, the question of her social status has generated a major controversy. While some scholars painted a lamentable picture of the life of the Athenian woman, others argued that despite her formal handicaps she was neither despised nor secluded. Most modern treatments taking the latter position go back to the radical essay of A. W. Gomme, "The Position of Women in Athens in the Fifth and Fourth Centuries B.C.," *CP* 20 (1925), 1-25 (reprinted in his *Essays in Greek History and Literature* [Oxford: Blackwell, 1937], 89-115). The many advocates of Gomme's position include: Moses Hadas, "Observations on Athenian Women," *CW* 29 (1936), 97-100; H. D. F. Kitto, *The Greeks* (Harmondsworth, Middlesex: Penguin, 1951), 219-236; Charles Seltman (cited above, I, 1), 110-111, and "The Status of Women in Athens," *G & R* 2 (1955), 119-24; and Donald C. Richter, "The Position of Women in Classical Athens," *CJ* 67 (1971), 1-8, who gives a history of the controversy.

Taking a less sanguine position are W. K. Lacey (cited above II, 2), chapter VII, and V. Ehrenberg (cited above II, 2), chapter VIII, by calling attention to a life spent mostly inside a dark unsanitary house, to marriages between fourteen year old brides and thirty year old grooms, and to the wives' relative lack of access to the educational values of Athenian life. Ehrenberg, in fact, believes that women did not attend the theatre. Considered in these terms, even Xanthippe may lose her reputation as a virago and a laughing-stock, and may be viewed as a member of an oppressed and neglected class.

The wide divergence of scholarly opinion is puzzling, and cannot be attributed to sexist bias — for male partiality can be detected on both sides of the argument. The principal reason for the two viewpoints is the genre of the evidence consulted. Gomme and his followers, relying predominantly, or exclusively, on the evidence from classical tragedy, and believing that the heroines were modeled directly on Athenian women of the fifth century B.C., determine that women were respected and not secluded. Lacey (p. 50), who explicitly rejects the testimony of tragedy as not representative of normal people in a normal family, or Ehrenberg (p. 12), who accepts only Euripides, while finding Sophocles and Aeschylus less close to reality, paints a sorrier picture of the position of women.

Lacey and Ehrenberg rely heavily upon the Attic orators, while the majority of the followers of Gomme, in contrast, scarcely cite the orators. Hadas gives the reason that speeches are too polemical, and give a one-sided abnormal picture. The evidence from comedy is less decisive, and is cited in support of both positions.

Two prose passages are a staple of discussions on the social status of Women: Pericles' advice to women in his Funeral Oration (Thucydides, II, 45) that it would be best for them to have no reputation, either for good or evil, and the patronizing account of the training of a wife in Xenophon's *Oeconomicus*. Both pieces have been an embarrassment to those who argue for the high status of women. Gomme (pp. 101-02) merely assigns little significance to the two passages in comparison with the abundant testimony of tragedy. Richter (p. 4) condones the superior attitude of the husband toward his bride on the basis that the man [as usual] is sixteen years older than his wife. The standard device in explaining away Pericles' dictum is to call attention to his high regard for the notorious Aspasia. Of course, as even some of its proponents have confessed, the Aspasia argument is faulty in that it fails to distinguish between Pericles' attitude toward a foreign-born, highly educated hetaira, and his expectations of the proper behavior on the part of citizen women, the mothers of Athenian soldiers. In contrast, Lacey and Ehrenberg cautiously distinguish between wealthy and poor, citizen and non-citizen women. While seclusion was the preferable condition of citizen women, often economic or religious obligations, or occasions of stress interfered with this ideal. According to this argument, then, the women depicted in vase paintings engaged in all sorts of out-of-doors activities, and used by Seltman as evidence of the freedom of women, are more likely to have been poor citizens, or non-citizens both free and slave.

The preceding brief survey has demonstrated that the question of the social status of women is part of a larger dispute concerning the appropriate source of evidence for women's life in Athens. The critical factor appears to be the heroines of Aeschylus and Sophocles. The scholars who consider Antigone and Electra, for example, as "real" evidence for women of the fifth century B.C. will believe that the status of women was high. On the other hand, evidence from orators and other prose writers points usually to a low status, while comedy and Euripides give ambiguous testimony. The scholars surveyed do not give equal weight to all available evidence, but deliberately exclude, or explain away the literature not supporting their positions. Moreover, archaeological evidence is not widely used, Ehrenberg (pp. 5-6) even cautioning against trusting isolated pieces of material evidence.

For a unique psychoanalytic discussion of women in Athens using testimony from Aeschylus and Sophocles as evidence of a low status of women see also Philip Slater, cited above, II, 3, pp. 4-14, *et passim.*

None of the scholars named in the preceding discussion draws a clear distinction between the status of women in the fifth and fourth centuries B.C., some citing Aristotle, Theophrastus, Menander, and Demosthenes in support of their beliefs regarding the fifth century B.C. However, a more strictly chronological examination of Greek literature has generated the theory of the gradually improving status of women. Hadas (p. 98), to be sure, had suggested that the works of Aristophanes, Euripides, and Herodotus, as well as the *Republic*, all indicate an interest in women's rights at the end of the fifth century, but had not noted whether this interest produced any results. Arnold Toynbee, *A Study of History*, 2 (London: Oxford, 1939), 75-76, noted an actual rise in the prestige of both Athenian and Spartan women after the Peloponnesian War, reasoning that since women are less affected by the peculiarities of a civilization, they are better suited to survive disasters. The fullest development of the theory is in Joseph Vogt, *Von der Gleichwertigkeit der Geschlechter in der bürgerlichen Gesellschaft der Griechen* (Akademie der Wissenschaften und der Literatur in Mainz, Abhandlungen der Geistes und Socialwissensch.; Weisbaden: Steiner, 1960, 2), 211-255, who traces female emancipation from an origin in the last part of the fifth century B.C. under the influence of Euripides and Socrates through the Roman period up to Plutarch. R. Flacelière, "D'un certain féminisme grec," *REA* 64 (1962),109-116, while agreeing with Vogt for the most part, suggests that rather than being a founder, Euripides was publicizing an already-existent feminist movement.

The relationship of women to the traditional Greek and Roman census classes is explored by J. Le Gall, "Un critère de différenciation sociale," *Recherches sur les structures sociales dans l'antiquité classique (Actes du Colloque de Caen* 25-26 avril 1969; Paris: Centre national de la recherche scientifique, 1970), 275-286.

8. *Spartan women*

Worth special mention among the many brief studies of Spartan women is H. Michell, *Sparta* (Cambridge: Cambridge University Press, 1964), 45-61. Michell's footnotes refer to a variety of ancient sources, while other secondary studies seem to rely solely on Plutarch. While Michell does not answer the question of how the marriage was kept a secret if the wife's hair was cropped, he does discuss the status of children produced by wife-sharing. The Spartan family has also been recently studied by Lacey, cited above, II, 2.

IV HELLENISTIC

The abundant papyri of this period are a prime source of information about women. Among interpretative works of the highest value is Claire Préaux, "Le statut de la femme à l'époque hellénistique, principalement en Egypte," *Recueils de la société Jean Bodin,* 11, *La femme* (1959), 127-175. The recent work of Claude Vatin, *Re-*

cherches sur le mariage et la condition de la femme mariée à l'époque hellénistique (Paris: E. de Boccard, 1970) studies the changing male-female relationship through its various expressions in the law of marriage from classical through hellenistic Greece. A bibliography of earlier scholarship can be found in each of these works.

Somewhat antiquated is L. A. Post, "Women's Place in Menander's Athens," *TAPA* 71 (1940), 420-459.

Greek women in the Roman period are the subject of a brief study by O. Braunstein, *Die politische Wirksmankeit der griechischen Frau* (Leipzig: August Hoffman, 1911), based almost exclusively on evidence from inscriptions.

V ROMAN WOMEN

1. *General works*

For general studies of the women of both Greece and Rome see the first section of the present bibliography. A factually reliable but untheoretical work on the women of Rome is J. P. V. D. Balsdon, *Roman Women: Their History and Habits* (London: Bodley Head, 1962). This book can be read by undergraduates, while the footnotes will be of additional value to scholars. Balsdon is aware of the masculine prejudice of most ancient authors, and attempts to resurrect the reputations of some "notorious" Roman women.

2. *The Regal period, and Etruscan women*

The status of women in pre-Republican Italy is considered in many of the books cited in my discussion of matriarchy and matriliny, above, II. Among these works see especially G. D. Thomson for evidence for matriarchy and matriliny in Italy. J. J. Bachofen, *Die Sage von Tanaquil: eine untersuchung über den orientalismus in Rom und Italien* (Heidelberg: Mohr, 1870; reissued Basel: B. Schwabe, 1943-44), likewise argues the existence of Mutterrecht in pre-classical Italy. An excerpt from this work is translated in *Myth, Religion, and Mother Right: Selected Writings of J. J. Bachofen* (cited above, II, 1), 211-46. J. Heurgon, "Valeurs féminines et masculines dans la civilisation étrusque," *Mélanges d'Archéologie et d'Histoire de l'Ecole Française de Rome* 73 (1961), 139-60, confirms female eminence among the Etruscans by examining the necropolis at Caere where the tombs of males are clearly differentiated from the more elaborate tombs of females. [See further in this issue of *Arethusa*, Larissa B. Warren, "Etruscan Women," pp 91-101. *Ed.*]

3. *Daily life*

The everyday life of Roman women is discussed by J. P. V. D. Balsdon (cited above, V, 1), chapter XIII. General discussions of everyday life at Rome, including special treatments of women's life, may be found in such standard works as Jerome Carcopino, *La vie quotidienne à Rome à l'apogée de l'empire* (Paris: Hachette, 1939; Eng. tr., *Daily Life in Ancient Rome: The People and the City at the Height of the Empire*; paperback reprint, New Haven: Yale University Press, 1940); U. E. Paoli, *Vita Romana* (Florence: Le Monnier, 1958; Eng. tr., *Rome, its people, life and customs*, New York: McKay, 1963); and in L. Friedländer, *Sittengeschichte Roms*, 7th ed., (Eng. tr., *Roman Life and Manners Under the Early Empire*, London: Routledge, 1965). Owing to the nature of the sources, of course, the daily life described is overwhelmingly that led by women of the upper classes.

4. *Women of the upper classes: matrons and empresses*

For a thorough consideration of the pervasive influence of Roman matrons, especially in religious cults, the scholar should read Jean Gagé, *Matronalia: Essai sur les dévotions et les organisations cultuelles des femmes dans l'ancienne Rome* (Coll. Latomus 60, 1963), an exciting book, unfortunately without an index. Barbara Förtsch, *Die politische rolle der frau in der römischen republik (Würzburger Studien zur Altertumswissenschaft* 5; Stuttgart: Kohlhammer, 1935), surveys the political influence of famous women, and the status of women from legendary times to the late Republic. G. Ferrero, *Le donne dei Cesari* (Milan: Athena, 1925) is often cited in bibliographies, although the book is written in a popular style lacking scholarly annotation.

Noteworthy among shorter popular articles are M. I. Finley, "The Silent Women of Rome," *Horizon* 7 (1965), 57-64 = *Aspects of Antiquity: Discoveries and Controversies* (London: Chatto and Windus, 1968), 129-142, and J. P. V. D. Balsdon, "Women in Imperial Rome," *History Today* 10 (1960), 24-31. Finley interprets the notorious rebellion of a few women as testimony to the severe repression of the many, while Balsdon, questioning the anti-feminist tradition of such Latin sources as Juvenal, attempts to improve the reputation of Roman women by citing the complimentary evidence of sepulchral inscriptions.

M. P. Charlesworth, "Livia and Tranaquil," *CR* 41 (1927), 55-57 presents reasons for Tacitus' deliberate slandering of the character of Livia.

5. *Legal and economic*

Due to the efforts of scholars of Roman law, a prodigious number of studies have been devoted to topics pertinent to the legal and economic position of Roman women including *matrimonium, dos, tutela, manus, patria potestas, actio rei uxoriae,* and *divortium*.

The present bibliography will not attempt a comprehensive survey of Roman private law, but will merely guide the novice in the field to some useful studies. The non-specialist will be well advised to begin with a comprehensive general handbook with scholarly annotation such as Max Kaser, *Römisches Privatrecht*, 6th ed. (Munich: Beck, 1968; Eng. tr., *Roman Private Law*, 2nd ed., London: Butterworths, 1968), or J. A. Crook, *Law and Life of Rome: Aspects of Greek and Roman Life* (London: Thames and Hudson, 1967). For a consideration of the philosophy of Roman law as well as discussion of some specialized topics including dowry, see David Daube, *Roman Law: Linguistic, social and philosophical aspects* (The Gray Lectures, 1966; Edinburgh: The University Press, 1969). A standard reference is Adolf Berger, *Encyclopedic Dictionary of Roman Law* (Philadelphia: American Philosophical Society, 1953).

The historical development of the *de facto* freedom of Roman women is traced from legendary times to the late Republic by Claudine Hermann, *Le rôle judiciare et politique des femmes sous la république romaine* (Coll. Latomus 67, 1964). The decline in the powers of the father and husband of a woman, and the break-up of the traditional Roman family are noted by Robert Villers, "Le statut de la femme à Rome jusqu' à la fin de la République," *Recueils de la Société Jean Bodin*, 11: *La femme* (1959), 177-189. For a brief discussion of the status of women in the empire based on legal sources see Jean Gaudemet, "Le statut de la femme dans l'Empire romain," *Recueils de la Société Jean Bodin,* 11: *La femme* (1959), 191-222. Gaudemet takes note of the development of reciprocal obligations of spouses in divorce. He carefully distinguishes the status of women in Rome from their status in the provinces.

The specialized range of topics which are considered may be demonstrated by the articles cited in the present paragraph. A woman's ability to inherit is considered by J. A. Crook, "Patria Potestas,"

CQ 17 (1967), 113-22. The postponement of the execution of a pregnant woman, on the theory that the baby is innocent, is discussed by J. Quaesten, "Mutter und Kind in der Passio Perpetuae et Felicitas," *HJ* 62 (1952), 50-55. Among the studies by David Daube can be cited "The marriage of Justinian and Theodora. Legal and theological reflections," *CULR* 16 (1966-67), 380-99, in which he discusses Justin's decree eradicating the permanent social stigma from women who had led a disreputable life, but wished to reform. Daube in "Licinia's dowry," *Studi in onore di B. Biondi* I (Milan: Giuffrè, 1965), 197-212, considers whether the dowry of the widow of C. Gracchus should be confiscated with her husband's other possessions, or whether she should be compensated for its loss, as being truly her possession. On the relevance of the censorial definitions of class to Roman women see the article by Le Gall cited above at the end of III, 7.

6. Medical

The life cycle of Roman women has received special attention in recent years in a number of scholarly articles. For a discussion of the age of menarche and whether puberty was a prerequisite of marriage see M. K. Hopkins, "The Age of Roman girls at marriage," *Population Studies* 18, 3, (1964-65), 309-27. The discrepancy between the age of menarche cited in the legal sources, and the age in medical writers is investigated in D. W. Amundsen and C. J. Dieis, "The age of menarche in classical Greece and Rome," *Human Biology* (U.S.A.) 41, 1, (1969), 125-32. The same authors discuss "The age of menopause in classical Greece and Rome" *ibid*. 42, 1 (1970), 79-86. *

The topic of contraception is thoroughly treated by Keith Hopkins "Contraception in the Roman Empire," *Comparative Studies in Society and History* 8 (1965), 124-51. This article catalogs and evaluates contraceptive methods both medical and magical, and will direct the reader to a variety of Greek and Latin writers on gynecological topics. Hopkins states that the Romans confused contraception with abortion.

On the subject of abortion, the scholar should look into Enzo Nardi, *Procurato aborto nel mondo greco romano* (Milan: Giuffrè, 1971), reviewed on pp 159-166 in this issue of *Arethusa*. Some brief comments on the theory and practice of abortion in classical antiquity can be

* I have not seen this work.

found in John T. Noonan, Jr., "An absolute Value in History," *The Morality of Abortion* (Cambridge, Massachusetts: Harvard University Press, 1970), 1-59.

Caesarian section is discussed by J. P. Pundel, *Histoire de l'opération césarienne. Etude historique de la césarienne dans la médicine, l'art et la littérature, les religions et la législation. La prodigieuse évolution de la césarienne depuis l'antiquité jusqu'aux temps moderns* (Brussels: Pr. Acad. européennes, 1969).* The employment of women as physicians and midwives is noted by J. Le Gall, "Métiers de femmes au corpus inscriptionum Latinarum," *Mélanges Marcel Durry* (= REL 47, 2), 123-130.

The life expectancy of Roman women is discussed by Iiro Kajanto, *On the Problem of the Average Duration of Life in the Roman Empire (Annales Academiae Scientiarum Fennicae*, Ser. B, 153, 2; Helsinki: Suomalainen Tiedeakatemia, 1968). From the evidence of sepulchral inscriptions Kajanto determines woman's greater rate of mortality during her child bearing years, but finds her life expectancy equal with men in old age. M. K. Hopkins, "The Age of Roman girls at marriage," cited above, points out the pitfalls of drawing conclusions from sepulchral inscriptions, and also discusses the age of widowhood, likelihood of remarriage, age of remarriage, and the modal ages of pagan and christian marriages.

7. Erotic

There are no studies of the erotic life of Roman women which may be recommended without reservations. The books in this field tend to be popular in nature, the obvious example being O. Kiefer, *Kulturgeschichte Roms unter besonderer Berücksichtigung der Römischen Sitten* (Berlin: Aretz, 1933; Eng. tr. *Sexual life in Ancient Rome*, London: Routledge, 1934). Kiefer's work includes an interesting discussion of the relationship between sex and cruelty among the Romans. A popular work is Pierre Grimal, *L'amour à Rome* (Paris: Hachette, 1963; Eng. tr. *Love in Ancient Rome*, New York: Crown, 1967).

8. Women in Latin literature

For literary studies of the women of both Greece and Rome see the end of section I of the present bibliography. The women depicted

---

* I have not seen this work.

in Latin literature could be the subject of an extensive bibliography. I shall limit myself here to the citation of several recent studies with sociological implications.

Sara Lilja, *The Roman elegists' attitude to women (Annales Academiae Scientiarum Fennicae,* Ser. B, 135, 1; Helsinki: Suomalainen Tiedeakatemia, 1965) discusses Tibullus, Propertius, and Ovid as poets rather than as historical personages. Although some may disagree with her conclusions, Lilja's book is an extremely useful reference work for the elegists. For example, in the index under "feminine beauty" are classified references to Ovid's view, Propertius' view, Tibullus' view on such matters as complexion, eyes, hair, natural beauty, height, teeth. Unfortunately the social status of the women immortalized in elegy is barely investigated by Lilja. Susan Treggiari, "Libertine Ladies," *CW* 64 (1971), 196-198, briefly discusses the social consequences of marriages between *libertinae* and *libertini* or free born Roman citizens.

E. E. Best, "Cicero, Livy and educated Roman women," *CJ* 65 (1970),199-204, discusses the favorable attitudes of Cicero, Tacitus and Livy towards some women. In another brief article A. L. Motto, "Seneca on Women's Liberation," *CW* 65 (1972), 155-57, traces Seneca's relatively generous opinion of female capabilities. Evidence from Catullus, Terence, Plautus, and Propertius is employed by G. Williams, "Some Aspects of Roman Marriage Ceremonies and Ideals," *JRS* 48 (1958), 16-29. This article investigates marriage rituals as well as the wifely virtues of marriage to one husband, eternal marriage of wives (whereas widowers may remarry), and humble obedience.

In the Jungian tradition, Erich Neumann, *Amor und Psyche, mit einem Kommentar von Erich Neumann: Ein Beitrag zur seelischen Entwicklung des Weiblichen* (Zurich: Rascher, 1952; Eng. tr. *Amor and Psyche: The Psychic Development of the Feminine, A Commentary on the Tale by Apuleius;* Bollingen Series 54; Princeton: Princeton University Press, 1956; paperback reprint, 1971) considers at length the myth of the "Golden Ass" in terms of the psychological maturation of the woman.

VI WOMEN UNDER CHRISTIANITY *

Among the general works on ancient women (cited above I, 1) of some use are Seltman, who comments on the social and psychological ef-

---

* Section VI was written by Michael Southwell, York College, C.U.N.Y.

fects of the church's developing anti-feminism, Leipoldt, and the *Histoire Mondiale de la Femme*. Balsdon (cited above, V, 1) surveys the involvement of women in paganism, Judaism, and Christianity, and offers a reminder of the importance of Christianity in overturning the rejection of unmarried women in the Augustan marriage legislation.

Of feminist literature, Georgia Harkness, *Women in Church and Society* (Nashville: Abingdon, 1972), although somewhat simplified, provides a useful overview of Christian attitudes, both ancient and modern. Mary Daly, *The Church and the Second Sex* (New York: Harper, 1968), is valuable, though only briefly historical. Rosemary Radford Ruether, "Women's Liberation in Historical and Theological Perspective," *Women's Liberation and the Church*, ed. Sarah Bently Doely (New York: Association Press, 1970), pp. 26-36 (reprinted in *Soundings*, 53[1970], 363-373), more anthropological-psychological than historical-theological, is worth reading.

Much specifically Christian material, chiefly concerned with dogma, is of little value for this bibliography; virtually all the writings on Mary, for example, or marriage, or the ordination of women, fall into this category. Still, useful literature does exist. Most important is D. Sherwin Bailey, *Sexual Relation in Christian Thought* (New York: Harper, 1959; also published as *The Man-Woman Relation in Christian Thought*, London: Longmans, 1959), a basic book on early Christian female-male relationships. Almost as essential is William E. Phipps, *Was Jesus Married?* (New York: Harper, 1970), an informal but thorough examination of virtually every aspect of the relationship between the sexes in the early church, with extensive notes. Charles Caldwell Ryrie, *The Place of Women in the Church* (New York: Macmillan, 1958), is perhaps the most complete survey of the role of women in the first three centuries of Christianity. Krister Stendahl, "Bibelsynen och Kvinnann," *Kvinnann-Samhället-Kyrkan* (Stockholm: Svenska Kyrkans Diakonistyrelses Bokförlag, 1958, 136-167; Eng. tr., *The Bible and The Role of Women*, Philadelphia: Fortress, 1966), contains a useful survey of New Testament attitudes toward women, and an annotated bibliography. L. J. Swidler, "Jesus was a Feminist," *South East Asia J. Theol.* 13 (1971), 102-110, though simplified, is the clearest statement of Jesus' repudiation of traditional anti-feminist attitudes; a brief summary of the article appeared in *The New York Times*, 18 December 1971, p. 29.

Some material on miscellaneous subjects, even though less important, deserves mention. André Dumas, "Biblical Anthropology and the Participation of Women in the Ministry of the Church," *Con-*

340

cerning the Ordination of Women (World Council of Churches; Geneva, 1964), 12-40, surveys the extent to which women were ordained in the early church. William Graham Cole, *Sex in Christianity and Psychoanalysis* (New York: Oxford University Press, 1955), describes Christian attitudes toward women and sex from a rather naive psychological point of view. W. Derek Thomas, "The Place of Women in the Church at Philippi," *Expos. Times* 83 (1972), 117-120, suggests that Christianity was particularly receptive to women where the influence of Judaism was weak. E. O. James, *The Cult of the Mother Goddess* (New York: Barnes & Noble, 1959) discusses the assumption of the Magna Mater into the early church.

Thomas David Boslooper, *The Virgin Birth* (Philadelphia: Westminster, 1962), is the authoritative book on the subject of virginity, with a 20 page bibliography. Boslooper compresses a hugh amount of material, with the inevitable simplifications, but pays virtually no attention to the status of women. Lucien Legrand, *The Biblical Doctrine of Virginity* (New York: Sheed & Ward, 1963), is a polemical but thorough exposition, with careful attention to Hebrew and pagan attitudes. Robert Schillin, "Vestales et vierges chrétiennes dans la Rome antique," *RSR*, 35 (1961), 113-129, contrasts the status of pagan and Christian virgins. Raphael Patai, *Sex and the Family in the Bible and the Middle East* (Garden City: Doubleday, 1959), is valuable, with extensive notes, despite its primary emphasis on the Old Testament world.

The question of Paul's attitude toward women has occasioned much controversy. Else Kähler, *Die Frau in den paulinischen Briefen unter Besonderer Berücksichtigung des Begriffes der Unterordnung* (Zurich: Gotthelf, 1960), attempts an exhaustive exegesis of the important Pauline passages, with a lengthy bibliography; a brief summary of the book appeared as "Zur 'Unterordnung' der Frau im Neuen Testament," *Z. f. Evangelische Ethik* 3 (1959), 1-13. Daniel van Allmen, "L'homme et la femme dans les textes pauliniens," *Foi et Vie* 70 (1970), supp. vol.), 157-181, contains a useful synopsis of Pauline passages on marriage. Madeleine Boucher, "Some Unexplored Parallels to 1 Cor 11, 11-12 and Gal 3, 28: The New Testament on the Role of Women," *Cath. Bib. Q.* 31 (1969), 50-58, in a brief but important study with useful bibliographical footnotes, proposes Judaic sources for Paul's apparently conflicting theories of the subordination and the equality of women in the New Testament.

There is also some work on the attitudes of the church fathers toward women. Sister Mary Lawrence McKenna, *Women of the Church*

(New York: Kenedy, 1967), is an enthusiastic view of the role of women in the early church, useful primarily for its collection of relevant patristic passages, and for its notes. Gerald J. Campbell, "St. Jerome's Attitude Toward Marriage and Women," *Am. Eccles. Rev.* 143 (1960), 310-320, 384-394, usefully surveys Jerome on women, concluding, rather surprisingly, that he was not anti-feminist. Rev. Louis A. Rongione, in a letter printed in *The New York Times Magazine*, 11 June 1972, p. 36, suggests that Augustine was the first Christian feminist, a theory quite opposed to the traditional view.

— — — — — — — — — —

SELECTED BIBLIOGRAPHY

ON WOMEN IN CLASSICAL ANTIQUITY

Sarah B. Pomeroy

Index

Since 1973, the field has burgeoned. The Women's Classical Caucus, founded ten years ago, has sponsored an annual panel for the presentation of papers on some aspect of women in antiquity. Classicists have also been well represented at the five Berkshire Conferences on the History of Women. Panels dealing with the history of women in antiquity occasionally appear at the annual meetings of the Association of Ancient Historians, the American Historical Association, and other fora too numerous to mention. French and British scholars are publishing a steady stream of articles, but the expansion in this field is primarily due to North Americans.

Because women pervade nearly every aspect of antiquity, Part II will be selective, and much material, even newly-published, will be left unconsidered. Preference will be given to publications that look at a topic that was previously unconsidered, that use a new methodology, or that for some reason have attracted the attention of scholars in the field. No publication will be cited under more than one rubric.

I GENERAL WORDS ON THE WOMEN OF BOTH GREECE AND ROME

1. *Bibliographies and surveys*

Sarah B. Pomeroy, "Selected Bibliography on Women in Antiquity," *Arethusa* 6 (1973), 125-52 (= Part I, above pp. 315-342). The first modern bibliography on this subject presented a historical survey of the field and introduced the viewpoint of scholars in disciplines other than classical studies.

Leanna Goodwater, *Women in Antiquity: An Annotated Bibliography* (Metuchen, N. J., 1975). Some information may be gleaned from this uncritical compilation by a librarian.

Sarah B. Pomeroy, "Women in Antiquity" (Study guide of the American Philological Association, 1976). This guide was designed to aid the Classicist who wanted to introduce a course on women in

I am grateful to Ross S. Kraemer for writing the section on women and religion, to Natalie Kampen for writing the section on women in art, to Marylin Arthur for her suggestions, and to Helene Foley for supplying information on a recent volume which she has edited. This bibliography was written during the tenure of a fellowship from the National Endowment for the Humanities to whom I wish to express my gratitude.

345

antiquity or to include more material on women in existing Classics courses. It also provided a check-list of works published since my first bibliography in *Arethusa*.

Marylin B. Arthur, "Review Essay: Classics," *Signs* 2 (1976), 382-403. This essay is devoted primarily to a discussion of theories of matriarchy, a review of Sarah B. Pomeroy, *Goddesses, Whores, Wives, and Slaves*, and a perceptive analysis of methodological issues and future directions in the study of women in antiquity.

Sarah B. Pomeroy, "Classical Antiquity," in *History of the Family and Kinship: A Select International Bibliography*, ed. Gerald L. Soliday (Millwood, N. Y., 1980), 159-67. Family history is a close relative of women's history. This bibliography includes rubrics for "Demography," "Psychoanalysis and Psychohistory," and "History of Childhood." The volume has a bibliography on the family in Italy compiled by Ruth Liebowitz and one on the family in Greece compiled by Jill Dubisch. Barbara Sicherman, E. William Monter, Joan Wallach Scott, and Kathryn Kish Sklar, *Recent United States Scholarship on the History of Women* (American Historical Association, 1980). This report places the work of scholars of women in antiquity in the context of the new scholarship on the history of women, and draws attention to the ways in which ancient historians exploit historical evidence which is prescriptive or idealized.

2. Books

Verena Zinserling, *Women in Greece and Rome* (Leipzig, 1972; New York, 1973), 32 color pls., 80 black and white pls., and 12 drawings. This book is useful, not for the brief text, but as a source of representations of Greek and Roman women in the visual arts.

Sarah B. Pomeroy, *Goddesses, Whores, Wives, and Slaves: Women in Classical Antiquity* (New York, 1975; London, 1976; paperback, New York, 1976; Italian translation, Turin, 1978; Greek translation Dodone; Dutch translation, Bijleveld; German translation, Medusa (Greek, Dutch, and German translations to be published), "the first really scholarly work on the subject of women in classical antiquity. . . . Pomeroy discusses the mythology, history, and literature of antiquity and traces the role of women in society and politics from the Bronze Age through the Roman period. She has assembled an impressive amount of information" (Marylin Arthur, *Signs* [1976], 391). "As for the thoroughness of the author's research and the high quality of her own classical scholarship, there cannot be a moment's doubt. In an informative way (even on so traditionally unacademic a topic as eroticism, natural and unnatural) this is, in general, an authoritative book" (J. P. V. D. Balsdon, *CR* 27 [1977], 207). "Professor Pomeroy has written a serious and amazingly comprehensive study . . . , especially valuable for its use of primary sources in the text and notes" (Elaine Fantham, *Phoenix* 30 [1976], 80). Other longer reviews include: Hugh Lloyd-Jones, *Times Literary Supplement* (September 26, 1975), 1074-75, Ernst Badian, *New York Review of Books* (October 30, 1975), 28-31, Maria-Victoria Abricka, *AJP* 97 (1976), 310-12, and W. den Boer, *Mnemosyne* 29 (1976), 319-23.

Mary R. Lefkowitz and Maureen Fant, *Women in Greece and Rome* (Toronto, 1977), a selection of primary sources in translation, most valuable for the excerpts from medical authors.

II THE BRONZE AGE

Questions regarding the roles of Bronze Age women, especially touching matriarchy and matriliny, continue to attract attention. Serious historians are once again entertaining the theory that the social structure of Crete in the Bronze Age was matriarchal. Although anthropologists (e.g., Joan Bamberger, "The Myth of Matriarchy: Why Men Rule in Primitive Society," in *Woman, Culture, and Society*, eds. Michelle Zimbalist Rosaldo and Louise Lamphere [Stanford, 1974], 263-80) have been able to provide cross-cultural explanations of the function of matriarchy as a myth, and have declared that it is impossible to find a society where women actually rule, several historians have recently asserted that such a society did exist, or may have existed, at Knossos. In the revised edition of *Cambridge Ancient History*. ("The Zenith of Minoan Civilization." *CAH* 3d ed. [London, 1973], 11, pt. 2, 573) F. Matz states tentatively, "it has even been suggested that Minoan society as a whole had a matriarchal basis, but there is no clear proof that this was so." More decisively, Carol G. Thomas ("Matriarchy in Early Greece: The Bronze and Dark Ages," *Arethusa*, 6 [1973], 175-79) has argued that Minoan society was matriarchal.

Professor Thomas proposes three criteria which she uses to identify Minoan society as matriarchal: 1) the representation of women in art and artifacts; 2) the religion that is oriented toward the cult of a

347

supreme mother goddess; and 3) the economic rights exercised by women. As Thomas admits, the third criterion can be examined only in the light of provisions in the Law Code of the town of Gortyn. This code can be dated, at the earliest, to the seventh century B.C. Yet, that the Code should not be examined in the hope of finding survivals from Minoan Crete should be apparent, not only because of the approximately 800 years that separate the Minoan world from the creation of the Code, but also because of the successive devastating upheavals that took place in the Greek world at the end of the Bronze Age and that gave rise to "the discontinuity in Greek culture."

The study of art and artifacts from Knossos depends upon the publications of Sir Arthur Evans who completed the publication of the site in 1935. In his views on women, Evans was a Victorian in the conventional sense of this word. His half-sister Joan Evans, in *Time and Chance: The Story of Arthur Evans and his Forebears* (London, 1943), reports that he considered women a hindrance and an undesirable presence, at an excavation, or among the scholars at the British School in Athens. Some absurdities in the restoration and explanation of the Palace of Minos should be attributed to Evans' Victorian view of women. Of major importance is his determination that one section of the domestic quarters was the "Queen's Megaron." It must be understood that this room was not found with a label on it. Indeed, king and queen might just as well have shared a room, as Odysseus and Penelope do in the *Odyssey*. Evans' decision that the hall that he subsequently named the "Queen's Megaron," had been used by women was the result of a remarkable bit of detective work. In the first year of the excavation (1899) he uncovered a chair that he called a "throne." He believed, unequivocally, that the throne was intended for a man, as the name he gave to the site, "Palace of Minos," indicates. His reasons for naming one hall the "Queen's Megaron" are published in his excavation reports of 1900 and 1901 (*BSA* 6 and 7). In 1900, he had uncovered a seat with a larger hollowed space than the seat of the throne. The next year, in the same hall, he found a second seat of similar dimensions, again lower and wider than the throne. He reasoned that Mycenaean (as he called them) women are often shown squatting and therefore would have been comfortable on lower seats than men would use. He delicately avoids discussing the gender difference implied by the width of the seat. He records the width of one of the women's seats as 55cm, and the depth as 46cm. The throne was only 45cm wide and 32cm deep.

348

The seat of the dimensions he considered suitable for females identified the women's quarter of the Palace beyond a doubt. In *BSA* 8 (1902), 42; he refers to the women's quarter as the "Queen's Megaron." Evans designated a small, inner room off the Queen's Megaron as the Queen's Bathroom and merely stated that this hall had an adjacent bathroom. His assistant, Duncan Mackenzie, had first identified the bathroom as a lightwell. Leonard R. Palmer, *A New Guide to the Palace of Knossos* (London, 1969, 85), who was uneasy about Evans' work for other reasons, suggested, many years later, that the Queen's Bathroom may have actually been another bedroom or alcove. Evans took a particularly fine bathtub from a nearby hall, described the tub as "portable," and had it placed in the so-called Queen's Bathroom.

One would not surmise from the plan of the palace that Evans published how much of the nomenclature was due to the remains themselves, and how much was due to guesswork. Yet Evans' plan is reproduced without cautionary statements in scholarly works on ancient history, archaeology, and architecture including the *Cambridge Ancient History*, 3d ed., 11, pt. 2; D. S. Robertson, *A Handbook of Greek and Roman Architecture*, 2d ed. (London, 1964), plans 2a and 2b; and J. D. S. Pendlebury, *the Archaeology of Crete: An Introduction* (London, 1939), figure 30a and b.

A number of historical theories describing the social role of Minoan women have been devised on the supposition, that the queen actually inhabited the room designated as the "Queen's Megaron," and that frescoes peculiarly relevant to female life were not relegated to this vicinity. The location of the Queen's Megaron has been used, on the one hand, to show that Minoan women were modest creatures, and, on the other hand, to show that they were independent. James W. Graham accepts Evans' identification of the Queen's Megaron because it was the main room of a fairly private suite, but was not totally cut off from the rest of the palace. Graham's reason is that "one can hardly avoid seeing in this arrangement a nice respect for the privacy of the fair sex, as well as a due appreciation of their company" (*The Palaces of Crete* [Princeton, 1962], 87-88). Thomas quotes Graham, but, in contrast, she uses the location of the Queen's Megaron as evidence that Minoan women were not secluded in a remote area of the palace since frescoes showing women were not found exclusively in the Queen's Megaron.

In his excavation report for 1903 (*BSA* 9, 76-80), Evans published the snake goddess and her votaries. The snake goddess has appeared in so many publications that by now she has come to symbolize Minoan Crete. Yet all the figurines required extensive refabrication. Evans twice described the goddess figure as "reconstituted," (*ibid.*, 76 and *The Palace of Minos*, 1, 500) and related in detail the complete restoration of the votary from a torso, right arm, and the bottom flounces of a skirt (*BSA* 9, 78 and *The Palace of Minos*, 1, 500-06). The head was entirely modern. A crown was pieced together from a circlet that had a rivet hole which matched the rivet hole in a small figure of a lion found in the same deposit (*BSA* 9, 78 and *The Palace of Minos*, 1, 505-06). He does not give any reason for considering one figurine a goddess and the others her attendants. Perhaps he thought that their status was indicated by their sizes: although the one he called a goddess was only 34.2 cm., the votary was only 20 cm. to the neck. In his discussion of the goddess worship, Evans refers to similar figurines, for example, in museums in Toronto and Boston. Unfortunately, as A. J. B. Wace in a review of *The Palace of Minos at Knossos*, 4, pts. 1 and 2 in *The Burlington Magazine*, 67 (1935), 234-35 has pointed out, none of the figurines were discovered at sites that were excavated in a properly scientific manner. The Toronto Goddess, whom Evans named "Our Lady of Sports" suddenly appeared in Canada, where museum officials were able to say only that it had been owned privately in Crete until then. The Boston Goddess, in its original fragmentary condition, was seen in Heraklion only some twelve years after it was said to have been discovered.

In this discussion, I do not intend to denigrate Evans' achievement, but merely to caution scholars of women's history about the evidence that is vital to them. For example, anthropologist Ruby Rohrlich-Leavitt, in "Women in Transition: Crete and Sumer," in R. Bridenthal and C. Koonz eds. *Becoming Visible: Women in European History* (Boston, 1977), 36-59, a book that is used as a textbook, suggests *the Palace of Minos* as recommended reading, and trustingly refers to "the queen's suite," and "the Snake Goddess, a skillful and commanding figure."

Evans noted that the mother goddess appears without a male consort, since "fatherhood is unknown in matriliny" (*The Palace of Minos* 3, 466). Elsewhere he often confuses the term "matriliny" with the term "matriarchy," but this may have been characteristic of the period in which he began his work. Lewis Farnell, the historian of religion who was Evans' contemporary at Oxford, isolated the two ideas, for he thought it lamentable that the word "matriarchy" was employed to refer to the determination of descent through the female line, and pointed out that the connotations of female supremacy implied by this term were not inevitably bound to the determination of descent through women ("Sociological hypotheses concerning the position of women in ancient religion," *Archiv für Religionswissenschaft*, 7 [1904], 70, n. 1.), Farnell's published work shows that, at Oxford, the two terms were distinguished by 1906-07 (Review of J. G. Frazer, *Adonis, Attis, and Osiris: Studies in the History of Oriental Religion*, in *The Hibbert Journal*, 5 [1906-07], 8. 690.)

Yet Evans certainly thought both matriliny and matriarchy had existed at Knossos—though he used the word "matriarchy" to refer to both patterns. Certain iconographic features struck him as characteristic of matriarchal society. These included the mingling of the two sexes in some of the frescoes—a mingling that showed that women were not kept in a harem-like seclusion, as well as the separation of the sexes in the Grand Stand fresco, so that women occupied the front seats. He also reports that in the Grand Stand fresco the women are more carefully drawn than the men, although the men are more numerous. (*The Palace of Minos* 3, 46, 49, 227). For Evans, sitting in the front seats was a more precise indicator of social status than mere numbers. Evans was probably thinking of classical Greece where priests and priestesses sat in the front row of the theater, and where the granting of the front seats at public events *prohedria* was bestowed as an honor on distinguished men. The *prohedria* of women—whoever they are—is significant, even if we cannot explain the precise significance, but of course classical Greece was not Minoan Crete and Evans' analysis leaves unanswered the question of where the rest of the Minoan women were. Several other theories might explain the Grand Stand fresco: perhaps men were more numerous because, with the exception of priestesses or women who lived in the palace, most women stayed at home, or perhaps men were more numerous in the society as a whole because female infanticide was practiced.

Evans never defined the word "matriarchy," though he used it with frequency. Perhaps he accepted Bachofen's view, in part, where the head of the primitive horde would have been a powerful man. But for Bachofen, such a tyrant would have been able to dominate the women through physical strength. Evans, on the other hand, always describes the status of Minoan women as high. In his report of 1900 he stated "the prominence of the female sex in the Mycenaean period . . . the leading part played by Goddesses and female votaries in the cult-scenes may have been due to the longe (*sic*) survival in the domain of religion of ideas attaching to the matriarchal system." It would seem, then, that in 1900 he thought that a king ruled in Knossos, but that a matriarchal religion remained as a survival from an earlier matriarchal system. Yet, throughout the final publication of *The Palace of Minos*, Evans called the social system of the Minoans, matriarchal, and stated that the Minoan religious system owed its origin to this matriarchal stage of society, (vol. 3, 406).

In Evans' assertion that the cult of the mother goddess was the outcome of matriarchy, he was following the thought pattern of the Kekrops myth that indicates that women, when they have political power, will vote for a supreme divinity, who is female. James George Frazer, came to another conclusion. Frazer was born three years after Evans; both died in 1941. Both Frazer and Evans were heirs to the same nineteenth-century evolutionary theories stating that in primitive societies matrilineal reckoning, or mother-kin, preceded patrilineality. Both had the same archaeological evidence available to them. But Frazer specifically denied that women rule at any stage in the development of primitive society, even if such a society worshipped female divinities. Frazer wrote, "the theory of a gynaecocracy is, in truth, a dream of visionaries and pedants. And equally chimerical is the idea that the predominance of goddesses under a system of mother-kin . . . is a creation of the female mind. If women ever created gods, they would be more likely to give them masculine than feminine features . . . Men make gods, and women worship them. The combination of ancestor-worship with mother-kin furnishes a simple and sufficient explanation of the superiority of goddesses over gods in a state of society where these conditions prevail. Men naturally assign the first place in their devotions to the ancestress from whom they trace their descent" (*The Golden Bough*, 3d ed. [London, 1907-15], 6: *Studies in Oriental Religion*, 211).

M. I. Finley, "Archaeology and History," *Daedalus*, 100 (1971), reprinted in *The Use and Abuse of History* (London, 1975), declared that material remains tell us very little about the social institutions or the ideas of a society. No one had dared to say this before, and for a neo-Marxist like Finley, to reject the testimony of material evidence, is quite astonishing. Yet he uses this data himself when he states that of the total number of neolithic Cretan anthropomorphic figurines only 28 are certainly female, 5 male, and 28 sexless, and when he proceeds to deduce from these ratios that the notion of a Great Mother Goddess is nothing but a "remarkable fable."

The various interpretations of the role of women in Minoan society and religion developed independently of any knowledge of the material remains at Knossos. Bachofen's theory of matriarchy predated the excavation by half a century. Arthur Evans' theory is no more plausible than any other theory. He apparently based his interpretations and restorations on a matriarchal historical model current in the nineteenth century. Some subsequent scholars, in turn, have used Evans' interpretations and restorations to support the matriarchal historical model. This argument is circular.

It would seem that only the written record could give some reliable testimony about women in the Palace period, and that we must await the decipherment of linear A before venturing to write of women and goddesses in the days of Minos. See also the brief response to Thomas' article by Sheila Dickison, "Forum," *Arethusa* 9 (1976), 119-20.

Jon-Christian Billigmeier and Judy A. Turner, "The Socio-Economic Roles of Women in Mycenaean Greece: A Brief Survey from Evidence of the Linear B Tablets," *Women's Studies* 8 (1981), 3-20 and *Reflections of Women in Antiquity* (London, 1982), report that matrilineal naming was employed in the listing of craftswomen (who may have been slaves) and their children. Workers of both sexes received the same rations and women were as prominent as men among religious personnel. These facts suggest the possibility at least of a more equal social status for women in Mycenaean than in classical Greece. Simon G. Pembroke, "The Early Human Family: Some Views 1770-1870," *Classical Influences on Western Thought A.D. 1650-1870* (Cambridge, 1979), continues his work on theories of matriarchy and matriliny. In this article he discusses the intellectual careers of social anthropologists including Bachofen and McLennan, and the influence of evolutionary theory on the thinking of Marx and Engels. The Marxist debate on prehistory continues, see, e.g., Carolyn Fluehr-Lobban, "A Marxist Reappraisal of the Matriarchate," *Current Anthropology* 20 (1979), 341-59 with comments and discussion by Bettina Aptheker, Lawrence Krader, Joan Landes, Raoul Makarius and others.

Amazons and Centaurs who purportedly lived in the Bronze Age are examined in the light of their representations in the art and literature of the classical period. Mandy Merck, "The City's Achievements: The Patriotic Amazonomachy and Ancient Athens," in *Lifting the Veil* ed. Susan Lipshitz (London, 1978), 93-115 concludes that "the Amazon myth cannot be separated from a context of patriarchal dominance," but analyzes the ways in which the myth functions in feminist history. Page duBois, "On Horse/men, Amazons, and Endogamy," *Arethusa* 12 (1979), 35-49, and *Centaurs and Amazons* (Ann Arbor, 1982), employs a structuralist approach in considering the juxtaposition of Centaurs and Amazons in art and literature. The myth of the Centaurs deals with marriage, i.e., exchange of women and a golden age pre-dating marriage.

III ARCHAIC GREECE

The archaic period, before the Athenian domination of literature, is a fruitful one for the scholar of women's history. The majority of the works cited in this section show the influence of French thought, particularly C. Lévi-Strauss or J.P. Vernant.

Hugh Lloyd-Jones, *Females of the Species: Semonides on Women* (London, 1975), gives the Greek text and translation, and the first separate and detailed commentary in English. Lloyd-Jones suggests that the purpose of the poem was amusement. The book is illustrated by sculptures of each type of woman by Marcelle Quinton. Claude Calame, *Les Choeurs de jeunes filles en Grèce archaïque. I Morphologie, II Alcman* (Rome, 1977), collects the allusions to girls' choruses in Greek literature. The elucidation of the educative function of the chorus, in turn, sheds light on the old question of the relationship of Sappho to younger women. Eva Stehle Stigers, "Sappho's Private World," *Women's Studies* 8 (1981), 47-63 and *Reflections of Women in Antiquity* (London, 1982), analyzes the poet's romanticization of erotic life in a totally female context. Private space is the chief metaphor for love in Sappho's poetry. Jack Winkler, "Gardens of Nymphs: Public and Private in Sappho's Lyrics," *Women's Studies* 8 (1981), 65-91 and *Reflections of Women in Antiquity* examines the poet's reaction to male public culture (as epitomised by Homeric epic) and the complex sexual relations of women in a totally female world.

James Redfield, "The Women of Sparta," *CJ* 73 (1978), 146-61, examines the role that Spartan women play in Greek utopian and political theory. Although the women were themselves undisciplined they upheld Spartan discipline for men. In "The Homeric Hymn to Aphrodite: A Structuralist Approach," *CW* 67 (1974), 205-13 Charles P. Segal interprets the poem as a mediation between civilization and mortality. E. J. Bickerman in "Love story in the Homeric hymn to Aphrodite," *Athenaeum* 54 (1976), 299-54 asserts that the hymn expresses romantic love, the youthfulness of passion, the willingness to die if love goes unrequited, and the deification of the beloved woman. Marylin Arthur, "Politics and Pomegranates. An Interpretation of the Homeric Hymn to Demeter," *Arethusa* 10 (1977), 7-48 gives a psychoanalytic interpretation, stating that the poem reveals the psycho-sexual development of the female leading to the bonds of female solidarity. The female element is finally incorporated into a male-dominated world, but is honored and respected. D. Asheri, "Tyrannie et Mariage Forcé," *Annales, ESC* 32 (1977), 21-48 gives a structural analysis of themes of women's heroism especially in opposition to marriage by conquest.

IV CLASSICAL GREECE

1. *Medical*

Ann Ellis Hanson, "Hippocrates: Diseases of Women 1," *Signs* 1 (1975), 567-84 gives a translation of the treatise and discusses the obstetrical and gynecological works in the Hippocratic corpus. Sarah B. Pomeroy, "Plato and the Female Physician (*Republic* 454d2)," *AJP* 99 (1978), 496-500, discusses the evidence for female obstetricians in fourth-century Athens. Marie-Thérèse Fontanille, *Avortement et Contraception dans la Médecine gréco-romaine* (Paris, 1977), includes fifty-eight pages of charts listing methods of preventing conception and producing abortion from the Talmud, Hippocrates, Dioscurides, Soranus, et al. E. Eyben, "Geboortebeperkung in de Grieks-Romeinse Oudheid," *Kleio* 7 (1977), 97-127 discusses contraception, abortion, and exposure of newborns. A more extensive study by Eyben appears in *Ancient Society* 11-12 (1980-1981), 5-82. Donald Engels, "The Problem of Female Infanticide in the Greco-Roman World," *CP* 75 (1980), 112-20 argues that a high rate of female infanticide was demographically impossible, assuming a low rate of natural increase in antiquity. A. Rousselle, "Observation féminine et idéologie masculine: le corps de la femme d'après les médicins grecs," *Annales, ESC* 5 (1980), 1089-1115 discusses the influence of contemporary attitudes toward women on the medical writers' interpretations of women's physiology.

2. Women poets

Charles P. Segal, "Pebbles in Golden Urns: The Date and Style of Corinna," *Eranos* 73 (1975), 1-8 argues for a fifth rather than third century date for Corinna on the basis of an echo in her poetry of a voting procedure used in fifth-century Athens. M. L. West, "Erinna," *ZPE* 25 (1977), 95-119 gives a revised text of "The Distaff" with detailed commentary. The ancient biographical testimony and the epigrams are also discussed. West concludes that the works attributed to Erinna must have been written by a man or men. Sarah B. Pomeroy, "Supplementary Notes on Erinna," *ZPE* 32 (1978), 17-22 argues that women's access to education improved in the fourth century and that a woman was quite able to write the poetry attributed to Erinna. Illustrations of handlooms demonstrate the physical resemblance of the tortoise-lyre and loom: the game of Tortoise is an aspect of the weaving motif in "The Distaff." Marylin B. Arthur, "The Tortoise and the Mirror: Erinna *PSI* 1090," *CW* 74 (1980), 53-65 discusses the tortoise as a symbol in women's lives. Arthur also applies a Lacanian model and argues that Baucis serves as a mirror of self-discovery for the poet. Sylvia Barnard, "Hellenistic Women Poets," *CJ* 73 (1978), 204-13 reviews the lives and works of Anyte, Erinna, and Nossis.

3. Male authors' views of women

S. I. Oost, "Xenophon's Attitude Toward Women," *CW*, 71 (1977), 225-36 finds that in the Socratic works and the *Oeconomicus* Xenophon takes a favorable view of women's equality, while in his other works he seems to share the attitudes of contemporary upper-class Athenians. Michèlle Rosellini and Suzanne Saïd, "Usages de femmes et autres nomoi chez les sauvages d' Hérodote. Essai de lecture structurale," *ASNP* 8 (1978), 949-1005 and *Aristophane: les femmes et la cité (Les cahiers de Fontenay* no. 17, 1979), edited by Pierre Vidal-Naquet containing: 1) a brief introduction by Vidal-Naquet; 2) Michèlle Rosellini, "Lysistrate: une mise en scène de la féminité;" 3) Suzanne Saïd, "L'Assemblée des Femmes: les femmes, l'économie et la politique;" and 4) Daniele Auger, "Le Théâtre d'Aristophane: Le mythe, l'utopie et les femmes," share several characteristics. All the works are in the structuralist tradition. They argue that these works are not about women, but rather about how Greek authors use women as a means of structuring their thoughts about politics and society. All the essays are too long and lack adequate scholarly annotation of secondary literature not written in French. Although these works lack the thoroughness of some of the others cited in this bibliography they do offer some interesting theory and speculation. Nicole Loraux, "Le lit, la guerre," *L'Homme* 21 (1981), 37-67 documents and discusses the opposition between war and childbearing in the context of a general opposition between masculine and feminine in ancient thought. In "Travesties of Gender and Genre in Aristophanes' *Thesmophoriazusae*" *Critical Inquiry* (Winter, 1981), and *Reflections of Women in Antiquity* (London, 1982), Froma Zeitlin explores the relationship between the feminine and mimesis. Transvestism and parody together expose the relationship between the crossing of genders and the crossing of genres. Helene Foley, "The Concept of Women in Athenian Drama," *Reflections of Women in Antiquity* (London, 1982), deals with the conflict between the images of women presented in Athenian drama and in other contemporary, primarily prose, sources. Foley examines the success of both psychoanalytic and structuralist approaches and develops aspects of the latter as the basis of future research.

4. *Economic*

David M. Schaps, *Economic Rights of Women in Ancient Greece* (Edinburgh, 1979), reviews the evidence for women and property control in Classical and Hellenistic Greece. The book is based on a Harvard dissertation completed in 1972, and, with the exception of two articles by the author himself, the most recent work cited appeared in 1974. The work is sound but lacks theory and interpretation. For example, Schaps shows that some women owned slaves and movables acquired or produced during marriage and might take them in case of divorce but fails to notes that no woman took her children.

5. *Legal and historical*

Douglas M. MacDowell, *The Law in Classical Athens* (London, 1978), is intended to be an introduction to Greek law. Chapter VI "The Family," deals with the relationship of the *oikos* to women. W.

K. Lacey, "The Family of Euxitheus (Demosthenes LVII)," *CQ* 30 (1980), 57-61 argues that this family provides evidence for child mortality among poor Athenians. J. Modrzejewski, "La Structure juridique du mariage grec," *Scritti in Onore di Orsolina Montevecchi* (Bologna, 1981), 231-68, gives a useful survey of Greek marriage law in the Classical and Hellenistic periods, paying particular attention to the changing position of women. David M. Schaps, "Women in Greek Inheritance Law," *CQ* 25 (1975), 53-57 argues against Willetts' idea that the Gortynian Code preserves matriarchal traditions. Women's rights to inheritance are not equal to men's. In "The Woman Least Mentioned: Etiquette and Women's Names," *CQ* 27 (1977), 323-30 Schaps points out that the names of respectable women were seldom mentioned in public. Therefore instead of focussing on the few women whose names are known, attempts should be made to study women who are identified only through a family role, e.g., Democrates' sister and Mexiades' daughter. Susan Guettel Cole, "Could Greek Women Read and Write?" *Women's Studies* 8 (1981), 129-55 and *Reflections of Women in Antiquity* (London, 1982), surveys the evidence for women's literacy from the seventh century B.C. to the fourth century A.D. Chester G. Starr, "An Evening with the Flute-Girls," *PP* 33 (1978), 401-10 discusses facts about flute-girls including their social status, and salary. K. J. Dover, *Greek Homosexuality* (Cambridge, Mass., 1978), has a short section on women and homosexuality. The brevity is due to the scarcity of literary and pictorial sources; the existing evidence, particularly the work of Sappho is carefully scrutinized.

J. P. Gould, "Law, custom and myth: aspects of the social position of women in classical Athens," *JHS* 100 (1980), 38-59 and Roger Just, "Conceptions of Women in Classical Athens," *Anthropological Society of Oxford Journal* 6 (1975), 153-70 both discuss the problems confronted by the scholar who attempts to study what E. Ardener has aptly termed a "muted group." Gould endeavors to use the data from law, custom, and myth as evidence for the social position of women while Just uses as his criteria: 1) social organization — the extent to which women are incorporated into the polis and family structure; 2) popular morality; and 3) myth as a reflection of reality. Neither Gould nor Just pay sufficient attention to non-literary evidence. Yet vase paintings and terracottas give valuable testimony concerning women's literacy. The excavations at Brauron have already yielded vases that supply information about girls which was not previously available. Unlike the interpretation of the artifacts from Knossos, the interpretation of classical material can be checked and complemented by the testimony of written evidence. It is to be hoped that more art historians and archaeologists take an interest in the history of women. Only then will we have more data (and a different kind of data) available than Gomme had in 1925 when he considered "The Position of Women in Athens in the Fifth and Fourth Centuries."

V HELLENISTIC GREECE

M. Keith Hopkins, "Brother-Sister Marriage in Roman Egypt," *Comparative Studies in Society and History* 22 (1980), 303-54 asserts that siblings married one another because they wanted to. Hopkins draws attention to romantic themes in Egyptian literature. Sarah B. Pomeroy, *"Technikai kai Mousikai*: The Education of Women in the Fourth Century and in the Hellenistic Period," *AJAH* 2 (1977), 51-68 discusses women's expanding opportunities for education and their entrance into the liberal professions and creative arts. Elaine Fantham, "Sex, Status and Survival in Hellenistic Athens: A Study of Women in New Comedy,"*Phoenix* 29 (1975), 44-74 analyzes law, custom, and romance as they affect women from hetairas to housewives. Rape is often an essential prerequisite to a marriage based on love.

F. T. Griffiths "Home Before Lunch: The Emancipated Women in Theocritus," and Alan Cameron, "Asclepiades' Girl Friends," in *Reflections of Women in Antiquity* (London, 1982), both look at women in Alexandrian poetry. For Griffiths, interpretation of Theocritus II and XV must balance off the new realism concerning ordinary life in Hellenistic poetry with the sophisticated aims of a poet writing for learned colleagues and a royal court. Cameron finds that few of the women described by Asclepiades fit the stereotype of the hetaira in search of financial remuneration. They may not be chaste, but they are not prostitutes.

VI ROME

1. *Literary*

D. Konstan, "Plot and theme in Plautus' *Asinaria*," *CJ* 73 (1978), 215-21 finds that one of the themes of this play is an attack on the dowry system. E. Schuhmann, "Zur sozialen Stellung der frau in den Komödien des Plautus," *Altertum* 24 (1978), 97-105 asserts that Plautine comedy gives a conservative view of women, presenting two opposed types—the respectable woman and the prostitute. Patricia A. Johnston, *"Poenulus* I, 2 and Roman Women," *TAPhA* 110 (1980), 143-59 considers this play in the context of contemporary debates between the elder Cato and L. Valerius Flaccus over women and luxury. Phyllis B. Katz, "The Myth of Psyche: A Definition of the Nature of the Feminine?" *Arethusa* 9 (1976), 111-18 gives a structuralist analysis of the myth. Psyche is a hero who, through toil, passes from one state to another. Matthew S. Santirocco, "Sulpicia Reconsidered," *CJ* 74 (1979), 229-39 asserts that Sulpicia was a competent poet who has been previously underestimated.

2. *Historical*

Paul Veyne, "La famille et l'amour sous le haut-empire romain," *Annales, (ESC),* 33 (1978), 35-63 discusses the changes in marital and sexual relations that led to a new morality, predating, but resembling the Christian view of marriage. Leo Ferrero Raditsa, "Augustus' Legislation Concerning Marriage, Procreation, Love Affairs and Adultery," *ANRW* 2, 13, 278-339 reviews the recent historiography, the historical background, and the substance of the legislation. The legislation institutionalized the dissociation of love from sexuality which was intended to create people incapable of dealing with the real world. Amy Richlin, "Approaches to the Sources on Adultery at Rome," *Women's Studies* 8 (1981), 225-50, and *Reflections of Women in Antiquity* (London, 1982) weighs the value of the evidence for heterosexual adultery appearing in literary, legal, historical, anecdotal, rhetorical, slanderous, and satirical sources. Judith P. Hallett, "Perusinae Glandes and the Changing Image of Augustus," *AJAH* 2 (1977), 151-71 discussed critical views of Augustus' sexuality and obscene attacks on Fulvia. Sarah B. Pomeroy, "The Relationship of the Married Woman to her Blood Relatives in Rome," *AncSoc* 7 (1976), 67-79 traces the changing roles of the Roman woman as wife and daughter from the XII Tables to the SC Orfitianum of A.D. 178.

A prosopographical question is posed by R. G. M. Nisbet, "Felicitas at Surrentum (Statius, *Silvae,* II.2)," *JRS* 68 (1978), 1-11. Was Polla married first to Lucan and then to Pollius? R. Syme, "Sallust's Wife," *CQ* 28 (1978), 292-95 shows that Cicero's wife Terentia could not have married Sallust. Possibly another Terentia was married to Sallustius Crispus, the great-nephew of the historian. A. E. Gordon, "Who's who in the Laudatio Turiae," *Epigraphica* 39 (1977), 7-12 revives the idea of Mommsen that Turia was the wife of Q. Lucretius Vespillo, consul in 19 B.C.

Thomas Africa, "Psychohistory, Ancient History, and Freud: The Descent into Avernus," *Arethusa* 12 (1979), 5-33 asserts that the insights of modern psychology can illuminate historical events. In "The Mask of an Assassin: A Psychohistorical Study of M. Junius Brutus," *Journal of Interdisciplinary History* 8 (1978), 599-626 Africa gives a case study. He analyzes the close relationships that Roman matrons enjoyed with their sons and views the murder of Caesar in the context of Oedipal conflict between a son and his mother's lover. Jasper Griffin, "Propertius and Antony," *JRS* 67 (1977), 17-26 uses psychological insight to discern the historical figures of Antony and Cleopatra as the models for the poet's presentation of Cynthia and himself.

Women in the provinces provide the theme of three publications by Anthony J. Marshall. In "Roman Women and the Provinces," *AncSoc* 6 (1975), 109-27, Marshall points out that women were not permitted to make any real contribution to Rome's imperial mission. Literary sources treat wives of senators as merely extensions of their husbands. In "The Case of Valeria: An Inheritance-Dispute in Roman Asia," *CQ* 25 (1975), 82-87 Marshall discusses a conflict in Asia over the estate of an obscure woman, Valeria, wife of Sextilius Andro. In "Tacitus and the Governor's Lady: A Note on *Annals* iii. 33-4," *G & R* 22 (1975), 11-18 Marshall asserts that in Caecina's speech the presence of wives in the provinces is symptomatic of the decline of Roman *virtus*. Ramsay MacMullen, "Women in Public in the Roman Empire," *Historia* 29 (1980), 208-18 declares that one would have seen plenty of women in public in the Empire. In the provinces lower class women wore veils, but others, imitating the fashions established in Rome, were fully visible. Elizabeth Lyding Will, "Women in Pompeii," *Archaeology* 32 (September/October, 1979), 34-43 reviews the archaeological evidence for women of all classes at Pompeii. Sarah B. Pomeroy, "Women in Roman Egypt: A Preliminary Study Based on Papyri" *ANRW* 2, 10, 1 discusses the ways in which the release of land for private ownership affected women's participation in the economy. Because illiteracy rates were higher among women than men, women's increased economic activity and its concommitant documentation raised the illiteracy rate which we can perceive in Roman Egypt. An expanded version in *Reflections of Women in Antiquity* (London, 1982) adds a discussion of dowries in immovables and movables and contrasts the ways in which each type of dowry can affect a married woman's relationship with her husband and father respectively.

3. *Women of the Lower Classes*

Susan Treggiari continues her epigraphical studies which provide invaluable evidence for woman's occupations, demographic facts, slave marriage, and even women as slave owners. Her recent publications include: "Jobs for Women," *AJAH* 1 (1976), 76-104, "Jobs in the Household of Livia," *PBSR* 43 (1975), 48-77, "Questions on Women Domestics in the Roman West," in *Schiavitù, manomissione e classi dipendenti nel mondo antico (Università degli studi di Padova pubblicazioni dell'istituto di storia antica* 13, 1979), 185-201, and "Contubernales in *CIL* 6," *Phoenix* 35 (1981), 42-69. On contubernium see also Beryl Rawson, "Roman Concubinage and Other *De Facto* Marriages," *TAPhA* 104 (1974), 279-305. Rawson points out that status prevented many couples from marrying legally. This fact has important implications for Roman attitudes about morality and illegitimacy. In "The Age at Time of Sale of Female Slaves" *Arethusa* 11 (1978), 243-53 Keith R. Bradley reviewed the evidence in papyri from Roman Egypt. He found that female slaves were bought and sold with their childbearing potential in mind. Andrew Dalby, "On Female Slaves in Roman Egypt," *Arethusa* 12 (1979), 255-59 asserts that it was more likely that they were selected for their ability to perform particular tasks. A rebuttal by Bradley follows Dalby's note.

VII WOMEN IN RELIGION
(prepared by Ross S. Kraemer, Stockton State College)

1. *Graeco-Roman*

Most of the research that may be categorized under the heading of women and Greco-Roman religions other than Christianity and Judaism may be divided into two categories: 1) research on goddesses and 2) research on women's religious activities. While the two are often related, they are by no means synonymous, and very few studies have considered sufficiently the relationships between goddess worship and women's status, nor examined the actual roles and functions

of women in goddess cults as compared with cults of male divinities.
Until very recently most studies of goddesses from the Greco-
Roman world were undertaken by Jungian scholars. K. Kerenyi wrote
a number of studies on Greek goddesses, including one in collabora-
tion with Jung himself, (*Essays in the Science of Mythology: The Myth
of the Divine Child and the Mysteries of Eleusis*, New York, 1950).
Kerenyi's works compile much fascinating material, but his un-
critically Jungian perspective and often enigmatic writing style leaves
much to be desired. (*Eleusis: Archetypal Image of Mother and
Daughter*, Princeton, 1967; *Zeus and Hera: Archetypal Image of
Father, Husband and Wife*, London, 1975; *Goddesses of Sun and
Moon: Circe/Aphrodite/Medea/Niobe* Irving, Texas, 1979; *Athene:
Virgin and Mother in Greek Religion*, Irving, Texas, 1979.
Research on goddesses in the last ten years has taken a different
direction, focussing more on new archaeological findings and literary
texts. The Egyptian goddess Isis, most popular in her Greco-Roman
incarnation, has been the subject of so much research that Leclant's
bibliography, covering work through 1969, is already substantially
out of date (*Inventaire bibliographique des Isiaca [IBIS]. Répertoire
analytique des travaux relatifs à la diffusion des cultes isiaques,
1940-69 AD*, Etudes préliminaires aux religions orientales dans l'empire Romain [EPRO] 18, Leiden, 1972-74). The major studies on Isis
include J. Bergman, *Ich Bin Isis. Studien zum memphitischen
Hintergrund der griechischen Isisaretalogien*. Uppsala, 1968; R. E.
Witt, *Isis in the Graeco-Roman World*, Ithaca, 1971; Francoise Dunand, *Le culte d'Isis dans le bassin oriental de la Méditerranée*.
[EPRO] 26, Leiden, 1973; F. LeCorsu, *Isis mythe et mystères*, Paris,
1977. Only two authors have paid much attention to the roles of
women in the cult of Isis, Sharon Kelly Heyob, *The Cult of Isis
Among Women in the Graeco-Roman World*, [EPRO] 51, Leiden,
1975, and Francoise Dunand, "Le statut des hiereiai en Égypte romaine," in *Hommages à Maarten J. Vermaseren*, M. B. de Boer and
T. A. Edridge eds. [EPRO] 68, Leiden, 1978, I:352-374.
The cult of Demeter has also been the subject of study. Joan
Engelsman, *The Feminine Dimension of the Divine* (Philadelphia,
1979) contains a chapter on Demeter and Isis, again from a Jungian
perspective. Zuntz' study of Persephone includes some discussion of
earlier goddess worship, and considers the roles of women as devotees
of goddesses (*Persephone: Three Essays on Religion and Thought in
Magna Graecia*, Oxford, 1971). C. Sourvinou-Inwood, "Persephone

363

and Aphrodite at Locri. A Model for Personality definitions in Greek religion," *JHS* 98 (1978), 101-21 draws attention to local distinctions in goddess cults. At Locri Persephone presided over the world of women, especially marriage and child-rearing, while Aphrodite was associated with the cosmic and demiurgic aspect of love.

A select sampling of other studies on goddesses includes Paul Friedrich, *The Meaning of Aphrodite*, Chicago, 1978, an anthropological study; T. Hadzistelion, *Kourotrophos: Cults and Representations of the Greek Nursing Deities*, Leiden, 1978; M. Horig, *Dea Syria: Studien zur religiosen Tradition der Fruchbarkeitsgottin in Vorderasien*, Neukirchener Verlag, 1979; R. Mellor, *Thea Romē: The Worship of the Goddess Roma in the Greek World*, Hypomnemata, (Gottingen, 1975); Vermaseren, *Attis and Cybele: The Myth and the Cult*, London, 1977. Vermaseren has also compiled the *Corpus Cultus Cybelae Attidisque*, [EPRO] 50, Leiden, 1977-78.

Several studies have looked at the actual religious practices of women. G. E. Skov, "The Priestess of Demeter and Kore and Her Role in the Initiation of Women at the Festival of the Haloa at Eleusis," *Temenos* 11 (1975), 136-147; J. P. Johansen, "The Thesmophoria as a Women's Festival," *Temenos* 11 (1975), 78-87; Bruce Lincoln, "The Rape of Persephone: A Greek Scenario of Women's Initiation," *Harvard Theological Review* 72 (1979), 223-235; and R. Kraemer, "Ecstasy and Possession: The Attraction of Women to the Cult of Dionysus," *Harvard Theological Review* 72 (1979), 55-80. A recent essay by Susan Guettel Cole sheds light on the religious practices of women, ("New Evidence for the Mysteries of Dionysos," *GRBS* 21 [1980] 223-238). Albert Henrichs, "Greek Maenadism from Olympias to Messaline," *HSPh* 82 (1978), 121-60, criticizes Dodds' interpretation of maenadism and rejects Euripides' *Bacchae* as a source for actual cult practices. Robert E. A. Palmer, "Roman Shrines of Female Chastity from the Caste Struggle to the Papacy of Innocent I," *RSA* 4 (1974), 113-59 discusses the historical development of the cults of Plebian and Patrician Chastity respectively. Certain Fortunae with sexual functions are also studied. Mary Beard, "The Sexual Status of Vestal Virgins," *JRS* (1980), 12-27 analyzes the sexual identity of the Vestals according to three aspects: the virginal, the matronal, and the male.

Although this bibliography represents only a sampling of the literature, it is clear that much work remains to be done, both on the study of goddesses and of women in Greco-Roman religions. Recent dissertation titles suggest an encouraging trend (C. L. Trachy, *The Mythology of Artemis and Her Role in Greek Popular Religion*, Florida State University, 1977; M. B. B. Hollinshead, *Legend, Cult and Architecture at Three Sanctuaries of Artemis*, Bryn Mawr, 1979; J. A. Dutra, *Hera; Literary Evidence of Her Origin and Development as a Fertility Goddess*, Tufts University, 1966; D. D. Boedeker, *Aphrodite's Entry into Greek Epic*, St. Louis University, 1973).

2. Early Christian

Since Pomeroy compiled her select bibliography on women in antiquity in *Arethusa* 6 (1973), the literature on women in early Christianity has become so extensive that here I can only highlight some of the major works that have appeared.*

Most of the research on women in early Christianity has grown out of the contemporary debate over the ministry and priesthood of women, with the result that the literature is heavily weighted in favor of first-century Christianity. While many researchers have an explicitly feminist orientation, many others do not. Constance F. Parvey, ("The Theology and Leadership of Women in the New Testament," in Rosemary Ruether, ed. *Religion and Sexism; Images of Women in the Jewish and Christian Traditions*, New York, 1974, 117-149) focusses on the attitudes towards women, and their status in the writings of Paul and the *Gospel According to Luke*. George Tavard, (*Woman in Christian Tradition*, Notre Dame, 1973) devotes his second chapter to a discussion of the New Testament influence on later concepts of actual women and ideal womanhood. Raymond Brown looks at women in the community of the writer of the *Gospel According to John* ("Roles of Women in the Fourth Gospel," *Theological Studies* 36, 1975, 688-699). Elizabeth Schüssler Fiorenza has written a number of exemplary articles from the vantage point of a feminist scholar. "Women Apostles: The Testament of Scripture," in A. M. Gardiner, ed. *Women and Catholic Priesthood, An Expanded Vision* (New York, 1976) 94-102; "Women in the Pre-Pauline and Pauline Churches," *Union Seminary Quarterly Review* 33 (1978), 153-166;

---

*I am currently preparing a fuller review and critique of the literature on women in the religions of the Greco-Roman world for *Religious Studies Review*.

Sarah B. Pomeroy

"The Apostleship of Women in Early Christianity," in Leonard Swidler and Arlene Swidler, eds. *Women Priests. A Catholic Commentary on the Vatican Declaration* (New York, 1977) all explore the roles and status of women in earliest Christian communities. Several of her other essays ("The Study of Women in Early Christianity: Some Methodological Considerations," in J. T. Ryan, ed., *Critical History and Biblical Faith: New Testament Perspectives*, Villanova, 1979, 30-58 and "You are Not to be Called Father: Early Christian History in a Feminist Perspective," *Cross Currents* 1979, 301-323) examine the issues in the study of women in early Christianity, and their implications for early Christian history as a whole. Roger Gryson has written a useful chronological survey of the texts pertaining to the ministry of women in the early Christian churches through the sixth century, as an explicit prelude to the consideration of contemporary Christian ministries for women (*The Ministry of Women in the Early Church*, trans. Jean Laporte and Mary Louise Hall, Collegeville, Minn., 1976). Early Christian women have rarely figured in the research of classicists, but recently Averil Cameron has written a brief, provocative and insightful article, which suggests that studies of early Christian women would benefit from a more thorough consideration of the contemporaneous Greco-Roman world ("Neither Male Nor Female," *G & R* 27 [1981], 60-68).

Perhaps the single largest category of studies on women in early Christianity has been that devoted to the attitudes towards women, and the roles and status in the Pauline communities, particularly as evidenced by the letters of Paul. The controversy over Paul's teachings noted by Southwell in the first *Arethusa* bibliography has intensified. A host of pertinent articles and books have appeared on the topic since 1972, and sufficient literature had been published by the mid-1970s to warrant the review essay by Ronald W. Graham, ("Women in the Pauline Churches: A Review Article" *Lexington Theological Quarterly* 11 [1976], 25-33). This literature tends to be highly technical, resting finally on careful textual analysis of several key and controversial passages.

Among the earliest of these was Robin Scroggs ("Paul and the Eschatological Woman," *Journal of the American Academy of Religion* 40, 1972, 283-303) who notes that most of the passages which restrict the roles of women in the community are found in those letters whose genuine Pauline authorship is doubted. Scroggs thus claims that Paul asserted the freedom and equality of women in the

Christian eschatological community. James B. Hurley considers the problematic passages in I Corinthians, and attempts to minimize the force of those texts regulating women's head-covering and calling for their "silence" in church ("Did Paul Require Veils or the Silence of Women? A Consideration of I Corinthians 11:2-16 and I Corinthians 14:33b-36," *Westminster Theological Journal* 35, 1973). William O. Walker ("I Corinthians 11:2-16 and Paul's Views Regarding Women," *Journal of Biblical Literature* 91, 1975, 94-110) goes one step farther and argues that this controversial text on the veiling of women is a non-Pauline interpolation. His hypothesis is challenged by J. Murphy-O'Connor, ("The Non-Pauline Character of I Corinthians 11:2-16?" *Journal of Biblical Literature* 95, 1976, 615-621) and expanded and defended by G. W. Trompf, ("On Attitudes Toward Women in Paul and Paulinist Literature: I Corinthians 11:3-16 and its Context" *Catholic Biblical Quarterly* 42, 1980, 196-215). Wayne Meeks tries to resolve some of the contradictions of the Pauline corpus by contending that while Paul insisted on the "preservation of the symbols of the present, differentiated order," together with "the equality of role of man and woman," in the Christian community, the authors of the deutero-Pauline letters rejected the "equivalence of role accorded to woman," ("The Image of the Androgyne: Some Uses of a Symbol in Earliest Christianity," *History of Religions* 13, 1974, 165-208).

While many authors have tended to preoccupy themselves with Paul's teachings about women, several feminist scholars have considered the evidence for historical women in the Pauline communities (Fiorenza, "Women in the Pre-Pauline and Pauline Churches," [cited above]. Bernadette Brooten, ("Junia . . . Outstanding Among the Apostles [Romans 16:7]," in L. and A. Swidler eds. *Women Priests. A Catholic Commentary on the Vatican Declaration*, New York, 1977, 141-144) contends that Paul's co-worker commended in Romans 16 was not the man Junias, as the verse is usually translated, but rather a woman, Junia. Although the debates generated by the Pauline texts seem likely to continue, the reflections of Elaine Pagels ("Paul and Women: A response to Recent Discussion," *Journal of the American Academy of Religion* 42, 1974, 538-549—published together with a rejoinder by Scroggs to his earlier article [532-537]) make explicit and challenge some of the contemporary concerns which underlie research into the Pauline problems.

Despite the emphasis on earliest Christianity, some work has been done on women in Christian communities from the second through the fourth centuries. Rosemary Ruether has written two good introductory surveys of the attitudes towards women and the history of women in this period ("Misogynism and Virginal Feminist in the Fathers of the Church," in *Religion and Sexism*, 150-183, and "Mothers of the Church: Ascetic Women in the Late Patristic Age," in Ruether and McLaughlin, *Women of Spirit*, 71-98). Also pertinent are the studies by JoAnn McNamara ("Wives and Widows in Early Christian Thought," *International Journal of Women's Studies 2*, 575-592 and "Sexual Equality and the Cult of Virginity in Early Christian Thought," *Feminist Studies 3*, 145-158).

Studies of post-first-century Christian communities have yielded some of the more synthetic and analytic studies, including Frederick C. Klawiter, "The Role of Martydom and Persecution in Developing the Priestly Authority of Women in Early Christianity: A Case Study of Montanism," *Church History*, 49 (1980), 3:251-261; Mary R. Lefkowitz, "The Movations for Saint Perpetua's Martyrdom," *Journal of the American Academy of Religion*, 44 (1976), 417-421; and Anne Yarbrough's fascinating study of the economic and social patterns of upper class Roman Christian families in the fourth century, "The Christianization of Rome: The Example of Roman Women," *Church History* 45 (1976), 149-165. Steven Davies has recently published *The Revolt of the Widows: The Social World of the Apocryphal Acts* (Chicago, 1980) which focusses on the pervasive presence of women in the *Apocryphal Acts*, and argues for their probable female authorship. I have also briefly explored the functions of asceticism for the conversion of women to Christianity in the legends of the *Acts* (R. Kraemer, "The Conversion of Women to Ascetic Forms of Christianity," *Signs* 6, 1980, 298-307.) One of the few studies to blend research on Christian women with the study of pagan women is M. Lightman and W. Zeisel, "Univira: An Example of Continuity and Change in Roman Society," *Church History*, 46 (1977), 19-32.

Limited research has also been published on feminine aspects of the divine in early Christianity, particularly in light of the gnostic library discovered at Nag Hammadi. Elaine Pagels explores the gnostic expressions of God as a Dyad encompassing masculine and feminine aspects (*The Gnostic Gospels*, N. Y., 1979, ch. 3 and "What Became of God the Mother: Conflicting Images of God in Early Christianity," *Signs* 2 [1976], 2, 293-303). Meeks' article, cited above, explores the significance of the androgyne as a redemptive symbol.

More recently, Jorunn Jacobson Buckley has suggested that in the gnostic Gospel of Philip, "the resurrection comes about in the restoration of the unity of the sexes through the sacrament of the bridal-chamber," a claim which alludes to a feminine element in the gnostic concept of divinity ("A Cult-Mystery in the Gospel of Philip," *Journal of Biblical Literature* 99, [1980], 4, 569-581). Joan Engelsman devotes one chapter of *The Feminine Dimension of the Divine* (Philadelphia, 1979) to the Jewish figure of Wisdom/Sophia, with a subsection on "The Repression of Sophia in the New Testament," and another to Mary. Averil Cameron has written an important series of articles on the iconography of the Virgin and on Marian imagery in Greek and Latin Byzantine poetry. These works include: "The Theotokos in Sixth-Century Constantinople," *JTS* n.s. 29 (1978), 79-108; "A Nativity Poem of the Sixth Century A.D." *CP* 79 (1979), 222-32; and "The Virgin's Robe: An Episode in the History of Early Seventh-Century Constantinople," *Byzantion* 49 (1979), 42-56. Overall, though, the figure of Mary, the mother of Jesus, has received relatively little attention, in part because earliest Christian writings have relatively little to say about her. Marina Warner, a nonspecialist writing for a literate lay audience, has compiled most of the Christian traditions about Mary, with several chapters on early Christian materials (*Alone of All Her Sex: The Myth and the Cult of the Virgin Mary*, N. Y., 1976). R. Brown, K. Donfried, J. A. Fitzmeyer and J. Reumann have edited *Mary in the New Testament: A Colloborative Assessment by Protestant and Roman Catholic Scholars* (Philadelphia, 1978), a sober, useful discussion of the early Christian traditions on Mary, though uninformed by feminist research or perspective. The figure of Mary Magdalene has also received relatively short shrift, although Fiorenza presents a cogent argument for an early and continuing conflict between Mary and Peter as sources of authority and power in early Christianity ("You Are Not To Be Called Father," cited above.)

VIII WOMEN IN ART
(prepared by Natalie Kampen, The University of Rhode Island)

1. *Etruscan*

Larissa Bonfante, "The Women of Etruria," *Arethusa* 6 (1973) 91-101 and this volume, "Etruscan Women: A Question of Interpretation," *Arch* 26 (1973), 242-49, and "Etruscan Couples and Their

Aristocratic Society," *Women's Studies* 8 (1981), 157-87 and *Reflections of Women in Antiquity* (London, 1982) forges a new methodology, using art—mostly funerary—to study women in Etruscan society. Critical views of Etruscan women by Greek authors are also scrutinized. See also Bonfante, *Etruscan Dress* (Baltimore, 1975).

2. *Greek*

Basic works on style and typology include: G. Richter, *Korai* (London, 1968) and R. Kabus-Jean, *Studien zu Frauenfiguren des 4 Jh. V.C.* (Freiburg diss., 1965). On hair and clothing see M. Bieber, *Enturicklungsgeschichte der griechischen Tracht* (Berlin, 1967).

Sheila McNally, "The Maenad in Early Greek Art," *Arethusa* 11 (1978) 101-35 and this volume relates changes in iconography of female followers of Dionysus to social change. Amy Swerdlow, "The Greek Citizen Woman in Attic Vase Painting: New Views and New Questions," *Women's Studies* 5 (1978), 267-84 examines the portrayal of women in art to find evidence for a separate female culture. Natalie Kampen, "Hellenistic Artists: Female," *ArchClass* 27 (1975), 9-17 reviews the traditions for Timarete, Aristarete, Olympias, *et al.* and discusses the emergence of female artists in the context of the status of women in the Hellenistic period.

3. *Roman*

The following publications represent a sample of work on imperial and royal portraiture; they make no contribution to feminist methodology or analysis and could as easily be about men as women. They do supply raw material, however. An enormous amount of work remains to be done on female portraiture and iconography from a feminist point of view, including questions of the ideal of beauty and how it was communicated at various times and in various places and for what goals, and of the issues of appropriation of divine iconographies and of political propaganda.

Works on portraiture published in the past twenty years include: H. Bartels, *Studien zum Frauenporträt der Augusteischen Zeit* (Munich, 1963); A. Bellezza, "Cecilia Paolina," *Tetraonyma* (Genoa, 1966), 75-83; A. Carandini, *Vibia Sabina* (Florence, 1969); G. Daltrop, et al., *Die Flavier* (Berlin, 1966); W. H. Gross, *Julia Augusta: Untersuchungen zur Grundlegung einer Livia-Ikonographie* (Göttingen, 1962); K. Polaschek, *Studien zur*

Ikonographie der Antonia Minor (Rome, 1973); and H. B. Wiggers and M. Wegner, *Caracalla, Geta, Plautilla; Macrinus bis Balbinus* (Berlin, 1971). On hair and clothing see C. Barini, *Ornatus muliebris* (Turin, 1958).

Works on broader topics which contain essential information on female imagery include: O. J. Brendel, "Scope and Temperament of Erotic Art in the Greco-Roman World," in T. Bowie and C. Christenson eds. *Studies in Erotic Art* (N. Y., 1970), 3-107 — The most interesting article on the subject, comparing Greek and Roman erotica and giving ideas for future work; R. Brilliant, *Gesture and Rank in Roman Art* (New Haven, 1963) — a basic dictionary of gestural language in its relationship to social standing; and H. Gabelmann, *Die Werkstattgruppen der oberitalischen Sarkophage* (Bonn, 1973) — important insights on female iconography and portraiture outside the aristocracy, especially in northeastern Italy. D. E. E. Kleiner, *Roman Group Portraiture. The Funerary Reliefs of the Late Republic and Early Empire* (N. Y., 1978) discusses portraits of women and men of the lower classes and in "The Great Friezes of the Ara Pacis Augustae. Greek Sources, Roman Derivates, and Augustan Social Policy," *MEFRA* 90 (1978), 753-85 Kleiner relates Augustus' family policy to the iconography of family, women, and children. G. Mansulli, *Le Stele romano del territorio ravennate e del Basso Po* (Ravenna, 1967) includes important ideas about non-aristocratic female portraits and iconography as well as images of women in a variety of roles. E. E. Schmidt, *Römische Frauenstatuen* (1967) is a typological and stylistic study. H. Wrede, "Stadtrömische Monumente, Urne and Sarkaphage des Klinen typus in den beiden ersten Jahrhunderten n. Chr.," *ArchAnz* (1977), 395-431, in passing makes some crucial remarks about poses and attributes associated with sex and age categories. P. Zanker, "Grabreliefs römischer Freigelassner," *JDAI* 90 (1975), 267-315 makes some passing comments on freedwomen's images, status, and iconography of upward mobility.

Several publications focus more specifically on women. J. Gagé, *Matronalia* (Brussels, 1963) has a discussion of the imagery of matrons. N. Kampen, *Image and Status: Representations of Roman Working Women at Ostia* (Berlin, 1981) combines an art-historical and sociological approach to study six reliefs. See also C. Panella, "Iconografia delle Muse sui sarcofagi romani," *StudMisc* 12 (1966-67), 11-43. S. Wood, "Alcestis on Roman Sarcophagi," *AJA* 82 (1978),

499-510 discusses female mythological iconography, giving an important model for further work with mythological sarcophagi.

IX RECENT AND FORTHCOMING BOOKS

Mary R. Lefkowitz, *Heroines and Hysterics* (New York, 1981) is a collection of the author's essays on women, four of which have not been previously published. Lefkowitz and Fant's *Women's Life in Greece and Rome* (London and Baltimore, 1982) replaces *Women in Greece and Rome* and contains more information about women's occupations. *Reflections of Women in Antiquity* (London, 1982), ed., Helene Foley includes the articles in *Women's Studies: Special Issue on Women in Antiquity*, 8 (1981), with the addition of articles by Alan Cameron, Helene Foley, F. T. Griffiths, Sarah B. Pomeroy, and Froma Zeitlin. *La Donna Antica* (Turin, 1982) eds. M. Vegetti and D. Lanza, advisory eds. J.-P. Vernant, A. Momigliano, and S. C. Humphreys with introduction by Humphreys is a collection of essays, many of which have been cited in the present bibliography. *Feminism and Art History* (N. Y., 1982, eds. N. Broude and M. Garrard, includes C. M. Havelock, "Mourners on Greek Vases: Remarks on the Social History of Women," and N. Kampen, "Gender and Class in Roman Art: The Case of the Saleslady."

Hunter College C.U.N.Y.

SUGGESTED UNDERGRADUATE SYLLABUS FOR "WOMEN IN CLASSICAL ANTIQUITY" *

Sarah B. Pomeroy

Catalog description: The status of women in antiquity will be examined in the light of modern thinking on the subject of women's roles in society. Formerly, women in Greece and Rome have been studied from a masculine point of view; thus, the course will also be a critique of the sexist bias inherent in traditional classical scholarship. This course will be a comparative study, covering the development of attitudes towards women from the matrilineal memories of the Bronze Age though fully developed patriarchal society. Both literary and archaeological evidence will be examined. Readings may be in English translation. No prerequisites.

I   Sources of our Knowledge of Women in Antiquity
   A. Archaeological and literary
   B. Male orientation of classical literature and of traditional scholarly interpretation
   C. The need for new approaches to the study of women in antiquity.

II   Prehistoric Greece
   A. Speculation on the organization of earliest societies
     1. Evidence from primate studies
     2. Evidence from present-day primitive societies
     3. Archaeological evidence from antiquity
   B. Role and status of women: viewpoint of 19th century anthropologists and of historical materialism that prehistoric Greek society was often matriarchal, matrilineal and matrilocal; rebuttal by 20th century anthropologists.

III Bronze Age
   A. Mother goddesses and their human surrogates, role of male consort, sex symbols
   B. Vestiges of matrilineal and matriarchal legends in epic: Helen, Penelope, Arete, Jocasta, Clytemnestra, Amazons
   C. Women in Minoan and Mycenaean art.

* This syllabus is based on one used for my course "Women and Slaves in Classical Antiquity" at Hunter College in both fall and spring 1971-72, augmented by topics from the Honors Colloquium "Women in Antiquity" taught by Meyer Reinhold at the University of Missouri in winter 1972.

IV Transition to Patriarchal System
    A. Historical causes, theory of invasion
    B. Social causes, discovery of paternity of the male
    C. Economic causes, rise of capitalism
        1. Role of woman as breeder of the legitimate heir; virginity, chastity and monogamy required for reputable women
        2. Role of slavery in declining economic role of women
    D. Religious revolution
        1. Subordination of female deities
           (a) As chthonic powers, Eumenides, Fates, Hours, Moira preserve traditional morality
        2. Division of integrated mother goddess into specialized female divinities: e.g., Hera, wife; Aphrodite, whore; Athena, masculine intellectual; Hestia, virtuous old maid
    E. Anti-feminism in patriarchal society
        1. Masculine heroic ideal of epic
        2. Misogyny of Hesiod and Semonides
    F. Psychological consequences of male domination
        1. Sex antagonisms in the Greek family: Oedipus and Electra complexes
        2. Female revolts against male repression: Antigone, Danaides, Bacchae.

V Developed Functioning of Patriarchal System
    A. Differing opinions of modern scholars on the status of women in classical Greece, e.g., Kitto, Gomme, Seltman, Richter
    B. Private life of Athenian women
        1. Dress, toilette, contraception, abortion, childbirth, exposure of infants
    C. Political, legal and economic aspects of the life of the Athenian woman
        1. Influence of Solonian reforms
        2. Women as citizens in democratic Athens
        3. Legal minority of women: guardianship, inheritance, the epikleros
        4. Marriage: betrothal, dowry, marriage ceremony, adultery, divorce, widowhood
        5. Economic role at home and in the polis
    D. Religious life: cults, magic, tabus
    E. Hetairas, prostitutes, polygamy
    F. Women in the visual arts, nudity

G. Homosexuality or bisexuality of Athenian intelligentsia in relation to status of women

H. Heroines of tragedy and comedy, and female stereotypes in Greek mythology: witches, maidens, monsters, wives, devouring mothers, prophetesses, Maenads

I. Philosophical inquiries on whether the inferiority of women is the result of nature or custom
   1. Views of Sophists, Euripides, Plato, Aristotle
   2. Males as culture bringers: Prometheus, Daedalus, Cadmus, Triptolemus
   3. Relationship of the low status of women in Athenian society to the high civilization created by Athenian males
   4. First ideas of emancipation of women: *Thesmophoriazusae, Ecclesiazusae, Lysistrata, Republic, Laws.*

VI Women in the Hellenistic World
   A. Hellenistic queens
   B. Daily life in Alexandria and in the Fayum
   C. The bourgeois love ideal and the happy marriage in Hellenistic literature.

VII Functioning of the Patriarchal System in Rome (where topics differ from Greek, above, Unit V)
   A. Economic, political and legal aspects (the letter of the law and the reality compared)
   B. Distinctive character of Roman love poetry
   C. Misogyny and sexual perversions in Roman satire
   D. The role and life style of women in different social classes: Matron, Empress, Hetaira, Prostitute, slaves and free women
   E. Legislation on sexual morality
      1. The emancipated woman of the late Republic and early Empire
   F. Some famous Roman women in literature and the visual arts
   G. Religions of women and women in religion
      1. Pagan cults: Bacchus, Isis
      2. Judaism
      3. Christianity
         (a) Early equality, feminism of Christ
         (b) Influence of St. Paul in subjection of women
         (c) Asceticism, sex and marriage

  (d) The 'Virgin' birth in the New Testament and earlier Pagan myth
  (e) Religious women: nuns and mystics
  (f) The rival masculine cult of Mithra.

VIII Ancient Alternatives and Counter-Cultural Examples
  A. Women in the Commune: Sparta, the *Republic, Ecclesiazusae*
  B. Lesbianism, Sappho
  C. Women without men: myths of Amazons and the Lemnian women
  D. Etruscan women
  E. Barbarian women in the Mediterranean world.

— — — — — — — — — —

SUGGESTED READING LIST

The following reading list is to be assigned to undergraduates taking the course "Women in Classical Antiquity," and follows the topic outline of the preceeding syllabus. Obviously, it will be too lengthy for the average three credit college course, if papers and other forms of independent study are assigned.

  Because one of the advantages of this course is that it provides an attractive and stimulating mode of introducing students to the Classics, only primary source readings are assigned. Secondary source material is of course consulted for class lectures and for student reports.

I No assignment.

II No assignment.

III Homer, *Iliad* I; III, 121-90; VI 315-502; XVIII, 22-137; XXII, 82-130; *Odyssey*, I-VII; VIII, 416-530; X-XII; XV, 14-26, 170-78; XVII, 84-165, 498-588; XIX; XXI, 67-357; XXIII, 63-309.

  Herodotus, *History*, I, 2-4; II, 118-20.

  Thucydides, *History of the Peloponnesian War*, I, 9.

IV Hesiod, *Theogony*, 585-612; *Works and Days*, 53-82, 373-75, 695-705.

  Semonides, *Iambics*, fragment 7.

  Aeschylus, *Eumenides*.

Sophocles, *Antigone; Oedipus*.

Euripides, *Bacchae*.

V   Xenophon, *Oeconomicus*.

Lysias, *On The Murder of Eratosthenes*.

Euripides, *Alcestis; Hippolytus; Medea*.

Aristophanes, *Lysistrata; Ecclesiazusae; Thesmophoriazusae*.

Plato, *Symposium; Republic* V.

Aristotle, *Politics* I; *Generation of Animals*, excerpts.

Demosthenes, *Against Neaera*.

VI   Theocritus, *Idyll,* XV.

Plutarch, "Advice to Bride and Groom," *Moralia*, Vol. II.

Menander, Plautus, or Terence, selection.

VII   "Marriage Regulations of Romulus," and "The XII Tables," in N. Lewis and M. Reinhold, *Roman Civilization*, Vol. I, (New York: Columbia University Press, 1951), 58-60, 101-109.

Cicero, *For Caelius*.

Catullus, Propertius, Sulpicia, Ovid, selections.

Vergil, *Aeneid*, I, IV.

Livy, I.

Pliny, *Epistulae* I, 14; III, 16; IV, 19; VI, 7, 24, 26, 31, 32; VII, 5; VIII, 5, 10, 11.

Juvenal, 6.

Petronius, *Satyricon*.

Paul, I Corinthians.

VIII   Sappho, *Lyrics*.

Plutarch, *Life of Lycurgus*.

Hunter College C.U.N.Y.